GREAT IDEAS

IN

PSYCHOTHERAPY

RICHARD D. CHESSICK, M.D.
Professor of Psychiatry
Northwestern University
Evanston, Illinois

Jason Aronson Inc.
Northvale, New Jersey
London

TO LINDA, BRENDA, AND CYNTHIA
for their future . . .

New Printing 1987

ISBN: 0-87668-787-7

Library of Congress Catalog Number: 87-71335

Manufactured in the United States of America.

People were scurrying about, horses running around, and dogs, and on my girls' faces was all that anxiety, terror, entreaty, who knows what; my heart was wrung when I saw those faces. My God, I thought, what more will these girls have to go through, in a long life! I grabbed them, ran and kept thinking one thing: What more will they have to live through in this world!

Anton Chekhov, *Three Sisters*

There is a great realm in which the intelligent mind finds it necessary to move, where the principles of conduct and of understanding cannot be determined by scientific experiments and objective tests. In this realm the only weapon is man's reason—his intuition and his powers of logical construction, as these are cultivated in the most intelligent beings by a long process of training and constant exercise, a continuous communion with the experiences of life and science, and also with those experiences as they have been distilled for us by the great minds of the past. The schools, universities, and churches of the later Middle Ages and early modern times made a grievous error when they allowed little room for experiment or even for observation. We are in danger today of falling into the equally serious error of allowing no room for the independent mind. It is not a want of science on which despotism has fed as much as a want of balance in matters of the intellect.

John Nef
The United States and Civilization

Contents

Introduction

I am most happy to introduce the reader to the second printing of *Great Ideas in Psychotherapy,* which is one of the most wide ranging and most popular of my publications. The purpose of this introduction is to comment briefly on each chapter in the light of the changes in our field and my current thinking and clinical experience over the past decade, in order to bring the reader up to date.

The reader will note that I have taken a historical approach, emphasizing the important figures over the centuries who in my opinion made substantial contributions to the current technique and practice of psychoanalytic psychotherapy. In Chapter 1, I began with the Greeks, especially the pre-Socratic philosophers. Since that time, coming under the influence of Heidegger, I would be even more inclined to stress the sense of wonder felt by the pre-Socratic philosophers when they began to think about the world in nonmagical terms. It is this sense of wonder and curiosity that forms the starting point of any genuine inquiry; without it, regardless of the infantile roots from which it springs, a person cannot be an effective psychotherapist. Furthermore, to really understand the world in which modern man must survive, one needs to go back either in time to a situation like that of the pre-Socratics, when humans experienced a far greater closeness between the earth, the sky, the mortals, and the gods than they do today, or geographically travel to places like Africa and wander among the Masai, who live in close contact with the land and the sky and the animals and their gods. I believe even more than I did ten years ago that a thorough understanding of modern man's predicament is vital if one is to help troubled individuals find some meaning to their lives in the turmoil of the late twentieth century, at a time when civilization is in a serious decline. Just as the pre-Socratics wrote during the spring of civilization, so Socrates attempted to find meaning during a winter of the civilized world similar to ours, carrying out his relentless inquiry as the classical Greeks committed mutual suicide in the Peloponnesian War. Since the original publication of this book, I have discussed the figure of Socrates at great length in another book (1983a), and the reader is urged to become familiar with the struggles of that enigmatic individual, who was really the founder of our discipline.

The discussion of mental health in Chapter 2 can be made immensely more sophisticated by turning to the work of Kohut (1971, 1977, 1978, 1984) on the subject. I have reviewed his work at length in another book (1985a) and wish here only to urge the reader to study Kohut's contribution. In his "psychology of the self in the broader sense of the term," Kohut points out that although individuals may have many neurotic symptoms, if they have a cohesive self they can still get a sense of enjoyment out of life; conversely, we see a number of patients who have no complaints of neurotic symptoms but who are depressed, empty, and "burned out" because of the impending fragmentation of their selves. According to Kohut the central tasks to achieve joy in life are (1) the development of continuous activity that forms a bridge between the nuclear ambitions pole and the nuclear ideals pole of the self, and (2) the development and establishment of an empathic selfobject matrix throughout one's life. This raises the entire issue of mental health to a much more sophisticated plane, and avoids a rigid or stereotyped depiction of the "normal" or "healthy" person.

Chapter 3 could be expanded by turning to the work of Heidegger in greater detail, as I began to do in recent papers (1986, 1987a). It was Heidegger who enlarged on Spengler's idea and proposed the thesis that we have lost contact with Being as a consequence of being immersed in the age of technicity. Heidegger would say that Being shows itself through the present era of technicity, but the threatened destruction of the human race due to the "technology frenzy" of the superpowers, as Heidegger describes it, brings us closer and closer to the final calamity of a nuclear holocaust. This would orient the philosopher *and* psychotherapist to a greater appreciation of the crisis in the human community that looms up in the 21st century; Heidegger said that "only a god can save us," but I (1988a) have argued that we must certainly take a more active approach to this crisis. It becomes increasingly problematic, as Kohut (1984) suggests, whether a psychoanalyst who pays no serious attention to world affairs can be called a healthy model and can be said to have completed a successful training analysis.

Since the time I wrote Chapter 4, predominantly on Confucius, I have become increasingly impressed with the potential of eastern philosophy, if one can unravel some of the mystical language and get through the vast cultural difference that is involved. The eastern philosophers from India, China, Japan, and other countries have approached the same human condition in their own characteristic way, and a definitive text remains to be written on their contribution to both philosophy and psychotherapy. For example, the Japanese at present are developing indigenous psychotherapeutic models, which in some instances are quite different from our psychoanalytic approach and are complementary to it. Eastern philosophy stresses in its own characteristic way the unique value of the human spirit and in that sense is an anodyne to our current western technological and materialistic frenzy. It was badly distorted by the drug culture of the 1960s, but that only represented a confused and autistic melange of some important eastern ideas. Professional philosophers such as Copleston (1980) have only recently started to explore eastern thought in a meticulous fashion, and much scholarly work remains to be done to bridge the gap separating the cultures of the world.

Chapter 5 on the Renaissance, which stresses the expression of humanistic ideals and the humanistic solution in the outpouring of art at the time, is parallel to Heidegger's development of philosophy in his later work — focusing on the expression of Being in literature and art, especially poetry. Heidegger speaks of the direct therapeutic value of poetry, literature, and art for troubled humanity, and suggests that the arts offer alternative "lightings" of Being. Even in self-analysis (Chessick 1988b) the importance of the influence of the arts cannot be sufficiently emphasized.

Furthermore, both Foucault and Kohut pointed out the role of modern artists in stressing the "episteme" (Foucault 1973) of the future, the contemporary ubiquitous threat of the fragmentation of the personality, and the trend towards the erasure of humans (Chessick 1985a). Thus the focus in understanding humans, heralded by authors such as Foucault, Kohut, and Heidegger, has increasingly centered on artistic productions, which have a very special link to the human spirit. This is in sharp contradistinction to the more classical theories of art developed by Freud and expanded by Hartmann (Greenberg and Mitchell 1983), which stressed the sublimation of infantile desires in the production of art to the exclusion of the transcendent aspects. It offers a complementary theory of art to that of traditional psychoanalysts and is coming to be taken with increasing seriousness by thinkers of all orientations.

Chapter 6 on "Confessions, Soliloquies and Persuasion" can be amplified by a study of Foucault's (1980) *History of Sexuality*, especially Volume 1, which stresses the development of western man as a "confessing animal." The rise of the "expert" in hearing such confessions and the subsequent study of the changing history of how humans view the development of their selves has been eloquently outlined by Foucault's research in this volume and then much amplified in his recently published three final volumes on *The History of Sexuality*. One warning is in order about these final (some even posthumously) published works of Foucault; they are sketchy, unfinished, and the scholarship has come under considerable question, since Foucault leaned heavily on idiosyncratically selected Greek and Roman sources and was not a classical scholar.

One of the most controversial issues in current psychotherapeutic work is that of the "physicianly vocation" discussed in Chapter 7. The development of a "physicianly vocation" in the psychotherapist is the most important aim, in my opinion, of the education of any psychotherapist. It is the best protection for the patient against being either exploited or retaliated against. This kind of education runs directly contrary to the entire trend of modern western civilization, the "culture of narcissism" as described by Lasch (1979). His book should be read by all psychotherapists, with a caveat that the minor discussions of Kohut and Kernberg in Lasch's book are inaccurate. To develop a physicianly vocation and maintain it against all the pressures of our modern era is the hardest and yet the most vital requirement for the correct technique and practice of psychoanalytic psychotherapy and, indeed, such psychotherapeutic practice can be thought of as one of the few remaining humanizing forces in the modern world.

Since the writing of Chapter 8, I have expanded at length (1980a, 1985a) on the importance of Kant and the relationship of Kant's phenomenal and noumenal self to Kohut's concept of the self. The diagram in the present book (p. 166) attempts to show the unavoidable interrelationship between one's philosophy and one's practice of psychoanalytic psychotherapy; those who ignore the study of first principles do so at their own risk because such principles are invariably embedded in any form of therapeutic practice and will appear to the patient whether the therapist attempts to hide them or not.

The thought of two major predecessors of Freud, Schopenhauer and Nietzsche, has been outlined in Chapters 9 and 10. I have expanded at length on this in my book (1983a) on Nietzsche, which presents the link between the thought of Socrates, Schopenhauer, and Nietzsche and serves as a preface to the understanding of Freud's position in the history of western civilization. Freud was far more than just another scientist; his collected works represent an entire philosophical system as illustrated, for example, in Ricoeur's (1970, see also Chessick 1987b) well-known study. A thorough understanding of Freud's work from the point of view of the psychotherapist was hopefully developed in my book (1980b) on Freud; the treatment of Freud in *Great Ideas in Psychotherapy* is deliberately cursory because it is assumed that the psychotherapist will spend a substantial portion of his or her time in reading and rereading Freud over a professional lifetime.

Since the contribution of Sullivan was described in Chapter 12, the evidence for a biological and genetic basis in schizophrenia has become overwhelming. However, an important link between Sullivan's thought and modern traditional psychoanalysis may be found in the work of Gill (1982) and his followers, who have studied the transference from the point of view of the here-and-now interaction between the therapist and the patient. This is close to Sullivan's "interpersonal" approach to therapy and indicates the viability of Sullivan's orientation. A more extreme example of this approach is found in the various publications of Langs (1982), for whom treatment is centered entirely on the interaction between the patient and therapist, rather than viewing the therapist as relatively neutral and the patient as bringing into the treatment mostly reenactments of past situations.

The most serious omission in the book is a description of the work of Kohut, which would belong in Chapter 13 for our purposes. It is Kohut who carried the principles reviewed in that chapter to a much more sophisticated development and, after my introductory book (1985a) on the subject, the reader is urged to turn directly to Kohut's (1971, 1977, 1978, 1984) work for details. Basch (1981) offers some excellent clinical examples of the application of Kohut's principles to the practice of psychoanalytic psychotherapy.

The Chapter 14 topic of feminine psychology has received significant attention over the past decade (Chessick 1983b, 1984a); for a complete update on current psychoanalytic thinking on this topic, see the paper by Chehrazi (1986). I believe that a consensus is gradually being reached on this topic among experienced psychoanalytically oriented psychotherapists that remains consistent with the psychoanalytic approach but corrects a number of Freud's contentions in the light of modern research. Freud would have welcomed this since he freely admitted that his knowledge of female development, especially in the preoedipal period, was quite deficient.

The most important updating of Chapter 15 would be to include a section on Lacan. Lacan is only now beginning to be introduced to American psychotherapists, and I believe that his work will have an important influence in sharpening our attention to the vicissitudes of language and the importance of careful psychoanalytic listening; I have reviewed Lacan and discussed this topic in other publications (1985a, 1985b, 1987c). Of all the authors mentioned in *Great Ideas in Psychotherapy*, Lacan would be the most difficult; those wishing a general introduction to his work beyond my brief reviews are referred to Muller and Richardson (1982), with the caveat that *all* interpretations of Lacan are open to debate since he was such an ambiguous writer. The correct and definitive explication of Lacan's orientation remains for the future; much of his work remains untranslated from his difficult French.

The issue of psychoanalysis as a science, discussed in Chapter 16, remains as controversial as ever. A whole host of publications on this subject have appeared (Eagle 1984), stimulated primarily and most recently by the erudition and energy of Grünbaum (1984). This topic is so vast that it cannot be reviewed in this introduction, but Grünbaum's work contains all the pertinent references for those who are interested in this technical subject. I cannot say there has been much consensus on the issues raised in this chapter in 1977, nor has the term *metapsychiatry,* as I attempted to use it in this and other books, received much attention.

The subject of Chapter 17, especially the issue of inner sustainment, would be much enhanced by a study of Kohut, as I have mentioned before. This would also be the place to turn to my (1984b, 1985a) subsequent discussions of Sartre and R. D. Laing. I did not give sufficient attention to these authors in *Great Ideas in Psychotherapy;* one of the reasons for this is that Sartre's (1981) magnificent study of Flaubert had not yet appeared in English translation. It was this study that sent me back to Sartre and subsequently again to R. D. Laing, and the reader is advised to do the same. Barnes (1981) presents an excellent review of Sartre's approach to human development most pertinent to psychotherapists, and is mandatory reading.

In Chapter 18 I lean heavily on the thought of Jaspers, but over the past decade I have found a study of Heidegger to be more useful because it is so rich, sophisticated, and detailed. There is a certain vagueness to Jaspers's presentation, such that it does not withstand repeated scrutiny. Considering the terrible conditions of the Nazi regime that oppressed him, this is not surprising and constitutes a significant loss to western civilization. The detailed explication of Heidegger would require a book all to itself, and the best clear introduction is by Richardson (1974).

I had the most fun writing Chapter 19 and was surprised that reviewers overlooked this amateur effort to copy Book I of Plato's *Republic*. Since that time I have begun increasingly to question whether accurate writing on the human condition can be contained either in the standard psychiatric case history format or the scholarly paper, and, perhaps influenced by Sartre, I have cast about for other forms such as the drama. The question of whether insights from literature, poetry, drama, and the arts can be encompassed in standard scholarly or scientific writing remains completely open; I have received some interesting responses to dramatic presentations that I gave in lieu of scientific papers, ranging from great rage and insult ("This was not a scientific presentation.") on the one hand, to exuberant praise with a sense of release from the constrictions of standard technical presentations of the human spirit and the phenomena of human living on the other. One could easily argue, as did Freud, that Shakespeare was the greatest psychologist who ever lived.

The discussion of Heidegger in Chapter 20 is very brief and was only presented to stimulate the reader (and myself) to further investigation of this very difficult thinker. Some of the comments I have made on Heidegger in this introduction are already mentioned in this final embryonic chapter, but the chapter can only serve as an all-too-brief preamble to the topic (see also Chessick 1986, 1987a).

I stand completely behind my comments on Soviet psychiatry — which regrettably has not much changed in the past decade — in the *Epilogue* to this book, but as a postscript to the epilogue I have made a study (1985c) of the current state of American psychiatry, which I believe is also in danger, and I hope to bring this to the attention of the reader. By the proper use of the references that immediately follow this introduction, the reader of *Great Ideas in Psychotherapy* may update the book and acquaint himself or herself with the current state of the art.

Richard D. Chessick
June 2, 1987

REFERENCES

Barnes, H. (1981). *Sartre and Flaubert*. Chicago: University of Chicago Press. *Critique*. Berkeley: University of California Press.

Basch, M. (1981) *Doing Psychotherapy*. New York: Basic Books.

Chehrazi, S. (1986). Female psychology: a review. *Journal of the American Psychoanalytic Association* 34:141–162.

Chessick, R. (1980a). The problematical self in Kant and Kohut. *Psychoanalytic Quarterly* 49:456–473.

———— (1980b). *Freud Teaches Psychotherapy*. Indianapolis: Hackett.

———— (1982). Psychoanalytic listening: with special reference to the views of Langs. *Contemporary Psychoanalysis* 18:613–634.

———— (1983a). *A Brief Introduction to the Genius of Nietzsche*. Washington, D.C.: University Press of America.

———— (1983b). Marilyn Monroe: psychoanalytic pathography of a preoedipal disorder. *Dynamic Psychotherapy* 1:161–176.

———— (1984a). Was Freud wrong about feminine psychology? *American Journal of Psychoanalysis* 44:355–38.

———— (1984b). Sartre and Freud. *American Journal of Psychotherapy* 38:229–238.

———— (1985a). *Psychology of the Self and the Treatment of Narcissism*. Northvale, New Jersey: Jason Aronson.

———— (1985b). Psychoanalytic listening II. *American Journal of Psychotherapy* 39:30–48.

———— (1985c). The frantic retreat from the mind to the brain: American psychiatry in *mauvaise foi*. *Psychoanalytic Inquiry* 5:369–403.

———— (1986). Heidegger for psychotherapists. *American Journal of Psychotherapy* 40:83–95.

———— (1987a). A comparison of the notions of self in the philosophy of Heidegger and the psychoanalytic self psychology of Kohut. *Psychoanalysis and Contemporary Thought*. In press.

———— (1987b). Prolegomena to the study of Paul Ricoeur's "Freud and Philosophy." *Psychoanalytic Review*. In press.

_____ (1987c). Lacan's practice of psychoanalytic psychotherapy. *American Journal of Psychotherapy*. In press.

_____ (1988a). Matthew Arnold, the death instinct, and the future of man. *American Journal of Social Psychiatry*. In press.

_____ (1988b). Self analysis: fool for a patient? *Psychoanalytic Review*. In press.

Copleston, F. (1980). *Philosophies and Cultures*. New York: Oxford University Press.

Eagle, M. (1984). *Recent Developments in Psychoanalysis*. New York: McGraw-Hill.

Foucault, M. (1973). *The Order of Things*. New York: Vintage.

_____ (1980). *The History of Sexuality*. Vol. 1. Trans. R. Hurley. New York: Vintage.

Gill, M. (1982). *Analysis of Transference*. Vol. 1. New York: International Universities Press.

Greenberg, J., and Mitchell, S. (1983). *Object Relations in Psychoanalytic Theory*. Cambridge, MA: Harvard University Press.

Grünbaum, A. (1984). *The Foundations of Psychoanalysis: A Philosophical Critique*. Berkeley: University of California Press.

Kohut, H. (1971). *The Analysis of the Self*. New York: International Universities Press.

_____ (1977). *The Restoration of the Self*. New York: Universities Press.

_____ (1978). *The Search for the Self*. New York: International Universities Press.

_____ (1984). *How Does Analysis Cure?* Chicago: University of Chicago Press.

Langs, R. (1982). *Psychotherapy: A Basic Text*. New York: Jason Aronson.

Lasch, C. (1979). *The Culture of Narcissism*. New York: Norton.

Muller, J., and Richardson, W. (1982). *Lacan and Language: A Reader's Guide to Écrits*. New York: International Unversities Press.

Richardson, W. (1974). *Heidegger: Through Phenomenology to Thought*. The Hague: Martinus Nijhoff.

Ricoeur, P. (1970). *Freud and Philosophy: An Essay on Interpretation*. New Haven: Yale University Press.

Sartre, J. (1981). *The Family Idiot*. Vol. 1. Trans. C. Cosman. Chicago: University of Chicago Press.

Part I
CLASSICAL THOUGHT

Chapter 1

Dialectic and
the First Metapsychology

Socrates: *Beloved Pan, and all ye other gods who haunt this place, give me beauty in the inward soul; and may the outward and inward man be at one. May I reckon the wise to be the healthy, and may I have such a quantity of gold as a temperate man and he only can bear and carry. Anything more? The prayer, I think, is enough for me.*
Phaedrus: *Ask the same for me, for friends should have all things in common.*

Plato, *Phaedrus*

CLASSICAL GREECE

The area comprising present day Greece was first taken over about 3000 B.C. by the Achaeans, who invaded from the North and overran the Neolithic culture already there. The invaders were led by a small noble or warrior caste that used bronze shields, swords, and armor. Around 1700 B.C. this group also invaded Crete. They found a highly developed Minoan culture (the name derived from the great Cretan King Minos) and influenced this culture to the extent that the palaces at Knossos and other places on Crete, rebuilt after their invasion, show a distinct Grecian turn.

Thus the Minoan Age in Crete from around 2500 to 1400 B.C. may be considered the very first phase of Aegean Bronze Age civilization.

The palace at Knossos was elegantly decorated with wall paintings, while others were four stories high and showed remarkable plumbing. Religion was highly ritualized and centered in the palaces. The man-bull Minotaur and the myth of the Labyrinth dramatized in two novels by Mary Renault (1959, 1972) are from Knossos.

Simpson explains, "There was a cult of the bull, and dancer-like figures are shown catching the horns and bull-vaulting. Minoan civilization, in contrast with later Greek, seems to have been peace-loving as well as pleasure-loving. Crete had wide shipping commerce and a protective navy. It traded with Egypt, and Minoan influence spread to Aegean islands that may have been Cretan dominions, and to the Greek mainland. Writing found in Crete scratched on clay tablets (Linear B.), has been deciphered as an early form of Greek" (1968).

The present day palace at Knossos, though a poor restoration, maintains a certain beauty. The ancient, primitive Minoan civilization that abided here and evolved from 2500 to 1400 B.C. was a truly astounding achievement. It created a peerless world which if compared with contemporary or slightly earlier civilizations stands out as unique. It was achieved by the Minoan pre-Hellenes—a spirited, active, intelligent people with marvelous artists, outstanding sailors, wonderful craftsmen, and genial architects, who attained a remarkable standard of living in a state of leisure, comfortable joy, and continuous peace among themselves. They were a merry and expressive people, fond of colors, movement, and of their physical environment.

A terrible catastrophe hit Crete around 1450 B.C. and cities, palaces, mansions, and settlements were transformed into ruins or destroyed completely by fire.

About 1400 B.C., there was probably a massive invasion of Crete by the mainland Greeks. This time the Asian bureaucratic methods that had been developed in the Minoan culture under the influence of trade with Egypt and Libya were carried back to the Greek mainland. Thus began what may be called the Mycenaean phase of Greek culture as the power center shifted from Crete to Mycenae and other cities in the southern Peloponnese; even Athens was Mycenaean in culture at this stage. At this time there were several significant population centers: Athens, Pylos (King Nestor), Sparta (King Menelaus, brother of Agamemnon and married to Helen), Ithaca (Odysseus), and most powerful of all, Mycenae (King Agamemnon).

The most impressive aspect of the famous palace of the kings at Mycenae is the building of the Cyclopean walls. Not much is left of the inner castle except the burial circle, although the less recent but more complete construction set on an imposing hill commanding the plains of Argolis is impressive indeed. At the top one is surrounded by great natural beauty and can hear just for a moment the voices of men long ago. The line between history and poetry in Greece cannot be drawn, and hence much of ancient history like much of psychoanalysis as Freud said is creative reconstruction, whether one likes it or not.

Under the influence of Minoan beaurocratic techniques imported into Greece, these population centers developed rapidly into highly stratified aristocracies, centering around the king. These centers allied loosely to wage war against Troy for ten years. About 1160? B.C., Troy fell to the combined Grecian invaders.

Some eighty years later the entire area of Greece was rapidly over-whelmed and essentially destroyed by the Dorians, who invaded from the North. Sudden destruction resulted from the discovery of iron, with which the Dorians could arm every able-bodied man and thus overwhelm the small Bronze Age caste of warriors. The survivors of this destruction fled to Asia Minor and probably put together their story under the name of Homer. These Homeric epics were written by about 800 B.C.

The period beginning around 1100 B.C. with the Dorian invasion is often known as the Dark Age of Aegean civilization. In 800 B.C. the work of Homer and Hesiod signalled a coming renaissance. Civilization slumped under the Dorian invasion to the extent that writing, even the scratched form on clay tablets, temporarily disap-peared.

In the era of the famous Greek city-states, temples began to be built and art revived. The term "archaic" is mainly used for the sculpture of this age. As no life-sized statues are known to have been carved in Greece before 650 B.C. Simpson explains, "Archaic stone figures show Egyptian-Mesopotamian influence, but they are distinctive in being free-standing and (in the case of males only) nude. Bronze casting came from Egypt and was not much practiced in Greece until after 600" (1968). There was important Greek colonization in Ionia and up through the sea of Marmara to the Bosporus where, about 660 B.C., the Greeks built Byzantium (Constantinople) and settled later in various colonies along the shores of the Black Sea. They spread west to Sicily and southern Italy.

From 650 to 600 B.C. is sometimes called the age of law-givers in Greek history, and to Thales and Solon are attributed the maxims "Know Thyself" and "Avoid Excess." Tyrannies arose in the various city-states. In Athens, kingship was succeeded by oligarchy. About 600 B.C., Solon wrote the famous constitution for Athens, and this city eventually became the first prosperous democracy in a limited sense, after first being consolidated as a city under the constitutional tyranny of Pisistratus.

The phase of classical Greece from about 500 B.C. to 323 B.C., obviously only a small segment of the history of the Aegean civilization, began officially in 480 B.C. with the defeat of the great Persian empire by the Greek city-states united under the leadership of Athens in the famous battles of Thermopylae, Salamis, and Plataea. From about this time to the rise of Macedonia, Athens experienced about 150 years of a cultural explosion which rose to its first peak under the leadership of Pericles and ended with the final eclipse of Athens by Alexander the Great. The spectacular flowering of dramatists, rhetoricians, enlightened political leaders, philosophers, and sculptors made this one of the greatest periods of civilization for those lucky enough to be enfranchised citizens of Athens.

The Peloponnesian War from 431 B.C. to 404 B.C. resulted in the destruction of the Athenian democracy and the temporary ascendance of Sparta over Athens, but it introduced a new phase of Athenian greatness. Bury, in the most comprehensive and scholarly history of Greece, explains, "It was not until Athens lost her empire that she began to exert a great decisive influence on Greek thought and civilisation." This influence was in part due to the literary school of Isocrates and the philosophical school of Plato (founded in 387 B.C.) which attracted to Athens men from all quarters of the Hellenic world. Athens began to become truly cosmopolitan, a tendency promoted by a philosophical speculation which rose above nationalism and by the extremely widespread influence of the theatre, at the time the most effective instrument for spreading ideas. "They were all dominated by the influence of Euripides, the great teacher of rationalism, the daring critic of all established institutions and beliefs" (1913). Cultural growth was accompanied by that of individualism and a demand that the state be for the education and service of the citizen, not, as it had been, the other way around.

The close of the golden age in Greece corresponded to the rise of Macedonia and Alexander the Great, lasting until his death in 323 B.C. During this period, Alexander through his famous military conquests carried Greek civilization all over the world. Alexander's generals divided and fought over his empire at his death, and new and Hellenized spheres of influence arose outside of the Aegean civilization. Greece was then fatally divided against itself and was eventually swallowed piece by piece through Roman conquests. The suicide of the Hellenized Cleopatra in 30 B.C. may be taken as the final close.

A great tendency to glamorize life in ancient Greece, especially in the golden age of Athens, has produced a plethora of impressive picture books on the subject (Warner 1973, Bowra 1965). The actual Athens of Pericles was somewhat different. For example, the population of three-hundred thousand consisted of about one-third slaves, who usually worked a ten-hour day in the rich Athenian silver mines. Simpson writes, "At law a slave had certain rights, but not many. He could be whipped, but to kill a slave was illegal. If he was a witness in a court case, his evidence was required to be taken under torture. If he was permanently injured by this, compensation had to be paid to his master" (1968).

Politically, women were not citizens and they could not bring actions at law. They were not even allowed to do the shopping, which was done by men and carried home by slaves. No change was made or even contemplated in the status of all these unfranchised people during the fifty years of the Golden Age. The repeated abuses of their democracy, for example, the trial and execution of Socrates in 399 B.C., are well known. On the other hand, there is no doubt that this complicated people gave rise to the whole western philosophical, scientific, and psychotherapeutic tradition and deserve our careful attention.

The Greek approach was characterized by prudence, forethought, rationality, and a devotion to theoretical science which appeared first as a trend in the philosophical method of Thales and other Ionian philosophers. However, the Greek mind was much more complicated than first appears. According to McNeill, "from very ancient times, Greek religion had manifested a double character: the pantheon of Olympus confronting what the Greeks called the 'mysteries.' In fact, the gods of Olympus were themselves a mixed assemblage, derived partly from Indo-European sky and nature dieties and partly from autochthonous protectresses worshipped by pre-Greek populations. Yet the poets, especially Homer and Hesiod, brought a certain order and stability to Greek conceptions of the Olympians; and the supreme artistry of the *Iliad* and the *Odyssey* made it certain that Homer's relentlessly anthropomorphic theology could never be forgotten. The mysteries, however, bore little relation to this theology. Some, like the Orphic and Dionysiac rites, seem to have originated in the Orient and spread widely throughout Greece in the eighth or seventh centuries B.C. Others, like the mysteries of Eleusis, were apparently indigenous, originating in Mycenaean or pre-Mycenaean times, and may have been related to fertility cults professed by Neolithic agriculturalists as early as the third milleneum B.C." (1963, p. 206).

In Greek orgies, even before the days of Homer, the emphasis was on a fusion with the god Dionysus or Bacchus. These rituals were not thought of as pleasure in the physical sense but rather as purification. The original meaning of the word orgy was sacrament. The rituals enabled the votary to escape from the wheel of birth and become as one with the divinity, Dionysus, and temporarily possess his powers. The etymological meaning of the word "enthusiasm" is "union with god." The Bacchic ritual produced what was called "enthusiasm" in which the god was supposed to enter the worshipper. Homer in the *Iliad* speaks of Dionysus as "raging," an epithet that indicates that the orgiastic character of his worship was already recognized. Homer did not consider him very important, nor did Hesiod, who first called wine the gift of Dionysus.

Women played a prominent part in the ritual of worship. At its base was a savage form of sacramental communion in which a human, and later an animal victim, was torn to pieces raw and eaten. This victim was regarded as the incarnation of the divinity, so that his ingestion enabled the votary to gain his strength.

The spectacular wild ecstacy and orgiastic self-abandonment practiced at these rituals is perhaps most magnificently described by Euripides in his play *The Bacchae*. These women companions of

Bacchus were also called Maenads and took a major part in his festivals. In the course of time the mysteries celebrated became occasions for intoxication and great licentiousness.

One can see why Durant (1939) calls Dionysus "The most troublesome, the most popular, the most difficult to classify of all the Greek gods." The worshippers were seeking *ecstasis,* a going out of their souls to meet and be one with Dionysus; thus they felt free from the burden of the flesh, they acquired divine insight, they were able to prophesy, and they took part in being a god. This passionate cult, coming from Thrace into Greece like an epidemic, dragged one region after another from the cold and clear Olympiana of the state worship into a faith and ritual that satisfied the craving for excitement and release, the longing for enthusiasm and possession, mysticism, and mystery. Durant writes, "The priests at Delphi and the rulers of Athens tried to keep the cult at a distance, but failed; all they could do is to adopt Dionysus into Olympus, Hellenize and humanize him, give him an official festival, and turn the revelry of his worshippers from the mad ecstacy of wine from the hills into the stately processions, the robust song, and the noble drama of the Great Dionysia. For a while they won Dionysus over to Apollo, but in the end Apollo yielded to Dionysus' heir and conqueror, Christ."

PRE-SOCRATIC PHILOSOPHY

The antidote to the Orphic religion was the philosophy of Ionia, for in Asiatic Greece the Orphic religion and mysteries could not take root in the atmosphere of skeptical questioning already started by Thales and Anaximander and continued by Xenophanes and Heraclitus as the crucial sixth century B.C. drew to a close. The power of their skeptical challenges to all mysteries and religious superstitions produced a major turning point in history.

Russell writes, "In all history, nothing is so surprising or so difficult to account for as the sudden rise of civilization in Greece. . . . Homer as a finished achievement was a product of Ionia, i.e. a part of Hellenic Asia Minor and the adjacent islands. Some time during the sixth century at latest, the Homeric poems became fixed in their present form. It was also during this century that Greek science and philosophy and mathematics began. . . . Now almost all the hypotheses that have dominated modern philosophy were first thought of by the Greeks: . . . theories which have had an independent life and growth, and which, though at first somewhat infantile, have proved capable of surviving and developing throughout more than two thousand years" (1945). As an example of this it is truly impressive to see Freud (1937a) in "Analysis Terminable and Interminable," one of his last great papers, refer excitedly back to the Presocratic philosopher Empedocles of Acragas (c. 484-424).

Pre-Socratic is the term commonly used to cover those Greek thinkers from approximately 600 B.C. to 400 B.C. who attempted to find universal principles which would explain the whole of nature, from the origin and ultimate constituents of the universe to the place of man within it. This group includes the early Ionian philosophers, who have been called natural philosophers, since they saw a single material principle for all things and processes.

It is important to note that the term *pre-Socratic* indicates not a chronological unit in time but rather a type of outlook and range of interests. This outlook was deliberately attacked and opposed by Socrates, as I shall discuss later, for Socrates condemned natural philosophy as worthless compared with the search for the good life, the discussion of social and political questions, and individual morality. Socrates also dismissed the explanations of the pre-Socratics as inadequate, and for the last sixty years of the fifth century B.C., both points of view existed and a lively controversy went on between them. As Guthrie states, "It was not that the natural philosophers excluded human nature from their investigations but that they saw man and society in a larger framework as a particular late stage in cosmic development, whereas the others deliberately turned their back on the external world" (1965).

HERACLITUS

In the Ionian city of Ephesus, all religions mixed, blended, were compared, and all might seem nonsense to a good mind. There all the questions began in the marketplace, on the road to the seaport, and at the theatre. Everything and everybody mixed together in great flux. No religion clearly appeared the only one or sacred, and the natural tendency in the face of so much might be to doubt all. The inevitable flux and change of this great commercial center naturally led to a search for permanence. The idea of the 'laws of change' or the 'formula of change' being that which is permanent, however, had to come from the genius of Heraclitus. He walked the streets of this big bustling metropolis in the heat and in disgust with himself and everybody else.

Of the interesting variety of pre-Socratic philosophers, the one of greatest importance to psychotherapists is Heraclitus of Ephesus, who lived around 500 B.C. (At least there is some evidence that he reached the peak of his powers, around that time at age forty.) The surviving work of this mysterious and rather cantankerous philosopher amounts to only about a hundred fragments (Wheelwright 1968). One of the great tragedies of human intellectual history is the loss of his book, *On Nature,* a work of so great a reputation that it inspired disciples, the Heracliteans. The problems of interpreting the extant fragments are deepened by frequent metaphors and obscured statements, often made deliberately difficult in order to stir up thought within the reader.

One of the central concepts of Heraclitus is that of *'Logos,'* a term left largely undefined and untranslatable but which implies something common to all existing things that could be accessible to men if it were not for their folly. The Greek term should not be confused with the Logos of Christian theology, a different and much later concept. The Greek word *Logos* can mean proportion, and some authors tend to use the term "formula" to translate it. In Heraclitus, however, 'Logos' is given a corporeal existence and symbolized or associated with fire.

Heraclitus has frequently been misquoted or misinterpreted in his famous statement that one does not step into the same river twice. This theory of flux was brought forward to demonstrate the necessity for the mind, as an interpreter behind apparent continuous change, not to support some form of the impossibility of any knowledge. For him it was the measure inhering in change and the stability that persists through it that were of vital importance. Another basic concept of Heraclitus, 'the unity of opposites,' includes the notion of a necessary tension between opposing forces as vital to producing harmonious functioning, a concept clearly at the basis of modern psychodynamics. Guthrie points out that "the hidden law of nature which he claimed to have discovered seems to have been that all things live by conflict, which is therefore essential to life and thus good. . . . The basis of equilibrium is struggle, which is therefore good in itself, since it is the source of life, . . . We must picture, I take it, a bow ready strung but not in use. As it leans against the wall, one sees no movement and thinks of it as a static object, completely at rest. But in fact, a continuous tug of war is going on within it, as will become evident if the string perishes. The bow will immediately take advantage, snap it, and leap to stretch itself" (1960).

Copleston explains, "The intellect constantly strives to conceive a unity, a system, to obtain a comprehensive view to link things up; and this goal of thought corresponds to a real unity in things: things *are* interdependent" (1962a).

The 'One,' according to Heraclitus, is the differences and the differences are themselves one, they are different aspects of the one: "Neither of these aspects, neither the upward nor the downward path can cease: if they were to cease, then the one itself would no longer exist. . . . Things taken together are whole and not whole, something which is being brought together and brought apart, which is in tune and out of tune; out of all things there comes a unity, and out of a unity all things" (Kirk and Raven 1971).

A fundamental preliminary state of western science is implied here, a fork in the road of the history of the intellect. Heraclitus insists that an intuitive method is necessary to get at the 'one,' rather than only the method of scientific observation and experiment. Heraclitus asserts that men should try to comprehend the underlying coherence of things as expressed in the 'logos,' the formula or element of arrangement common to all things. He regarded himself as having access to, and trying vainly to propagate, an all important truth about the constitution of the world while the great majority of men forever fail to recognize this truth, this 'logos,' this measure, this proportion. Heraclitus considered 'logos' an actual constituent of things and coextensive with his primary cosmic constituent, fire.

When Heraclitus writes "The wise is one thing, to be acquainted with true judgment, how all things are steered through all," he explains that wisdom and consequent satisfactory living consist of understanding and becoming acquainted with the 'logos.' Thus the real motive of his philosophy, as Kirk and Raven (1971) point out, is "not mere curiosity about nature, but the belief that man's very life is indissociably bound up with his whole surroundings." Though such thought is quite foreign to the scientific method and difficult for modern man to appreciate, a return to the kind of thinking demonstrated by Heraclitus, Parmenides, and other pre-Socratics has been made by the modern philosopher Heidegger (see Chapter 20).

Perhaps the most spectacular contributions of Heraclitus rest on his fragments "I searched out myself" and "Man's character is his daemon." Searching out one's self implies that man's inner nature ranges outside the self and manifests itself in interpersonal relations with others as well as in what Searles (1960) has called our relationship with the nonhuman environment. *Daemon* simply means a man's personal destiny is determined by his own character, over which he has some control, and not by external gods or capricious powers. This is a flat denial of the Homeric view, and the starting point of psychotherapy.

Though Heraclitus has been somewhat misunderstood and neglected for 2000 years, he is, in my judgment, the Greek father of dynamic psychiatry. His tone is not that of disinterested science or academic philosophy, as Cavendish (1964) points out. He has an urgent message and what seems to strike him most strongly is mankind's ignorance and lack of understanding. In particular, man does not understand "the purpose which stirs all things through all things." Lack of understanding on this score engenders arrogance and lack of moderation, which to the Greeks were the greatest of sins.

Heraclitus introduces a vital element into Western thought that has been neglected until recently. The object of the pursuit of knowlege is not simply factual or quasi-factual information but rather the acquisition of wisdom and understanding which will yield the fruits of moderation and modesty. The way to this wisdom is not what we would today call rational process, but rather a "breathing in the logos" or intuition—looking into one's self to understand the human and nonhuman world by understanding one's own inner processes. His basic purpose, however, like all of the pre-Socratic philosophers, was to understand nature as a whole. As we turn now to that great transition figure Socrates, I would stress that to work in psychotherapy, one must be willing to tackle the problems of knowledge and truth from many points of view and not insist only on an empirical, scientific approach.

SOCRATES:
UNDERSTANDING AS THE RESULT OF DIALOGUE

The Agora in Athens was actually the birthplace of the modern scientific attitude. As Leonard describes it, ". . . the inquiring intellect of the Athenian . . . was awake in the Agora, where, under the plane-trees or within neighboring porches and porticos, the citizen—whether in his busy hours he were an artisan in gold-work or ceramics, or importer of Pontic grain, or wine-merchant, or shipper at Piraeus, or banker, or physician, or farmsteader of Attica, or keeper of bees in Hymettus, or pilot, or soldier, or public official—still found leisure for friend and stranger and for exchange of news and views. We of a colder zone, of a more secretive and sullen temper, and of a more competitive civilization, can scarcely grasp the educative function of the Agora, but unless we do we cannot understand Socrates" (1915).

There strolled Socrates (470-399 B.C.), a native Athenian with a wife and three children, behaving as a self-appointed gadfly asking questions of anyone who would listen. He was an ugly man with bulging eyes. His stub nose, thick lips, big belly, and squat build suggested a satyr, but he had a rugged constitution and could take considerable cold and hardship, wearing the same cloak winter and summer.

Jaspers (1962) explains that Socrates' father was a stonemason, his mother a midwife. He lived frugally on a small inheritance which along with certain state subsidies paid out to all Athenians enabled him to be materially independent. He fought as a hoplite in the Peloponnesian War and served as chairman of the council in 406 B.C. He refused to take part in the arrest of an innocent man and showed incredible moral courage to the day of his death. His wife Xanthippe has been characterized as a terrible shrew, but the evidence upon which this stands is highly questionable.

Socrates grew up during the powerful, prosperous golden age of Athens. He was about forty when the Peloponnesian War broke out in 431 B.C., and experienced the decline and defeat of Athens in 404 B.C. At the age of seventy, during the second phase of Athenian greatness, he was accused of impiety and corrupting the youth, tried, and condemned to death in the famous trial depicted in Plato's *Apology*. He chose to die rather than to run away from Athens, and in 399 B.C., he took a fatal dose of hemlock. This in turn is described in Plato's Crito.

McInerny (1963) reminds us that Socrates wrote nothing and it is very difficult to know much about him except through the biased eyes of those who came later and wrote about their experiences with him. There are four sources of information: the dialogues of Plato, various writings of Xenophon, particularly his *Memorabilia, The Clouds,* by Aristophenes, and a few important remarks by Aristotle. Aristophenes' comedy is a successful lampoon and caricature and probably bears some relation to the historical Socrates, but it can be hardly taken as a principle source of our knowledge. Since Aristotle writes very little about Socrates, we are actually left with extensive accounts only by Plato and Xenophon.

Xenophon primarily defends Socrates against the charges in his trial and gives little personal recollection. Plato spent much time with Socrates but uses him as a literary character and does not give us verbatim reports of his philosophical activities. The Socrates of Plato's later dialogues is often simply a convenient vehicle for Plato's personal thought. The dialogues, however, vary in the artistic liberty taken with Socrates. Probably the three that, taken together, most accurately recreate the historical Socrates are the *Euthyphro, Apology,* and *Crito.*

Socrates, if he were interested, could have attended some of the works of Aeschylus. He saw the Parthenon and many statues of Phidias started and completed during his lifetime. He was known for his endurance and was allegedly capable of intense and sustained concentration. According to Plato, on one occasion, he stood in deep contemplation for a day and night. "Til dawn came and the sun rose: then he walked away after offering a prayer to the sun." He at times received messages or warnings from a mysterious voice that he called his *daemon.* It is hard to know just what this represents, since it comes to us indirectly and it may have been simply a figure of speech used by Socrates. Others have claimed this to indicate Socrates as a visionary who received a message from God, and it is certainly true that he seems to have had the supreme confidence in his approach and goals characteristic of a man who feels fundamentally he has a divine mission. His confidence is in the *Apology* and *Crito.*

Socrates was certain that the teachings of the Sophists were wrong and that by using his method one could arrive at universal knowledge and could be persuaded to find within the self an inner vision of what is good and true. Copleston asks, "What was Socrates' practical method? It took the form of "dialectic" or conversation. He would get into conversation with someone and try to elicit from him his ideas on some subject. . . . The dialectic, therefore, proceeded from less adequate definitions to a more adequate definition or from consideration of particular examples to a universal definition (1962a). Furthermore, this method, that Socrates called midwifery, also expressed his intention of getting others to produce true ideas in their minds with a view to right action. Socrates was not being pedantic in his attention to definitions; he was convinced that a clear knowledge of the truth is essential for right control of life.

Stumpf claims that Socrates created the Western conception of the soul, the *psyche*. "For him the soul was not any particular faculty, nor was it any special kind of substance, but was rather the capacity for intelligence and character; it was man's conscious personality" (1966). Socrates turned the attention of Western thought away from the facts of the natural world outside of man, which had preoccupied the pre-Socratics, and directed attention to within man himself. Socrates' notion of the soul can be understood as the first primitive metapsychology in the sense that Freud defines metapsychology (see chapter 11).

The dialogue *Euthyphro,* a good example of Socrates' method, has special interest for psychotherapists. It involves a discussion with the youth Euthyphro, who is attempting to prosecute a suit against his own father. He has charged his father with impiety, a capital offense, the same charge brought against Socrates. Thus Euthyphro was attempting to bring about a state murder of his father. This dialogue represents the first example of psychotherapy in Western thought and ends with the unwilling "patient" Euthyphro abruptly leaving Socrates, and for all we know never seeing him again. It is a good example of resistance and of the kind of effect Socrates must have had upon his less sympathetic Athenian audience.

Socrates had a teleological orientation—a view that things have a function or purpose. The diversity of things in the universe are not a haphazard mixture, argued Socrates; each thing does one thing best, and all of them acting together make up the order of the universe. Stumpf writes, "Clearly, Socrates could distinguish two levels of knowledge, one based upon the *inspection* of facts and the other based upon an *interpretation* of facts, one based upon particular things and the other based upon general or universal ideas or conception" (1966).

In the far more complicated dialogue *Theaetetus,* Plato has Socrates describe at some length his own method of interrogation. This maieutic method as practiced by Socrates purports to release what is *already in the mind* of the one being questioned. Socrates claims he has nothing positive to teach, there is no question of transferring something from his mind into that of the person he has questioned: "The irony of Socrates appears most forcibly when one, who with some condescension has agreed to enlighten Socrates, finds himself revealing that he does not possess the knowledge he has so confidently admitted to possessing" (McInerny 1963). Socrates believed that in man's self resides the knowledge of the true and the good, and only the man who pursues his method and is determined to be guided by the truth is truly himself. He is aiming like a true psychotherapist at the independence that comes from self mastery *(eukrateia),* the true freedom that grows with self knowledge.

Probably the best total description of Socrates is in a little book by Taylor (1953). He reminds us that the dialogue *Phaedo* gives a fairly full account of the nature of the Socratic method. Socrates starts from some initial hypothesis which on any grounds appears true, and proceeds to deduce its consequences, "What must follow if this is admitted?" This method, explains Taylor, ". . . is clearly in principle that which has proved itself the one path to truth in scientific theory down to our own time."

The contrast between the directly assertive procedure of the Ionian pre-Socratic philosophers, which had led nowhere, and the Socratic method of studying things in the "statements" we make about them, shows clearly the difference between the Socratic and pre-Socratic approaches. Of course what is missing from both approaches is methodical verification of theory by the confrontation of theoretical consequences with observational facts and experiments.

PLATO: DREAMS AND
FUNCTIONING DIVISIONS OF THE MIND

In turning to a discussion of Plato's philosophy we are interested here mainly in the great ideas that have influenced the development and practice of psychotherapy. Plato wished to take up Socrates' task at the point of Socrates' death, to consolidate his master's teaching and defend it. At the same time he was trying o defend his own idea of the city state as an independent, political, and economic and social unit; in spite of his effort the doom of the city-state was sealed by the conquests of Philip and Alexander.

Plato (428-347 B.C.) is considered one of the very greatest Western philosophers and an enormous amount of philological and philosophical investigation devoted to him has produced agreement on matters of external fact, but still there is no agreement on certain questions fundamental to an understanding of this philosopher. Part of this is Plato's fault since the dialogues which present his emerging and changing philosophy are not always consistent and on some subjects he employs only myths or flatly refuses to explain his views.

Plato came from the high Athenian aristocracy. When he was twenty, he became a follower of Socrates although little is known of their association. In 399 B.C., Plato, along with other supporters of the martyr, fled the city of Athens after the death of Socrates. For twelve years, he traveled throughout various parts of the Mediterranean world. During this time, he wrote the famous dialogues. When he was forty he visited southern Italy and Sicily and while in Syracuse he met the tyrant Dionysius and won the friendship of his brother-in-law Dion, who became his devoted follower.

On his return to Athens around 367 B.C., Plato founded an academy and when Plato was sixty, Aristotle, then a young man of twenty, joined the academy and belonged to it for twenty years until Plato's death in 347 B.C.

Dion and Dionysius the Second invited Plato back to Syracuse and the philosopher took this as an opportunity to put his ideas into practice, but he was twice unsuccessful: once when he was sixty-two and again when he was sixty-seven. Both times the philosopher was bitterly disappointed. It seems that his failure in politics in Syracuse is related to his refusal to accept compromise. He refused to content himself with the best possible under the circumstances and wanted everything or nothing, until his old age.

There is considerable disagreement among scholars as to the chronology of the dialogues. The earliest dialogues in which Socrates' thought is most faithfully rendered are *Apology, Euthyphro, Crito, Charmides, Laches,* and *Protagoras.* This may be termed the Socratic period, and many of these dialogues end without any definite result having been obtained.

The dialogues that characterize the transition period in which Plato was finding his way to his own opinions are the *Georgias, Meno, Euthydemus, Hippias I and II, Cratylus,* and *Menexenus.* Plato's full maturity is reflected in the spectacular dialogues the *Symposium, Phaedo, Republic,* and *Phaedrus.* The remainder are the works of his old age, including the *Theaetetus,* considered by many modern scholars his most important and lasting contribution to philosophical thought and epistemology, the *Parmenides, Sophistes, Politicus, Philebus,* in which he discusses the relationship of pleasure and the good life, the *Timaeus, Critias, Laws,* and *Epinomis.* The first two of these last four dialogues explore cosmological implications of the theories developed in the middle dialogues; the last two are more practical sequels to the *Republic.*

Klein (1970) points out the remarkable parallel in many of the basic notions of Plato and Freud, although he agrees that Freud was not consciously influenced by Plato. For example, both Plato and Freud have presented some of their key concepts as myths. We shall shortly discuss the famous myth in the *Phaedrus* as a convenient introduction to Plato's psychology. Klein points out the relation between Freud's concept of the unconscious and Plato's concept of the two irrational souls: "Both concepts refer to non-cognitive or orectic aspects of human nature. Furthermore, just as Plato attributed higher and lower impulses to the irrational side of human nature, so Freud attributed both id and superego forces to man's unconscious."

The struggle between good and evil desires, between reason and instinct, between disciplined self-control and unbridled impulsiveness, is clearly presented in Plato's mythological account of the soul in the *Phaedrus.* For Plato the attainment of happiness and harmony demands self-control, which in turn requires subordination of the irrational soul to the rational soul. Without this, unhappiness and disharmony from irrational impulsiveness or persistent conflict could result. "In the language of Freud, instinctual id forces are urging one course of action while those of the superego urge an opposite course of action. What Plato described in terms of an irrational soul, Freud described in terms of the unconscious or the amoral id or the dynamism of repression."

Furthermore, both Freud and Plato called attention to the great importance of dreams, and this represents on the part of Plato a remarkable anticipation of Freud's view. Plato refers to desires which find expression in dreams as "terrible, savage, and irregular," and ". . . just as Freud devoted much of his theorizing to an elaboration of the influence of libidinal or erotic forces, so Plato was much concerned with the description and analysis of different ways in which love or Eros may shape the character of men."

Klein even aruges that Plato's notion of the tripartite soul is quite parallel to Freud's depiction of the ego, id, and superego, but I think this involves a misunderstanding of what Plato said. I base this statement on Crombie, who has presented the most careful examination of Plato's philosophy of mind. He points out that most of what Plato has to say about the mind or soul or psyche is said with "moral or religious considerations in view, and not primarily as a contribution to what we now call psychology." So although in the *Republic* Socrates has something to say about the psychology of character and makes use of the tripartite notion of the soul in this discussion, "he derives little from it, and his remarks do not rise above the level of common sense, somewhat simpleminded common sense at that. Indeed one is inclined to say of Plato's psychological observations in general that they are vitiated by the assumption that human nature is a readily intelligible mechanism" (1966).

Thus although Plato gets credit for indicating a definite need for a science of psychology and metapsychology, he really does not go deeply into the subject; he establishes the first formally written metapsychology but on a very simple and primitive level.

Although most texts cover Plato's metapsychology, the clearest presentation is found in Copleston (1962a). In the *Republic* and again in the *Timaeus* we find the doctrine of the tripartite nature of the soul, said to have been borrowed from the Pythagoreans. The soul consists of three parts: the rational part, the courageous or spirited part, and the appetitive part. In the *Phaedrus,* the celebrated msth occurs in which the rational element is likened to a charioteer, and the spirited and appetitive elements to the horses. The one horse is good, the spirited element, which is the natural ally of reason and "loves honor with temperance and modesty; the other horse is bad, the appetitive element which is "a friend to all riot and insolence." While the good horse is easily driven according to the direction of the charioteer, the bad horse is unruly and tends to obey the voice of sensual passion, so that it must be restrained by the whip. Thus Plato takes the point of view that "there are frequently rival springs of action within man; but he never really discusses how this fact can be reconciled with the unity of consciousness, and it is significant that he expressly admits that 'to explain what the soul is, would be a long and most assuredly a godlike labor.' . . . We may conclude, then, that the tendency to regard the three principles of action as principles of one unitary soul and the tendency to regard them as separable remain unreconciled in Plato's psychology" (Copleston 1962a).

A detailed discussion of the horses and charioteer myth may be found in Stumpf (1966). The essence is that just as there can be order between the charioteer and the horses only if the charioteer is in control, so also with the human soul, it can achieve order and peace only if the rational part is in control of the spirit and the appetites.

It is most important for the psychotherapist to understand the Greek notion of the driving force of life or *eros,* defined differently by a variety of Greek writers, a concept at the basis of all mental health. To Bowra:

These different forms of *eros* agree in making it a power which drives a man to throw his full personality into what he does, which sustains him in powerful exertions and impels him to unusual efforts, which sets his intelligence fully and actively to work and gives him that unity of being, that harmony of his whole nature, which is he spring of creative endeavour. It not only removes many doubts and hesitations but by concentrating all a man's faculties on a single point sharpens his vision of it and enriches his understanding. If the complete force of a man's nature works as a single power, he is a full man, and no Greek of the great days would have denied that this was the right and natural way to behave.

This sounds simple enough, and would indeed be so, if in the fourth and later centuries philosophers had not tried to dismember the self, or at least to subordinate active parts of it to some central principle other than an over-riding harmony. When Plato classed all the emotions, except proper pride, as appetites and said that they were naturally hostile to the reason and should be subordinated to it, he robbed the reason of its main source of strength and prepared the way to that hardening and stiffening of it which became characteristic of the exclusively philosophical life. (1962, pp. 209-210)

THE THERAPEUTIC CONTRACT

In addition to establishing the first primitive metapsychology, Plato initiates the tradition of scientific literature, that is the writing down and recording of the details of the atmosphere of the dialogue and the depicting of the fundamental requirements or *therapeutic contract* that must be agreed upon for such an encounter or dialogue to take place. The poetry of Plato presents a therapeutic encounter between two individuals, one of whom, Socrates, is a gifted and intuitive therapist.

What are the terms of the therapeutic contract as presented in Plato's dialogues? In order to improve or heal the soul, there are several conditions which must be met in order to undertake the therapy or investigation by the maieutic method. Abernethy and Langford describe it: "First one must admit that he does not have knowledge and must be willing to seek it . . . Second, there must be . . . a proper disposition of the mind toward true reality. One must admit that he has some awareness of a standard of value or of moral knowledge. Third, the participants in the inquiry must be willing to consent to the guidance of the evidence. In other words a man cannot close his mind to what can or must be found. Rather, at every point of inquiry he must be ready to admit the truth as he finds it and willing to investigate the implication of that truth. . . . Plato wrote dialogues and not philosophical treatises; it is his effort to make the reader an active participant in the discussion, since ultimately the reader is philosophically serious only as he willingly engages in the discussion" (1970).

Jaspers (1962) discusses this Socratic therapeutic contract in even greater detail. The first requirement for a dialogue is the *ability to listen*. One who wishes to speak with other men must remain open to persuasion and not suppose himself to be in ultimate possession of the truth. Mere polemic discourse which serves no other purpose than to annihilate the enemy is a very different matter from discourse aimed at communication to view the truth. Jaspers points out that, "True conversation also requires *good manners.* It requires candor and an attitude of benevolence toward the other. Not only the logical forms, but an understanding of their place in conversation is prerequisite to the discovery of truth in dialogue. Socrates is a picture of urbanity, of freedom from malice even in the most impassioned debate, of communication cloaked in questions, and of the possibilities of playfulness. Bad manners in discussion include: speaking though as handling out orders; refusal to stick to the subject; wanting to be right at all cost; breaking off the discussion with a 'what you say is of no interest to me' or an 'I simply don't understand you' " (1962).

Clearly we have in this material the fundamentals of what today we call the therapeutic contract leading to the therapeutic alliance as discussed in my previous publications (1969a, 1971c, 1974g). It is interesting that although Plato has been given a great deal of credit for his rather simplistic depiction of the tripartite soul as a forerunner of modern psychology, remarkably little has been said about his contribution of formalizing the dialectical method and the therapeutic contract it implies.

This chapter began with a fundamental review of the history of the complex Aegean civilization that represents one of the high points of human development. I introduced Heraclitus and his concepts, especially his contentions that character is fate, and there is much that men could know if only they would not sleep and would be willing to look inward and use their intuition.

Socrates, although he was interested in an entirely different area of knowledge than Heraclitus, developed a method of turning inward known as the maieutic method, in which an interpretation of inward data was attempted for the first time in an effort to resolve questions of ethics.

Plato gained everlasting fame for formulating this method, writing it down, transmitting it, developing the therapeutic contract, and introducing the first metapsychology. It has often been remarked that all western science and philosophy is a series of footnotes to Plato, and this is equally true for the science of psychotherapy. There is a long gap in human history before the various hints of Plato are picked up again by Freud and developed into a formal discipline, but the parallel between Plato's thinking and Freud's approach is inescapable.

Chapter 2

Mental Health, the Good Life, and Happiness

But here in London streets I ken
No such helpmates, only men;
And these are not in plight to bear,
If they would, another's care.
They have enough as 'tis: I see
In many an eye that measures me.
The mortal sickness of a mind
Too unhappy to be kind.
Undone with misery, all they can
Is to hate their fellow man;
And till they drop they needs must still
Look at you and wish you ill.

A. E. Housman, *A Shropshire Lad*

MENTAL HEALTH

It is common knowledge that patients come to psychotherapists for a variety of reasons, most often hoping to be the beneficiary of the therapist's supposed omniscience and omnipotence. Wheelis (1958) and many other authors have pointed out the recent marked shift in what patients are seeking from psychotherapy, from the removal of symptoms to the removal of vague conditions of maladjustment and discontent. He writes that the change is from symptom neuroses to character disorders; to get well these days is to get well from loneliness, insecurity, doubt, boredom, restlessness, and marital discord. The confusion in our society about what psychotherapy can and cannot do about these problems is illustrated by the frequent synonymous use of three terms by philosophers, psychiatrists, and many lay persons. These terms, "mental health," "happiness," and "the good life" are assumed to be either identical or overlapping in meaning, and to be attained by essentially the same means. For example, it is assumed that the good life leads to happiness, that mental health leads to the good life and so on. Patients bring these terms up again and again, for they are vaguely unhappy, certainly not leading what they would call a good life, and hoping that getting well, that is, finding mental health, will mean finding happiness and the good life.

Society reinforces this confusion by the current fashion of bringing psychiatrists (some of whom seem quite willing) into every conceivable kind of community problem as authorities, on the assumption that the psychiatrist has the key to all the variegated difficulties of living that Freud called "everyday misery." The patients so preoccupied with these problems are also intensely watching the psychotherapist consciously and unconsciously to see what kind of a person he is, what kind of life he leads, and whether he appears to have found happiness. This can lead to considerable confusion, since a therapist presents a double message to the patient if he pretends to be omnipotent or have the answer to the quest for the good life and happiness (Chessick 1969a).

From various fields of creative endeavor have come clear and increasingly unrelieved statements regarding the utter meaninglessness and ultimate irrationality of life. Science is of very little avail. As Bertrand Russell (1961) repeatedly points out, increase in science by itself cannot guarantee any genuine progress, for it can in no way help us to find a right conception of the ends of life. Only wisdom can, for above all else, it consists of a right conception of the ends of life. As our world knows only too well, scientific knowledge does not necessarily lead to wisdom.

Camus (1955), in *The Myth of Sisyphus,* deals at length with the concept of absurdity. If God does not exist, then everything is absurd, and to decide whether or not life is worth living becomes the crucial problem of philosophy. Many authors insists that eventually man must face the truth about himself in this new dark age; he is alone in a universe indifferent to his fate, pushed by "a system which has no purpose and goal transcending it, and which makes man its appendix" (Fromm 1955).

Some thinkers have tried to use the intense despair arising from man's hopelessness to revive religious faith. This solution, sometimes called fideism, is very tempting and suggests a reliance on faith as opposed to reason; it takes a variety of forms. Generally speaking, there are two categories of fideism, which may be termed the "institutional" and the "individualistic." One example of individualistic fideism is Tolstoy's rather eccentric and literal form of Christianity. The neo-Thomists, such as T. S. Eliot and a number of outstanding philosophers, prefer to give up science and rational philosophy completely as a foundation for our lives and return to the situation of basing our premises on the blind Catholic faith prevalent in the Middle Ages. Other thinkers have adopted individualistic forms of fideism, in which they develop rather unique and personal views of religion which they practice as they see fit. Wheelis (1958) calls dogmatic systems such as organized religion or Communism "institutional solutions." In the past such systems insisted on having *the* right answer to problems of mental health, the good life, and happiness. Individuals questioning these matters were treated to renew their faith or destroyed as devils, heretics, or enemies of the state.

The problem of evil and injustice in a world supposedly created by a benevolent god is an ancient debate. Only recently have institutional solutions broken down and men turned to find new solutions in directions ranging from leaps into faith to various drugged states. This chapter shall not dwell on fideistic solutions to mental health, the good life, and happiness for three reasons. First, those who have adopted fideistic solutions do not raise therapeutic issues regarding the good life and happiness with the same urgency as those who have not. Second, although the fideistic solutions of thinkers such as Kierkegaard are of interest, there is no way to regard their answers in the light of reason. Either one "believes" or not. Third as Alexander (1951) has pointed out, fideism, especially the institutional forms, represents a regressive solution which refuses to utilize the great technical and scientific advances of our time to establish a new and better life. He views institutional fideism especially as an attempted return to a more immature but happier condition. There is every indication, however, that if such solutions were possible, they would simply make things worse (see Dewey et al. 1943).

Perhaps it is most appropriate for Alexander, a psychiatrist (see chapter 13), to challenge this type of solution. Psychiatrists in clinical practice become all too soon impressed by the eagerness with which patients turn to fantasies and misperceptions based on wishes to solve very frustrating problems. Psychiatrists spend day after day tearing down such castles in the air constructed by patients to protect themselves from recognizing the harsh and sobering facts of their existence. The thoughtful psychotherapist, on the other hand, should never depreciate the intellectual and spiritual attractiveness of the magnificent system of Thomas Aquinas, which exerts an eternal magnetism.

The existential crisis of contemporary culture and the numerous unsatisfactory solutions that have been proposed are reviewed by W. Jones (1969, Vol. 1, Introduction and chapter 1) in an unusually clear form of special interest to psychotherapists. He concludes that what was once merely considered personal catastrophe or disappointment is seen today as a deep sense of cosmic meaninglessness: "The pains we suffer, the misfortunes we encounter, the defeats we experience, including that most final of all defeats—death—are literally meaningless, since the universe is neither beneficent nor hostile, but merely indifferent to us" (1969).

Existential concerns are even more psychoanalytically complex than originally believed, because they often represent a displacement from anxiety over unconscious conflicts (Chessick 1969a). Thus, as conversion symptoms were the fashion in the Victorian era, existential nausea is the current vogue.

Unconscious mental conflicts must be resolved before a person can be considered as genuinely concerned with problems of the good life and happiness. Mental health, as well as physical health and a certain minimum of material prosperity and political freedom, is a condition that must be achieved prior to the pursuit of either the good life or happiness. Otherwise the energies of the individual are bound up in the problems of simple survival. Many philosophers have overlooked this point. A person can have mental health without having the good life or happiness, but he cannot have the good life or happiness without first a reasonable degree of mental health.

MENTAL HEALTH

What is mental health and how is it attained? Roazen (1968) calls it "the capacity to endure—to tolerate frustration, delay, ambiguity, separation, depression." He reminds us of one of Freud's favorite sayings, "One must learn to bear some portion of uncertainty," and of Freud's well-known characterization of mental health as being able to love and to work. In trying to assess a person's mental health more formally, Hartmann (1960) asks, "How secure is the autonomy of the nondefensive functions of the ego, and how well are they protected against being weakened by the energic demands of the defensive structures?"

Saul conceives of mental health as developing naturally if certain fundamental conditions are met during childhood. These are adequate physical care, good feelings toward the child, and positive examples of mature behavior on the part of those responsible for the child and closest to it. He writes: "The child's pattern of feeling toward its parents and siblings, which is formed by about age six, remains constant for life in its essentials. This pattern sets channels for the child's developing feelings toward others and toward itself. And it continues as a permanent nucleus, mostly unconscious, in the personality. The child we once were lives on in each of us however much the rest of the personality matures" (1966).

From severe disturbance of the early mother-child symbiosis with a subsequent warp, as Saul calls it, in the childhood nucleus, the entire variety of impaired ego structures and the fixation on magical operations arise. Of course a great many influences later in life can determine the final set of feelings with which an individual is endowed. A healthy father or a change of mother, for example, can ameliorate an impaired early childhood. A fortunate identification with a relative or teacher in adolescence, marriage to a healthy loving person, or even a lucky circumstance such as an empathetic or understanding employer can do much to cover or even neutralize a pathological childhood nucleus.

In psychotherapy we attempt either to ameliorate the childhood warp through various supportive techniques or to actually reduce the extent of the warp through intensive uncovering techniques. The more serious the warp, the more vital will be the actual human interaction between patient and therapist as a factor in the cure, whether this be characterized as the internalization by the patient of the more benevolent and nonanxious attitudes of the therapist, or in other ways (Chessick 1969a, 1974, Bruch 1974).

Clearly psychotherapy has nothing to say about the good life or about happiness, except to comment that mental health is a necessary precondition to these phenomena. The psychiatrist is no more trained or equipped to lead people to the good life or happiness than anybody else. His solutions are no better and he is no more a winner in the battle of life than many other people. We expect only that the child in the man will be "a little less fractious, unruly, and disruptive in those whose profession it is to help others in life's journey" (Saul 1958).

The most reliable test of mental health is the capacity to exchange love with other persons. If the individual is unable to exchange mature and selfless love with others, there is no point whatever in talking about the good life or happiness. Perhaps Lucretius about 55 B.C. offered the most dramatic description of such a life:

> If only men . . . would not pass their lives as now for the most part we see them; knowing not each one what he wants, and longing ever for change of place, as though he could thus lay aside the burden. The man who is tired of staying at home, often goes out abroad from his great mansion, and of a sudden returns again, for indeed abroad he feels no better. He races to his country home, furiously driving his ponies, as though he were hurrying to bring help to a burning house; he yawns at once, when he has set foot on the threshold of the villa, or sinks into a heavy sleep and seeks forgetfulness, or even in hot haste makes for town, eager to be back. In this way each man struggles to escape himself: yet despite his will he clings to the self. (1924, pp. 141-142)

The question What is love? can be answered in many ways and by a variety of psychological systems (see, for example, Fromm 1963). Anyone capable of love and who has experienced the give and take of mature love knows intuitively the sense of fusion, of belonging, of exchange of feelings with another person or persons on the deepest possible level of intimacy, in which, as Sullivan describes it, "the satisfactions and security which are being experienced by someone else, some particular other person, begin to be as significant to a person as his own satisfactions and security" (1947).

When a patient has become genuinely capable of achieving the selfless exchange of love, I know that my task as his psychotherapist is successfully being accomplished. Pieper, writing from an entirely different starting point, arrives at a similar conclusion: "All neuroses seem to have as a common symptom an egocentric anxiety, a tense and self-centered concern for security, the inability to 'let go'; in short, that kind of love for one's own life that leads straight to the loss of life" (1954). It follows that problems involving the capacity to love others must be resolved first before any discussion of happiness can be meaningful in any context.

The patient, however, will not keep still about matters of the good life and happiness. In fact, as he improves and his energies are released, he begins the process of searching and scanning, so typical in adolescence, for his own identity, his own good life, his own happiness. In the therapy of many patients as it progresses into later stages, an intellectual phase is often necessary, in which the patient is eager to engage in searching discussion, intellectualization, and identification with the therapist on these matters. This phase is useful, although of course from the dynamic point of view it is a more mature version of the mother-child symbiosis; it permits solidification of identity and sets the stage for eventual separation from the psychotherapist. Now although there is a substantial area of agreement on what is mental health and how to attain it (with some glaring exceptions on the part of certain authors), there is no agreement on either what constitutes the good life and happiness or how to attain them. For our purposes it is useful to begin with an idea of the kinds of solutions to these problems that are available; people often try them all at one time or another.

THE GOOD LIFE

The phrase 'the good life' has an archaic and unpleasant ring to many people today for a variety of reasons. It is used here as a technical phrase traditional in philosophy. It is very difficult to completely separate discussion of 'the good life' from a discussion of 'happiness,' but it is necessary to try, for we must carefully avoid the controversial implication that one leads to or is coincidental with the other.

What is the good life, and how is it attained? The first application of reason to these questions began with the Greeks. Every psychotherapist, serving whether he likes it or not as a model of human living for his patients and participating in and observing their struggle to find a good life and happiness, is following a tradition in philosophy that began with Socrates and Plato and was developed at length by Aristotle.

The extent of Aristotle's final revision and reorientation of all classical Greek thought is presented by Farrington. He speaks of the "Aristotelian revolution," which also may be thought of as beginning the tradition of scientific psychotherapy: "For him, knowledge was more than information. His interest was in the interpretation of the facts, the penetration of them by the mind in order to classify them and reveal their interconnections" (1969). Thus Aristotle brought to the highest fruition the tradition of exciting intellectual exploration arising from the Greek mind.

As Jones explains, the typically classical Greek view of human life lies in the notion that man is different from the rest of nature. He has an obligation to live in a characteristically human way, to do certain acts and abstain from others. "Man must live up to his responsibilities as man. . . . No one expects animals to temper their violent impulses; the law for them is such that they must devour one another in order to survive. But men are capable of an inner discipline, a self-restraint in their dealings with one another. They ought to live by this uniquely human law; when they do not, they sooner or later pay for their violation" (1969). The two basic classical Greek approaches are to be found in Plato and Aristotle, and each will now be discussed along with an example of a recent approach based on the same principles—Santayana as a follower of Plato and Veatch as an interpreter of Aristotle.

For Plato, there is an eternal 'form of the Good,' existing separately from the sensible world. It cannot be fully realized in nature, and it is unchanging as an ideal. Arnett points out that the good life, according to Plato and Santayana, is "something whole, complete, ordered, and perfect; many possibilities must be considered, but finally one must choose a particular *form* of life for his own and labor toward that goal" (1955). However, the result is an ideal that is not only a goal but has aesthetic value; thus, the good life for Plato and Santayana is both an art to be practiced and an ideal to be contemplated.

Santayana is a theoretical man, not a man of action. For him fine art "is the delightful *consummation* that makes life finally and wholly worth living" (Arnett 1955). The good life, from this point of view, is an aesthetic vision involving a rational ordering of the parts of the mind and a contemplation of the "human pageant." Arnett insists that it is a misunderstanding of Santayana to assert that this later philosophy represents an abandonment of concern for humanistic values and an immersion in the contemplation of timeless essences. Yet Friess and Rosenthal (Schilpp 1951) make just such a criticism, and one cannot read Santayana without being impressed by the lack of concern for a struggling humanity in his discussion of the good life. We are aware of the withdrawal from interpersonal relations into a more contemplative existence stressing, for example, the pleasures of aesthetic as the keystone of the good life. Santayana writes: "The appreciation of beauty and its embodiment in the arts are activities which belong to our holiday life, when we are redeemed for the moment from the shadow of evil and the slavery to fear, and are following the bent of our nature where it chooses to lead us" (1938).

To put it simply, this view holds that the misery of man cannot be alleviated so therefore let us contemplate the imaginary. It is not necessary for our purposes to compare and contrast Plato and Santayana; it is sufficient to understand their basic approach and not to fall into the error of calling this a neurotic retreat. Essential to their conviction is a fundamental division between the sensible world of everyday perception and the intelligible world of divine essences. The good life for them is characterized by reason establishing an inner harmony in the personality and guiding the individual to focus attention and interest on the essences of beauty and goodness rather than on striving in this world.

ARISTOTLE: THE GREEK IDEALS

The opposing classical view is based, of course, on the work of Aristotle, especially *The Nicomachean Ethics* (1941). A modern interpretation of this point of view is presented by Veatch (1966, 1974). Aristotle's basic premise states that there is *no* 'eternal Good' outside of nature; the good is instead what is most natural. What is uniquely natural to man is to use reason. Therefore, according to Veatch's interpretation of Aristotle, the good life for man is one that uses intelligence to decide upon goals. It is this kind of rational activity that determines the good life, not passive contemplation.

Aristotle (384-322 B.C.) is not so clear as Veatch would have him. Born in the Ionian city of Stagira, his father died when he was a boy and he was brought up by a guardian who sent him to Athens where he joined Plato's Academy. He remained there from 367 B.C. to 347 B.C. when Plato died, becoming thoroughly imbued with Plato's philosophy. Thereafter he became the first professional philosopher, systematizing and correcting Plato's work and building upon it in his own way. At one point he spent a notable three years tutoring the thirteen-year-old son of Philip II of Macedon, who later protected Aristotle as Alexander the Great but paid no attention to his *Ethics.* From 335 B.C. to 323 B.C. he presided over his famous peripatetic school in Athens but left at the death of Alexander the Great. He died in exile in Chalcis at age sixty-two.

A full understanding of Aristotle's contribution to psychology really requires a thorough familiarity with his total system beyond the scope of this book and demanding more study than can be reasonably expected from the nonprofessional philosopher. From our point of view, Aristotle's works on psychology *(De Anima: Parva Naturalia,* including "On Memory and Reminiscence," "On Dreams," and "On Prophesying by Dreams") do not represent an important advance on Plato's basic metapsychology since they require an acceptance of Aristotle's entire philosophical system in order to make sense. Sullivan (in Wolman 1972) would disagree, and Watson points out that *De Anima* is "the first systematic treatise on psychology in that it deals with the functioning of the individual organism as a whole. . . . With this book psychology as a discipline consciously differentiated from other field comes into being. In writing it, Aristotle became the first psychologist and the founder of psychology" (1963).

Plato conceived of the soul as an individual "entity" which existed before birth and continued to exist after death; his tripartite soul discussed in the *Republic* and again in the *Phaedrus,* consisted essentially of a rational, a spirited, and an appetitive part. These were really principles of action which involved the bodily drives or needs, the passions and emotions, and human reason, which Plato hoped would rule over the whole. The driving force of the soul was defined by

Plato in the *Symposium* as Eros, and each aspect had its own proper drive or desires, for example, the rational part has a passion for truth. Whether the three aspects are separable or inseparable is never worked out, but at least Plato represents an advance over Socrates in that Plato's soul can suffer inner conflicts—the problem of reason as the charioteer, with one good and one bad or unruly horse, described in the *Phaedrus.*

Aristotle denied the Platonic notion of the soul as a separate entity having an eternal separate existence, although he was not consistent on the subject. He developed the notion of a multifaceted soul at greater length, resting his description on the hierarchy of a nutritive faculty; a faculty involving sense perception, animal desire, and local motion; and a rational faculty peculiar to humans. For Aristotle the soul or psyche represented the actualization or "entelechy" of an organic body potentially endowed with life. As he explained it in *De Anima,* the soul is the raison d'être of the body.

Aristotle's *De Anima* deals with the soul of *all* living things and the notion of "life" is not clearly distinguished from "psyche," except that "life" seems to represent the manifestations of a power or powers that enable a creature to grow and reproduce, whereas the soul or psyche represents a form or essence—a cause and moving principle in every living body.

Even the ancient Hebrews distinguished in a vague way between the soul *(nephesh)* and the spirit *(ruach).* The spirit (meaning literally "wind" or, in a person, breath) denotes that which is the mark of the living as opposed to that of the dead. At other times it is used to represent the motivating power or the life force of the soul, somewhat akin to Plato's use of Eros in the *Symposium.*

Reason *(nous)* is divided by Aristotle into a passive and active faculty of the human soul. In a much disputed passage in *De Anima,* Aristotle mentions that "active reason" might have some eternal existence of its own, and it participates in some way with the eternal Unmoved Mover. Later Christian theologians rejected this notion, but there is a curious inconsistency in Aristotle's position about active reason and the rest of his philosophy, which regards essences as inseparable from matter. Furthermore, he uses the concept of reason *(nous)* in two ways, sometimes as scientific intellect and practical deliberating power and at other times as what he might call intuition or the mysterious power of grasping self-evident truths, through some combination of intuition and induction. This is as far as Aristotle's psychology goes, and he explains that "to attain any assured knowledge about the soul is one of the most difficult things in the world."

No new great ideas fundamental for psychotherapy are contained in Aristotle's psychological works; it is rather to the *Nicomachean Ethics* that the psychotherapist should turn. Here the first systematic attempt is made in Greek thought to deal with the identical clinical problems that patients present to the psychotherapist today. It remains the best treatise on human living antecedent to the idea of the unconscious mind.

Bertrand Russell, before he had formed his final opinion on the matter complained, "The views of Aristotle on ethics represent, in the main, the prevailing opinions of educated and experienced men of his day. . . . The book appeals to the respectable middle-aged, and has been used by them, especially since the seventeenth century, to repress the ardours and enthusiasms of the young" (1945). O'Connor on the other hand agrees with me that "the *Nicomachean Ethics* is still, at least in some of its parts, a very influential book. Echoes of its doctrines can be found in a good deal of present-day ethics" (1964). He continues, significantly, "The rest of his philosophy, however, is vitiated by a fatal flaw. It is very closely tied up with an entirely false scientific picture of the world."

Let us have a closer look at the *Nicomachean Ethics*. In Book I, Aristotle reviews the three approaches to the good life—the pursuit of sensual pleasure, the pursuit of power and honor, and the contemplative life. Happiness is the highest good and can be attained by the active practice of the proper function of a human being. He rejects the Platonic idea of the absolutely fixed Good as of little value in everyday affairs—an attitude which marks Aristotle's basic pragmatic, common-sense approach to life.

The psyche, according to Aristotle, consists of two elements, one rational and the other irrational. Whether these are physically separate or only abstractions of functioning entities is irrelevant. The rational and irrational elements of the psyche are each subdivided into two parts. The irrational part contains both a vegetative striving and a source from which all emotional desires spring. The vegetative aspect is shared completely with animals; the emotional part can be made submissive to reason, and when we have made it submissive to reason, we have achieved "virtues of character."

The rational part (Book VI is divided into the "scientific faculty," by which one contemplates first principles, and the "calculative faculty," by which man deliberates contingent or varying things. The development of these scientific and calculative faculties to the utmost represents the achievement of "intellectual virtue." Thus the good life consists of activity based on virtues of character and on intellectual virtues—the achievements most proper to human beings.

The virtues of character are based on the famous and usually misunderstood doctrine of the golden mean. Intellectual virtues are the result of learning, but virtues of character are the result of habit and practice. Thus man must actively work at *both* understanding *and* the development of his character in order to achieve the good life.

At the end of the *Ethics* (Book X) Aristotle arrives at an untenable and inconsistent conclusion. If the scientific faculty as defined above is the highest faculty of the psyche, the most divine, then it would follow that the greatest happiness would consist of the exercise of this faculty. Thus the contemplative life is the best life and the happiest life. The continuing contemplation (not pursuit or discovery) of first principles or absolute truths becomes the greatest happiness.

Aristotle's practical and active approach shows itself in his repeated stress on possession of friends and certain basic material things as a down-payment on happiness. The life of the businessman, however, can obtain only a limited happiness, because he is pursuing as an end, wealth, what ought to be a means. Aristotle realizes that a certain basic material well-being is necessary to permit leisure to develop the intellectual and character virtues. He also suggests that "the man who is very ugly in appearance or ill-born or solitary and childless is not very likely to be happy. . . . Happiness seems to need this sort of prosperity in addition."

It is hard to do justice to Aristotle's magnificent intellectual edifice in such a short presentation. He fully recognizes the "human-ness" of human beings, and because of this he agrees that attainment of the virtues of character is necessary for the good life; in fact he believes that most people have to settle for this. Beyond the virtues of character, however, Aristotle believes that a privileged few can develop the virtues of intellect and in so doing strive to transcend the "human-ness" of their species. A fascinating inconsistency is present here in Aristotle's philosophy, for it is based on the notion that each individual of a species attempts teleologically to attain to the best actualization of the form of that species. An exception is made for humans in his notion of their possession of an active or separable reason which is an element that has a spark of the divine. Because of this, humans have the additional drive to transcend their own species and attain to the divine. The ambiguous character of the human species is not clearly worked out in Aristotle, but it provides the first philosophical approach to the notion of transcendence which is very important in psychotherapy and will be discussed in detail in later chapters.

The objections to Aristotle's *Nichomachean Ethics* are many, and not always fair. At least two basic categories of complaints can, however, be raised. The first category I label "emotional objections." Many critics have complained of a curious aloofness, aristocratic snobbery, and lack of compassion in Aristotle's *Ethics*. His approach seems to be suitable for only the small portion of mankind predisposed to turn their back on suffering and perhaps on all object relations in general and to seek happines from predominantly intellectual proceedings. This approach is not intrinsically wrong; it simply is irrelevant and useless to the vast majority of people.

Ross (1963) presents formal philosophical discussion and thorough review of Aristotle's philosophy. He describes Aristotle's not surprising transition from viewing the contemplation of the truths of metaphysics and mathematics as the highest form of happiness to arguing for contemplation and worship of God as the ideal in his *Eudemian Ethics*. Ross also notes the serious omission of aesthetic contemplation as a factor in happiness according to Aristotle's theory. He correctly points out that the word "happiness" is a mistranslation, and prefers "well being" to emphasize that happiness is a state of feeling differing from pleasure only by its suggestion of permanence, depth, and serenity; Aristotle's term implies an *activity:* the greatest good for man is rational activity in accordance with virtue.

Randall (1960) in chapter 12 of his outstanding book on Aristotle presents the best short summary of the spirit and content of the *Nichomachean Ethics*. He makes the important point that the coolness of the *Ethics* is "apt to seem disappointing on first reading." There is a lack of fervor: "Where is the fire, the enthusiasm, the compelling force, the *eros* of Plato?" The sober sanity and wisdom of Aristotle seem foreign to our Age of Anxiety, as Randall calls it. He argues that "Aristotle is not a system, but a spirit, a method, an intellectual technique." Readers tend to miss the point that Aristotle insists on the acceptance of brute given facts as the only possible starting point for thought and action. Readers are disappointed because "They fail to discover Aristotle's basic conviction that wisdom is learning how to deal, not with what might be, but with what is." To put it simply, for happiness we need not only intellect but practical sense, and this is not very romantic. The resemblance to Freud is unmistakable.

Russell as indicated previously, dislikes Aristotle's *Ethics*. He insists that the *Ethics* has no intrinsic importance and contains an "emotional poverty" that is not found in the earlier philosophers. There are two basic complaints. First, a certain snobbery is implied in the *Ethics,* in that the contemplative life of highest happiness is obviously available only to the few, especially to the philosophers. Second, the *Ethics* offers little to help the man of strong passions: "He has nothing to say to those who are possessed by a god or devil, or whom outward misfortune drives to despair." Furthermore, Russell accuses Aristotle of "an almost complete absence of what may be called benevolence or philanthropy. The sufferings of mankind, in so far as he is aware of them, do not move him emotionally; he holds them, intellectually, to be an evil, but there is no evidence that they cause him unhappiness except when the sufferers happen to be his friends" (1945).

Allen presents a diametrically opposite opinion and devotes an entire chapter in his book on Aristotle to the *Ethics.* He underscores Aristotle's views that the purpose of the teacher is not only to learn the truth but to improve men and make them happier. He writes: "Comprehensiveness of view, tolerance and humanity, great acuteness in psychological analysis, a judicious and consistent view of the scope of *Ethics* and its method of procedure are the good points in Aristotle's work; they are also the qualities most conspicuously lacking among contemporary moral philosophers" (1952).

Bonnard (1961) ignores Aristotle's discussion of happiness but levels major criticism at the Aristotelian concept of scientific thought and the conclusions of Book X. Obviously, a life devoted to contemplation of the already known tends to choke off the process of scientific discovery. He also makes a curious differentiation between Aristotle the "savant" and Aristotle the "philosopher." In the latter role, Aristotle appears as distasteful to Bonnard as to Russell, although for different reasons. It is interesting that so many authors admire Aristotle's consistency and reasonableness but cannot emotionally accept the conclusions of Book X. Though it seems clear these conclusions are based in part on a misconception of science and in part on certain erroneous premises in Aristotle's metaphysical system (W. T. Jones 1969) and that Book X needs revision in the light of modern science, this certainly does not nullify the whole of Aristotle's thought.

A more fundamental category of objection rests on the logical structure of Aristotle's argument. The argument that what *is* natural *ought to be* has been attacked in many ways. G. E. Moore (1966) calls this "the naturalistic fallacy," and Veatch's (1966) attempt to refute Moore is not very convincing.

Moore brings us to the modern approaches to the problem of the good life. He severely criticizes Aristotle's *Ethics* and flatly claims that reason cannot establish what is meant by "good." In an important sense, however, "good" is indefinable, simple, and unanalyzable. When we say a state of affairs or thing is "good" or not, the quality "good" is known by direct apprehension or intuition and cannot be defined. Later on in his book Moore insists: "By far the most valuable things, which we know or can imagine, are certain states of consciousness, which may be roughly described as the pleasures of human intercourse and the enjoyment of beautiful objects. No one, probably, who has asked himself the question, has ever doubted that personal affection and the appreciation of what is beautiful in Art or Nature, are good in themselves; nor, if we consider strictly what things are worth having *purely for their own sakes,* does it appear probable that any one will think that anything else has *merely* so great a value as the things which are included under these two heads." Thus "personal affections and aesthetic enjoyments include *all* the greatest, and *by far* the greatest, goods we can imagine," worth having purely for their own sake. (1966)

Moore is very important historically because of his great influence on modern English philosophy. It is possible to argue that after Moore all confidence that by reason alone one can find the good life is gone, although Moore carefully points out that *the* good, that which is good, *is* definable. (For a basic summary of Moore's extremely technical and difficult views see Castell [1966], and for a more technical and formal discussion and summary see Schilpp [1968].)

Maugham carries this view further. Having lived among those who made the contemplation of art the main business of life, he found "little to admire in them." They are "vain and self-complacent" as well as "inept for the practical affairs of life." He sees aesthetic contemplation only of value if it moves us to right action and argues that "loving kindness is the better part of goodness," an extenuation of life and an affirmation of our independence. Yet even Maugham ends on a sour note, for he points out that "goodness is shown in right action and who can tell in this meaningless world what right action is" (1946). The problem of the good life, unanswerable by reason alone, remains unsettled in our time. All we can say is that our notion of the good life assumes the presence of and must be consistent with our notion of mental health.

HAPPINESS

Disagreement and confusion on the subject of happiness is even more widespread: The term is badly misused and must be carefully defined in any discussion. Do we mean, for example, temporary happiness or a long-term state? There is certainly no compelling reason for the assumption on the part of many philosophers that the good life brings happiness.

There are four alternatives on this subject, only two of which are consistent with our notion of psychodynamics and mental health. The first is expressed by Sophocles in *Oedipus at Colonus:*

Not to be born surpasses thought and speech.
The second best is to have seen the light
And then to go back quickly whence we came.
The feathery follies of his youth once over,
What trouble is beyond the range of man?
> (Grene and Lattimore 1959, Vol. 2, p. 134)

Or as Camus (1955) states, "There is but one truly serious philosophical problem, and that is suicide." To answer this question in favor of suicide is not consistent with mental health.

A second alternative is stated by Kant, who argues that pleasure or private happiness is the direct opposite of the principle of morality, and therefore man should not make happines his direct goal (defining happiness as the satisfaction of all our desires). This can be easily carried to a logical absurdity; it is like insisting that a waterfall should flow upward (Russell 1962). All men strive for what gives them a sense of personal happiness—even the philosopher who tells them not to do so and the religious ascetic who tortures and starves himself.

The idea that man is capable of an enduring happiness if he lives a certain type of life represents the third alternative. True and enduring happiness for both Plato and Aristotle is the true end of man; it is sharply distinguished from a life of physical pleasure, which, for different reasons, both philosophers consider to be inferior. "Aristotle agreed with Plato that the activities of reason are not only qualitatively different from the satisfactions of appetite but also superior to them" (Jones 1969).

The sophists argued, in contrast to this approach, that every man is a measure of his own good; whatever feels good to a man is good to him. This titillation of the senses is defined as pleasure, and happiness consists in getting as much pleasure as possible. Plato's disagreement with the sophists was based on his concept of the 'Form of the Good' which was "real" and universal for all and which had little room for the pleasures of the body. The good life is an organic whole for Plato and based on harmonious balance among components in the soul.

Plato's views *changed* in the various dialogues and are often presented in mythological form, making exact interpretation impossible. Plato viewed happiness as a reward for living the good life, in contrast to Aristotle, who saw happiness as the end for which the good man aims. For Plato there are two levels of goodness, that of the philosopher and that of the ordinary man. Happiness as a reward, or at least satisfaction or enjoyment, comes to the ordinary man as the result of temperance and balance. For the philosopher, a higher form of happiness is possible, coming through love of wisdom and indifference to the things of this world.

In a later dialogue, the *Philebus,* the good life is viewed as a "blended life"; both pleasure and intellectual activity are seen as important, but an order of priority is established, with intellect at the top. Pleasures must never interfere with our intellectual activity; the latter is more "noble," distinguishes us from the beasts, and is related to Plato's mystical theory of the soul. The philosopher knows this, and "devotes himself to the study of matters so momentous that they must make all temporal matters seem of no significance in the light of the soul's ultimate destiny" (Crombie 1966).

Some modern philosophers have followed this third alternative also. For example, Santayana would agree that a stable and enduring happiness is possible as a result of "rational discipline" and leading the good life as he conceives of it. Yet reason is not enough in his view; aesthetic pleasure is needed also; in fact, beauty is more fundamental than truth in regard to enduring human happiness.

Aristotle, Veatch, and Russell are agreed that living a good life gives the best guarantee that happiness can occur, or at least that certain habits and activities guided by reason can increase the chances of happiness. Aristotle argues more extremely that living the good life automatically brings happiness. Veatch repeats Aristotle's argument that the good life is equivalent to the happy life but holds considerable reservations about the "incredibly varied and frightful and unforseeable misfortunes that can befall a man in the course of his life." The argument rests on Aristotle's assumption that although a man may declare he is happy, he is not "truly happy" unless the satisfactions he possesses are those of his "natural aspirations and strivings and tendencies" and are characteristic" and consist of "living intelligently."

Freud (1930) expresses the fourth alternative, viewing happiness as only periodic. He offers a very clear discussion of happiness: "What we call happiness in the strictest sense comes from the (preferably sudden) satisfaction of needs which have been dammed up to a high degree, and it is from its nature only possible as an episodic phenomenon." Thus, any situation of prolonged pleasure can only offer us "mild contentment," according to Freud, and we are "so made that we can derive intense enjoyment only from a contrast and very little from a state of things." The way we are constituted restricts the possibility of happiness.

Freud defines happiness as, at best, the attainment of pleasure through direct or indirect gratification of drives, or, at second best, as the avoidance of unpleasure. He enumerates a variety of ways that men have avoided unpleasure in their own body, in the external world, and in their relationships with other men. With the aid of sublimation the individual tries to become as independent of fate as possible and to actively seek the pleasures of fulfillment of sublimated drives.

Freud makes few value judgments but does imply that "working with all for the good of all" and creative work or the scientific pursuit of truth have intuitively a "finer and higher" quality. He, therefore, views the problem of happiness to be basically the problem of avoiding unpleasure or deriving gratification of (usually) sublimated drives and admits to many sources of temporary happiness, which is all that is possible. He advises a sort of diversification of techniques and is against any golden rule that holds for all: "Every man must find out for himself in what particular fashion he can be saved. All kinds of different factors will operate to direct his choice. . . . The man who is predominantly erotic will give first preference to his emotional relationship to other people; the narcissistic man, who inclines to be self sufficient, will seek his main satisfactions in his internal mental processes; the man of action will never give up the external world on which he can try out his strength" (1930). Freud recognizes this to be an unfinished discussion, and at a number of points he indicates that metapsychological characterization of these various techniques to attain happiness has not been worked out. He dogmatically insists that institutional solutions such as religion have a definitely hampering effect on the attainment of happiness.

To summarize, there is a serious confusion in the mind of many people about what psychotherapy can and cannot do. This is illustrated in the overlapping and fuzzy use of the terms "mental health," "the good life," and "happiness" in everyday speech, in the literature of psychiatry and philosophy, and in the popular press. For example it is frequently assumed that all three concepts are attained by a similar means such as psychotherapy, positive thinking, and so forth.

This problem is especially pressing in our time, because the complaints of people have sharply changed from expression in classical symptoms, such as hysteria, to so-called characterological or existential preoccupations involving vague feelings of despair and maladjustment. The breakdown of faith in religious and political institutions has accelerated this change and increased the urgency of the problem, requiring a clear notion of these concepts. Furthermore, whether the psychotherapist likes it or not, his patients are constantly scrutinizing him in order to discover and identify with his life patterns and solutions. The therapist must be aware of these problems in himself and not present the patient with a double image.

Mental health is a condition that must be achieved prior to the successful pursuit of either the good life or happiness, just as physical health and a certain minimum of material prosperity and political freedom are necessary. Otherwise the energies of the individual are bound up in the problem of simple survival. Mental health is today conceived basically along the lines of Freud and Saul, involving impairment of early ego functions and so leading to inability to cope with the problems of adult life and reduced capacity to endure frustration. The best measure of mental health is the capacity to exchange mature love; without it, the entire discussion of the good life and happiness becomes meaningless.

Two classical Greek approaches to the good life are reviewed in this chapter. They are based on the attempt to find a solution more or less through the use of reason. These solutions primarily involve passive other-worldly contemplation (Plato, Santayana), and activity based on practical wisdom (Aristotle, Veatch). Modern philosophers have indicated that no absolute solution based purely on reason is possible and that intelligent opinion rather than either pure reason or psychotherapy is the best approach we have to the good life. Even the phrase "the good life" is of debatable meaning.

One must distinguish between the concept of a permanently happy life and momentary happiness. Platonists and neo-Platonists seek a stable and enduring happiness; at the other extreme, authors like Sophocles or Kant feel that the entire concept of personal happiness is either illusory or of secondary importance. Other philosophers argue that living a good life gives the best although quite uncertain guarantee that enduring happiness can be attained, while Freud conceives of temporary happiness in terms of the pleasure principle.

Chapter 3

The Philosopher as Psychotherapist

In the life of a man, his time is but a moment, his being an incessant flux, his senses a dim rushlight, his body a prey of worms, his soul an unquiet eddy, his fortune dark, and his fame doubtful. In short, all that is of the body is as coursing waters, all that is of the soul as dreams and vapours; life a warfare, a brief sojourning in an alien land; and after repute, oblivion. Where, then, can man find the power to guide and guard his steps? In one thing and one alone: Philosophy. To be a philosopher is to keep unsullied and unscathed the divine spirit within him, so that it may transcend all pleasure and pain, take nothing in hand without purpose and nothing falsely or with dissimulation, depend not on another's actions or inactions, accept each and every dispensation as coming from the same Source as itself—and last and chief, wait with a good grace for death, as no more than a simple dissolving of the elements whereof each living thing is composed. If those elements themselves take no harm from their ceaseless forming and re-forming, why look with mistrust upon the change and dissolution of the whole? It is but Nature's way; and in the ways of Nature there is no evil to be found.

Marcus Aurelius, *Meditations*

BEYOND THE PLEASURE PRINCIPLE

From the spring of 1919 to the spring of 1920 Sigmund Freud wrote one of his most remarkable, fertile, and speculative books, entitled

Beyond the Pleasure Principle (1920). Three years later he developed a serious case of carcinoma of the jaw and underwent the many well known surgical procedures and adventures as outlined in the recent book by Schur (1972), his personal physician.

Schur sees Freud's formulation of the death-instinct concept as having steeled him for the sixteen year ordeal of his cancer and also as having prepared him for his belief in the supremacy of the ego or the intellect as the only force with which to face one's fate. He writes, "We may thus modify Freud's statement of 1913 and say that in recognizing death intellectually man can hope to overcome not *death* but his *fear* of it." Of course all later Hellenistic philosophy also deals with this problem, but first for comparison let us have a look at how Freud approached the matter.

Beyond the Pleasure Principle (1920) begins by relating pleasure and unpleasure to the quantity of excitation present in the mind and relating "them in such a manner that unpleasure corresponds to an *increase* in the quantity of excitation and pleasure to a *diminution.*" The pleasure principle follows from the principle of constancy, that is to say the tendency towards stability, towards keeping the quantity of excitation of the mental apparatus low and constant, so that anything that increases this quantity of excitation is "bound to be felt as adverse to the functioning of the apparatus, that is as unpleasurable." Up to the time of this writing by Freud, it was believed that there exists in the mind an exclusively strong tendency towards obedience to the pleasure principle; the pleasure principle was believed to dominate mental life.

Freud goes on to argue in the second and third sections of his work that the *repetition compulsion,* manifest in the dreams of traumatic neuroses and transference phenomena, seem to argue against the pleasure principle, and he gives the famous example of the child who attempts to actively master unpleasure by repetition. In the transference and in the so-called fate neuroses, unpleasant past experiences are recalled: "The impression they give is of being pursued by a malignant fate or possessed by some 'daemonic' power; but psychoanalysis has always taken the view that their fate is for the most part arranged by themselves and determined by early infantile influences. The compulsion which is here in evidence differs in no way from the compulsion to repeat which we have found in neurotics, even though the people we are now considering have never shown any sign of dealing with a neurotic conflict by producing symptoms." He concludes from this that there must be *another* principle at work in these phenomena beside the pleasure principle.

It is interesting that he uses the same terminology as Heraclitus (see chapter 1)—character is daemon for man. He also refers to the famous myth of Plato in the *Symposium* that living substance at the time of its coming to life was torn apart into small particles which have ever since endeavored to reunite through the sexual instincts. In the final sections of this important work he sets up the beginnings of modern metapsychology and concludes with a long section which he himself labels as essentially speculation.

He summarizes his argument in a later work, *An Outline of Psychoanalysis* as follows: "After long hesitancies and vacillations we have decided to assume the existence of only two basic instincts, *Eros* and *the destructive instinct*. ... The aim of the first of these basic instincts is to establish ever greater unities and to preserve them thus— in short, to bind together; the aim of the second is, on the contrary, to undo connections and so destroy things. In the case of the destructive instinct we may suppose that its final aim is to lead what is living into an inorganic state. For this reason we also call it the *death instinct"* (1940).

Freud points out in *Beyond the Pleasure Principle*, "*It seems, then, that an instinct is an urge inherent in organic life to restore an earlier state of things* which the living entity was obliged to abandon under the pressure of external disturbing forces; that is, it is a kind of organic elasticity, or, to put it another way, the expression of the inertia inherent in organic life" (1920). In *Eros* this would take the form of the tendency to pursue the development of life and to repeat the process of creation of life; in the death instinct the compulsion to repeat would take the form of the tendency to return to the inorganic state. It is clear that these instincts are only to be found in fusions of varying proportions, for the individual would quickly die if the death instinct were not bound or neutralized by the life instinct. Thus the concept of fusion is an indispensable assumption in instinct theory.

Writing near the end of his life in "Analysis Terminable and Interminable" (1937a) Freud himself realized his link to the pre-Socratic philosophers. In a remarkable paragraph he reminds us of the theories of Empedocles of Acragas (in Sicily), born around 400 B.C.

(see chapter 1). Freud points out that one theory of Empedocles very closely approximates the final psychoanalytic theory of the instincts; he is even tempted to maintain that the two are identical except that the Greek philosopher's theory is a cosmic fantasy while "ours is content to claim biological validity."

Empedocles taught that two principles govern events in the life of the universe and also in the life of the mind and that those principles are everlastingly at war with one another. He called them "love" and "strife" and Freud admits that these two fundamental principles of Empedocles are both in name and function the same as his own Eros and Thanatos, the destructive instinct, "The first of which endeavors to combine what exists into ever greater unities, while the second endeavors to resolve those combinations and to destroy the structures to which they have given rise" (1937a). The debate over Freud's separation of instincts into Eros and Thanatos is unsettled today. It is usually difficult to accept the possibility that a death instinct is operating as Freud described and that there could be some kind of longing for the state of death or the inorganic state in every living thing.

SPENGLER: DECLINE OF THE WEST

Before we again approach ancient history directly, a remarkable phenomenon deserves mention, the meteoric work of Spengler (1880-1936). His first volume appeared in 1918 at the moment of his country's defeat in World War I, and not long before Freud began work on *Beyond the Pleasure Principle.* This visionary German obtained his doctorate in 1904 with a thesis on Heraclitus and embarked upon a career as a high school teacher, but in 1911 he abandoned teaching to take up the penurious life of a private scholar in Munich. His major work, *The Decline of the West* (1962), has been mercilessly criticized on all sides and is best appreciated as poetic vision rather than scientific study of history. It contains numerous lapses in scholarship and inattention to detail, but it has an unmistakable fascination for the open mind.

Spengler calls for a revolution in our way of viewing human history, away from the linear interpretation of progress. He sees an indefinite number of cultural configurations, of which western Europe is only one, that "grow with the same superb aimlessness as the flowers of the field." The organic unfolding, flowering, and dying of these cultures is outlined as Spengler's theory of history and it is this biologizing of history for which he has been most criticized.

Actually Spengler was only familiar in detail with two cultures—the classical Greek and the modern Western. Borrowing from Nietzsche he refers to classical man as Apollinian—a man who conceived of himself as living in a local finite space exemplified by the life-sized nude male statues and the small columned temple. In contrast, modern Western man is Faustian, with an urge to reach out and fill boundless space with his activity. Typically Faustian are long range weapons, the conquest of space, and the Gothic cathedrals with their spirals soaring skyward.

Spengler speaks of cultural cycles in terms of the succession of the four seasons. For example, in the Apollinian culture the spring of the culture—an early heroic, rural, agricultural, and feudal time—is marked by the inspiring epics of Homer, powerful mystic religion, and the work of anonymous artists. The summer of the culture is characterized by towns which are still tied to the country, like Athens and the plains of Attica, the evolution of an aristocracy of manners, and the work of named geniuses in art. Early city states reach a full ripening in the autumn of the Apollinian culture. Spengler calls this civilization, a hardening and congealing in which the cities grow, religion is challenged by philosophy, and tradition is undermined. The Apollinian culture is reflected in the work of Socrates and Plato. Finally in the winter of the culture, the decline of civilization is marked first by a brief romantic stage of nostalgia and then by the evolution of the megapolis, the mob, the strong-minded antimetaphysical man, the money spirit, *panem et circenses,* imperialism and energy directed outward, the cessation of great music, painting, and architecture, and what Spengler calls megapolitan philosophy—practical, irreligious social and ethical philosophy, such as that of the Stoics, Epicureans, and Schopenhauer. In the Apollinian culture this is the age of late Hellenic times and the Roman empire.

The Faustian culture saw its spring in the high Gothic middle ages, its summer in the geniuses of the Renaissance, its autumn in the high Baroque and Rococo work of Kant, Mozart, and Goethe, and its winter ushered in by Napoleon and awaiting now, Spengler predicted, world conquest by a Ceasar-like figure that he hoped would be German.

Spengler never gives any explanation as to why cultures undergo this transformation, but of course the parallel to Freud's concept of the fusion and interplay of Eros and Thanatos is very apparent.

These visions of both Freud and Spengler should help us grasp the *Zeitgeist* of the late Hellenic and Roman period. As Rodes (1970) points out, "it seems undeniable that the total ambience of a given period profoundly affects as well as reflects the lives of the people."

During the lifetime of Epicurus, Athens had forty-six years of wars and uprisings from 307 to 261 B.C.—wars which obliterated even the sense of common Greek ties. Bonnard describes the period: "Greeks were no more taken prisoners, women no longer respected—nothing but the sword, rape, and slavery. In the public life of the cities, the parties of what remained of them fought for a semblance of power. Four times in Athens, the foreigner intervened, occupied the city, and modified a phantom constitution which was never put in force. Three times there were insurrections. Four times the cities stood a siege. Blood, fire, slaughter, pillage—such was the moment of Epicurus" (1962). This was also the ambience of Europe right after the First World War, a period which produced *Beyond the Pleasure Principle* and Spengler's *Decline of the West.*

Along with the passing of the golden age of the city states, a general decline in freshness and vitality overtakes the Greek world. If there is one outstanding features that all the great Athenian philosophers had in common, it was a boldly cheerful attitude to life. As Hamilton writes in *The Greek Way,* "To rejoice in life, to find the world beautiful and delightful to live in, was a mark of the Greek spirit which distinguished it from all that have gone before. It is a vital distinction. The joy of life is written upon everything the Greeks left behind and they who leave it out of account fail to reckon with something that is of first importance in understanding how the Greek achievement came to pass in the world of antiquity" (1973).

When one compares the philosophic speculation of the late Hellenistic age with that of the great golden age of Athens one is forcibly struck by the wan and tired look of the age of decadence. Philosophy in the golden age was an adventure requiring the alertness and adventure of the pioneer. Later, philosophy displays the courage of resignation and patient endurance of an age where the old society has crumbled and there is a sense of the civilization's oncoming winter in the air. Men sought primarily peace and made a virtue out of putting up with hardships that could not be avoided. For example, the central aim of the doctrine of Epicurus was the attainment of an undisturbed condition of peacefulness, *ataraxia*. Today Bertrand Russell's philosophy returns again and again to the search for what he calls "unselfconscious alertness," the same state that Epicurus is seeking, except that Russell insists that such a state can be attained by "disinterestedly striving for understanding." The late Hellenistic age was marked by the lack of security. Since nothing seemed rational in the ordering of human affairs, people took to worshipping the goddess of fortune or luck, *Tyche*. There was no longer any incentive to take an interest in public life.

The Hellenistic world sank into chaos after the death of Alexander for lack of a despot strong enough to achieve stable supremacy or a principle powerful enough to produce social cohesion. There was widespread social discontent and fear of revolution or conquest on all sides. This general confusion brought moral decay and intellectual enfeeblement as all ages of prolonged uncertainty seem to do, inimical as they are to the prosaic everyday virtues of respectable citizens. There is no use in thrift when tomorrow all your savings may be dissipated by economic conditions. There is no advantage in honesty when the man toward whom you practice it is pretty sure to swindle you. There is no point to steadfast adherence to a cause when no cause is important. Such confusion led men like the early Cynics and Skeptics of the Hellenistic age to despair of the world and to feel that life on earth is essentially bad. The purpose of life is simply to escape misfortune rather than to achieve any positive good; fear takes the place of hope.

Klein points out that philosophy under these conditions becomes what we call today psychology of adjustment. The important question becomes, How can a person best promote his own welfare? Klein writes, "In the language of Freud, the Cynics urged conduct governed by the reality principle as contrasted with the Cyrenaic preference for indulgence of the pleasure principle. For the Cynics this meant the acquisition of virtue as the best protection against the vicissitudes of fate in a world of strife and uncertain fortune. On the other hand the Cyrenaics believed the pursuit of pleasure and the concomitant avoidance of pain are a better way of coming to terms with such a world" (1970). These issues were subsequently elaborated in the later rivalry of the Epicurean and Stoic movements, which differed from one another regarding the means to be employed but which agreed that philosophy had to be the art of achieving personal happiness.

Spengler explained that as a culture reaches the noon culmination of its being we get strict, measured, self-confident, and finally sweet and fragrant art such as the Cnidian Aphrodite, the Hall of Maidens in the Erechtheum, and the art of Watteau and Mozart, but in the grey beginning of civilization, the fire dies down, romanticism looks sadly back and life becomes weary, reluctant, cold, and dies. As the world city or megapolis grows, philosophy centers its interest in the individual, endeavoring to meet his demands for guidance in life. For in the large society there is not room to feel part of the community; rather the individual is cast adrift and loosed from his moorings. In such situations, the great thinkers repeatedly return to the pre-Socratics, Stoicism, for example, having recourse to the physics of Heraclitus, and Epicurianism to the atoms of Democritus.

Three phases of late Hellenic philosophy are usually distinguished. The first phase extends from about the end of the fourth century to the middle of the first century B.C. It is characterized by the Greek founding of the Stoic and Epicurean philosophies which placed emphasis on conduct and the attainment of personal happiness and returned to the pre-Socratics for the cosmological bases of their systems.

Set against these systems were the rival schools of Skepticism and Cynicism, which led to a certain eclectic approach in the later phase from about the middle of the first century B.C. to the middle of the third century A.D. Cicero is an example of such an eclectic. Later on more religious, mystical elements were introduced into these systems. The final period, from the middle of the third century A.D. to the middle of the sixth century A.D., is represented by neo-Platonism and represents a full turn to esoteric mysticism. In this period, I will concentrate on the doctrines of Epicurus and the Stoics as most pertinent to the great ideas in psychotherapy.

EPICURUS

I have already described the time of Epicurus, who lived roughly a century after Plato at the very end of the fourth and in the first third of the third century B.C. His thought and his life of suffering (he was a sick man) make a rejoinder, austere and serene, to the idealistic dreams of Plato. Born at Samos in about 341 B.C., he went at eighteen to Athens for his military service and finally in 306 B.C. opened his own school there in a garden that was bequeathed to him and his disciples. For his work in this school, Epicurus received great fame. In contrast to the Stoics, strict philosophic orthodoxy was maintained among the Epicureans more than any other school. The chief doctrines were given to the pupils to learn by heart. It is said that Epicurus was a voluminous writer, but most of his writings are lost and it is mainly through his famous Roman disciple Lucretius that we have some details of his thinking.

Epicurus took a new direction in philosophy, for he focused upon the individual and his immediate desire for bodily and mental pleasures instead of upon abstract principles of right conduct or consideration of God's commands. The ultimate pleasure human nature seeks is repose, which Epicurus claims can be achieved by scaling down our desires, overcoming useless fears, and turning to the pleasures of the mind which have the highest degree of permanence. His doctrine includes the denial of sexual pleasure; at very best, his disciple, Lucretius, sees no harm in sexual intercourse provided it is divorced from passion. The safest social pleasure is friendship and there is a very strong emphasis on its importance. Like Freud, Epicurus holds that the two greatest sources of fear are religion and the dread of death. These are connected since religion encourages the view that the dead are unhappy. The fear of death and the fear of divine intervention in the natural processes of the world are two worries which, according to Epicurus, if removed would make it easy for us to achieve mental repose.

His turn to the pre-Socratics was in an effort to demonstrate on cosmological grounds that both great fears are merely false superstitions. There is a clear relationship between Epicurus' notion of pleasure and Freud's pleasure principle. Both are based on what might be called egocentric hedonism. On the other hand, Epicurus should not be identified with advocates of living from moment to moment in the pursuit of as many and as violent pleasures as possible. This is a gross distortion of his doctrine. He agrees that the satisfaction of any desire is *per se* pleasant but thinks that the enlightened pleasure seeker will avoid violent and extreme pleasures because of their adverse after-effects. Thus it is better to lead a simple and frugal life of self denial. He found his greatest satisfaction in conversation with his friends.

Thus the Epicurean ethic leads to a moderate asceticism, self control, and independence. Virtues such as simplicity, moderation, temperance, and cheerfulness are the most conducive to pleasure and happiness and even Epicurus' concentration on friendships is based on the search for pleasure in the sense that the happiest men are they who have arrived at the point of having nothing to fear from those who surround them.

Similarly, in *De Rerum Natura,* the famous philosophic poem of Lucretius, we find an entire work dominated by the Epicurean desire to free mankind from superstition and the fear of death. Death is merely the dispersion of a particular combination of atoms which go to make up the human soul and hence is really nothing and cannot be feared. Lucretius (99 B.C. - 55 B.C.) portrays a sense of the organic returning to the inorganic, strikingly parallel to the arguments in *Beyond the Pleasure Principle.* He accepts the hope of nonexistence as a deliverance and describes (see chapter 2) how men seek escape from themselves when they are victims of inner conflict and vainly seek relief in a change of place.

STOICISM

The Epicurean school survived until the fourth century A.D. By way of contrast to the *ataraxia* of the Epicureans, the Stoics extolled the ideal of *apatheia* or emotional detachment in the sense of a cultivated indifference to changing events whether good or bad. Klein points out that it would be misleading to confuse this word *apatheia* with its English derivative "apathy" in the sense of listlessness or lack of ambition. Stoics were anything but listless or lethargic. Klein writes, "Their chief concern was to foster an inner life of rugged personal integrity that would be immune to the lusts, hungers, and cravings associated with pleasure-seeking impulsiveness. They were apathetic with respect to the pleasures of the table, the thrills of becoming wealthy or famous, and the joys of gratified desire. But they were not apathetic about resolute devotion to the cultivation of virtue. For them, such cultivation called for suppression of desire and emotion by disciplined thinking and willing. . . . In line with this viewpoint, the Stoic, aiming at improvement of his mental health—what he called the health of his soul—found himself at war with his emotions" (1970). These philosophies took over the priestly functions of bolstering self-confidence, aiding in the solution of personal problems, and assuaging guilt. In Roman times the Stoic philosophy was especially influential, and its practitioners functioned frankly as psychotherapists.

Individual well-being for the Stoic was contingent upon the sovereignty of reason or upon insight into the probable consequences of yielding to given impulses. Self-mastery was seen as a function of such insight. Klein writes, "Broadly considered, such a Stoic teaching is in line with some modern views regarding the promotion of individual well-being. At all events, it is not uncommon for psychotherapists to stress attainment of insight as a *sine qua non* of therapeutic progress. . . . There may thus be something in common between Freud's reference to, 'the voice of the intellect' and the ancient Greek injunction 'Know Thyself' inscribed in golden letters on the Temple of Delphos" (1970).

Freud relied upon the primacy of the intellect as eventually developing a reasonable understanding and evaluation of one's own mental processes in order to attain mastery over unconscious conflicts. As Klein points out, "In brief, modern man's quest for mental health and the good life continues to reflect insights dating back to the similar quest of Stoic and Epicurean philosophers. Seen in this light, it is an open question whether the past is illuminating the present or the present is illuminating the past. It is probably safer to conclude that the applied psychology of the ancient 'healer of souls' and the applied psychology of the modern psychotherapist reflect what is common to all human beings—especially when they are troubled, anxious, confused, and possibly in search of the *apatheia* of the Stoics or the *ataraxia* of the Epicureans or the *integrated personality* of the moderns" (1970).

Klein overstresses the parallel between Stoic and Epicurean philosophy and modern psychotherapy, but there is no doubt that courage in the face of danger and suffering, indifference to material circumstances, and the Socratic way of life in general are the virtues that the Stoics valued. There is a recognition that in some sense the internal good of virtue is more vital than other things. Losses of material possessions in some measure can always be repaired, but if one loses his self-respect, he becomes less than human.

The Greek founder of the Stoic school was Zeno (not to be confused with Zeno the pupil of Parmenedes, who posed the famous "Zeno's Paradoxes"). Zeno was born about 336 B.C. in Cyprus and died in 263 B.C. at Athens. He went to Athens as a young man just after Aristotle's death and founded his own school about 300 B.C., taking the name from the place where he taught—*stoa,* a porch or open collonade. It was the simple ethical opinions of Socrates rather than the elaborate metaphysical theories of Plato and Aristotle that were the primary inspiration of Zeno's views. He was also influenced by the arguments of the Cynics, who state that since poverty, suffering, and death obviously do come to good men, none of these are really bad and the truly virtuous man will be indifferent to everything that happens to him. Though this was too anarchical a doctrine for Zeno, happiness for the Stoics basically represents the peace of mind that comes through acceptance of the universe as it is and a corresponding indifference to the course of events.

Zeno was succeeded in the leadership of the school by Cleanthes of Assos, and Cleanthes by Chrysippus of Soloi, who was called the second founder of the school because of his systematization of the Stoic doctrines. He is said to have written more than seven hundred and five books.

The Stoics maintained a rationalism which was scarcely consistent with their empiricist position, and indeed the Stoic doctrine, always evolving, was constantly plagued by internal inconsistencies which were never quite resolved. The earlier Stoics believed that the virtues are all connected as expressions of one and the same character, so the presence of one virtue implies the presence of all. Conversely, when one vice is present all the vices must be present, and therefore either a man is completely virtuous or he is not virtuous at all. So a man who has almost completed the path of moral progress is not yet virtuous and has not achieved true happiness. A consequence of this doctrine is that very few attained to virtue and then only later in life. "Man walks in wickedness all his life, or at any rate, for the greater part of it. If he ever attains to virtue, it is late and at the very sunset of his days." This quotation is attributed to Cleonthes. There is an unbearable coldness in the early Stoic conception of virtue. Not only bad passions are condemned, but all passions. The Stoic does not feel sympathy; when his wife or his children die, he reflects that this event is no obstacle to his own virtue and therefore he does not suffer deeply. Friendship, so highly prized by Epicurus, is all very well but must not be carried to the point where your friend's misfortunes can destroy your holy calm, and so on.

The moral theories of the Stoics could not be integrated with their mechanistic determinism. For the will cannot be thought of as being free if its milieu is a universe whose operations are all fatally predetermined. Thus Stoics argue that since the universe is good there is actually no evil in it and if anything is interpreted as evil the thinker is obviously making an erroneous judgment. He must endure whatever comes to him in the way of pain and suffering and all other things that are normally accounted as evil. Oates points out, "Though everything in the universe is determined, nevertheless there remains to the individual the power to use correctly or incorrectly his impressions. If he concludes that there is no evil in the universe, he has used his impressions correctly and he is 'living in accordance with nature' in the deepest sense" (1940). This theory, though obviously paradoxical, had a wide emotional appeal to the early adherents of the Stoic philosophy. As time passed, the paradoxes become more and more intolerable to the spirit of rational metaphysics, and since the creed continued to exert its emotional and moral appeal, frequent efforts were made to mend the rational inconsistencies by borrowing doctrines from various schools. As a result the Stoicism of the first century B.C., for example, presents an incredible patchwork of beliefs.

The most important Stoic philosopher of the late classical period is of course Epictetus (A.D. 50-138). All that is really known about his early life is that he was a slave in Rome during the reign of Nero. Later he acquired his freedom and taught in Rome until A.D. 98, when the emperor Domitian expelled all philosophers from the city. The whole of Epictetus' teaching is summed up in the phrase "bear and forbear." If a man will only have this at heart and heed it carefully he will for the most part have a life that is tranquil and serene.

Epictetus was the head of his school until his death, but we have no writings extant from him, only lecture notes taken by his pupil Arrian.

Arrian also published a small catechism or handbook of his master's doctrine, the well known *Enchiridion,* which according to Copleston (1962) was given customarily by the director of a Swiss mental hospital to his neurasthenic patients and who found it to be a valuable aid in effecting a cure. The word *Enchiridion* is an adjective meaning "in the hand" or "ready at hand." Epictetus in the *Discourses* often speaks of the principles which his disciples should have ready at hand, and it was thus natural that Arrian after putting together the notes of his master's discourses or lectures should attempt to embody his teaching in the manual or *Enchiridion.* On the other hand, I wonder if the director of the mental health sanatorium in Switzerland ever read what he had handed over to his patients. For example, it is written, "If you kiss your child or your wife, say to yourself that you are kissing a human being, for then if death strikes it you will not be disturbed." And, "It is better for your son to be wicked than for you to be miserable."

Actually the Roman Stoics did not practice what they preached, and their personalities, from Epictetus to Seneca to Marcus Aurelius, often showed marked contrast to the coldness of their doctrines. These authors must actually be read to get the flavor of their personalities; no summary or abstract discussion of their doctrines really gives a fair picture of the Stoic way of life.

The noble morality of the Stoics is strikingly displayed in the life of three great Romans: the classless Seneca, the slave Epictetus, and the emperor Marcus Aurelius. Seneca was tutor and minister to the emperor Nero, opening his veins in obedience to Nero's command in A.D. 65. He has been accused of inconsistency and hypocrisy as courtier and tutor to Nero, but it must be remembered that the contrast between surroundings of great wealth and splendor on the one hand and the constant fear of death on the other would very much help a man of his temperament to realize the ephemeral nature of wealth, position, and power. He had unrivalled opportunities of observing human degradation, lust, and debauchery at close quarters. Seneca tempered the strict moral idealism of the earlier Stoics. He knew too much about the moral struggle to suppose that man can become virtuous by sudden conversions and so he distinguishes classes of proficiency and approximations to wisdom or perfect virtue. He is one of the first authors to emphasize the use of daily self-examination, which he himself practiced.

MARCUS AURELIUS

The Stoic philosophy is brought to its highest development by the emperor Marcus Aurelius, who lived A.D. 121 to 180 and reigned from 161 to 180. His book is usually translated under the title of *Meditations* but he seems to have called it *To Himself*. It is interior dialogue partly written down and Highet (1971) suggests that it ought to be called "Conversations With Himself." Highet points out that it is not really a book in the sense of having a beginning, a middle, and an end, and it is a mistake to read it straight through except to get the spiritual flavor of the man's mind and a general view of the book's character. He writes, "After that it should be sipped, not drunk down at a draught; chewed and digested, not swallowed at a gulp. To read one section and think it through provides almost enough healthy intellectual and moral nourishment for one day." This book emphasizes that we are liable to be afflicted and injured by spiritual diseases which are self-caused and self-inflicted and have to spend much time and much effort in trying to treat and cure them. A healthy body seems to live on almost automatically and will do its best to repair minor injuries, but the human spirit often seems to try to tear itself apart, to make itself sick, to wound and destroy itself. Marcus Aurelius even attempts to classify the destructive impulses.

Although the sad bearded face of his portrait and the sombre thoughtful words of his meditations gives us the impression of a retiring intellectual, Highet writes, "He was also a superb military commander, a fine disciplinarian, a master of tactics and terrain, and a first rank strategist for the long term" (1971).

Marcus Aurelius was the last thinker for many centuries to confirm the old ideal of moderation, and he is a fitting symbol of the close of the classical world. The sense of law and order, of balance and moderation, was one of the principle marks of the classical spirit. The Stoicism of Marcus is already quite different than that of Zeno and he seems to stand at a point of transition. The famous essay by Matthew Arnold portrays him as wise, just, self-governed, tender, thankful, blameless; yet, with all this, agitated, stretching out his arms for something beyond. The antique Stoic self-sufficiency is replaced in him by a diffidence and consciousness of his own imperfections, and the whole tenor of his writing suggests to some that a short step forward would have carried him across to Christian humility. He writes, for example, "Remember, it is the secret force hidden deep within us that manipulates our strings; there lies the voice of persuasion, there the very life, there, we might even say, is the man himself." And, "Accustom yourself to give careful attention to what others are saying, and try your best to enter into the mind of the speaker" (1964).

There are innumerable quotations dealing with the ephemeral nature of worldly goods and the transience and foolishness of ambition and power. There is an emphasis on integrity, on goodness, on a simple life with no fear of work, and on serenity of temper.

AESCULAPIUS:
FIRST ATTEMPTS AT PSYCHOTHERAPY

At Epidauros in Greece is the sanctuary of Aesculapius, the god of healing and son of Apollo by a mortal mother. Aesculapius was compassionate and kind and strove to alleviate man's suffering. Here was the most famous healing center of the ancient world, effecting cures of not only the physical health but also the psychic harmony of the patient, regenerating him completely. The Aesculapia of Epidauros was a religious institution of higher spirituality and artistic beauty, marked by remarkable achievement in the physical and spiritual reformation of men. Its history lasts from the end of the sixth century B.C. to the end of the fifth century A.D.

The priests of Aesculapius, who were not primarily physicians, had advanced towards contemporary science in *Nootherapia* or mind-healing, in psychosomatic healing, and in the search for and comprehension of the spiritual laws regulating the universe. They claimed to know about the great influence exerted by harmony and order in the universe on the psychic harmony and the physical health of men and about the unlimited potentialities in spiritualized thought to restore the body and the mind. Apparently they perfected practical methods for the application of this knowledge at the sanctuary of Aesculapius. Plato writes in the *Symposium*, "Medicine must indeed be able to make the most hostile elements in the body friendly and loving toward each other. . . . It was by knowing the means by which to introduce 'Eros' and harmony indeed that, as the poet here says and I also believe, our forefather Aesculapius established this science (art) of ours." These methods consisted mainly of attempting to influence the mind, for the belief was that it was the mind that basically governs the body. Considering that the cause of disease is mainly mental, the method to cure it must also be mental or spiritual. The patient in failing to guard his mind has let himself become sick either because he did not know how to protect himself or because his spiritual resistance was lessened.

Patients were healed at the Aesculapion through the high spirituality of the priest and the artistic and harmonious atmosphere of the place, which attempted to help him cast out all his erroneous beliefs and illusions and so recover his natural and harmonious condition. A part of this cure was sleeping at the Aesculapion during which dreams took place. An analysis of the dreams was employed to try to understand what was wrong and what needed to be done to help the sick dreamer. This sleeping procedure in the Abaton in the sanctuary of Aesculapius was called *enkoimisis* and although it was not the basic and always necessary means to cures, it was considered the culminating or last phase of a long series of purifications.

A healing was considered to be a success only when the mind itself was cured; when there was a change of mind, *meta-noia*. It was believed that the body of course could be cured directly with various medicines, but this cure was only temporary. Since the generative cause dwelling in the mind is not eliminated this way, it may at any time call forth new disharmonies in other parts of the body.

In addition to this procedure, the priests used the harmony and rhythm of music, dance, and poetry for character-building efficacy and for the immediate healing influence they asserted upon the mind and the body. Gymnastics and athletic games were also utilized because they disciplined the movements and the inner rhythm of the body, strengthening the psychic and physical capacity in man. Artistic creation and contemplation and enjoyment of the beautiful through the masterpieces of architecture, sculpture, and painting were employed because they were considered an important factor for the elevation and spiritualization of human thought and the restoration of health of both mind and body. It was believed that active contemplation of the beautiful and the good brings harmony and health to every individual. The more man's thought communes with the divine harmony the more spiritual, powerful, and healthy he becomes.

It should be pointed out that the worshippers in Aesculapios were not uneducated, naive or credulous people; they included distinguished men of great culture like the tragic poet Aristarchos, the orator Aristides, and even Marcus Aurelius, and Sophocles; the latter actually ministered personally as a priest at the Aesculapion in Athens and composed a well known song in honor of the god, which unfortunately has not been preserved.

The healings of the body and the mind that occurred in the sanctuary of Aesculapius were the natural and necessary outcome of the worship of Aesculapius and emphasized a spiritual awakening from sleep through the dreaming which took place, and through which the individual identified himself and became conscious of his true nature.

This chapter deals with a problem that has to be faced by anyone who practices psychotherapy. This existential problem is essentially based on the decay, destruction, and death that are inevitable in every human life and probably inevitable in every culture. The attitudes and approach that the psychotherapist takes toward these inevitable problems inevitably serve as an example to the patient. The outcome of the struggle against certain return from life to death is always known in advance but it makes the difference to be willing to grapple with the problems of life and the inevitable decay of both individual and culture. Spengler explains, "We have not chosen this time. We cannot help it if we are born as men of the early winter of full civilization, instead of the golden summit of a right culture in a Phidias or a Mozart time. Everything depends upon our seeing our own position, our destiny, clearly on our realizing that though we may lie to ourselves about it we cannot evade it" (1962).

In contrast to this passive recognition, we have the courageous attempts of the Stoics and Epicureans to preserve life and to enhance it in a similar age.

Erikson's (1959) concept of the late stage of life as being characterized by either integrity, or despair and disgust helps clarify this distinction. Such despair is often hidden behind the show of disgust, a misanthropy, or in chronic contemptuous displeasure with particular institutions and particular people—a disgust and displeasure which if not allied with constructive ideas and a life of cooperation only signify the individual's contempt of himself. The psychotherapist who has not grappled with these problems and is unable to empathize with them will inevitably have a difficult time.

In this historical material, the profound polarity between the empirical materialist visible world and the invisible spiritual world of being is manifest. The invisible world reigned in the middle ages; now science reigns. Spengler's thesis is that the pendulum swings back and forth. In any case, we must be aware of the profound influence of both aspects of human living.

Chapter 4

The Teacher as Model

I did not understand, until I read Confucius, the impact of one man upon another.

Ezra Pound

ANCIENT CHINA

Confucius (551-479 B.C.) was undoubtedly China's most famous man; his ideas influenced the civilization of all Eastern Asia. He has fallen into some obscurity in Western civilization today, and he is under attack by the current Chinese government. Thanks to the poet, Ezra Pound, we have been recently reminded of the pertinence and importance of the thoughts of Confucius.

By 1500 B.C. a civilization under the Shang dynasty (1523-1028 B.C.) was in full swing in China. It flourished mainly along the valley of the Yellow River; the excavated capital of this civilization is called Anyang. The Shang dynasty gave way to the Chou dynasty, which lasted in a declining form from about 1000 B.C. to 256 B.C. After a series of wars among princes, Shih Huang-ti in 221 B.C. became ruler and instituted important reforms, including the building of the Great Wall of China. However, he believed in an absolute emperor and burned the books of Confucius. He died in 210 B.C., and his successors were overthrown by Kao-tsu, founder of the Han dynasty, in 202 B.C. During this militarily powerful dynasty, Confucianism became

official, and all China was converted to Confucian decorum and
stability.

TAOISM AND CONFUCIANISM

Chinese thought began to flower during the Chou dynasty. The
oldest sage was Lao-tze (605-517 B.C.) who presented the concept of
Tao, meaning essentially "the way" and implying moral guidance or a
code of behavior. This philosophy stressed inner freedom and
tranquility. The original Taoists thought ill of government and of all
interferences with nature. They complained of the hurry of modern life
which they contrasted with the calm existence of those whom they
called "the pure men of old." There is a flavor of mysticism in the
original doctrine of the Tao, and it soon took a highly mystical
direction, becoming for many a system of private magic.

Lao-tze composed the *Tao-teh-king* (Bahm 1963; Waley 1965), the
bible of Taoism, which is so cryptic it can be interpreted in an endless
variety of ways. It stressed simplicity, humility, contentment, and
allowing the laws of nature to carry one through life. It opposed the use
of force. Its spirit of quiet meditation was replaced by a great many
primitive magical practices and later rejected altogether by the
aristocrats of China, who adopted the rules and regulations of
Confucius.

Confucius departed from the original Taoists in rejecting the idea
that nobility was inborn. Nobility was for him a matter of education
and conduct. The marks of gentility were goodness, wisdom, and
courage; the importance of cultivation of these virtues was stressed as
the way to happiness. For him Tao meant the practice of all the virtues
becoming to a gentleman. He was adverse to theologic speculation,
devoted to decorum, and reluctant to resort to violence. Under his
influence the rulers of China for two thousand years gave a remarkable
stability and coherence to Chinese culture and politics.

There are important differences between Confucians and Taoists,
reflected for example, in disagreement about *Te* (virtue). Kaltenmark
points out: "To Confucius, *Te* was a quality acquired by living nobly in
cultured company. As the possessor of *Te,* the sage exemplifies an ideal
of civilization and becomes a model of behavior for all around him: his
virtue is thus contagious, efficacious" (1969). For the Taoists, virtue

centers on an inner quietude, humility *(wu-wei),* and simplicity, and all class distinctions are considered irrelevant. In a probably apocryphal meeting between Confucius and Lao-tze, the latter is reported to have said: "I have heard it said that a good merchant hides his wealth and gives the appearance of want; if endowed with a rich supply of inward virtue, the superior man has the outward appearance of a fool. Get rid of that arrogance of yours, all those desires, that self-sufficient air, that overweaning zeal; all that is of no use to your true person" (Kaltenmark 1969).

Koller points out that "the basic aim of Chinese philosophy has not primarily been that of understanding the world, but of making man great. Although the various Chinese philosophies share this common aim, they differ considerably as a result of different insights into the source of man's greatness. Thus, in Taoism, the emphasis is upon becoming great by becoming one with the inner way of the universe. On the other hand, in Confucianism, the emphasis has been upon developing man's humanity by cultivating human-heartedness and the social virtues" (1970).

Recently Tseng (1973) has supported this view of the basic humanism of Confucius. He contrasts the emphasis of Freud and Erikson on the earlier part of a person's life with the concern of Confucius over the latter part of life and contrasts the Chinese lack of urgency about hurrying the young toward early social independence and emotional maturity with the frenetic approach of the West. Western authorities are increasingly concerned with this tendency and its dangers (see, for example, Blos 1971), and are turning more toward an investigation of the middle and late years of life.

Tseng explains that "one of the most valuable contributions made by Confucian thought is its suggestion that obtaining internal satisfaction is the essential way to achieve happiness. Power, wealth, or honor do not alone make a person happy; they may contribute to happiness, but they are secondary to the condition of obtaining internal satisfaction. As long as a person is diligently making use of his potentiality to obtain knowledge, to develop his talents, to cultivate his own personality, to be good to others and to himself, and to 'know' how to be satisfied with this condition of striving itself, disregarding the outcome of it, then he is gaining the real happiness of life" (1973).

Confucianism and Taoism were later fitted together into the peculiar symbolism known as Yang-Yin, which combines private, mystical magic with public display of gentility and decorum. This symbolism is charged with a great many often incomprehensible meanings. Everything in the universe shows the interplay of these forces. Yang is the Confucian, positive, or masculine, force. It is found in everything that is warm and bright, firm and dry and steadfast. Yin is the Taoist, negative, or feminine force. It is found in everything cold and dark, everything soft, moist, mysterious, secret, and changeable. At one time Yin may be stronger, at another time Yang. In each person's life the changing balance of Yin and Yang brings now failure, now success, now flowering, finally decay. Yang and Yin do not represent good and evil, and in this the religion differs from so many others. They are both seen as necessary to the order of the universe. When they are in harmony, they are always good.

Bertrand Russell during his visit to China in 1922, was quite impressed with Taoism, although not pleased with Confucianism. He thought that the Chinese civilization was most like that of the Greeks, since both shared a profound sense of ethics, but that the Chinese showed very little depth in the way of religion and science. He believed the Chinese were happier because of the influence of Lao-tze, which stressed "production without possession, action without self-assertion, development without domination." He pointed out the radical contrast between Lao-tze and Western ideas about the ends of life: "Restlessness and pugnacity not only cause obvious evils, but fill our lives with discontent, incapacitate us for the enjoyment of beauty, and make us almost incapable of the contemplative virtues. In this respect we have grown rapidly worse" (1961). He saw the Chinese as aiming more at enjoyment of life, while the West aims more at power.

CONFUCIUS

The facts about the life of Confucius have been lost or blended with legend over the ages, and it is very difficult to put together much biographical information about him. We know that his father died when he was three years old and that Confucius was the child of his father's old age. As a small boy, after the death of his father, he became considerably preoccupied with rituals and postures of ceremony. Little is known about his schooling, but apparently he was largely self taught. On the other hand he was a diligent scholar and seems to have acquired considerable knowledge.

He was deeply distressed by the misery he saw all over China. The feudal states were divided between powerful nobles who did as they pleased. The aristocrats made war as a hobby, taxed their subjects, exhausted them with forced labor and oppressed them at will. Starvation was common; Confucius spent a great deal of time attempting to influence the political situation and government in the China of his day, but as we might expect, little attention was paid to him.

While waiting for the opportunity to become an important minister and thus influence the government, which never came, he talked to younger men about his principles and gradually a group of disciples formed around him. As the years passed he considered himself definitely to be an unsuccessful man. Even in his fifties he set off on a decade or more of arduous and sometimes dangerous travels through various states to find a ruler who could confide to him the administration of his state. He died at 72, convinced he was a failure. He was married at the age of nineteen and fathered one son and two daughters. His relationships with his wife and children were apparently poor, and there is some talk even of a divorce.

An interesting anecdote is provided by Legge (1935) about Confucius and his son. Apparently Confucius spent some time badgering his son to read the Confucian writings, to learn the Odes and to study the Proverbs. His son, like so many sons who have followed him, kept putting the assignment off. He was repeatedly told by his father that he would not be fit to converse with and would have a bad character if he did not learn these things. It is unlikely that his son ever bothered to do so; their relationship was not cordial.

Understanding Confucius is immensely complicated by the difficult translation problem involved. I have at hand three translations of the Analects and none of them are really very satisfactory. Let us compare the opening lines of two.

In the third translation by Ezra Pound (1951a), there is no question, as commentators have pointed out, that the translation is unorthodox and exciting. Unfortunately he translates Confucius in a very idiosyncratic way, and his rendering is unreliable. (For a defense of Pound's translations, see Brooke-Rose 1971.)

Arthur Waley's translation tends to be dry and technical.

The master said, To learn and in due times to repeat what one has learnt, is that not after all a pleasure? That friends should come to one from afar, is this not after all delightful? To remain unsoured even though one's merits are unrecognized by others, is that not after all what is expected of a gentleman?

(Confucius 1938)

Probably the most famous translation of the *Analects* is by James Legge (1935), who has produced five volumes of translation known as the *Chinese Classics,* published by Oxford University Press. These are beautiful books and contain both the Chinese and the English translations as well as commentary by Legge in footnotes. Besides being somewhat out of date—this translation was made in the nineteenth century—Legge's commentary is damaged by a nineteenth century Christian bias in which everything said by Confucius that doesn't agree with the Christian fundamentalist view makes Confucius obviously wrong. The opening to the *Analects (Lun-Yu)* translated by Legge is as follows:

1. The Master said, 'It is not pleasant to learn with a constant perseverance and application?
2. 'Is it not delightful to have friends coming from distant quarters?
3. 'Is he not a man of complete virtue, who feels no discomposure though men may take no note of him?

(Legge 1935)

On the whole, the Legge translation is the most reliable and useful despite its moralizing. The five volumes contain the four Confucian great books *(Lun-Yu, Chung-Yung, Ta-Hsiao* and *Book of Mencius),* which form the basis of Confucian thought plus much ancillary material.

The problem of translation is vastly increased by the fact that the Chinese written character has its own mystical and difficult aspects. The most important of these written characters, *jên,* will serve as an example of the difficulties involved. Waley points out that *jên* represents man at its earliest derivation, but with a slight modification the character means good in the most general sense of the word, that is to say, possessing the qualities of one's tribe. Waley writes, "It seems to me that 'good' is the only translation of the *jên* as it occurs in the *Analects*. No other word is sufficiently general to cover the whole range of meaning; indeed terms such as 'humane,' 'altruistic,' 'benevolent' are in almost every instance inappropriate, often ludicrously so. But there is another word *shan,* which though it wholly lacks the mystical and transcendental implications of *jên,* cannot conveniently be translated by any other word but 'good.' For that reason I shall henceforward translate *jên* by Good with a capital; and *shan* by good with a small g" (Confucius 1938).

The difficulties of all this are obvious and become more devastating when we turn to a far less scholarly exposition of Confucius such as that of Jaspers (1962). He translates *jên* as the nature of man, and sees it as "representing humanity and morality in one." He claims the ideogram means "man" and "two," "that is to say: to be human means to be in communication. The question of the nature of man is answered, first in the elucidation of what he is and should be; second in an account of the diversity of his existence."

Creel (1960) in his well known book on *Confucius and the Chinese Way* translates *jên* as virtue, which is even more unsatisfactory. He points out that many scholars have written at great length about this ideogram, and he sees it as simply representing "complete virtue." The great problem in making sense out of the written Chinese character is illustrated by all this disagreement.

In studying these various translations, certain important facts and stimulating ideas do somehow manage to emerge. For example, it is clear that Confucius was sincerely preoccupied with the problem of knowing men and trying to change them. Because of this fact he becomes pertinent and relevant to psychotherapists. In fact, it may be argued that Confucius' main preoccupation was in how to change men, for it is clear that he believed that in order to rule men one had to have the capacity to be able to change them. There is a clear affinity here to Freud's concept of "after-education" in which the therapist is seen as being placed in a governing position by the patient and so being given an opportunity to correct the blunders of the parents.

Confucius seems to have had a similar idea in his concept of how men are changed. In the *Analects* (Bk. I: Ch. XVI) he writes: "I will not be afflicted at men's not knowing me; I will be afflicted that I do not know men" (Legge 1935). He goes on to insist one should watch what a man does, mark his motives, examine in what things he rests; if we do this he will be unable to conceal his character from us.

In the *Chung-Yung (The Doctrine of the Mean)* he points out, in one of the most important passages (Ch. XXIII) in this work, how he conceives of men being changed: "Next to the above is he who cultivates to the utmost the shoots *of goodness* in him. From those he can attain to the possession of sincerity. This sincerity becomes apparent. From being apparent, it becomes manifest. From being manifest, it becomes brilliant. Brilliant, it affects others. Affecting others, they are changed by it, they are transformed. It is only he who is possessed by the utmost complete sincerity that can exist under heaven, who can transform" (Legge 1935). In this passage discussed further below, one senses the impact of the method of Confucius. There is a marked methodological parallel to change through identification as it occurs in the process of psychoanalytic psychotherapy (Offenkrantz and Tobin 1974). In the four classic books of Confucian thought, the basic notion of helping men change for the good through a leader who presents the example of absolute sincerity, never lying to himself, clearly emerges.

The philosophy of Confucius suggests the tranquil capacity necessary to the therapist if he is not to be thrown by confrontation with the patient's passions. It shows the need to have good faith that the humanity or virtue of the patient will, given a chance in the proper atmosphere, ultimately express itself. In fact, the following character could very well be used as the motto for psychotherapists:

This character, sometimes known as *Hsin* illustrates man *(jen)* at the side of his word *(yen).* It stands for good faith, the keeping of promises, and the fulfilling of undertakings or, translated into psychotherapeutic terms, adhering to the therapeutic contract, doing our best to develop "sincerity," and carry the patient through to the end of his therapeutic endeavors regardless of the difficulties involved.

From another point of view one can easily emphasize the ethical aspects of the writings of Confucius. The principle of Reciprocity as it appears in the *Analects,* (Bk. XV: Ch. XXIII) is the famous golden rule: "What you do not want done to yourself, do not do to others" (Legge, 1935). The five steps towards virtue which have been frequently quoted from the writings of Confucius, include gravity, generosity, sincerity, earnestness and kindness.

Perhaps even more interesting is the skeptical tradition of the Confucian writings. Although Confucianism has sometimes been called a religion, Confucius considered a large part of the religion of his day to be sheer superstition and there is no supernaturalism to be found in his philosophy. On the contrary, the whole tradition is strongly imbued with the spirit of skepticism, which forms a stimulus to scientific inquiry. The ancient doctrine of the investigation of things, found throughout his writings, is essentially scientific in outlook and procedure.

The *Chung-Yung* can quite justifiably be called the first treatise on the human mind. To the psychotherapist, a study of the *Chung-Yung,* which is usually translated as *The Doctrine of the Mean* (also significantly translated by Ezra Pound as *The Unwobbling Pivot),* is extremely important. This work was allegedly written by the grandson of Confucius, Tsze-tsze (483-402 B.C.) and contains some important thoughts of Confucius. It is difficult to grasp in many of its aspects because it combines the practicality and wisdom of Confucius with a certain metaphysical streak in his grandson, and any statements about the meaning of some of the comments are much open to debate. Regardless of this, the *Chung-Yung* cannot help but stimulate considerable thought in psychotherapists about the subject of *how* one changes one's self and subsequently others. The book is based on the difficult concepts of equilibrium and harmony. The author opens (Ch. I, 4): "While there are no stirrings of pleasure, anger, sorrow or joy, the mind may be said to be in the state of **equilibrium.** When those feelings have been stirred, and they act in their due degree, there ensues what may be called a state of **harmony.** This **equilibrium** is the great root *from which grow all the human actings* in the world, and this **harmony** is the universal path *which they all should pursue"* (Legge 1935).

To give the reader an idea of the complexity and difficulty here, in the far more metaphysical Pound translation, the author wants the student to seek not a surface or a single stratum of himself, but to find his plum center, making use of himself. Thus he would abandon every clandestine egoism and move toward things representing the real core of man in order to realize to the full their true root. As he sees it, the two ideograms *Chung* and *Yung*, "represent most definitely a process in motion, an axis around which something turns. *The master man's axis does not wobble"* (1951b).

One could argue that the fundamental principles of psychodynamics are implied in this, although it would be very difficult to prove, since there is a complex metaphysical implication to this allegory also. The answer probably is that Confucius was interested in changing the individual man and subsequently the individuals around him, but his grandson was attempting to express a much more grandiose metaphysical scheme.

The concept of sincerity is emphasized throughout the *Chung-Yung.* Creel (1960) states, "The basic point that he pounded at his students again and again and again, was sincerity, sincerity, sincerity." The concept of sincerity is difficult to understand and it is never really made clear just how Confucius expected a man to develop it. He felt that some people are born with it and others can expand it within themselves. There must be no lingering remnant, no last inward glimmer of self-deception if you are going to travel in the way of truth. If the states of equilibrium and harmony exist in perfection, a happy order will prevail.

It is "sincerity" or "singleness" (Legge) by which the virtues of knowledge, benevolence, and energy are able to be carried into practice. The sincere or perfect man of Confucius is he who satisfies completely all the requirements of duty in various relations of society and in the exercise of government; the sincere man or Tsze-Tsze is also given an actual potency in the universe, a concept which constitutes obsolete metaphysics.

The important point emphasized repeatedly is that if one is to change other men, one must develop as the major technique for such change, a total sincerity in one's self: "Its starting point is an unconditional sincerity toward itself. Only if one does not lie to oneself can one hope to be master of one's own mistakes and weaknesses, which can be perceived in the mirror of others. What is necessary is not a theoretical knowledge for its own sake, but a practical exercise in and from communion with other men" (Wilhelm 1931). It is through the example of the master's sincerity that the pupil changes. Confucius' emphasis on this theme has been somewhat neglected by authors who have attempted to apply Confucian writings to Western philosophy.

Other aspects of Confucian thought are also pertinent to psychotherapists. For example, "Happy union with wife and children, is like the music of lutes and harps. When there is concord among brethren, the harmony is delightful and enduring. *Thus* may you regulate your family, and enjoy the pleasure of your wife and children" *(Chung-Yung,* Ch. XV: 2; Legge 1935). This interesting quotation condenses Confucius' great interest in healthy object-relations, his emphasis on music, and his willingness to accept the impact of music upon the human mind. The enjoyment of music, harmony, and equilibrium plays a critical role along with the pursuit of knowledge, the scientific spirit, and self-examination in developing what Confucius would consider to be the sincere man. To furnish and deepen his students' minds, he had them study history, poetry and music. To equip them to act effectively in the world he schooled them in the theory and practice of human relations. The sincere man is the *only* kind of man who has the potency to change others, according to his view.

An interesting extension of the thought of Confucius is presented by two of his famous disciples. The unanswered question in the writings of Confucius is specifically *how* one becomes a superior sincere man. He seems to imply that man is good by nature, but it is necessary to explain how we know that man can be good.

Mencius (372-298 B.C.) argued that the superior man is one who develops his mind to the utmost and nourishes his inner nature. He believed that man's nature is originally good, possessing humanity, rightousness, propriety and wisdom, plus an innate knowledge of the good and the ability to do good. He blamed evil on bad environment, lack of education, and "casting one's self away."

Hsun-Tzu (313-281 B.C.) contended that the original nature of man is evil and that by nature man seeks gain and is envious. He sees the rules of propriety and rightousness as formulated to control evil and train men to be good, and conceives of these not as major characteristics but artificial effects of education. These sages are in direct opposition but are both truly Confucian because their central objective is the attainment of the good man. This question of the basic nature of man is still uncertain and debated today. If time is available, study of the book of Mencius, especially in the Legge translation, which also contains a number of interesting commentaries by other sages, is well worthwhile, and is still pertinent to considerations of instinct theory.

Wing-tsit Chan (1968) in an excellent article on Confucianism in the *Encyclopaedia Britannica,* points out that two clearly divergent tendencies are present in the 5th century B.C. as represented in the writings of the Confucian School. *The Doctrine of the Mean* emphasizes central harmony, "that is, the full realization of the self through the harmony of the emotions, and the development and operation of all things in their harmonious relationship." Sincerity as the way of all existence, is absolute, intelligent, and indestructible. "Only those who are absolutely sincere can develop fully their own natures, the natures of other people, the nature of things and finally partake in the creative work of Heaven and Earth." Mencius elaborates on the idea of sincerity and carries the doctrine of human nature to new heights.

Another tendency is found in the *Great Learning* or *Great Digest (Ta-Hsiao)* which is more a social and political text. It aims at "manifesting one's clear character, loving the people, and abiding in the highest good" for the purpose of ordering the state and bringing peace to the world.

The following quotation from *The Doctrine of the Mean* (Ch. XXVII: 6) makes an excellent summary and illustration of the relevance of Confucius and his great ideas for use in psychotherapy: "Therefore, the superior man honors his virtuous nature, and maintains constant inquiry and study, seeking to carry it out to its breadth and greatness, so as to omit none of the more exquisite and minute points which it embraces, and to raise it to its greatest height and brilliancy, so as to pursue the course of the Mean. He cherishes his old knowledge, and is continually acquiring new. He exerts an honest, generous earnestness, in the esteem and practice of all propriety" (Legge 1935). This is the fundamental conviction of Confucius, that by cultivating his human-ness (Koller's 1970 translation of *jên),* man can perfect society and achieve happiness. The stress is on education through imitation of humane individual and social models.

Chapter 5

The Renaissance Ideal:
Essere Umano

In contrast with the person whose purpose is esthetic, the scientific man is interested in problems, in situations wherein tension between the matter of observation and of thought is marked. Of course he cares for their resolution. But he does not rest in it; he passes on to another problem using an attained solution only as a stepping stone from which to set on foot further inquiries.

The difference between the esthetic and the intellectual is thus one of the places where emphasis falls in the constant rhythm that marks the interaction of the live creature with his surroundings. . . . The odd notion that an artist does not think and a scientific inquirer does nothing else is the result of converting a difference of tempo and emphasis into a difference in kind.

Inner harmony is attained only when, by some means, terms are made with the environment. When it occurs on any other than an "objective" basis, it is illusory—in extreme cases to the point of insanity. . . . Pleasure may come about through chance contact and stimulation, . . . but happiness and delight are a different sort of thing. They come to be through a fulfillment that reaches to the depths of our being—one that is an adjustment of our whole being with the conditions of existence. In the process of living, attainment of a period of equilibrium is at the same time the initiation of a new relation to the environment, one that brings

with it potency of new adjustments to be made through struggle.
The time of consummation is also one of beginning anew.

John Dewey, *Art as Experience*

PSYCHOTHERAPY AND THE LANGUAGE OF ART

One of the basic premises developed in my previous work (Chessick 1971c) is the value to the therapist of immersion in the arts. It must be made clear that no amount of writing about the arts can possibly serve as a genuine introduction to immersion in the arts because it is not really possible to translate from the language of the arts into the spoken word. *(Art* in this chapter means all the arts including the plastic arts, music, and literature.) As Dewey points out, "Because objects of art are expressive, they are a language. Rather they are many languages. For each art has its own medium and that medium is especially fitted for one kind of communication. Each medium says something that cannot be uttered as well or as completely in any other tongue. The needs of daily life have given superior practical importance to one mode of communication, that of speech. This fact has unfortunately given rise to a popular impression that the meanings expressed in architecture, sculpture, painting, and music can be translated into words with little if any loss. In fact, each art speaks an idiom that conveys what cannot be said in another language and yet remain the same" (1958, p. 106).

The therapist who is in agreement with the principles behind the argument for immersion in the arts must actually go and experience and immerse himself in the arts seeking both as wide a variety of the arts as possible and becoming thoroughly familiar with certain selected works of arts. Any works may be selected, but there must be certain art works in all areas that are returned to again and again. Thus he has the experience of actually being immersed in these works and can watch his reactions and interactions with them as they change through the phases of his life.

In *How Psychotherapy Heals* (Chessick 1969a), I described how the psychotherapist moves rapidly back and forth between the role of scientist and artist during the psychotherapy process itself. The therapist can be criticized by the scientist as performing an unscientific discipline and yet not be accepted by the artist because the many scientific aspects of his work restrict his creativity. These restrictions arise from the fact that psychotherapy is basically teleological. It is not art for art's sake, nor is the goal of creation left completely up to the choice of the artist. The result of the psychotherapy is judged not on the basis of esthetics, but on the basis of the relief from suffering that it can achieve. At the same time the task confronting the psychoanalytically oriented psychotherapist is remarkably similar to the task confronting the artist in certain ways. For example, picking the crucial themes out of the myriad of communications and interactions and presenting these back to the patient in an effective way combined with a proper sense of timing as to when the patient is ready for them, constitutes the essential creative aspect of such psychotherapy. Thus therapists are closely akin to artists and may learn by being familiar with them.

In *Why Psychotherapists Fail* (Chessick 1971c) I reviewed the many important functions that art can be used for by the individual, and I tried to give theoretical foundation to the importance of immersion in the arts for the therapist. All appreciation of beauty is a temporary escape from everyday problems, and art can take a person temporarily outside of himself, enabling him to immerse himself spiritually with the cultural achievements of others. If art allows one to escape temporarily, calms one, excites and refines one, or improves one, it often is called beautiful, and thus beauty can be defined by its capacity to produce certain effects. By this definition many things partake of beauty, which is primarily an intuitive conviction about the effect of a given experience. As a pleasure of the mind, esthetic appreciation is closely related to happiness, and both are important in assessing the quality of a person's life.

Dewey strongly believes that there is a continuity between esthetic experiences and practical living. He views human life as rhythmic movement from experiences qualified by conflict, doubt, and indeterminateness toward experiences qualified by their integrity, harmony, and funded esthetic quality. We are constantly confronted with problematic and indeterminate situations, and in so far as we use our intelligence to reconstruct these situations successfully, we achieve consummation. He was concerned both with delineating the methods by which we can most intelligently resolve the conflicting situations in which we inevitably find ourselves and with advocating the social reforms required so that life for all men would become funded with enriched meaning and increased esthetic quality.

ART AND HUMAN ENCOUNTER

Art As Experience by Dewey should form a part of the early curriculum of reading for the psychotherapist. As he points out, "works of art are the only media of complete and unhindered communication between man and man that can occur in a world full of gulfs and walls that limit community of experience." Art, according to Dewey, is a good measure of the quality of the culture that produces it, and this gives the therapist a way of evaluating the milieu from which his patients come: "The final measure of the quality of that culture is the arts which flourish" (1958).

The close affinity between the artist and the therapist is touched on at many points by Dewey. For example, he writes: "Moreover, I do not think it can be denied that an element of reverie, of approach to a state of dream, enters into the creation of a work of art, nor that the experience of the work when it is intense often throws one into a similar state. Indeed it is safe to say that 'creative' conceptions in philosophy and science come only to persons who are relaxed to the point of reverie. The subconscious fund of meanings stored in our attitudes have no chance of release when we are practically or intellectually strained. For much the greater part of this store is then restrained, because the demands of a particular problem and particular purpose inhibit all except the elements directly relevant. Images and ideas come to us not by set purpose but in flashes, and flashes are intent and illuminating, they set us on fire only when we are free from special preoccupations" (1958, pp. 275-276).

Dewey touches at many points on the special theory of psychotherapeutic interaction presented in *Why Psychotherapists Fail* (Chessick 1971c) and expanded upon in *The Technique and Practice of Intensive Psychotherapy* (Chessick 1974g). In this theory it is made clear that because of the nuclear operations of the mind, there are two languages which compete as descriptive maps of reality: one, sober, factual, claiming to be custodian of the literal truth; the other, mythical, playful, but claiming to point the way to deeper wisdom. Scientific understanding and humanistic imagination are fundamentally different and each provides "knowledge" that the other is unable to account for.

Dewey gives an example of two men meeting in which one is the applicant for a position while the other has the disposition of the matter in his hands. There is a certain similarity between this encounter as described by Dewey, and the encounter described in Volume I of Jaspers' *Philosophy* (1932) between a physician and his patient. At any rate the interplay that takes place must be accounted for, and Dewey asks,

> Where should we look for an account of such an experience? Not to ledger-entries nor yet to a treatise on economics or sociology or personnel-psychology, but to drama or fiction. Its nature and import can be expressed only by art, because there is a unity of experience that can be expressed only as an experience. The *experience* is of material fraught with suspense and moving toward its own consummation through a connected series of varied incidents. The primary emotions on the part of the applicant may be at the beginning hope or despair and elation or disappointment, at the close. . . . As the interview proceeds, secondary emotions are evolved as variations of the primary underlying one. It is even possible for each attitude and gesture, each sentence, almost every word, to produce more than a fluctuation in the intensity of the basic emotion; to produce, that is, a change of shade and tint in its quality. The employer sees by means of its own emotional reactions the character of the one applying. He projects him imaginatively into the work to be done and judges his fitness by the way in which the elements of the scene assemble and either clash or fit together. The presence and behavior of the applicant either harmonize with his own attitudes and desires or they conflict and jar. Such factors as these, inherently esthetic in quality, are the forces that carry the elements of the interview to a decisive issue. They enter into the settlement of every situation, whatever its dominant nature, in which there are uncertainty and suspense. (1958 p. 43)

Dewey's description ties together the importance of esthetics and the language of the humanistic imagination on the one hand and the understanding of the scientific data of an interview on the other. Art serves the function of transforming knowledge into experience. The interview then becomes something more than factual knowledge, because such knowledge is merged "with non-intellectual elements to form an experience worth while as an experience." As Dewey points out, "Friendship and intimate affection are not the result of information about another person even though knowledge may further their formation. But it does so only as it becomes an integral part of sympathy through the imagination. It is when the.desires and aims, the interests and modes of response of another become an expansion of our own being that we understand him. We learn to see with his eyes, hear with his ears, and their results give true instruction, for they are built into our own structure" (1958, p. 336).

I have belabored this subject at length because my whole conception of reducing failure by psychotherapists is based on the hope of improving the psychic field one has to offer the patient. Any and every way in which the therapist can be trained and matured to be able to empathically experience the patient, engage in a human encounter with the patient, and reflect back to the patient this deeper understanding, will increase the possibilities that the therapist has to help the given patient. Immersion in the arts has something to offer the therapist in this area that no other type of training or experience can provide.

There are many other aspects of the understanding and importance of art; these are somewhat peripheral to the purpose of the present book, which is to outline the great ideas of psychotherapy. Art has an important value in the actual life of the individual and since the psychotherapist is also a human individual, art will function in his life as in anyone else's. Pater wrote in 1873 that we are all under sentence of death but with a sort of indefinite reprieve: "Some spend this interval in listlessness, some in high passions, the wisest, at least among 'the children of this world,' in art and song. For our one chance lies in expanding that interval, in getting as many pulsations as possible into the given time. Great passions may give us this quickened sense of life, ecstacy and sorrow of love, the various forms of enthusiastic activity, disinterested or otherwise, which comes naturally to many of us. Only be sure it is passion—that it does yield you this fruit of quickened, multiplied consciousness. Of this wisdom, the poetic passion, the desire of beauty, the love of art for arts sake, has most, for art comes to you, proposing frankly to give nothing but the highest quality to your moments as they pass, and simply for those moments' sake" (1959).

This view, debatable but very interesting, is worth considering by the therapist. Other various interpretations and understandings of art, including the important and difficult view of Croce, in which the role of intuition and expression are stressed, are vital to the therapist's considerations of the meaning of art and the role of artistic procedure in psychotherapy. There is an excellent summary of these various approaches in chapter 10 of Brennan (1967).

It is unfortunately most debatable whether or not immersion in art also has a direct humanizing effect on the therapist; nothing would be more important than this. Berenson insists that no artifact is a work of art if it does not help to humanize us. He points out that much time is wasted in reading about art and what we must do is "look and look and look till we live the painting and for a fleeting moment become identified with it. If we do not succeed in loving what through the ages has been loved, it is useless to lie ourselves into believing that we do. A good rough test is whether we feel that it is reconciling us with life. . . . Art teaches us not only what to see but what to be" (1952).

THE RENAISSANCE IDEAL

To give a brief illustration of the principles involved in this discussion let us review the Italian Renaissance ideal as it expressed itself in the great artists from the end of the fourteenth century, through the fifteenth century, and into the sixteenth century. The most famous authors who have conveyed in writing the spirit of the Italian Renaissance are probabably Alberti (1966) and Castiglioni (1967).

"A man can be all things if he will"—Alberti in his life and writings typifies the spirit of the Italian Renaissance ideal, that of *l'uomo univerale,* combining an "impulse to the highest individual development" with "a powerful and varied nature, which has mastered all the element of the culture of the age" (Burckhardt 1958).

Berenson describes this ideal figure: "Towards the end of the fourteenth century something happened in Europe that happens in the lives of all gifted individuals. There was an awakening to the sense of personality. Although it was felt to a greater or less degree everywhere, Italy felt the awakening earlier than the rest of Europe, and felt it far more strongly. Its first manifestation was a boundless and insatiable curiosity, urging people to find out all they could about the world and about man. They turned eagerly to the study of classic literature and ancient monuments, because these gave the key to what seemed an immense storehouse of forgotten knowledge; they were in fact led to antiquity by the same impulse which, a little later, brought about the invention of the printing press and the discovery of America" (1952, pp. 4-5).

Berenson goes on to explain that the natural outcome of this development was the production of painting, "for it is obvious that painting is peculiarly fitted for rendering the appearance of things with a glow of light and richness of color that correspond to warm human emotions." For example, much art of the remarkable Venetian painters can be understood by the development in the Venetians of "a love of comfort, of ease, and of splendor, a refinement of manner, and humaneness of feeling, which made them the first modern people in Europe." At the same time, the spirit of analysis which is perhaps more marked in the Florentines, produced patient studies of the face. Their art enabled them to give the features "that look of belonging to one consistent whole which we call character (1952, pp. 8, 16-17).

Thus at a time when painters had not yet learned to distinguish between one face and another, "Donatello was carving busts which remain unrivalled as studies of character, and Pisanello was casting bronze and silver medals which are among the greatest claims to renown of those whose effigies they bear" (1952, p. 17). Of course, the summit of this kind of remarkable preoccupation with personality and character, and of psychological perception in the artist, is reached with Leonardo Da Vinci, who was to Alberti "as the finisher to the beginner" (Burckhardt 1958). In his *Last Supper* he showed us a critical emotional moment. In the *Mona Lisa* he wanted to and did depict a definite personality. DeWald points out, using the *Mona Lisa* as an example, "that the human individual personality is, or can be, one of the subtlest things in creation, that personality is something that cannot be pinned down and pigeonholed, because the moment you say it is one thing it can turn around and be another. That is the so-called enigma of the Mona Lisa, and that was Leonardo's supreme problem, the subtlety of the individual personality. The sheer difficulty of the problem fascinated Leonardo" (1961). Thus the painters of the Italian Renaissance were unquestionably the master psychologists of their time.

The best review of both the spirit and the history of the Renaissance in Italy, studied from all directions is to be found in the two volume classic by Jacob Burckhardt (1958). A simple review of the chapter titles of Volume Two conveys rather quickly the spirit of the Italian Renaissance: "The Discovery of Natural Beauty," "The Discovery of Man—Spiritual Description in Poetry," "Biography," "The Description of Nations and Cities," "Description of the Outward Man," "Descriptions of Life in Movement," "The Equalization of Classes," "The Outward Refinement of Life," "Language as the Basis of Social Intercourse," "The Perfect Man of Society," and so forth. In fact this explosion of interest in the human being in every aspect of his character and personality and this insatiable curiosity to find out how things work, what makes them up, and which causes lead to what effects—the spirit of the Italian Renaissance—represents one of the most remarkable flowerings in history. The sudden appearance of so many geniuses in such a brief period of time has the same awesome effect on the student of history and the arts as discovering the sudden spread of Christianity around 400 A.D. often has on the student of religion. Let us take a careful look at the beginnings of this explosion of the Renaissance spirit.

GIOTTO

The Madonna Enthroned with Angels by Cimabue (c. 1272-1302) in the Uffizi Gallery in Florence is the painting with which many courses on Italian painting begin. DeWald (1961) describes Cimabue as being "both the culmination of the old style and a pathfinder in the direction of the new" and reminds us of the contemporary comment that Cimbaue was "a proud and impetuous person who would destroy any of his paintings no matter how good if an adverse remark about it was made." In fact Cimabue means "de-horner of oxen" or "violent man" (Hartt 1969). Venturi (1950) points out that what gives Cimabue's art its exceptional power is "its expression of the sublime," which in a fashion sums up all the tendencies of his predecessors, but I don't think that words can do justice to his painting nor can they adequately describe the difference between Cimabue and those who went before.

It is clear that an element of Cimabue's work represents a sharp difference from the previous far more stereotyped and symbolic Gothic art. He was an artist of great dramatic capacity, and his "penetrating intelligence enables him to analyze and differentiate psychological types with considerable effect, as for example the fresh, even a bit foppish, young angels and the weary, disillusioned prophets" (Hartt 1969).

Another important painter who departed from the Gothic tradition is Pietro Cavallini, whose work (around 1290) is almost entirely lost. His most important remaining work is a fragmentary fresco in Santa Cecelia in Trastevere, in Rome, extremely difficult to see because it is bisected horizontally by the nuns' chapel and the nuns are in *clausura*. These two painters are the crucial transition figures who paved the way for the genius most commonly given credit for beginning Italian Renaissance art, Giotto.

The reader must go to Padua and stand in the Arena Chapel (built on a Roman circus arena) in order to experience Giotto (c. 1267-1337) at the height of his powers about 1305. Stand before the picture of Mary Magdalen from the *Noli me Tangere* in the Arena chapel and experience this work slowly for yourself. DeWald explains the psychological impact: "Giotto was a master at portraying the simple fundamental human emotions, and in order to express these most effectively he embodied them in simple, bulky, earthy forms. In general he achieved for the episodes he was painting an expressive psychological unity far surpassing a mere color and pattern unity by blending with his subject content remnants of Byzantine abstraction, the Classical sense of the universal, and Gothic naturalism and movement. He gave Florentine art the direction it was to follow for several centuries—that is, the use of the human figure as the chief element in a pictorial composition" (1961).

Canaday agrees that "there is no way to understand Giotto without visiting the Arena Chapel." He points out that photography and reduction in size somehow produce a heavy outline that flattens the roundness of the figures: "The camera tends to make Giotto's full volumes seem merely bulky, and the pearly colors lose both their strength and their subtlety. Nor can individual scenes from the cycle give any impression of the majestic progression of the story from one section to the next along the chapel walls, with each incident conceived in its own appropriate emotional air as a unit in a—the word is inevitable—symphony. The story is told with such tenderness and passion that we are moved as human beings, whatever our religion" (1969). To understand Giotto's step forward, compare his *Enthroned Madonna,* finished a few years after the Arena Chapel with the Cimabue *Madonna* mentioned above. Both are in the Uffizi Gallery. The difference is unmistakable, from visionary transcendence to warm humanity.

It is important to recognize, as Berenson points out, that Giotto's claim to everlasting appreciation is that his "thorough-going sense for the significant in the visible world enabled him so to represent things that we realize his representations more quickly and more completely than we should realize the things themselves, thus giving us that confirmation of our sense of capacity which is so great a source of pleasure" (1952). Thus it was Giotto who sharply turned the focus of all the painters and thinkers of the Renaissance to the subject of man himself. One of the most powerful artists who ever lived, he revolutionized the art of Italy.

An entirely different aspect of the spirit of the Italian Renaissance, which gets much less attention in the various books on art, is represented by Duccio (1278-1318) and his followers in the development of Sienese art. This art is of a totally different nature than Florentine and Venetian art: Duccio's work has had a rough time of it from the vicissitudes of history, so that he is poorly represented in various museums. One must imagine the day on June 9th, 1311 when Duccio's magnificent *Madonna* was carried through the streets in triumph, in a public procession from his workshop to the Cathedral of Siena. The story of this fourteen-foot-wide altarpiece gives us a good insight into the relationship of the artist and the society that produced him. Canaday quotes a contemporary account of the occasion:

On the day when it was brought to the Cathedral, the shops were shut and the Bishop decreed a solemn procession of a large and devout company of priests and friars, accompanied by the nine Signori, and by all the officers of the Commune and all the populace; and one by one all the most worthy persons approached the picture with lighted candles in their hands and behind them came the women and the children in devout attitudes. And they accompanied the said picture to the Cathedral, marching in procession round the Campo, as is the custom, while the bells sounded the Gloria, in homage to so noble a painting as this is. And they remained all day praying and gave many alms to poor persons, praying to God and to his Mother, who is our patroness and with her infinite mercy defends us from every adversity and evil and preserves us from the hand of traitors and enemies of Siena. (1969, Vol. 1, p. 16)

This attitude toward art was typical in the cultures of all the various Italian city–states during the time of the Renaissance. The subsequent history of this work is painful to relate. It was taken down, sawed to several pieces, parts were lost and "all sadly butchered"; in 1878 it was put into the cramped little Cathedral museum, where it remains today.

Duccio begins that tradition of Italian Renaissance art commonly called transcendent which is to be found especially in the art of Duccio and his Sienese followers and, as we shall see, in the work of Piero della Francesca. Though sense of the transcendent in art is extremely difficult to write about, the reader is referred to chapters 19 and 20 for further modern discussion of this concept. In bringing up the art of Duccio at this point, I wish to illustrate again the extreme interconnection of immersion in the works of art and a variety of nonverbal experiences vital to the human understanding, such as a conception of the transcendent. An effective way to illustrate the significance of Duccio is to compare his *Rucellai Madonna,* also in the Uffizi Gallery, to the Madonnas of Cimabue and Giotto already mentioned (all stand together in one hall).

Entering the Brancacci Chapel of *Santa Maria Del Carmine* in Florence, containing the frescoes of Masolino (1383-1440), Filippino Lippi (1457-1504), and Masaccio (1401-1428), not only will the therapist be able to experience the best of Masaccio, but he will have the opportunity to compare side by side the works of Masaccio and Masolino, which present in the best possible way the special genius of Masaccio. The difference can be summed up in one word: psychology. Masolino's work makes no attempt at a psychological interpretation of a major event such as the expulsion of Adam and Eve from the Garden of Eden, whereas Masaccio's depiction of the identical event is overwhelming in its effect—the work of a master psychologist. Venturi (1950) contains an excellent section on the Brancacci Chapel as does Hartt (1969).

Masaccio died at age 28 after little more than six years of creative activity, but his effect on art was permanent. As is the case with Giotto a century earlier, he appears to represent the sudden unpredictable emergence of an artist of individual genius. Stand before the Brancacci Chapel frescoes and experience their charge of high dramatic tension.

To see how spectacular was the progress of painting in such a short time compare the *Madonna and Child* of Fra Filippo Lippi, c. 1455, with the other Madonnas previously mentioned, in the Uffizi Gallery. Note also the sense of wistful human melancholy that characterizes much of his work, so different from serene transcendence.

PIERO DELLA FRANCESCA

One of the most remarkable and disputed of the major geniuses of this time was Piero Della Francesca (1420?-1492), who at least trained in Florence but did not remain in the tradition of Florentine painting. He was an unusual and original genius with a style all his own. Berenson points out that being "the pupil of Domenico Veneziano in characterization, of Paolo Uccello in perspective, himself an eager student of this science, as an artist he was more gifted than either of his teachers. He is hardly inferior to Giotto and Masaccio in feeling for tactile values; in communicating values of force, he is the rival of Donatello; he was perhaps the first to use effects of light for their direct tonic or subduing and soothing qualities; and, finally, judged as an Illustrator it may be questioned whether another painter has ever presented a world more complete and convincing, has ever had an ideal more majestic, or ever endowed things with more heroic significance" (1952, pp. 108-109).

There is a quality about Piero that holds one "spellbound" as Berenson puts it, and he believes that this quality is shared with only two other artists, the one who carved the pediments of the Parthenon, and Velazquez, "who painted without ever betraying an emotion." There is both a transcending and a healing quality to Piero's art which is extremely difficult to convey to a reader. Canaday argues that his series of frescoes in the choir of the Church of San Francesco in Arezzo could be called "the greatest cycle paintings in the world." Also he wrote a treatise on pictorial perspective that has become the classic statement of that science as a form of philosophical mathematics.

The secret of Piero's art seems to be that he shared Plato's view that geometry alone is capable of imparting to form its absolute beauty, and in precise geometrical forms he embodies both his supreme ideal and his experience of reality. Venturi writes that he produces an effect "of serenity so all-pervasive, a calm so profound, that we feel we are translated out of space and out of time, on to a plane high above the vicissitudes of the ephemeral, in which the words 'eternal life' acquire their full and literal meaning" (1950). This begins to approach Jaspers' concept (see chapter 18) of the transcendent and represents a remarkable expression in art of the kind of "ciphers" that I think Jaspers is talking about. Although the therapist may not agree with his concept of the transcendent, it is certainly most important for him to know and to understand as much as possible about it, because it is a driving force in the lives of a great many people.

A further vital aspect of Piero's life, most significant to us, is his association with the remarkable Duke of Urbino (Hendy 1968). The reader must stand before the portraits of the Duke and Duchess of Urbino in the Uffizi Gallery in Florence. Every detail of the physiognomy has been set down with painful accuracy, with no attempt to beautify the subject. Duke Federigo was an ardent jouster. In one of the tournaments he sustained a broken nose and the loss of his right eye when he was struck by his opponent's lance. Piero shows the profile with the good eye, but delineates the notch of the broken nose. A remarkable far distant landscape fills each background of the portraits.

Clark points out that life in the court of Urbino was "one of the high-water marks of western civilization" primarily because it was this same first Duke of Urbino, Federigo Montefeltro, a highly cultivated and intelligent man as well as a defender of his city and dominions, whose own character permeates the whole building of his palace. When the duke was asked what is necessary in ruling a kingdom, he replied: *"essere umano* (to be human)." This life style and this approach pervades the spirit of the Italian Renaissance. It is no accident, as Clark writes, that "Raphael, one of the civilizing forces of the Western imagination, found his earliest impressions of harmony and proportion and good manners in the court of Urbino" (1969). *The Courtier* (1967) was written in this court under Federigo's son and successor, Guidobaldo. The happy fusion of Piero della Francesca and Federigo

Montefeltro in the court of Urbino must indeed represent a high point in civilization, and it deserves careful study by any therapist who is interested in the aspirations of human beings and in how far and toward what they may develop.

The same is true to a lesser degree of the court of Mantua. Although this court and palace lacked "exhilarating lightness and lucidity" (Clark) of the court of Urbino, it still contains a room in which more than anywhere else one can get an idea of civilized life. This room was decorated by the court painter Andrea Mantegna (1431-1506). It shows for the first time, remarkable psychological family scenes described in detail in Clark's book (1969). No greater masterpiece representing family interaction has ever been presented in the arts. Clark writes: "They show the Gonzaga family as large as life (perhaps the first life-size portraits in art), their dogs, their old retainers and one of their famous collection of dwarfs. In spite of the frontal formality of the Marcioness, the spirit of the whole group is remarkably natural. The little girl asks if she may eat an apple, but her mother is interested to know what news the Marquess has just received from his secretary—in fact it is good news: that their son has been made a cardinal. In another scene the Marquess goes to greet him, accompanied by his younger sons. What an agreeably informal reception. One of the younger children holds his father's hand and the little boy takes the hand of his elder brother" (1969, p. 111). It is remarkable that Mantegna, who achieved a great many unusual effects through his knowledge of perspective and whose paintings abound with dramatic power, could also paint this subtle, gentle, and psychological depiction of a civilized and happy family scene.

BOTTICELLI

One of the extremely important painters to be brought to the attention of psychotherapists is "little barrel" or Botticelli (1445-1510). Botticelli is known as one of the first great geniuses to undergo an existentialist crisis in his life; and his painting can certainly be understood as a representation of his existential preoccupations and concerns. The great critic Walter Pater noted that "his figures have the wistfulness of exiles, conscious of a passion and energy greater than any known issue of them explains, which runs through all his varied work with a sentiment of ineffable melancholy" (1959). Pater considered this to be decadent, but today we hopefully understand Botticelli much better, as an insufficiently appreciated universal genius.

Stand in the Uffizi before Botticelli's *Adoration of the Magi,* painted about 1478. To the right of the viewer at the edge of the picture a remarkable person looks out at us with a detached, somewhat scornful, and pained expression. This is Botticelli himself, who shortly after this painting began a series of allegories based on classic subjects including the famous *Primavara,* the *Birth of Venus,* and *Venus and Mars* in which an exquisite existential sadness is clearly present. The sight of youthful grace so fragile and so ephemeral, of beauty that must die, is a feeling that ever haunted the minds of the Florentines of the time. Venturi writes: "Here all is an exquisite awareness of the frailty of woman, infinite compassion for a loneliness that hides itself from the world, and indignation with that door forever closed against all human charity" (1950).

The appearance of Savonarola in 1489 signalled disaster for Botticelli. Savonarola's fanatical sermons of 1491, attacking the luxuries and vanities of life and prophesizing doom to come, fit all too well into Botticelli's depressive psyche; he even destroyed some of his own paintings. Those paintings done while he was under the influence of Savonarola present a remarkable emotionally disturbed quality. Perhaps the greatest expressions of the existential predicament are his *La Derelitta* in Rome and his famous *Pieta* of 1496 in Munich.

Suffering from premature aging, public neglect, and depression, Botticelli seems to have passed the last ten years of his life (55-65) with little productive accomplishment. Perhaps one of the most interesting ways to approach him for readers of this book, would be to compare his painting of St. Augustine with the painting of St. Jerome by Ghirlandaio (1449-1494). Both frescoes were done in 1480 and they show a remarkable difference. As DeWald points out, in contrast to Ghirlandaio, "Botticelli is not concerned at all with the minutiae of the setting but instead depicts St. Augustine as an inspired mystic filled with emotional fire" (1961). No good psychoanalytic study of Botticelli is in existence, and part of this may be because it is very difficult to get much information about his life. In fact some of the statements I have already made are open to dispute by various historians; even the title

Primavera given to his most famous painting was provided by Vasari (1967) and no one knows what the painting is really all about.

This brings us to the end of the quattrocento and the beginning of the Sixteenth century or cinquecento, the time of the high Renaissance in Rome especially, marked by the unbelievable presence together of Leonardo da Vinci (1452-1519), Raphael (1483-1520), and Michelangelo (1475-1564). At the same time the remarkable development of the Venetian school of painting reached an apogee. The roots of the high Renaissance in Rome were unmistakably Florentine, and some of the later Florentine painters have been neglected because of the overshadowing emphasis on the famous Renaissance giants in Rome at the time.

Among these later Florentines, the therapist will be especially interested in Piero de Cosimo (1462-1521), who painted a variety of strange, whimsical, symbolic paintings in Florentine during the time of the high Renaissance in Rome. Some of his work can only be called bizarre. His introverted imagination led him beyond the usual range of subjects to be painted, to the activities of primitive man and into the realm of the fantastic. Since we are dealing with the world of dreams and fantasies all the time, I think it is important for us to pay special attention to the masterpieces of Piero de Cosimo (and Hieronymus Bosch) who stand out in the history of art as two early fascinating dream painters.

MICHELANGELO, LEONARDO DA VINCI, AND RAPHAEL

Freud (1914a) wrote about the *Moses* of Michelangelo and the personality of Leonardo da Vinci (1910b). Both of these universal geniuses are absolutely impossible to discuss in a mere chapter. One can easily and quickly form an affinity with Michelangelo's works, but somehow the *corpus* of his masterpieces seem to me limited by the times and religious struggles of the era in which he lived. This is not true of Leonardo da Vinci. His contemporaries really did not appreciate him enough and even today much of his life and work is shrouded in mystery. Leonardo was, as Canaday (1969) points out, a defeated genius. "He was the apotheosis of the man of the Renaissance, an age that could still conceive of the possibility of universal knowledge, and did not recognize as we do today, that the individual's knowledge must remain fractional" (1969). He had to know the answer to everything. Difficulties merely stimulated his imagination the more. At the same time his life was a record of things left undone.

Even so Leonardo gave more attention to the study of human personality than did any other artist in Italy before his time. "The spirit in which he approached everything by attempting to describe, define, and understand must be emulated by any who wish to study nature and thoroughly grasp the recesses of the human mind. Berenson insists that "just as his art is life communicating as is that of scarcely another, so the contemplation of his personality is life-enhancing as that of scarcely any other man" (1952, p. 66).

I find myself troubled in different ways by these different Renaissance geniuses, and perhaps their very genius consists of the capacity to stir up thought and introspection and to leave a sense of a task unfinished. To my taste though Leonardo da Vinci was the greatest of all, he leaves one with a peculiar sense of incompleteness, poor comprehension, and dissatisfaction. He makes us wish for more understanding, more depth, as he conveys to us his restlessness and dissatisfaction with everything that he knows. Michelangelo disturbs me because in a sense he also is a failure. Although a genius of the highest order, he did not really resolve the psychological problems that he struggled with throughout his long life; the resolution that appears in the Sistine Chapel in his *Last Judgment* seems a retreat into frightened superstition. Perhaps in this work and in his final works in the Pauline Chapel, exhausted in his old age, he has sacrificed some of his usually unfailing artistic integrity to the demands of the church. My favorite Michelangeloes are the unfinished statues for the tomb of Pope Julius the Second (in the Accademia of Florence) and the other statues from the tomb project—above all the *Moses*. Here I think Michelangelo shows himself at his best, essentially unable to resolve the conflicts and problems that torment him.

Raphael's frescoes in the *Stanza della Segnatura* (Vatican) are obviously works of genius. We have, however, a great borrower, a great organizer, and a great summarizer of the Renaissance rather than a great originator of powerful and new ideas. For this reason, although I appreciate Raphael's transcendent beauty and the magnificence of his portraits, there is a certain lack of psychological conviction in his work, except perhaps in his portraits of Pope Leo X (Uffizi Gallery) and of Castiglione. Yet even these are oversimplified. For example, the Castiglione portrait (in the Louvre) illustrates the *riposo* or inner calm Castiglione recommends as one of the essentials of gentlemanly character but does not give a glimpse of all that goes into developing such a character and maturity. Compare it, for example, with Rembrandt's various self-portraits, or the *Mona Lisa*.

CORREGIO

Corregio (1494-1534), who came from Parma, was full of the joy of living as borne out by the suavity, charm and amiability of so many of his pictures. Venturi writes: "Though he began by using persistently a chiaroscuro of his own devising, in which the colors are brought out by glints of warmer tones, he subsequently practiced a franker statement of form, a subtler use of tones, and a more mellow and sensuous rendering of light which, flooding bodies, seems to impart to them its characteristic vibrancy" (1961). Although Berenson views the very sensuousness of Corregio's paintings as a detraction from his greatness and something which keeps him from the category of Raphael and Michelangelo, have a careful look at his work for the unusual heightening of sensibility that they present. Corregio is frankly out to charm and this sometimes is considered to be an affectation in his work.

GIORGIONE

Fleming (1968) points out that Venetian painting is marked by the refinement and perfection of painting with oil in canvas, since frescoes are unsuited to the damp Venetian climate. The Venetian school of painting is distinctive in itself and constitutes a long list of outstanding artistic geniuses. I shall only touch on a few of these of special interest to psychotherapists.

Giorgione (1477-1510), was a dream painter who worked in symbols and easily interchanged one symbol for the other. Some of his few paintings, including the most famous, *The Tempest* (faded and under glass) in the Accademia of Venice, seem to be totally unintelligible. In *The Tempest* Giorgione substituted a standing soldier for a seated woman in the final work. No one knows what this is supposed to represent. That a woman bathing should be deliberately changed into a soldier, proves there was no fixed subject in the artist's mind; this is borne out by Giorgione's other works and by Vasari's admission that he could not make sense of it at all.

Hartt writes of this masterpiece, "Apparently the picture is a caprice on Giorgione's part—an antisubject. He has given us the spare parts of a story, so to speak, which we can utilize as we wish. . . . Again, he shows us an unfriendly nature. The woman seems trapped in the unkempt, weedy natural world that has grown up around her. The trees are unpruned (Piero di Cosimo would have loved them), the bushes shaggy, the columns ruined, the bridge precarious, the village disheveled. And the whole scene is threatened by an immense, low storm cloud, which fills the sky and emits a bolt of lightning, casting the shadow of the bridge upon the little river and illuminating the scene with a sudden glare. . . . When the picture hung in the Accademia in a room by itself, with its own light, one could watch it for hours with inexhaustible fascination" (1969, p. 531).

Use of x-rays has revealed the change that Giorgione made. Canaday, writes, *"The Tempest . . .* points the way toward the complete abolition of subject matter in contemporary abstract art. The picture exists for itself, within itself; painting becomes a way of seeing and feeling, not auxiliary to thinking and clarifying. All normal relationships are ignored in order that everything—figures, landscapes, sky—may be united in a dream relationship born of sensual experience" (1969). Even in Florence painting had not reached this degree of independence.

Giorgione's life was short and few of his works, not a score in all, have escaped destruction. His accomplishment is characteristic of that phase of the Renaissance when the human species seemed so full of promise. It is for this reason that Berenson calls Giorgioni's work characteristic of the height of the Renaissance spirit.

But the reaction had already set in, as seen in the paintings of Lorenzo Lotto (1480-1556) who does not paint the triumph of man over his environment but shows us people desperately in want of the consolations of religion, of sober thought, of friendship, and of affection. Berenson (1952) writes, "They look out from his canvases as if begging for sympathy." This great north Italian painter, influenced by Giorgione and Titian, was an earnest, simple, good-hearted man. Titian called him "kindness itself" (1952). He was a man of the highest principles, of sensitive perceptions, and of a gift for spontaneous expression, yet he lacked a tenacity of purpose—which is a most important characteristic if the artist (or the psychotherapist) is to make steady progress toward a truly personal style—and therefore he cannot rank among the greatest painters of the Venetian school of the cinquecento.

TITIAN

This leads us to Lotto's great contemporary, another Renaissance giant, the long lived Titian (1488-1576). Hartt writes: "Titian is to be credited with one of the crucial discoveries of the history of art. He was the first man in modern times to free the brush from the task of exact description of tactile surfaces, volumes and details, and to convert it into a vehicle for the direct perception of light through color, and the unimpeded expression of feeling. . . . Brushwork was however, only the beginning of Titian's magic" (1969, p. 532). Critics are generally agreed that Titian presents the best grasp of the reality of life of any of the Renaissance painters. He represents a splendid example of an artist who lived a long life and adapted remarkably well to the changing of the times and the ideals of the milieu around him. The length of his inspired creative life, and the repeated rejuvenations with renewed and surprising heat and passion, ending only with his actual death, are almost unique.

Titian of course was the forerunner of modern impressionism. Throughout his long career the genius of Titian owed its compelling power to the warmth and directness of his response to life, and to his firm belief in the value of painting in itself. In many ways Titian is the most meaningful and modern of the Renaissance painters. As Berenson (1952) points out, "Titian then, was ever ready to change with the times, and on the whole the change was toward a firmer grasp of reality, necessitating yet another advance in the painter's mastery of his craft. Titian's real greatness consists in the fact that he was as able to produce an impression of inner reality as he was ready to appreciate the need of a firmer hold on life" (1952, p. 22). A suitable end point for the art tour of the psychotherapist might be in standing before Titian's moving and impressive self-portrait, in the Prado, Madrid; it is typical of Titian's knack of registering a face at that crucial psychological moment when the man's true nature reveals itself.

We finish with Veronese (1528-1588), who presents the last great attempt in Renaissance painting to uphold the spirit of the Italian Renaissance against the forces of darkness and superstition that were closing in on the culture from all sides. Venturi sees this as an attempt in the sixteenth century by man to assert his power in art at the very time, when, in reality he was experiencing so many setbacks. He writes that the Venetians, "employed all the nuances of tones, the vibrations of color and light in hymning their feeling for reality. . . . . With the coming of Veronese, painting took on a new lease of life; his talent was immense, his proficiency seems limitless. All the earlier discoveries were recapitulated in his art. . . . Thus he stood for a summing up and culmination of all the tendencies of a century, and it was difficult to go farther on the path that he had charted" (1961).

As the reader reviews the painters mentioned in this chapter it should become increasingly clear that *the problems they were struggling with are the same problems we are struggling with today.* The humanistic solution and the humanistic ideals—the reverence for human life—that they united in striving for still represent our greatest hope for developing social welfare and improving the lot of men on this earth (Chessick 1973). The humanizing ideal is a basic great idea for the psychotherapist, since history has proved repeatedly that the great advances in the practice of psychotherapy occur whenever there has been an increase in the capacity for humanistic feeling among those who make it their life's profession to help others who have been less fortunate than themselves. Many of the various thinkers reviewed in this book have all been united upon this one principle, and therefore it is of the utmost necessity that we strive toward the Italian Renaissance ideal both in the development of our personality and our therapeutic style: *essere umano.*

Chapter 6

Confessions, Soliloquies, and Persuasion

Whoever does not want to fear, let him probe his inmost self. Do not just touch the surface; go down into yourself; reach into the farthest corner of your heart.

St. Augustine, *Sermon*

For there are some things which with their full implications are not understood or are hardly understood, no matter how eloquently they are spoken, or how often, or how plainly. And these things should never, or only rarely on account of some necessity, be set before a popular audience. In books, however— which, when they are understood, hold the readers to them in a certain way, and when they are not understood, are not troublesome to those not wishing to read—and in conversations the duty should not be neglected of bringing the truth which we have perceived, no matter how difficult it may be to comprehend or how much labor may be involved, to the understanding of others, provided that the listener or disputant wishes to learn and has the capacity to do so no matter how the material is presented. The speaker should not consider the eloquence of his teaching but the clarity of it.

St. Augustine, *On Christian Doctrine*

AUGUSTINE

Kohut points out that assessment of the influence of the therapist's personality is of particular importance in the evaluation of treatment results: "There can be little doubt that a therapist's quasi-religious fervor or his deep feeling of inner saintliness provides a strong therapeutic leverage in the treatment of very disturbed adults and children which accounts for some striking therapeutic successes. The relevant influence may emanate from the charistmatic therapist directly, or it may be transmitted via the therapeutic team of which he is the leader" (1971). Kohut explains that no one should object to therapeutic success with "otherwise almost untreatable disorders" on the ground that these successes were achieved by the direct or indirect influence of the therapist's personality. He insists that the decision whether a specific form of therapeutic management is in essence scientific or whether it is inspirational is approached by answering the questions, (1) Do we have a systematical theoretical grasp of the processes involved in therapy? (2) Can the treatment method be communicated to others, i.e. can it be learned (and ultimately practiced) without the presence of its originator? And (3) most importantly, Does the treatment method remain successful after the death of its creator? It is specifically the last event which . . . seems . . . often to reveal that the therapeutic methodology was not a scientific one but that the success depended on the actual presence of a single, specifically endowed person" (1971).

The great therapy procedure originated by St. Augustine was patently antiscientific, but at the same time it set the tone of approach to the investigation of man for a thousand years. It embodied a new idea, which was in the air at the time, especially in the philosophy of Plotinus. Augustine's entire philosophy was a reaction to the close of the classic age, which was marked by successive groups of barbarians attacking and pillaging cities of the Roman Empire. In many respects it was construed as a response to the devastation and decadence that characterized the empire's decline and disintegration, and it represents the projection of an ideal world for the elect in a world to come. The philosopher Charles Frankel (Klein 1970) sees a parallel between the contemporary world with its "unsettled frame of mind" in the face of threatened atomic holocaust and the world of St. Augustine. Both can be described as ages of anxiety, and in both one can note a desperate search for means of coping with anxiety. Just as Augustine turned to God and the hope of eternal life, many moderns are turning to faith in "the courage to be" and "to the existential philosophies calculated to foster such courage," as well as to a variety of weird and quasi-mystical immersions and practices.

W. T. Jones explains that Augustine was not a thinker whose views evoke a neutral response. "Those who are not for him are likely to be dead against him. Thus, many people today regard Augustine's point of view as hopelessly unbalanced—a neurotic exaggeration of guilt and sin and an unhealthy otherworldliness that result in almost total neglect of the really serious social and political problems that it is the business of the philosopher to discuss. . . . Others, however, will argue that if Augustine went too far in one direction, the modern world has gone too far in another. Concentration camps, Hiroshima, and Nagasaki have shocked many of us into a painful recognition of man's inhumanity to man. The post-World War II generation is likely to understand Augustine's horror at the depths of iniquity of which men are capable; even those who reject his specifically Christian interpretations may feel that he gave a truer picture of human nature than that presented by eighteenth and nineteenth century philosophers of progress" (1969, Vol. 2, pp. 136-137).

Besides the fundamental idea of therapy for the troubled person through introspection, confession, soliloquy, and persuasion, Augustine made a number of significant contributions to modern psychology. He called attention to the broad question of the nature of infant behavior, although he misinterpreted it by confusing the immoral and amoral. He developed a distinction between inner sense and outer sense and regarded self knowledge through introspection as the basis for "one mind to know another mind." He repudiated astrological teachings in view of the divergent life histories of twins. For him furthermore, it was not will that determines character but character that determines will, an introspective observation that was not followed up until Freud (see chapter 11). His consideration of memory revealed his recognition of the influence of wishes on recall; he further distinguished between a recalled emotional experience and the original experience. He attempted to differentiate carefully between concepts and percepts and in so doing developed a fundamental theory of semiotic (see especially Books Two and Three of *On Christian*

Doctrine 1958, and Markus 1972). Wittgenstein begins his twentieth century *Philosophical Investigations* with a famous quotation from Augustine's *Confessions:*

> This I remember; and have since observed how I learned to speak. It was not that my elders taught me words in any set method; but I, longing by cries and broken accents and various motions of my limbs to express my thoughts, that so I might have my will, and yet unable to express all I willed, or to whom I willed, did myself, by the understanding which Thou, my God, gavest me, practice the sounds in my memory. When they named any thing, and as they spoke turned towards it, I saw and remembered that they called what they would point out by the name they uttered. And that they meant this things and no other was plain from the motion of their body, the natural language, as it were, of all nations, expressed by the coutenance, glance of the eye, gestures of the limbs, and tones of the voice, indicating the affections of the mind, as it pursues, possesses, rejects, or shuns. And thus by constantly hearing words, as they occurred in various sentences, I collected gradually for what they stood; and having broken in my mouth to these signs, I thereby gave utterance to my will. Thus I exchanged with those about me these current signs of our wills, and so launched deeper into the stormy intercourse of human life, yet depending on parental authority and the beck of elders. (1952, p. 8)

This magnificent quotation, two thousand years ahead of its time, gives the flavor of Augustine's introspection and his loving concentration on parent-child interaction in character formation. The subject of semiotic is discussed in detail in chapter 15. In another direction Augustine formulated some important basic issues in the study of the psychology of time perception and presented a relativistic theory of time centuries before Einstein. Clearly, Augustine may be called the greatest introspective psychologist before Freud.

Knowledge of Augustine's life is essential to an understanding of his method. Since there are numerous available descriptions of his life, I will not go into great detail here. He was born in A.D. 354 in North Africa. His pagan father was a lesser official—a sociable man who enjoyed life. Monica, his mother, was Christian and an extremely determined, rigid, and moralistic woman with an abhorrence of sexuality. He acquired a classical education in his native land, and as a young man he led the licentious life of a pagan. In 372 he fathered an illegitimate son. At the age of nineteen, Cicero's *Hortensius,* a skeptical work, now lost, inspired him with a passion for philosophy. He became a Manichaean but in 382 perceived that this viewpoint was untrue and became a successful teacher of rhetoric in Carthage, Rome, and Milan. Under the influence of the great Roman Christian, Ambrose, Bishop of Milan, he became a catechumen in 385. In 386 he gave up his post as a teacher of rhetoric and went with his mother and son to live in the country home of a friend near Milan where he devoted himself to philosophy. His mistress of fifteen years, the mother of his son, was summarily sent away.

In 387, after a remarkable conversion experience described in his *Confessions,* he was baptized by Ambrose. After his mother died, he returned to Africa. From 388 to 430 he lived in Africa and eventually became the famous bishop of Hippo. He died during the siege of Hippo by the Vandals. He produced an enormous amount of written work.

Jaspers describes the importance of Augustine's great conversion at thirty-three. Immediately after this conversion, he went to live with his friends in Milan and met with them daily in earnest discussion of the question of truth. Jaspers writes, "Their medium was the world of classical culture (they read and interpreted Virgil among other authors). In the early writings, something of the force of ancient philosophizing seems to be reborn; we perceive the ancient passion for clear thinking. But there has been a change. These early works disclose an ancient philosophy that seems to have lost its original vitality and become an empty idiom in which the young Augustine could no longer think of any fundamental or satisfying idea. A great new spiritual reality had dawned, bringing to philosophy new blood without which it would have died. ... Such conversion is not the philosophical turnabout that must daily be renewed, in which a man tears himself out of distortion, obscurity, forgetfulness, but a definite biographical moment, that breaks into his life and gives it a new foundation. After this moment, the philosophical transformation with its daily endeavor can continue, but it draws its force from a more radical and absolute foundation, the transformation of his whole being in faith" (1962, p. 177).

Augustine is not a likable figure. His attitude, for example, toward his mistress was base. In fact, his personality is a riddle. His nature discloses both noble and commonplace traits. Along with Kierkegaard (see chapter 17) and Nietzsche (see chapter 10), he begins a movement in philosophical and psychological thought that can be described as springing from deep personal emotions rather than objective reason. All three authors underwent radical transformations and wrote unremittingly. As Jaspers puts it, "They write with their blood." Their thinking with its many contradictory possibilities is like life itself. "Yet they think with an intensity that is always systematic, though the system is never completed." All three have a maximum of conscious self-understanding and self-control. "Augustine wrote the first true autobiography and (like Kierkegaard and Nietzsche) concluded his written work with a critical retrospect. They give the reader not a mere content, but an interpretation of it, a reflection on its meaning" (1962). Thus their life histories are inextricable from their thought. For this reason Augustine is sometimes classed along with Kierkegaard and Nietzsche as a founder of the existentialist movement in philosophy.

There are two obvious ways of interpreting the life of Augustine outlined in his *Confessions* that are of immediate interest to psychotherapists. The first of these is to view his work and life as a sincere intellectual and philosophical striving. A typical example of this is contained in the summary of his developing thought by Stumpf (1966). Augustine's essential premise was that true philosophy is inconceivable without a confluence of faith and reason. The striving for rest, completion, and satisfaction is seen as the motive power that drives all things in nature toward their purposes; the pursuit of happiness is "in the nature of man" and is the goal of philosophy, but it cannot be found, according to Augustine, without Christianity. The movement is from a rejection of the skepticism of Cicero's work, in despair of attaining happiness through rational philosophy, to a conversion in which peace, happiness, and blessedness are finally found.

A second, diametrically opposed view is presented as one might expect by psychoanalysis. While Kligerman, for example, respects Augustine greatly, he sees the *Confessions* as essentially a psychiatric personal history which has the spontaneous quality of free association. Kligerman analyzes Augustine's conversion in terms of his oedipal struggle, with the rather unsatisfactory resolution of an identification with the mother and a passive feminine attitude to the father, displaced to God. Kligerman goes so far as to claim that "many years later he fought the battle all over again in his monumental work, *The City of God,* in which he vindictively regarded the sack of Rome with an almost totemic glee. Rome was still the city of his father, and the 'City of God' the province of his mother" (1967).

It is not our purpose here to try to debate further the meaning and motivation behind Augustine's philosophical and religious position but to concentrate on the methodology that he introduces, as embodied in his *Confessions* and later on in his less productive *Soliloquies.* The *Confessions* is probably his most important and most influential work. In the first place, the *Confessions* establishes two basic principles of education. First it shows how much the learner must perform by his own unaided effort; at the same time it emphasizes the necessity and significance of divine illumination, related to the modern insight theory of learning. "Thus, the *Confessions* are a demonstration of the principle which Augustine was to argue more systematically in *The Teacher,* that learning is achieved by the personal activity of the learner and in an inner, voluntary movement of the mind, a movement in which external teachers and formal lessons play only a minor part" (Howie 1969).

The *Confessions* has much to do with Augustine's middle age crisis; it was written in his forties. Brown explains that "only a very profound, inner reason would have led him to write a book such as the *Confessions:* he was entering middle age. This has been considered a good time for writing an autobiography. Around 397, Augustine had reached a watershed in his life. Since 391, he had been forced to adjust himself to a new existence, as a priest and bishop. This change had affected him deeply. It had already driven him to anxious self-examination. . . . The *Confessions,* therefore, is not a book of reminscences. It is an anxious turning to the past. The note of urgency is unmistakable. . . . It is also a poignant book. In it, one constantly senses the tension between the 'then' of the young man and the 'now' of the bishop. The past can come very close: its powerful and complex emotions have only recently passed away; we can still feel their contours through the thin layer of new feeling that has grown over them" (1969, pp. 163-164).

The writing of the *Confessions* was an act of self-therapy. Brown insists that it was written in the spirit of a doctor committed only recently, and so all the more zealously, to a new form of treatment. "In the first nine books, therefore, he will illustrate what happens when this treatment is not applied, how he had come to discover it, and, skipping a decade he will demonstrate in Book Ten, its continued application in the present" (1969). The method of getting to know one's self by self–observation and self–examination resulted in brilliant introspections that give Augustine permanent status in the history of psychology. In his work introspection and self–examination are presented as a method of discovering truth and of communicating truth to others. The concept that the mind can discover itself in the very process of seeking itself is a new and great idea in sharp contrast to previous philosophical theories of psychology and truth. As we shall discuss later, it also illustrates how change occurs on the basis of knowledge gained through introspection and the role of so-called divine illumination.

Many of the themes of the *Confessions* are taken up on a broader plane in Augustine's *City of God* in which he makes the love of God the central principle of morality and sees in the conflict between the *City of God* and the city of the world a beginning philosophy of history. In seeing a meaning in history or a pattern put there by God, Augustine founded the philosophy of history. Similarly, Augustine became one of the first to introduce the idea of the human predicament. Jones explains that this idea "reflected the sense of insecurity and the pessimism with which man had come to look at his world. Augustine fully shared this mood. He never tired of enumerating the miseries of this life: the dangers by land and by sea, by day and by night; plague, famine, slaughter, bloodshed, social and civil war. . . . Nothing seemed to him more obvious than the misery of the human situation. . . . It was clear to Augustine that he could do nothing to extricate himself from this terrible situation. His sense of his own helplessness was one of the most vivid facts of his experience. He had struggled for years to lead a good life, but all in vain. When salvation finally occurred, it was none of his doing; it was something that came to him as a gift of God" (1969, Vol. 2, p. 106).

On the other hand, Augustine did have some definitive ideas on how man could be helped, educated, and changed. He declared that wisdom, by which he meant the understanding of absolute truth, is the ultimate goal of education. Wisdom *(sapientia)* is a higher value than science *(scientia)*, the former being "the intellectual understanding of eternal things" and the latter "the rational understanding of temporal things." He maintained "that at the heart of existence there must always be an area of mystery inpenetrable to the understanding of man. Scientific research cannot demonstrate everything; certain things must always be accepted on faith. Therefore, teachers must carefully nourish the precious sense of wonder in their students" (Howie 1969).

Augustine insists that education is founded on a personal relationship between teacher and pupil in which both learn from each other and is therefore as subtle and inexplicable as all personality interactions. The record of sustained and often painful self-examination effectively demonstrates Augustine's basic educational principle, that every man who learns must be his own teacher. He insisted that truth can be won only at the cost of arduous and prolonged personal effort aided by divine grace and that it cannot be directly communicated by any human teacher. Furthermore, education is not an irksome preparation for the happy life, but it *is* the happy life, according to Augustine. Henry writes that Augustine was "the first thinker who brought into prominence and undertook any analysis of the philosophical and psychological concepts of persons and personality" (1960). Earlier thinkers had looked to the cosmos to unfold the ultimate secrets of reality and of the divine nature, but for Augustine they are all within man himself.

MONTAIGNE

The tradition of self-study, inaugurated by Augustine was renewed by Michel Eyquem De Montaigne (1533-1592), the French essayist and skeptical philosopher, but without the religious preconceptions. The solution of Montaigne's quest allegedly appears in Book III of his *Essays* (1958). From self-study he derives the importance of having tolerance and living a good life, but he fails to really come to grips with the forces in the mind that stand in the way of reasonable living. He appeals essentially to stoical humanism in the earlier essays, but in Book III, as his biographer Frame explains, he insists "that man not be judged by standards not meant by him. Human ethics must be grounded securely in human psychology. The only useful and acceptable human morality must be a morality made for man" (1965). This is an enormous Renaissance step from the Medieval morality of Augustine.

The crucial psychological change in Montaigne's self-therapy is heralded in his long essay, *Apology for Raymond Sebond* (1958), which is primarily a treatise on human reason. Sebond was a fifteenth-century Spanish thinker who tried to establish the Christian religion on rational proofs which numerous critics felt were inadequate, as indeed all such proofs are. The princess to whom Montaigne addresses his warning of the impotence of unaided human reason, Margaret of Valois, simply asked him to defend Raymond Sebond, but Montaigne built upon this excuse an attack on Socratic ratiocination: "I do not believe that knowledge is the mother of all virtue, and that all vice is produced by ignorance."This essay, which is the longest of Montaigne's works, is mordantly critical and pessimistic, stressing man's arrogance, ignorance, and misery. It represents the fullest expression of the doubt expressed by the famous skeptical formula *Que sais-je?* engraved on a medal along with a pair of evenly balanced scales by Montaigne in 1576. As summed up by Frame, Montaigne's biographer and editor, the essay says that "man and his reason are presumptuous. He is neither wiser, happier, nor better than the animals. His self-conscious premeditation of troubles is less valuable than simple and trusting acceptance of life as it comes. Even the philosophers admit this without having to. Their dogmatic pride is absurd, since they have not found truth and cannot" (1965).

The puzzling inconsistencies in this essay probably result from its being a "command performance," for which Montaigne put together large parts of essays that had been composed or partly drafted a good deal earlier; one major section was written around 1573 and another around 1576. The frequent inconsistencies and lapses in the order and development of the themes in the essay support this idea. The long early essay probably was to be entitled "On Human Presumption." It is probably a mistake to be overly strenuous in interpreting this essay on Sebond as a consistent whole.

The essay stands basically as a challenge to the presumption of human reason and the limitations of rationalistic materialism. At the same time the essay is obviously very unsatisfactory. It leaves one with a sense of confusion and offers no constructive suggestions about obtaining happiness except the false implication that a simple or peasant type of life is best. The best psychiatric interpretation of this essay is that it represents a turning point in Montaigne's thought. It reflects a rather depressed state in a highly educated man who is beginning to turn his back on stoical humanism and his youthful hopes based on his readings of the classic Greek and Roman thinkers, that he could lift himself above human problems by his own reason. Montaigne himself in his later essays and in a less melancholy mood contradicts his own statements and the extreme Pyrrhonistic skepticism in this essay.

This destructive and pessimistic essay ushered in the new psychological resource for Montaigne to replace his abandoned stoical humanism, namely *self-study*. Thus years later in his final summing up in Book III of his *Essays,* he writes: "There is no knowledge so hard to acquire as the knowledge of how to live this life well; and the most barbarous of our maladies is to hate and disdain our being" (1958). Here one realizes how Montaigne has moved from a harsh intellectual melancholy to a gentle mature wisdom, marked by tolerance and the acceptance of our great human limitations. It is indeed one of the earliest examples of an at least partially successful self-analysis.

For a period of ten years Montaigne suffered repeated bereavements. He lost his father, his best friend, his brother, six of his infant children, and experienced the massacre of St. Bartholomew's Day in 1572. Finally at the age of thirty-eight, as described dramatically in his essay *On Solitude,* he retired from practical affairs into his "back shop," lined with thousands of books. For nine years he developed a unique and individualized technique of free–association in writing, resulting in the essays of Book I and Book II, published in 1580. Book III was written rather hurriedly some seven years later and published in 1588. It basks in the light of the confidence and greater happiness engendered by the success of the first two books and his self-analysis.

Montaigne is of interest to the psychotherapist for two special reasons. In the first place, he pioneered the exploration of human behavior and motivation in literature, departing from the classical tradition, which heavily emphasized the rational man's ability to solve all questions and problems of life and achieve happiness. By 1577, in *Of the Education of Children,* he stresses his belief that education should have as its method and primary objective the development of the child's judgment: "There are too many people with their pockets full of knowledge and too few who have really assimilated knowledge and gained wisdom." Thus for Montaigne, "Judgment and wisdom lie between ignorance and erudition; they represent an artistic, that is, carefully cultivated realization of the natural capability of a man" (1958).

In the second place, Montaigne, like Augustine, underwent a remarkable midlife crisis (Jacques 1964) that lead to a new burst of creativity based on previous and now abandoned beliefs and a subsequent overcoming of depression. An interesting parallel to Freud is present in the methodology employed to overcome the midlife crisis, in which self-analysis produces the solution. This crisis, as heralded in the *Apology for Raymond Sebond,* is resolved by a remarkably detailed study and description of every aspect of himself, even including his bowel habits. From this self-study he derives the importance of tolerance and living a good life, above sterile intellectualism. He fails, however, to come to grips with the unconscious forces that invariably disrupt the search for the good life. In this he represents a transition figure between early classical rationalistic psychology and modern psychodynamic psychology.

The vital role of confessions, soliloquies, and persuasion in modern psychotherapy has been best delineated by Frank (1961). In fact his general bias seems to be that this is the essence of *all* the various forms of psychotherapy. Breaking vicious circles of self-perpetuating and self-defeating behavior is seen by Frank as "the main goal of psychotherapy," and Augustine would completely agree.

Frank (1961) suggests that much of the effectiveness of different forms of psychotherapy may be due to those features that all have in common, rather than to those that distinguish them from each other. If he is right, we have not gone far beyond the contributions of St. Augustine. The reader must decide for himself whether the other great ideas described in the later chapters of this book make it possible to carve out a discipline of psychoanalytically oriented psychotherapy that is fundamentally different from inspirational forms of treatment characterized by confessions, soliloquies and persuasion.

Chapter 7

The Physicianly Vocation

Weyer's contributions can be summarized as follows: He was the first physician whose major interest turned toward mental diseases and thereby foreshadowed the formation of psychiatry as a medical specialty. He was the first clinical and the first descriptive psychiatrist to leave to succeeding generations a heritage which was accepted, developed, and perfected into an observational branch of medicine in a process which culminated in the great descriptive system of psychiatry formulated at the end of the nineteenth century. Weyer more than anyone else completed, or at least brought closer to completion, the process of divorcing medical psychology from theology and empirical knowledge of the human mind from the faith in the perfection of the human soul. He reduced the clinical problems of psychopathology to simple terms of everyday life and of everyday, human, inner experiences without concealing the complexity of human functioning and the obscurity of human problems. He left no theory, no dogmatic philosophy of his own. His was the task of combating misguided dogma, and he studied the field of human relations through free observation and objective evaluation of man in nature, rather than through consideration of what man might and should be and most of the time is not.

All this Weyer accomplished without developing that cold objectivity which betrays a frigid unconcern about man and which insists that the only thing which matters is the gratification of scientific curiosity. Instead, he repeatedly stressed the fact that he was a physician and that the 'sacred art of medicine' must be practiced on man and for man. 'Love man,' he admonished, 'kill errors, go into combat for truth without cruelty.' He studied theology and history and law because these had to do with man. To those who objected to his legal arguments, he merely replied that it was the duty of the doctor to look for the truth about man wherever he could find it. In this respect Weyer was also the forerunner of the great consciousness of our day that a psychiatrist must not limit himself to a knowledge of anatomy, physiology, internal medicine, surgery, and neurology, but that he must go further into those fields of human activity which reveal man in his totality, that he must acquire sound knowledge of history, sociology, and anthropology. . . .

The whole course of the history of medical psychology is punctuated by the medical man's struggle to rise above the prejudices of all ages in order to identify himself with the psychological realities of his patients. Every time such an identification was achieved the medical man became a psychiatrist. The history of psychiatry is essentially the history of humanism. Every time humanism has diminished or degenerated into mere philanthropic sentimentality, psychiatry has entered a new ebb. Every time the spirit of humanism has arisen, a new contribution to psychiatry has been made.

Gregory Zilboorg, *A History of Medical Psychology*

MACHIAVELLI:
UNROMANTIC AND REALISTIC STUDY
OF HUMAN BEHAVIOR

The Renaissance movement towards humanism, described in chapter 5, gave rise to three important themes, current in modern psychotherapy. In the previous chapter, I described one of these as embodied in the character of Montaigne, a psychological realist, concerned with the great richness of human feelings, character, and behavior, and not at all with general abstract principles. In so doing, Montaigne revived the tradition of concentration on the individual man and his inner life.

Parallel to this trend is that of an unblinking and unromantic examination of human motivation and human social behavior; in this tradition Machiavelli may be characterized as the first social psychologist and as the first student of interpersonal relations. Alexander and Selesnick explain that "to view natural phenomena dispassionately, without wishful distortions, is difficult enough; to study human behavior in the same objective manner is perhaps the most difficult of all scientific tasks" (1966).

Machiavelli (1469-1527) wrote *The Prince* in 1513 almost at the same time Thomas More (1478-1535) wrote *Utopia.* The contrast between these works, as Prezzolini (1967) points out, establishes most clearly the brilliance and originality of Machiavelli's thought. Benoit-Smullyan declares: "The difference in method and general spirit between his work and the work of his immediate predecessors is really astonishing. The difference may be summed up as a change from a religious, ethical approach grounded on faith and authority, to a naturalistic, matter-of-fact approach grounded on empirical evidence, and a somewhat cynical conception of human nature" (1966).

A correct judgment on Machiavelli requires a study of all his works. *The Prince,* most popular of his writings, can be understood best as an essay on human nature, produced for the advancement of his political ambitions during the composition of *The Discourses.* It stands in relation to the latter as the *Communist Manifesto* of Marx and Engels stands to Marx's *Capital:* it is an action pamphlet based on the thought of the much larger work. The larger work is more scholarly and reveals the true breadth of the author's efforts and thoughts. Since *The Prince* is an action pamphlet written to serve a political purpose, it is easily misinterpreted.

In attempting to ground his theories on historical evidence and personal experience, Machiavelli breaks from the Medieval tradition and becomes the first true political scientist. The parallel to Freud's approach to the neuroses is evident. However, although he was a great pioneer, Machiavelli's life reveals a serious flaw in his approach.

We owe almost the entire body of Machiavelli's work to one of the variegated twisting and turnings of Italian politics which caused him to lose both his political reputation and his government post. He wrote in exile, poverty, and overwhelming boredom, as he describes in a very famous letter:

On the coming of evening, I return to my house and enter my study; and at the door I take off the day's clothing, covered with mud and dust and put on garments regal and courtly; and reclothed appropriately, I enter the ancient courts of ancient men where, received by them with affection, I feed on that food which only is mine and which I was born for, where I am not ashamed to speak with them and ask them the reasons for their actions; and they in their kindness answer me; and for four hours of time I do not feel boredom, I forget every trouble, I do not dread poverty, I am not so frightened by death; I give myself entirely over to them. (Prezzolini 1967, p. 162)

This classic letter describes a situation comparable to Montaigne in his "back shop." An important difference is also found here, for Machiavelli, unlike Montaigne, was not at all satisfied with a literary or scientific life. At the time he was writing he considered himself a failure, and all his efforts were bent constantly toward getting back into active politics.

During his period of literary output, he was consumed with anger that the wickedness and stupidity of the human race had led to his undeserving downfall and torture on the rack. Four turns of the rack were considered severe torture for any man; Machiavelli is reported by one author (Ridolfi 1954) to have stoically endured six turns and even composed a poem about his imprisonment. He was preoccupied with innumerable schemes to restore himself to power, which included flattering the tyrants by writing whatever he thought they wanted to hear. It is a tribute to his genius that his anger, lust for power, and boredom could be transformed into a body of lasting literary work. In his writing Machiavelli identifies completely with the aggressor in his worship of success and power as the highest goods. He even distorts history or relies on mythology as historical fact when necessary to prove a point. He is ever preoccupied with human wickedness and corruption; his most famous play, *Mandragola* is a complete satire on human greed and corruption at all levels.

His political theory is fairly clear and simple. He proposes to ask why states rise and fall and how they can be made to defer as long as possible their inevitable decay. His answer, as Durant (1953) points out, is through a rejection of Christian ethics in favor of Roman ethics.

Preservation of the state and its leader becomes the supreme law; in war, Christian ethics are treason. Since a state must continue to expand or it will decay, a constant preparation for war is necessary, whether it be disguised under the term "deterrent" or not. The concept of *virtu* appears repeatedly, meaning not humility, gentleness, or peace but Roman *virtu*—virility, manliness, courage with energy, and intelligence.

His theory of human nature, at the base of his political theories, is not so clear and at times contains contradictions. The fundamental contradiction lies in the question of whether or not human nature is unchangeable. On the one hand, he seems convinced that man's nature is immutable and on the other, he firmly believes in the power of princes to modify people. It is easy to quote passages from Machiavelli in which he bases his whole argument for the possibility of a science of groups on the unchanging and fixed qualities in human nature. It is equally easy to quote passages demonstrating an almost mystical belief in the "strong man" or leader who brings about a renaissance in the state singlehandedly and after whose death there is relapse into former habits by the group.

There is no answer to this contradiction in Machiavelli except the psychological one that, on the one hand, he was bitter about what had happened to him but, on the other hand, identified with the aggressor by extolling the tyrannical prince. The general tenor of his works implies that any improvement in people's habits is not an improvement in human nature itself but a temporary uplifting of behavior under the passing influence of the strong prince. Such an improvement was probably not conceived by Machiavelli as a civilizing influence as I have defined it; more likely he meant an increase in Roman *virtu*.

Machiavelli's specific theory of human nature can be outlined as follows:

1. The desire to acquire and hold material property is one of the fundamental desires of man. Thus he writes that "men forget more easily the death of their father than the loss of their patrimony." (This point of view has been enlarged and carried to an extreme in Ardrey's controversial work on *The Territorial Imperative* [1966].)

2. "It may be said of men in general that they are ungrateful, voluble, dissemblers, anxious to avoid danger, and covetous of gain; as long as you benefit them, they are entirely yours; they offer you their blood,

their goods, their life, and their children when the necessity is remote; but when the danger approaches they revolt."

3. Men are wicked and they are fools. They are deceived by false glory and false good, and those few who do not agree do not dare to speak up because they are afraid of the majesty of the state and so do not dare to oppose themselves to the many.

4. Men resemble each other. As a group they may be loud and audacious in the denunciation of their rulers, but when punishment stares them in the face, then, distrustful of each other, they rush to obey.

5. Men's hatreds generally spring from fear or envy.

6. "As human desires are insatiable (because their nature is to have and to do everything, whilst fortune limits their possessions and capacity of enjoyment), this gives rise to a constant discontent in the human mind and a weariness of the things they possess; and it is this which makes them decry the present, praise the past, and desire the future."

7. Men are cowardly, avaricious, ungrateful, fickle, and deceitful so the prince should choose to be feared rather than loved since fear is a more stable and dependable motive of human action.

8. Fortune rules over men because men cannot change their conduct with the times. The reason men cannot change is due to the impossibility of resisting the natural bent of their characters and the difficulty in persuading themselves that a mode of proceeding which has been successful before will not work again.

One might be hard pressed to quarrel directly with these precepts; in many ways his pessimistic description of men resembles that of Freud. In a previous publication (Chessick 1969b) I have pointed out that something vital concerning the nature of man was left out of Machiavelli's work—the capacity for autonomous and creative functioning as individuals and as a group. This capacity represents the third trend in modern psychotherapy to originate in the Renaissance and may be best discerned in the role of man's "physicianly vocation."

VIVES AND WEYER:
ORIGIN OF THE PHYSICIANLY VOCATION

The Renaissance humanist Pico della Mirandola (1463-1494) espoused the doctrine that man alone above all other beings has no fixed state but is capable, because he is free, of realizing his ideal through education (Pico 1956). The Spaniard Juan Luis Vives (1492-1540), labelled "the father of modern psychology" by Zilboorg (1941), elaborated this idea. An associate of Erasmus and Thomas More, Vives lived a rather uneventful life. He was born in Valencia and died in Bruges at the age of forty-eight.

By offering a highly realistic description of human passions presented according to general principles such as those of physics, Vives paves the way for the science of psychodynamics. His contribution, however, rests in introducing and emphasizing a general attitude rather than in the achievement of solid knowledge based on systematic observation. Vives was a prolific writer who perpetuated a tradition of warmth and consideration for the insane. Viewing insanity as an unhealthy condition of the mind for which one ought to feel compassion, he insisted on humane treatment of the mentally ill. He wrote in criticism of scholastic psychology, attacking St. Augustine and others for their accent on the "soul" as a subject of psychological consideration, "What the soul is, is of no concern for us to know," argued Vives (Bromberg 1954).

Zilboorg maintains that the true importance of Vives has not yet been properly appreciated. For example, although Hobbes is generally credited with the discovery of mental associations, Vives, almost a century before, had a clear conception of associations, understanding their relation to remembering and forgetting and the influence of the emotions on the whole process. In his most significant book *De Anima et Vita* (published in Basel in 1538), he makes one of the first modern attempts to formulate principles of human psychology based on factual and descriptive considerations. He argues that the mind functions in accordance with definable laws and stresses the importance of psychological associations. Vives offers an illustration: "When I was a boy at Valencia, I was ill of a fever; while my taste was deranged I ate cherries; for many years afterwards, whenever I tasted the fruit I not only recalled the fever, but also seemed to experience it again" (Zilboorg 1941).

In 1563 Johann Weyer published his *De Praestigiis Daemonum* (Zilboorg 1941) declaring that witchery was either sickness or rascality; he attacked the burning of witches and asserted the right of the physician to delve into the treatment of the possessed. His treatise is commonly accepted today as the beginning of psychiatry as a medical discipline. For reward in his own time, he was attacked on all sides with jeers and disbelief and placed on the *Index Librorum Prohibitorum* so that reading any of his writings was forbidden. Born in Germany Weyer (1515-1576) devoted himself to the practice of medicine throughout his life. His method of study was basically that of clinical science, to search out cases of daemon-possession and investigate in painstaking detail with copious note-taking. Bromberg explains, "Weyer insisted on *individualization* of cases. . . . Weyer's plea that the patient be regarded as an individual heralded a medical psychology which three centuries later regarded patients as individuals with an emotional life and a set of reactions specific unto themselves. Weyer introduced a practical, clinical attitude, presaging the perception of individual differences and individual emotional needs" (1954). His masterpiece, *De Prestigiis Daemonum* is essentially a step by step clinical rebuttal of the *Malleus Maleficarum*. The dedication of his book illustrates his open and objective attitude: "If any arguments prove unsatisfactory to some learned and sensitive members of our profession to which, knowing my humble capacity, I freely accede—I offer them the opportunity to weigh and examine the matter with great precision, to employ a more scientific method, and a more systematic order. If I am admonished for having committed an error, I shall be grateful to those who will point it out to me; I shall never be ashamed to retract my mistakes, for I am not so good a friend of my own self that I would refuse to recognize my mistakes" (Zilboorg 1941).

PINEL: THE HUMANE TRADITION IN PSYCHOTHERAPY

In 1801 Philippe-Pinel published a volume that established the physicianly vocation at the *center* of psychiatric treatment. This treatise on insanity describes conclusions reached during his association with the Bicètre Hospital in Paris and later with the famous Salpetrière Hospital. It is well known how Pinel found conditions at the Bicètre in 1793—midway in France's reign of terror. A state of medieval horror prevailed that was also characteristic of most eighteenth century mental institutions. His unchaining of the mentally ill captured the imagination of many future generations of psychiatrists.

It is possible to debate (Alexander and Selesnick 1966) whether the credit for the humane tradition in unchaining the insane belongs entirely to Pinel. The psychiatric historian Schmitz states: "Not Pinel, but the physicians in Valencia in 1409 were the first to remove the chains and institute moral treatment. Free exercises, games, occupation, entertainment, diet, and hygiene were used" (Bromberg 1954). The isolation of Spain from the rest of Europe after the seventeenth century may explain why the reform did not spread directly to Europe but had to wait until the end of the eighteenth century for Pinel and the Grand Duke Pietro Leopoldo of Tuscany (1747-1792), an enlightened monarch who also shared the eighteenth century zeal for social reform.

It is perhaps less well-known that Pinel instituted painstaking scientific documentation of what he observed and the tradition of questioning knowledge derived from books and previous authorities on the subject of mental illness. Above all, he argued that the physician must be man in whom kindness and humanity predominate: "Such a physician must be able to project himself into the situation of the patient" (Bromberg 1954).

Pinel (1745-1826) died at eighty-one at his post in the living quarters at the Salpetrière. His brilliant and eventful career is summarized by Zilboorg (1941) at length. "The mentally sick," observed Pinel, "far from being guilty people deserving punishment, are sick people whose miserable state deserves all the consideration that is due suffering humanity." Zilboorg points out the direct descent of this quotation from the writing of Weyer, two hundred and thirty years before. Also in the tradition of Weyer, Pinel, by making personal notes for his own use, introduced the taking of psychiatric histories and the keeping of case records. The tradition was carried on by his famous pupil Esquirol (1772-1840), who further introduced the systematic study of a series of case histories. This idea, so obvious today, was revolutionary at the time. Finally, Pinel entered the battle regarding the *indiscriminate* use of drugs in the treatment of emotional disorders.

THE PSYCHOTHERAPIST'S PHYSICIANLY VOCATION IN THE MODERN AGE

The battle between society and the psychiatric physician who as part of his physicianly vocation has to almost forcibly annex psychiatry to medicine, often against the wishes of physicians in other specialties, continues even today. We still suffer the well known disputes between "antipsychiatrists" and numerous other movements, groups, and individuals who would do away entirely with the concept of mental illness and the physicianly treatment of mental illness on the one hand and the main stream tradition of psychoanalytically oriented psychiatry on the other.

Freud instituted the second great psychiatric revolution (see chapter 11) also on the premise that the physicianly vocation was implicit in the work of the intensive psychotherapist. The editor of the Standard Edition of Freud's works comments on the frequency with which Freud refers to the "physician" in his *Papers on Technique* (1911-1915) and on the complete replacement of this designation by "analyst" in the two late technical papers written in 1937 ("Analysis Terminable and Interminable," and "Construction in Analysis"). The diminishing emphasis on the physicianly vocation was developed by Freud in his attempt to establish the neutrality of the classical psychoanalyst so that he could be a better mirror for the transference. This tended to produce a certain distortion in the practice of others in the field, who interpreted Freud's description of a psychoanalyst as a neutral mirror or surgeon as an invitation to be cold and aloof and to hide from a human relationship with the patient in order to avoid countertransference problems. Even the briefest reading of Freud's famous case histories, however, at once establishes that the physicianly vocation formed the foundation of Freud's attitude and approach to all his patients.

It became necessary for this concept to have a formal or specific revival in the literature of psychoanalytic psychiatry. The credit for this revival is usually given to Zetzel and may be found in her collected papers: *The Capacity for Emotional Growth.* Zetzel suggested differentiating between transference neurosis and transference as therapeutic alliance. "Effective analysis depends on the sound therapeutic alliance, a prerequisite for which is the integration, before analysis, of certain mature ego functions. . . . It is important in the psychoanalysis of patients considered suitable for psychoanalytic procedure to make a distinction between therapeutic alliance, defined as as real object relationship which fosters mobilization of autonomous ego attributes in the patients, and the transference neurosis, in which the analyst is utilized as the displaced object of unresolved infantile fantasy" (1970).

She introduced the following extremely significant questions: What in short is the analyst's role in the development of therapeutic alliance? How is this activity to be distinguished from countertransference? How may this alliance be maintained at the height of an intense transference neurosis? Finally, how do interpretation and analysis of the object relationship implicit in the therapeutic alliance influence resolution of the terminal stages of an analysis? Zetzel convincingly demonstrated in a case presentation how a therapeutic alliance based on recognition of ego boundaries and objective reality testing may limit serious regressive tendencies and significant acting out. I have discussed this in detail in *The Technique and Practice of Intensive Psychotherapy* (1974g).

In addition to certain ego capacities brought by the patient to the therapy, the *real* personality features of the psychotherapist must be given full consideration in discussing the development of a therapeutic alliance. Zetzel explains, "In summary, neither Freud nor the other pioneer analysts bypassed the doctor-patient relationship as a necessary prerequisite to successful transference analysis. Like Freud, however, most contributors regarded the relationship either as an essentially stable, silent background which could take care of itself, or primarily as a feature of the opening stages of an analysis" (1970).

This physicianly vocation is approached from a somewhat different point of view in a classical monograph by Stone. It is not an excessive expectation, writes Stone, "that an analyst, in his capacity as physician, feel a kindly and helpful, broadly tolerant and friendly interest in his patients, expressed largely in the channels provided by his special work." This represents a lifelong vocation on the part of the psychotherapist, a profound sense of identity and commitment, and a real functional relationship to another individual, termed by Stone, "the physicianly vocation." It is essential to the successful outcome of psychotherapy since it produces formation of a fundamental therapeutic alliance. He continues, "I would regard the physician's attitude as not only more effective for the process but as somewhat better adapted to the emotional life of the therapist." Stone insists that the patient be permitted to experience his therapist's *physicianly vocation* as a stable and active reality of the relationship, to whatever degree it may be necessary, without yielding any of the crucial issues of nongratification in the sense of primitive transference wishes. This physicianly vocation has to do with the deep inner attitude of the psychotherapist and the kind of commitment he has to his work. Stone formalizes what every experienced clinician knows, that the small nuances of the psychotherapist's attitude "can determine the difference between a lonely vacuum and a controlled but warm human situation" (1961). Without this warm but controlled human situation, no therapeutic alliance can develop and no effective intensive psychotherapy can take place.

The importance of the physicianly vocation and the humanist tradition in intensive psychotherapy is most fully developed by Greenson (1965, 1967; with Wexler 1969, 1970). He explains that the daily work with the patient—the consistent and unwavering pursuit of insight in dealing with any and all of the patient's material and behavior—is a crucial factor, along with regular, consistent, and orderly work routines, in the establishment of a working alliance (Greenson's term for therapeutic alliance). Similarly, the importance given to each hour and the rarity of the therapist's absences and changes of the basic conditions of the therapy help to impress the patient with the need for serious cooperation.

This working alliance does not imply submission and compliance but rather cooperation in a relatively realistic and reasonable fashion: "Neither smugness, ritualism, timidity, authoritarianism, aloofness, nor indulgence have a place in the analytic situation." Thus the patient will be influenced not only by the content of our work but by how we work, the attitude, the manner, the mood, the atmosphere in which we work. Here the physicianly vocation has a crucial and central role in psychotherapy!

The metapsychological and technical details of the ego functions involved in the formation of a therapeutic or working alliance remain to be worked out by the experts in our field. The basic truth of this idea, however, has become indisputable. It is eloquently summarized by Greenson: "Essentially the humanness of the analyst is expressed in his compassion, his concern, and his therapeutic intent toward his patient. It matters to him how the patient fares, he is neither just an observer nor a research worker. He is a physician and a therapist, a treater of the sick and suffering, and his aim is to help the patient get well. However, the 'medicine' he prescribes is insight, carefully regulating the dosage, keeping his eye on the long-range goal, sacrificing temporary and quick results for later and lasting changes. The humanness is also expressed in the attitude that the patient has rights and is to be respected as an individual. He is to be treated with ordinary courtesy; rudeness has no place in psychoanalytic therapy. If we want the patient to work with us as a co-worker on the regressive material that he produces, we must take care that the mature aspects of the patient are consistently nurtured in the course of our analytic work" (1967, p. 213).

Part II
MODERN THOUGHT

Chapter 8

Metaphysics and Metapsychology

Accordingly, employing logical-philosophical, not psychological, terms, Kant became the first to recognize that our mentation is a synthesis between our autonomous psychological functioning and incoming stimuli. Thus the ancient problem of epistemology, or in other words, the problem of the nature of knowledge, or again in other words, the relation of the individual and his world, was formulated in logical-philosophical terms. Psychoanalysis taught another formulation of the same thing in terms of the psychology of instincts and wishes. One might say that psychoanalysis revealed the relativity of our view of the world in terms of the psychology of the id, while Kant revealed the same thing in terms of the psychology of thinking, that is, through a logical, philosophical analysis of thinking. Unhumble as it may seem, I would like to venture the suggestion that one of the royal roads toward a psychoanalytic psychology of thinking may lead through the discovery of the psychogenesis of the modes of apperception and the categories of pure reason which Kant postulated as the autonomous logical functions accounting for our view of the world.

David Rapaport, *The History of the Awakening of Insight*

KANT AS THE FOUNDER OF MODERN THOUGHT

It is now only a few years short of two centuries since Immanuel Kant announced a Copernican revolution in philosophy. His "critical philosophy," as he came to call his system, received its definitive statement in 1781 in the *Critique of Pure Reason* and in the series of works that he published during the next two decades. Virtually single handed, Kant destroyed the discipline of rational theology, to which the greatest philosophers of the preceedings 2,000 years had devoted their soberest attention. He transformed metaphysics, established epistemology on a firm theoretical foundation, discovered hitherto unrecognized problems in the philosophy of mathematics, and even gave moral philosophy a new direction. All philosophy before 1781 flows into Kant's great system, and it has been truly observed that in the modern world one can philosophize against Kant or with him, but never without him.

Kant's writing style is extremely obscure, and it is not recommended that the student first approach his work directly; rather he should study a number of commentaries and discussions first, such as those by Ewing, Weldon, Smith, and Paton, all listed in the bibliography. Kant undertook to make a new analysis of the nature of knowledge that would not only show its proper limitations, but that would also validate knowledge within its own proper field. The main reason for Kant's success in this study, as pointed out by W. T. Jones (1969) was his grasp of the role of experiment, his recognition that answers depend on the questions asked. The result of Kant's recognition of the mind's role as a "questioner" of nature was *a wholly new conception of the nature of the self and its object,* a conception that has important implications for almost every field of inquiry, from physics and psychology to ethics and art criticism.

In summary this original and revolutionary view demonstrates:

1. Self and not-self are *not* metaphysically distinct ultimates, but rather are constructs within the field of experience.

2. Experience is a spatiotemporal manifold in which distinctions are made, including the distinction between self and not-self.

3. The natural sciences are limited to describing and generalizing about this spatiotemporal manifold and the various constructs distinguished within it.

4. Experience, the spatiotemporal manifold, is dependent on transcendental conditions, i.e., conditions not in experience. Though these transcendental conditions are not in experience and hence cannot be objects of scientific cognition, we know that they exist, for they are *the necessary conditions* of experience.

5. These transcendental conditions validate the sciences in their own field, but at the same time limit them to this field.

6. Since our notions of God, freedom of will, and immortality fall *outside* this field, the sciences can say nothing one way or another about them, and it follows that God, freedom of will, and immortality are neither substantial nor causally efficacious, for substance and causality are concepts relevant only within the experiential field.

The net effect of all this philosophical work was to put a *sharp and unalterable barrier* between scientific thinking and scientific pursuit on the one hand and what Kant called "the dialectic of illusion" on the other.

Kant took as his starting point the skeptical philosophy of Hume, who Kant claimed "awoke me from my dogmatic slumber."Kant agreed with Hume that empirical knowledge involves connecting one part or element of experience with another; he agreed too that connection of this sort, "synthesis," proceeds on a principle that is neither analytically true nor empirically probable. But he refused to follow Hume in deriving the principles of connection or causality from "custom or habit," for the consequences of such a skeptical solution would be (a) that we should not only be deprived of any insight into the connection of things but also (b) that we should have no unitary consciousness of any sort.

The crux of his argument is that it is a necessary condition of having a unitary consciousness that we be able to relate to what is happening here and now to things that lie outside our immediate purview; "if the ability to relate is not a real possibility, than neither is unitary consciousness" (Walsh 1967). What Kant called "the thorough-going affinity of appearances," the fact that appearances are capable of being connected in a single experience, thus relates closely to the ability of the observer to recognize himself as a single person with diverse experiences. In fact the relation is one of mutual implication.

Of course the subject is even more complicated, and as Wolff points out, "Surprisingly, nowhere in the critical corpus do we find an extended, systematic discussion of the nature of the self, nor have modern students of Kant's philosophy concerned themselves especially with attempts to fill this gap by reconstructing a Kantian theory of the self. The reason for so striking a failure, I think it is fair to say, is the appalling difficulty of the task. Once we begin to itemize Kant's assertions about the self even within one work, such as the first

Critique, we discover that there are endless contradictions, complica-
tions, and unclarities" (1967). I hope the reader understands from even
this short discussion how extremely difficult it is to elucidate the
philosophy of Kant; in a sense the entire history of Western philosophy
from the time of Kant has been a series of attempts to clarify and
extend Kant's conceptions. Every scholar and reader of Kant,
including some very famous ones who should have known better,
approaches him as an individual and finds in him, to a certain extent,
what he is looking for. This is infinitely complicated by the fact that the
translation from German to English in the case of Kant's writings is
filled with pitfalls, and a certain philosophical position is already
implied in the way one translates Kant's work. It is, however, generally
agreed that the Norman Kemp Smith translation of the *Critique of
Pure Reason* (1965) is the best, and the reader must be *very* careful not
to attempt reading Kant in inferior translations or abridgements.

LIFE AND WORK OF KANT—AN OVERVIEW

Immanuel Kant (1724-1804) was born at Königsberg in East
Prussia, the son of a saddler and the grandson of an immigrant from
Scotland. He was educated locally and then at the University of
Königsberg, where he had the good fortune to encounter a first class
teacher in the philosopher Knutzen. After leaving the university
around 1746 he worked as a private tutor in Prussia and then began
lecturing in the university on a wide variety of subjects. His published
work is usually divided into the "precritical" writings before 1770, and
the "critical" writings, published after that time, but this doesn't give a
true picture.

The precritical writings are primarily contributions to natural
science or natural philosophy, the most famous being his *General
History of Nature and Theory of the Heavens* published in 1755; it was
not until 1760, that philosophical interests became dominant in his
mind. The publication of the physical and cosmological writings
earned for Kant an important reputation in Germany, and he was
repeatedly offered university positions. He wished, however, to remain
in Königsberg and, in order to do so, had to continue in the laborious
role of tutor until he was appointed to the chair of Logic and
Metaphysics in 1770. At his installation in this chair, he delivered the

customary inaugural dissertation, which contained the first announcement of revolutionary doctrines. Immediately afterwards, at the age of forty-six, he entered upon a ten year period of the most profound philosophical thinking, during which he published nothing. The critical writings represent the hastily written fruit of this period, and the publications followed one after the other in rapid succession.

He never married and lived a very regimented bachelor existence in which he carefully conserved his health until senility set in a few years before his death at eighty. His habits were so regular that the citizens of Königsberg set their clocks by him, and although he was extremely interested in all aspects of the world, he never left his native area.

Only this kind of a determined individual could maintain, during the ten years following his appointment, a period of literary silence while engaged in thinking about the issues first unfolded at length in the *Critique of Pure Reason*. This great work was eagerly awaited by Kant's friends and philosophical colleagues, but when it finally appeared in 1781 the general reaction was bewilderment rather than admiration. Kant tried to remove misunderstandings by restating the main argument in *Prolegomena to Any Future Metaphysics* in 1783 and by rewriting some of the central section of the *Critique of Pure Reason* for a second edition in 1787. On the whole this merely compounded the confusion and misinterpretation, for now there were three obscure texts for commentators to disagree about.

At the same time he continued to elaborate the rest of his system. By 1790, the *Critique of Practical Reason* and the *Critique of Judgment* were in print; shorter major treatises, *On Religion Within the Bounds of Mere Reason* in 1793 and *Metaphysic of Morals* in 1797, completed his major publications. In his declining years, he saw able young philosophers in his own country such as Fichte, Schelling, and Beck claim that he had not really understood his own philosophy and propose to remedy his deficiencies by transcendental systems of their own. The work of the last years of his life was probably intended as a counterblast to such critics, but it was never finished and was published finally in fragments under the title of *Opus Posthumum*.

Attention of philosophers has been focused on the later critical writings beginning with the *Critique of Pure Reason*. It is important to understand the three *Critiques* as constituting a vast and impressive philosophical system which responds to the challenge contained in the philosophy of Hume. Hume argues that there is nothing else but our sensory impressions and ideas. If we ever wonder about certain philosophical or scientific concepts, according to Hume, we only need to ask ourselves, "From what experience were these ideas derived?" If they do not go back to definite sense-impressions, then the ideas are meaningless.

Hume explains that the kind of reliability we can achieve depends on the kind of inquiry we are engaged in. Mathematical inquiry involves only the relation of ideas. These say nothing about the actual world and can neither be derived from or refuted by experience, for their truth is formal and systematic. Here we have absolute certainty but it is a sterile certainty, since it makes no reference to any situation in the factual world. Matters of fact are meaningful but always uncertain. Thus our sciences are doomed either to be true by empty or else to be meaningful but unsure. Hume in this way undermines our ideas of space, time, substance, causation, necessity, certainty, belief, prediction, science, mind, personal identity, and God. We are left with a complete skepticism, the antidote for which, according to Hume is living a pleasant, common life.

KANT'S ANALYSIS OF HUMAN MENTAL FUNCTIONING

As Kant points out in the Preface, the *Critique of Pure Reason* attempts a "Copernician revolution" in philosophy by asserting that things to be known must conform in advance with the mind. Space and time are like spectacles, with the aid of which the mind accomplishes its primary function, the organization of the world. In this case however, the mind is its own spectacle-maker. Notions of space or time represent a predicate, a visualization, an idea having all the earmarks of origin in the mind. In fact when "material things" are first perceived, they have already succumbed to the mind's arrangement for them, and all this is accomplished in advance.

Kant separates out the sensory manifold or field of sensory impressions as representing the impact on a person of the world as it appears before the mind takes charge. Thinking is what the mind does, and thinking is organization—the process of connecting disjoined impressions, perceptions, memories, and imagined data. Kant argues that the mind proceeds through understanding and imagination to organize this raw material under principles of general, abstract, and prior ideas, so that the mind's contribution is "organized unity." When the mind is finished with it, the raw material of the sensory manifold has acquired meaning, and refers to some identifiable "object." It is then knowledge, expressed in the form of judgments (Kant's term for what today we would call propositions).

How does anything ever come to be known? More accurately we can say that Kant sets out to determine what reason alone can achieve in the way of knowledge. He asks, "Can reason alone apart from experience give any knowledge?" In his Introduction to the *Critique of Pure Reason,* Kant explains that the most obvious kind of evidence on which we base our judgments (propositions) is experience; judgments based on experience are called by Kant empirical or *a posteriori* judgments. On the other hand, there is a kind of judgment that is independent of all experience, for instance, mathematical proofs. These kinds of judgments are known as *a priori* judgments. The two strict characteristics of *a priori* judgments that enable us to distinguish them with certainty from *a posteriori* judgments are that they are absolutely necessary and strictly universal: "If then a judgment is thought. . . . in such manner that no exception is allowed as possible, it is not derived from experience, but is valid absolutely *a priori.*"

Kant also distinguishes between analytic and synthetic judgments. In an analytic judgment the predicate is covertly contained in the subject and may be obtained by analysis of it, for example "Roses are flowers." The predicate follows from the definition and is part of the subject. In synthetic judgments the predicate is not contained in the subject, for example, "Some roses are red." Red is not a part of the definition of rose. The following table shows the two pairs of judgments, *a priori/a posteriori* and analytic/synthetic, yielding four logically possible classes of judgments:

	a posteriori	*a priori*
analytic	analytic *a posteriori*	analytic *a priori*
synthetic	synthetic *a posteriori*	synthetic *a priori*

An analytic *a posteriori* type of judgment is obviously impossible. There can be no analytic *a posteriori* judgments since all analytic judgments are universal and necessary and no judgments based on experience can be so. Thus there are only three kinds of judgments to examine. Analytic *a priori* judgments are all warranted by the law of contradiction, and indeed this class can be thought of as containing the basic rules of logic, universal and necessary. Synthetic *a posteriori* judgments are the usual ones from experience, what Hume calls "matters of fact."

The basic philosophical question is whether synthetic *a priori* judgments are possible. The basis of this type of judgment cannot be the law of contradiction because synthetic *a priori* judgments are not contained covertly in their subject. Nor can the basis be experience for "experience teaches us only that a thing is so and so," whereas *a priori* judgments assert a universal and necessary connection. Hume argues that there is *no* third type of basis other than experience or the law of contradiction that can establish judgments; he claimed that all judgments are either synthetic *a posteriori*, judgments about matters of fact, or analytic *a priori*, judgments about relations of ideas. This was the basis of Hume's skepticism regarding notions such as causality and inductive generalizations. He believed that there is no basis and could be no basis for such concepts, except habit or custom in everyday affairs.

Kant wanted to show that synthetic *a priori* judgments are possible in some areas but not in others, and this is the basic issue of the *Critique of Pure Reason*. His answer briefly is that synthetic *a priori* judgments are possible in mathematics and natural science but are not possible in metaphysics. In fact, he never even asked *whether* such judgments are possible in mathematics and natural sciences; he took this as self evident and merely asked *how* they are possible. He answered that these judgments represent, in mathematics and natural sciences, the organizing principles of the mind.

"THE TRANSCENDENTAL AESTHETIC"

Thus the first section of the *Critique of Pure Reason*, "The Transcendental Aesthetic," deals with "How are synthetic *a priori* judgments possible in mathematics?" Jones explains the term, "He called it 'aesthetic' because he believed the basis for this kind of knowledge to be immediate, nondiscursive, and sensuous; he called it 'transcendental' because he believed that such knowledge is not *in* experience but a necessary condition *for* experience" (1969). For Kant "immediate and sensuous" meant intuitive, as opposed to reasoned.

All mathematical judgments are synthetic, claims Kant, and contain the synthetic *a priori* notions of space and time—the two media in which experience appears. He calls space and time the forms of the outer and inner sense, respectively. This concept of space remains highly debatable in our day of relativity physics based on the employment of non-Euclidean geometry. Furthermore, for those who insist that all mathematical judgments are analytic or merely consequences of the laws of logic, this entire discussion of space is nonsense. For our purpose the important aspect of Kant's philosophy is his treatment of time, the order of our "inner sense" or form of our "awareness of ourselves and our inner states." This leads to a discussion of the nature of this inner sense and how one is "inwardly aware" of one's self. Heidegger (1962) has used this awareness as a starting point for his existential philosophy: "Time leads to self." I will return to this in detail later in chapter 20.

THE TRANSCENDENTAL LOGIC

In the second part of the first section of the *Critique of Pure Reason,* "The Transcendental Logic," Kant deals with "How are synthetic *a priori* judgments possible in physics?" Kant called it "logic" because it deals with the order in judgments discursive and reasoned rather than intuitive. He called it "transcendental" because he was concerned not with the content of experience but with the conditions that make an experience of objects possible.

"The Transcendental Logic" is in turn divided into two parts, "The Transcendental Analytic" and "The Transcendental Dialectic." "The Transcendental Analytic" is a study of the pure concepts of the understanding or the "categories" which deals with such synthetic *a priori* judgments in physics as quantity, quality, relation, and modality. It is subdivided into a "transcendental" deduction that is a general proof of the necessity of "categories" or pure concepts of the understanding, and then a deduction of the specific individual categories and a demonstration of the synthetic *a priori* principles that rest on the individual categories. "The Transcendental Analytic" is the most important part of the *Critique of Pure Reason* for our purposes here in this chapter.

"The Transcendental Dialectic" (the second part of "The Transcendental Logic") exposes the "dialectic of illusion" by showing that no synthetic *a priori* judgments are possible in metaphysics.

I shall discuss first the transcendental deduction of the categories, and second, the deduction of the specific individual categories and the establishment of the synthetic *a priori* principles of the understanding; together these constitute The Transcendental Analytic. Then I will discuss The Transcendental Dialectic.

THE TRANSCENDENTAL DEDUCTION OF THE CATEGORIES

The transcendental deductions or proofs represent Kant's methodology. They generally proceed by showing that if the principle he proves were not true of an object we could not "experience" that object. The transcendental deduction of the categories is the heart of the *Critique of Pure Reason,* which in turn is the cornerstone of Kant's philosophy and it is very difficult indeed.

Ewing (1967) points out that the basic premise of the transcendental deduction of the categories is that "there occurs awareness of a manifold in time." Kant asserts that unless the existence of a system of necessarily connected objects to which our thoughts refer is conceded, we are utterly unable to explain the existence of any coherent or unitary self at all. In the absence of such a system, we would have no experience, but only a "mere play of representations, less even than a dream."

Kant goes on to argue that among the conditions of human knowledge are included not only *a priori* intuitions of space and time but *a priori* concepts, for to know anything we require the concept of an object, and this cannot be formed without the use of the categories. *A priori* concepts are consequently necessary because they are conditions of experience.

Space and time are a form of our perception of outer objects and the flow of our consciousness, respectively. Both are a function of our mind. Thus the synthetic *a priori* truths of mathematics state conditions necessary for the occurrence of perception, according to Kant. The synthetic *a priori* truths of natural science similarly state the conditions necessary for the occurrence of discursive thought. On the other hand, the propositions of metaphysics such as God, free will, and immortality, express beliefs which have a *regulatory* function according to Kant, but do not represent synthetic *a priori* truth.

THE INDIVIDUAL CATEGORIES

In "The Transcendental Analytic," Kant argues that for our knowledge of the world about us, our mind provides twelve pure concepts of the understanding that organize human thought—the *categories.* These are abstract and prior and valid for the world of nature because the laws of the mind are also the laws of nature. Mind comes first and provides the means of assimilating the world to its own uses.

At this point Kant introduces his doctrine of the *schemata.* Mind and the sensory manifold as they are dissected out appear to be discreet. How then can the categories be applied to sense data? Kant's answer is, by means of a *third* entity in which both mind and the sensory manifold share. Sense data are fitted to space and time, which are universal requirements of the mind. The categories are also, by definition, universal concepts of the mind, but are restricted in application to possible objects of experience. At this point "reproductive imagination" plays a crucial role. The common properties shared by categories and sense data are discovered, and the former are applied through the work of the imagination to the latter. In specific cases of sense data to be organized, the reproductive imagination produces appropriate schematization of the categories.

THE KNOWING PROCESS

The knowing process, which is approximately instantaneous, can then be thought of as reassembled in a series of events. The first awareness of an object comes as a field of crude sense data to which mind applies the forms of space and time. Mind then organizes the field by means of its own pure concepts, the categories. This application of the categories to sense data is made possible by the participation of both categories and sense data in the work of the imagination, resulting in the schematization of the categories. "The schemata . . . are necessary to an intelligible account of the knowing process" (1960).

The notion of schemata, or schematized categories, and their relation to categories and sense data is simply not clear in Kant. Wolff (1969) describes Kant's explanation as "hopelessly murky" and suggest that Kant could have simplified the matter considerably by identifying the categories with their schemata, instead of maintaining the distinction between them, but he agrees that there are "powerful considerations" against it. I suggest the reader relegate this question to the realm of technical philosophy, and for the time being let us follow Kant's distinctions the best we can.

Synthetic *a priori* ('pure') principles of the understanding connect schemata to sense impressions. Schemata enable us to apply categories (pure concepts of the understanding), through the use of pure principles, to sense-impressions, especially by introducing the time element. Thus some authors write of "schematization" of the categories (Ewing 1967) when the time element is added.

Kant in his search for synthetic *a priori* knowledge progresses from "judgments" (scientific propositions) to categories, to schemata, to synthetic *a priori* principles of the understanding. This presents us with a structure in which each level connects the levels at either side. This is summarized in the following table (from Rauch 1965):

	Categories	Schemata	Principles
QUANTITY:	Unity		*Axioms of Sense-intuition: extensive magnitudes*
	Plurality	Number	
	Totality		
QUALITY:	Reality		*Anticipations of perception: intensive magnitudes*
	Negation	Intensity	
	Limitation		
RELATION:	Inherence	Permanence	*Analogies of experience: permanence, etc. in all changes*
	Causality	Succession	
	Community	Coexistence	
MODALITY:	Possibility	In time	*Postulates of empirical thought in general*
	Existence	Certain time	
	Necessity	All time	

The mind thus has certain principles or rules which describe its own character and delimit and predict the possibilities of knowledge. These rules or synthetic *a priori* principles of the understanding can be deduced from the way the mind presides over sense data by means of the schemata. Kant proceeds to what he calls "The systematic presentation of the organizing principles of the mind." Corresponding to the four major classes of categories (quantity, quality, relation, and modality) Kant lays out four sets of principles by which mind operates its categories. These principles of possible experience are the universal laws of nature, known *a priori* in this manner and imposed by the mind on the sensory manifold as a necessary condition for knowing.

The synthetic *a priori* principles of the understanding provide rules for the application of the categories to the sensory manifold, whereas the schemata merely give us images by which to apply these principles. Thus our experience as we experience it is actually structured in accordance with the categories. The answer to the question How is pure natural science possible? is thus provided in "The Transcendental Analytic." It is possible only because the phenomenal world conforms to certain *a priori* principles of our understanding, by which our objective experience is structured.

Kant's Copernican revolution consists of showing that the world must conform to our minds, rather than vice-versa, since otherwise it could not be experienced at all. *Thus once we know the formal patterns of our thinking we know to what forms the world must conform in order to be known by us.* This constitutes synthetic *a priori* knowledge and answers Hume's skepticism about the "universal" laws of nature.

NOUMENA

Does the world contain in addition real objects which are *not* possible items of experience, entities which may not be the phenomena of our sensory manifold? Kant asserts that it does, although he cannot tell positively what they are. He calls each of these objects the "thing-in-itself," or *noumenon,* in contrast to a phenomenon, which is in our experience and subject to the rules described above. This distinction marks the boundary beyond which mind cannot go because experience cannot follow. The logical development of Kant's thought has been criticized at this point, because logically one can assert nothing about a noumenon if one agrees with the Kantian system so far. At any rate it is a useful concept in "The Transcendental Dialectic" because Kant shows that the basic mistake of metaphysics and rational theology has been to attempt to develop a science of noumena, which is manifestly impossible.

There is penetrating insight in the *Critique of Pure Reason* that only a certain kind of world—one that produces phenomena suitable to our mind—could be for us an object of discourse and experience. Although we may feel that Kant's detailed tables of categories and schemata are artificial and contrived, nevertheless the general deduction that there are categories and the like represents an important advance over Humean skepticism and the tradition of naive empiricism.

THE PRE-SUPPOSITIONS OF ALL SCIENCE

Warnock points out: "Very much as the scientist approaches observational data with certain theoretical concepts and principles already in mind, so human beings bring to the diverse successive items of their experiences a predisposition to construe them in particular ways—as being, in fact, experiences *of* material things and objective happenings, describable in principle by everyone in a common vocabulary and locatable in one common space and time. If so, then there will indeed be fundamental concepts which would be better regarded as imposed upon, than as abstracted from our experience; and there will be certain very general propositions about our experience, which would be better regarded as defining its essential character than as merely recording the actual details of its course. Kant's perception of this was both profound and truly original" (1964). Kant showed that the presuppositions of physics have objective reference and why they have objective reference and yield knowledge, while at the same time, all can agree that pure empiricism is inadequate as a theory of knowledge.

One of the basic ideas that Kant has to offer us is that no "pure empirical" theory of human mental functioning is sufficient. His work offers a profound refutation of any purely behavioristic or stimulus-response human psychology, as well as of any attempt to build up the sum total of our knowledge and our personalities from the accretion of external sense impressions. It is impossible to maintain the old positivist argument that there cannot be such a thing as synthetic *a priori* judgments and that all synthetic *a priori* propositions turn out in the end to be either tautologies (open or concealed), or empirical generalizations, which may enjoy a very high degree of probability, but the truth of which cannot be known.

It should be clear that an analogous argument can be made against any effort to explain personality as strictly the result of experiences impinging upon Locke's *tabula rasa* of the mind and that all such theories are philosophically naive. In a previous book (1974g), I have devoted the final chapter to a detailed discussion of the naïvité behind a purely empirical psychology and attempted to present data from a variety of disciplines to demonstrate that there must be certain organizing principles of human mental functioning that are necessarily brought to the sensory manifold as a precondition for knowledge (see also Popper 1972).

THE TRANSCENDENTAL DIALECTIC

There is far more in Kant, the extraordinary man and prolific thinker, that must attract the attention of the psychotherapist willing to work his way through such difficult material. Midway in his section on "The Transcendental Dialectic," Kant inaugurates a confusing change of meaning: pure reason and mind are no longer equated with each other as they were in the first part of his *Critique of Pure Reason,* but reason now becomes one among other functions of mind. Reason now is the high court of mind and issues all inclusive organizing and unifying ideas which *do* transgress the rules of knowledge. Kant names three of these: God, soul, and universe. If a man looks up and off and out beyond, and is not content within the limits of experience, and then lets his reason freely operate, these three unifying ideas are the almost inevitable result, according to Kant. They are the result of the human mind not staying within the bounds of experience, but claiming autonomy whenever it is occupied with reasoning.

It is the nature of man's mind, that it will not stay within any formal bounds as long as knowledge is conditional, partial, or relational. Man cannot be satisfied short of reaching the top of the highest peak, where reality is met as unconditioned, whole, and unrelated. This belief is the main spring of German philosophy, and we will see it surface again in the philosophy of Jaspers (chapter 18).

Kant argues that these three ideas of pure reason are regulative: they are boundary markers, indicating the limits of human knowledge. They are illegitimate, however, when represented as being items of knowledge supported by experience. The "logic of illusion" represents the critical evaluation of the mind's operation in nonphysical matters, matters in which reason has transgressed beyond the limits of human knowledge. Kant demonstrates that reason alone cannot prove anything about these concepts because whatever can be proved about the world as a whole by unaided reasoning—the opposite can be proved just as well. Such opposites are called *antimonies* by Kant; a pair of apparently contradictory propositions based on the same assumptions.

The basic purpose of the entire *Critique of Pure Reason* now begins to emerge, and it is, according to Kant, to make room for faith. We begin to see that the project has been fundamentally aimed at reestablishing Kant's faith in essential human goodness and his hope that man exists as an end and must be never treated as a means alone. It is based on the doctrine of Rousseau, who argues that the intrinsic worth of a human being *qua* human being, the dignity of man, is part of man's innate nature. Furthermore, man's innate capacity for virtue is the reason for that worth and dignity. It is recognized by a corresponding sentiment, itself innate in human nature—the natural love of man for humanity. Kant's genius represents the high point of the age of enlightenment. The belief or faith Kant proposes as a replacement for discredited metaphysical knowledge can be neither strictly communicated nor learned from another person. It is something that has to be achieved by every man for himself.

Kant's basic humanism is obvious, and it is interesting to note that the key to his ideas are in his basic faith rather than justified by his philosophy itself. Kant's humanism is very important, especially his belief in the dignity of each man. He sees metaphysics as a natural disposition rather than a science and believes that human reason is naturally impelled to these problems which cannot be answered empirically. At the same time he argues that metaphysics cannot constitute a science capable of answering its own problems. One of the philosopher's main tasks is to expose the hollowness of every such claim. At the same time the human mind has a natural tendency to seek unconditioned principles of unity. These ideas, however, can possess only a regulative function and cannot be the source of any theoretical knowledge of corresponding realities. According to Kant, this opens the way for practical or moral faith. He has done away with scientific knowledge to make room for faith as he understands it.

Copleston says, "It is a great mistake to look on this theory as a mere sop to the orthodox and the devout or as a mere act of prudence on Kant's part. For it is part of his solution to the great problem of reconciling the world of science on the one hand with, on the other, the world of moral and religious consciousness. Science (that is, classical physics) involves a conception of causal laws which do not admit of freedom. And man, considered as a member of the cosmic system studied by the scientist, is no exception. But scientific knowledge has its limits, and its limits are determined by the *a priori* forms of human sensibility and understanding. There is thus no valid reason whatsoever for saying that the limits of our scientific or theoretical knowledge are identical with the limits of reality" (1964).

To say the least, Kant's point of view is certainly beset with difficulties. Not only do we have the division between sensible, phenomenal reality, and noumenal, purely intelligible reality, but we are also faced in particular with the difficult conception of man as phenomenally determined, but noumenally free, as determined and free at the same time, though under different aspects. At any rate it must be emphasized that this natural tendency or innate disposition of the human mind to reach unifying principles is an important aspect of human mental functioning—Jaspers has described this as the search for transcendence, and I have discussed it in detail elsewhere (1974g).

CRUCIAL IMPORTANCE OF
THE IMAGINATION IN PSYCHOTHERAPY

Kant's concept of the reproductive imagination is extremely important to psychotherapists. He changes his concept of the role of imagination when he moves from the *Critique of Pure Reason* to the *Critique of Judgment*. The latter *Critique* attempts to evaluate what Kant calls the faculties of judgment or what he now calls "reflective judgment." He felt he had proved in the first *Critique* that neither God nor beauty are established by pure reason alone; neither are they there solely because of man's desire or feeling. They appear from significant observations of the purposiveness or appropriateness in nature's parts, which are then judged to be either beautiful, good, or the work of God. Kant calls this "reflective judgment." It is just a way of thinking that is helpful and useful as long as the thought is not mistaken for fact.

Thus, writes Blakney, "Mechanism and teleology are not mutually any more inimical than arithmetic and algebra. For some scientific purposes, mechanistic explanations are not only adequate; they are simpler. Falsehood appears in mechanistic theories when their limited applicability, which in practice is quite abstract, is arbitrarily extended to brush aside as fakes such human qualities as freedom, morality, and spirit; where these factors are not considered fakes, a more capacious theory is required" (Kant 1960). Teleology is such a theory. It includes purposiveness or appropriateness where mechanism applies—a study of purpose not in the primitive sense in which individual human purposes are read into nature, but in the sense of the purposiveness or appropriateness that may be observed in nature's parts. No part in nature has a purpose of its own, but each part seems designed to fit into the total organic scheme or design of a final purpose.

In the last chapter of *Why Psychotherapists Fail* (1971c), I have taken up the suggestion, to my knowledge first advanced by Levi (1969), of basing our maps of reality on two different faculties of the mind, the understanding faculty and the imaginative faculty. As Levi sees it, extrapolating from the *Critique of Judgment,* the imagination is that faculty from whose active functioning the humanities stem. It must of course be made clear that no argument is involved here for the old fashioned faculty psychology—these "faculties" are abstractions made for the purpose of exegesis. In fact Levi claims that Kant's "faculty of judgment" does not make logical judgments at all, but is what Bergson and Cassirer have called the myth-making faculty.

The main point is that the differences between the sciences and the humanities are deeply grounded and motivated not merely in accidents of temperament but grounded and motivated in a basic commitment founded upon the structure of the human mind. The purposes of the two enterprises are different and they are grounded respectively in the nuclear operations of the understanding and the imagination. The language of the understanding and the language of the imagination represent different ways of looking at the same sensory manifold.

As Kant points out, our minds have an inborn propensity toward teleological interpretation. Levi argues that this propensity "coexists with equal dignity with the scientific understanding, although engaged in constant warfare with its conclusions. The real explanation for 'the antimonies of pure reason' is, then, not that they show a moral employment of pure reason in opposition to scientific, but rather that they insert the urgencies of teleological explanation into a domain preempted by the requirements of a mechanistic science" (1969).

This is a concept of considerable importance to psychotherapists and I have tried to show that much of the quarrel between the so-called opposing schools of psychotherapy really lies in the contrast between the method of science and the method of the literary arts, or the "faculties" of cognitive understanding and creative imagination. The two maps of reality and descriptions of what is going on are not fundamentally opposed and may be successfully blended with each other, provided the therapist is carefully aware of when and why he is using each competing map. If this is possible, then a greater understanding of patient material and patient problems can be achieved and a more effective psychic field can be presented to the patient.

THE SPECIAL THEORY OF PSYCHOTHERAPEUTIC INTERACTION

Some reviewers of *Why Psychotherapists Fail* (1971c) miss this main point that a humanistic education for the psychotherapist is not a luxury but a logical extension of the fundamental philosophical notions just described. A complete understanding of the patient *cannot* be achieved by a purely technical scientific education in dynamic psychiatry, no matter how thorough. If this basic theoretical philosophical orientation is correct, a corresponding education in the language of the humanistic imagination will have to be provided for the psychotherapist, so that he may move comfortably from one map of the sensory manifold to the other—from the language of science to the language of the creative imagination. After all, the genius of Freud was fundamentally grounded in his remarkable capacity to move back and forth from the faculty of scientific investigation to the faculty of the creative and humanistic imagination.

There will always be two fundamentally different and competing ways of describing the interaction between the psychic field of the therapist and the patient in the process of psychotherapy, based on the two fundamentally different and competing ways of describing the sensory manifold: the language of scientific investigation and the language of the creative imagination. These languages do not conflict with respect to truth or falsehood but merely illustrate the basic human need or innate disposition to describe reality in two radically different ways. Freud, because of his unusually wide erudition, had a tendency to switch back and forth between these languages in order to present as immediate and complete a description of the clinical phenomena as he possibly could. What happened is that the two languages became confused in the minds of his less erudite followers so that a number of problems or pseudoproblems (Chessick 1961) and animosities arose.

It is clear that for maximum effectiveness the therapist must be able to move back and forth comfortably in both languages, and his education must enable him to do so. An education which is exclusive in either area will leave a glaring deficiency in the therapist's capacity to interact with the patient. An education strictly confined to the technique and practice of scientific psychotherapy tends toward sterility and withdrawal from the encounter and from participation with the patient at a gut level. An education too heavily weighted in the humanities causes a loss of the scientific grounding and observation aspects of the psychotherapy, with a consequent tendency to go off the deep end by using bizarre and unjustifiable procedures with patients. Neither of these extremes is fair to the patient, and both of them represent a serious defect in the psychic field of the therapist.

In our discussion of the imagination we have now come a long way from Kant. Let us review his concept of the imagination as it appears in the *Critique of Pure Reason* and the *Critique of Judgment*. In the former, the imagination *(Einbildungskraft)* has a relatively non-creative function. It is introduced primarily as a mediating power or faculty between categories (pure concepts of the understanding) and the sensory manifold. The imagination is said to reproduce and bear the schemata: "This representation of a general procedure of the imagination for providing a concept with its image I call the schema for this concept." In other words, a schema is a procedure of the imagination for finding an image that will make a pure concept meaningful and connect it with our sense of reality, space, and time. In the *Critique of Judgment,* imagination is permitted to work *without* categories of the understanding. Here it is "creative" rather than "reproductive." It has its own playful imperatives, originating ideas "beyond the facts" and organizing experience into poetic "wholes." Kantian scholars have not been able to reconcile the two views of the imagination in the two *Critiques*.

In general, it is not so much the details of Kant's cumbersome description of mental functioning that concern us as psychotherapists but rather his basic focus and insistence on careful study of human mental functioning. These provide considerable stimulation to further exploration of the subject. Those who still wish to make an especially detailed study are referred to *Kant's Theory of Mental Activity* by Wolff and to an excellent brief review of the difficulties in Kant's psychological theories and general method of exposition presented in Wolff's introduction to *The Autonomy of Reason*. As Wolff explains, "When the confusions have been sorted out, and we have, in W. S. Gilbert's words, 'got up all the germs of the transcendental terms,' we are still left with the root difficulty of the work: Kant's own unclarity, and inconsistency about the doctrines he wishes to expound" (1973).

By far the greatest master of psychoanalytic theory who followed specifically in the Kantian tradition of investigating epistemology through a focus on our thought processes themselves was Rapaport (Gedo 1973). His four major books (1951, 1960, 1961, 1967) are very difficult but represent an important, though unfortunately unfinished, attempt to integrate psychoanalytic metapsychology with Kantian epistemology as well as with other psychological theories of learning, motivation, and development. This remains a vital task for the future. A really profound psychoanalytic metapsychology *must* be integrated with the best advanced approaches to epistemology and general mental functioning.

The inter-relationships between all these disciplines is illustrated and summarized in the following diagram, which is offered here to orient the reader. Detailed discussion of the inter-relationships will be found in chapter 16.

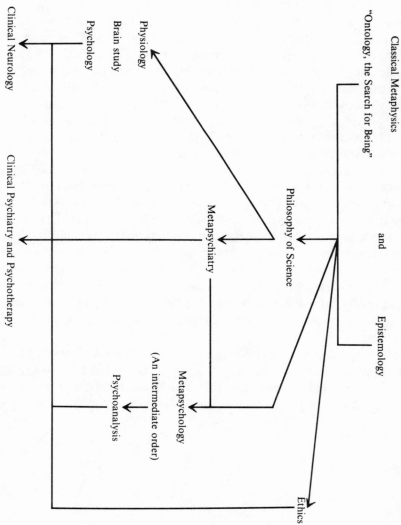

PHILOSOPHICAL FOUNDATIONS OF PSYCHOTHERAPY

Highest order	
First Principles	Classical Metaphysics
Epistémē	"Ontology, the Search for Being" and Epistemology
Second Order of Principles	Philosophy of Science
Third Order of Principles	Metapsychiatry
Science Research *Doxa*	Physiology Brain study Psychology
	Metapsychology (An intermediate order)
	Psychoanalysis
Clinical Application *Technè*	Clinical Neurology Clinical Psychiatry and Psychotherapy
	Ethics

Chapter 9

The Blind Force of Will

The Great War differed from all ancient wars in the immense power of the combatants and their fearful agencies of destruction, and from all modern wars in the utter ruthlessness with which it was fought. All the horrors of all the ages were brought together, and not only armies but whole populations were thrust into the midst of them. The mighty educated States involved conceived with reason that their very existence was at stake. Germany having let Hell loose kept well in the van of terror; but she was followed step by step by the desperate and ultimately avenging nations she had assailed. Every outrage against humanity or international law was repaid by reprisals often on a greater scale and of longer duration. No truce or parley mitigated the strife of the armies. The wounded died between the lines: the dead mouldered into the soil. Merchant ships and neutral ships and hospital ships were sunk on the seas and all on board left to their fate, or killed as they swam. Every effort was made to starve whole nations into submission without regard to age or sex. Cities and monuments were smashed by artillery. Bombs from the air were cast down indiscriminately. Poison gas in many forms stifled or seared the soldiers. Liquid fire was projected upon their bodies. Men fell from the air in flames, or were smothered, often slowly, in the dark recesses of the sea. The fighting strength of armies was limited only by the manhood of their countries. . . .

*Europe and large parts of Asia and Africa became one vast
battlefield on which after years of struggle not armies but nations
broke and ran. When all was over, Torture and Cannibalism were
the only two expedients that the civilized, scientific, Christian
States had been able to deny themselves: and these were of
doubtful utility.*

Winston Churchill, *The World Crisis 1911-1918*

BEGINNING OF TWENTIETH CENTURY THOUGHT

Lichtheim (1972) suggests that the 1914-1918 War left a deeper mark
on the consciousness of the belligerents than the far more destructive
second World War. Of the first World War, he writes, "In retrospect it
appears as the true dividing line between the nineteenth century and
the twentieth" (1972). The prophet of this true dividing line was the
dedicated philosopher Arthur Schopenhauer (1788-1860), whose work
has been rather underrated. It was not Freud but Schopenhauer who
broke decisively with the enlightenment tradition of optimism. His
work is essentially a pre-Bergsonian poetic vision, written in a
fascinating and clear prose style in dramatic contrast to that of his
murky contemporaries, the German academics such as Hegel and
Fichte.

Schopenhauer felt that a man's actions are *not* subject to the
direction of a free, controlling intellect capable of moulding character
and guiding behavior according to objective reason. He scornfully
rejected this entire optimistic picture of human nature, central to the
age of Enlightenment.

He bluntly accused his contemporaries of being dishonest and
mystifying readers with unintelligible language that left to them the
task of finding the meaning. He prided himself (as did Freud) on two
accomplishments: First, "he had not, in his thinking, set out with
certain fixed dogmas or preconceived ideas in mind, believing that
these must, by whatever means, be shown to be true; and secondly, he
had tried to express himself clearly and to eschew the cloudy
terminology behind which theorists too often seek to hide the errors
and illogicalities in their thinking, so that what he wrote could be put to
the test of serious criticism and discussion" (Gardiner 1971).

Perhaps in addition to his repulsive personality, the main reason for

Schopenhauer's neglect is his famous pessimism. Though this pessimism, of course, reflects his personality, it also follows intellectually from his doctrine. As a matter of fact the major technical error Schopenhauer made was not to see fully the pessimistic and hopeless consequences of his philosophy. Primarily, as we shall see, the Will, doomed to privation, is constantly striving and never satisfied. When it does find fulfillment, that fulfillment turns out to be illusion. Edman explains, "Schopenhauer sings a long dirge of sadness, a long lugubrious description of the way in which the human will oscillates between suffering and boredom. Half of life is the stinging pain of frustration, the other half the dull pain of boredom. Schopenhauer is the apotheosis of romantic irony expressing a romantic disgust over a world that does not meet the needs of the assertive will, and the irony of that will which finds the emptiness of what it thought it needed" (Schopenhauer 1928). Schopenhauer's descriptions of human life, as for example, presented in his essays "On the Vanity and Suffering of Life," "On the Suffering of the World," and "On the Vanity of Existence," are of course world-famous literary masterpieces.

SCHOPENHAUER

Schopenhauer's life has been described in great detail (for example Wallace 1890) but no one has attempted a really modern understanding of the psychological and philosophical roots of his pessimistic philosophy except for nonpsychiatrists such as Copleston (1946) and Gardiner (1971). He was born in Danzig in 1788 to a father who was a successful merchant with wide cultural interests and enlightened views. The father had a passionate temperament and increasing deafness made him more difficult as he grew older. His mother seems to have been marked by a certain hardness and inward complacency which later led a member of her circle to describe her as being without heart or soul. The marriage was not very successful.

Schopenhauer spent the first five years of his life in Danzig. In 1793 with the second partition of Poland and the Prussian annexation of Danzig, his father decided to move to Hamburg where he carried on his business for the next twelve years. During this time, Schopenhauer received an unconventional education in that his father was determined to train him for commerce, so that at the age of nine, a year after the birth of his only sister, he was put in care of a business friend in

France where he spent two years and acquired a thorough knowledge of the language. In 1803, he was taken by his parents on a protracted tour abroad during which time he spent three months at a very strict school in Wimbledon, England, run by narrow and unimaginative clergy. This left a disagreeable and lasting mark on the boy's mind.

His mother reported that by the age of sixteen Schopenhauer already showed signs of "a morbid tendency to brood over the misery of things." This strain of depression in his nature was strengthened by the sudden death in 1805 of his father, probably by a suicide, coming in the midst of an obviously already disturbed adolescence. Out of loyalty to a promise given his father, he worked two more years in the business in Hamburg, but in 1807, at the age of nineteen, he left to apply himself to the study of Greek and Latin.

After some moving about and some serious quarrels between himself and his mother, he received at twenty-one his share of his father's inheritance enabling him to become independent. He enrolled as a medical student but soon turned primarily to philosophy. His doctoral thesis "On the Fourfold Root of the Principle of Sufficient Reason" was finished in 1813 and published at his expense (Schopenhauer 1974). It attracted no attention, with the exception of some praise by Goethe. The satisfaction of being complimented by Goethe on what he had written probably led to his manuscript "On Vision and Colors," an essay which occupies only a peripheral place in the development of Schopenhauer's main philosophical position and seems to support Goethe's views.

In 1813 he received his diploma and attempted to resume relations with his mother, but they quarrelled again and he left in May 1814, and never saw her afterwards. From 1814 to 1818, he lived alone in Dresden and wrote *The World as Will and Idea*. Thus by twenty-eight, he had formulated every detail of his basic philosophy from which he never budged in the slightest. The book, when it appeared at the end of 1818, was an utter failure; nobody bought it, nobody read it, nobody reviewed it. Schopenhauer survived on his confidence that one day it would find its public and that one day he would be famous. In *The World as Will and Idea,* he felt he had expressed himself so completely that he published nothing further for eighteen years, and it took about twenty-five years before he attained any recognition.

In 1836 he published *On the Will in Nature,* designed to show that scientific knowledge corroborated his metaphysics. In 1838 Schopenhauer won a prize for an essay from a scientific society in Norway. He subsequently entered a second essay for a prize offered by the Danish Academy of Science. This essay, the only one submitted, was rejected because of his uncomplimentary remarks about other philosophers. Both essays were published in 1831 under the title *The Two Fundamental Problems of Ethics.* These essays, "On the Will in Nature," and "The Two Fundamental Problems of Ethics" are merely footnotes to *The World as Will and Idea.*

Despite continuing lack of success, he persuaded his publisher to bring out a second edition of *The World as Will and Idea* in 1844 containing a large number of supplemental essays and comment on the existing books (Schopenhauer 1958). After the appearance of this new edition, Schopenhauer attracted a little attention, but it was still not greatly forthcoming for another seven years until he published in 1851 his last major book *Parerga und Paralipomena (Essays and Aphorisms).* Although declined by three publishers and finally brought out by a fourth in return for ten free copies, this large, loose collection gained him wide popularity. Despite this recognition, he was never satisfied. He wanted nothing less than worldwide acclaim, for he felt he had discovered the key to the universe. In 1859 he brought out the third edition of *The World as Will and Idea,* which did not differ substantially from the second edition.

There are interesting gaps in his biography, especially in the 1820's, during which nothing worthy or of interest happened to him at all. As he said, "Life is a disagreeable thing and I have determined to spend it in reflecting on it." He seemed to idle many years away, although actually his love for reflecting and brooding was during these periods absorbing much of his time. There was a strong sensuous side to his nature and he apparently was involved in many erotic affairs, none of them lasting. He seemed capable of superficial relationships with friends and women but formed no deeper relationships. He was extremely sensitive to noise, and became involved in a famous lawsuit for attacking an old lady loudly gossiping outside his door.

For the last twenty-seven years of his life he lived alone in a room or apartment and followed an unvarying routine as described in an excellent brief introduction to Schopenhauer by Hollingdale:

He rose every morning at seven o'clock and had a bath and no breakfast: he drank a cup of strong coffee before sitting down at his desk and writing until noon. At noon he ceased work for the day and spent half an hour practicing the flute, on which he became quite a skilled performer. Then he went out for lunch at the *Englischer Hof*. After lunch he returned home and read until four when he left for his daily walk: he walked for two hours no matter what the weather. At six o'clock he visited the reading room of the library and read the London Times. In the evening he attended the theatre or a concert after which he had dinner at a hotel or restaurant. He got back home between nine and ten and went early to bed. He would deviate from this routine in order to receive visitors: but with this exception he carried it through for twenty-seven years. (Schopenhauer 1970, p. 25)

This description not only depicts Schopenhauer's dedication, obstinacy, and perseverance but also describes adherence to one of his most basic principles, namely, that one should systematically think through problems rather than just read about them. He was obsessed with the distinction between the academic philosophers who made their living studying the philosophy of others and writing books about other's philosophy, and people who were truly dedicated to the field. He wrote, "A man becomes a philosopher by reason of a certain perplexity from which he seeks to free himself ... but what distinguishes the false philosopher from the true is this: the perplexity of the latter arises from contemplation of the world itself, while that of the former results from some book, some system of philosophy which lies before him" (1970). Gardiner explains, "Mere scholarship and book-learning must in fact be wholly distinguished from what in the present context Schopenhauer calls *wisdom,* this being a profound deeply felt sense of how things are, of what the world is really like. It follows that learning, unlike wisdom, is always relative to an age, a period: learned men of the past, being for the greater part as children compared with us, need our indulgence; but the wise of earlier times do not" (1971).

Already from this review we can see Schopenhauer's attitude toward living producing an entirely different philosophical methodology than that of the traditional rational philosophers. It is in some ways unfortunate that Schopenhauer first became widely known through the essays *Parerga und Paralipomena* because they give little indication of the range of his knowledge of the history of philosophy, or the extent to which his own ideas developed out of a determined consideration of questions that had formed the focus of much previous philosophical inquiry and discussion. Schopenhauer himself explained in *Parerga und Paralipomena*:

> As the biggest library if it is in disorder is not as useful as a small but well-arranged one, so you may accumulate a vast amount of knowledge but it will be of far less value to you than a much smaller amount if you have not thought it over for yourself; because only through ordering what you know by comparing every truth with every other truth can you take complete possession of your knowledge and get it into your power. You can think about only what you know, so you ought to learn something; on the other hand, you can know only what you have thought about.
>
> Now you can apply yourself voluntarily to reading and learning, but you cannot really apply yourself to thinking: thinking has to be kindled, as a fire is by a draught, and kept going by some kind of interest in its object, which may be an objective interest or merely a subjective one. The latter is possible only with things that affect us personally, the former only to those heads who think by nature, to whom thinking is as natural as breathing, and these are very rare. That is why most scholars do so little of it. (1970, p. 89)

THE WORLD AS WILL AND IDEA

Let us turn directly to *The World as Will and Idea*. (*Idea* is a questionable translation. The term *vorstellung* means mental presentation, idea, or representation. The best modern translation, that of Payne (Schopenhauer 1958), uses the term "representation" for *vorstellung.*) *Vorstellungen* are the phenomenal world, the world studied by science, which seeks connections between these representations, and forms abstract concepts for the purpose of control and communication.

Thus the famous opening sentence, "The world is my idea" (representation), implies that all knowledge of objects is necessarily confined to the theory of ideas or representations of the perceiving subject and that this knowledge includes from one standpoint the knowledge we have of ourselves. Thus according to Schopenhauer, the world is only what it appears to be within the experience of the subject, and it is a gross error to imagine something independent of the subject as the "cause" of the appearances of things.

The world is the representation of the subject and bears a similarity to the world of our dreams. The only difference between the world of our waking hours and the world of our sleep is that our sleep dreams are not in continuous harmony with the spatio-temporal action of our waking life. Schopenhauer likens the difference between the world of our waking hours and the world of dreams to be the difference between reading a book in order, line by line, page by page; and reading a line here, a line there, a page in front of the book and a page in back of the book. Thus the order of events in our sleep-dreams is haphazard in relation to the order of events in that "long dream," our waking life.

The thing-in-itself *(noumenon)* postulated by Kant (see chapter 8) as the unknowable ground for all phenomena and as an initial cause and unknowable stuff is rejected by Schopenhauer. He never, however, claims that the world is *only* a dream or only "my idea." Taaffee explains, "The question should not be Does an independent world of objects cause the knowledge of the subject? Rather, the question should be Is this world which I see, touch, and smell anything else besides being my idea?" (1965). The answer is affirmative according to Schopenhauer; this world is not only my idea it is Will, and the world as Will is the subject of the second book of his philosophy and perhaps Schopenhauer's unique contribution to the history of philosophy.

How does Schopenhauer arrive at the conviction that Kant's thing-in-itself is Will? Copleston explains, "To find the key to reality I must look within myself. For in inner consciousness or inwardly directed perception lies 'the single narrow door to the truth.' Through this inner consciousness I am aware that the bodily action which is said to follow or result from volition is not something different from volition but one and the same. That is to say, the bodily action is simply the objectified will: it is the will become idea or presentation. Indeed, the whole body is nothing but objectified will, will as a presentation to consciousness.

According to Schopenhauer anyone can understand this if he enters into himself. And once he has this fundamental intuition, he has the key to reality. He has only to extend his discovery to the world at large" (1965, p. 37).

Schopenhauer proceeds to make this extension and sees the manifestation of the one individual Will everywhere. The Will and the "will to live" are for Schopenhauer one and the same thing. Thus Will is constantly working toward satisfying desires and maintaining the species. It is an endless striving, a blind urge, an impulse which knows no cessation and cannot find satisfaction or reach a state of tranquility. Thus Schopenhauer's pessimism is a consequence of the nature of the metaphysical concept Will. The thing-in-it-self being what it is, phenomenal experience *must* be marked with the black features which we actually observe and experience. Not only are we really Will according to Schopenhauer, the real world is Will.

SCHOPENHAUER'S METHODOLOGY

The basic methodology supporting this contention is to pay attention to our inner consciousness of our own existence. Through this we discover that the world is a duality. The world as idea is the outer physical world, the realm of time, space, and causation, appearance, Kant's phenomenal world; the world as Will is the inner subjective world, not subject to the forms of space and time, a unity, reality, Kant's *noumenal* world or thing-in-itself. It cannot be said that Schopenhauer uses the concept of Will in a fixed and constant way, for he often seems ready to mould and manipulate it to suit his purposes when the need arises. What is remarkable is his methodology: *"A way from within* stands open for us to that essential inner nature of things, to which we cannot penetrate *from without;* as it were, a subterranean passage . . . which, as if by a treachery, places us at once within the fortress which it was impossible to take by assault from without." Such intuitive methodology has influenced philosophers and psychologists from Freud to Wittgenstein and will be seen again and again in the remainder of the present book.

Perhaps no philosopher has felt more keenly than Schopenhauer a sense of dissatisfaction about the adequacy of scientific explanation, a dissatisfaction which the early Wittgenstein also was most concerned about. Wittgenstein (see chapter 15) in the *Tractatus* wrote: "We feel that even when all *possible* scientific questions have been answered, the problems of life have still not been touched at all." And this sentiment is a direct outgrowth of Schopenhauer's aphorism, "The fundament upon which all our knowledge and learning rests is the inexplicable. It is to this that every explanation, through few or many intermediate stages, leads; as the plummet touches the bottom of the sea now at a great depth, now at a less, but is bound to reach it somewhere sooner or later. The study of this inexplicable devolves upon metaphysics" (1970).

Thus through introspection, a fundamental intuition and entering into one's self, we are led to the discovery of universal Will, an endless meaningless struggle for existence—blind impulse, endless striving, the will to live, to maintain the species, to satisfy hunger and sex—which is never satisfied, for satisfaction soon turns to boredom. For Schopenhauer, "Thing-in-itself signifies that which exists independently of our perception, that which actually is. To Democritus it was matter; fundamentally this is what it still was to Locke; to Kant it was $=x$; to me it is *will*" (1970).

Thus reason has primarily a biological function. It is a practical instrument formed to be used at the service of Will. Secondarily, in Schopenhauer's view, it can be used as surplus energy to speculate and contemplate and to escape from subservience to the Will either temporarily through esthetic contemplation or permanently through asceticism. In either case this represents a profound dethroning of the sovereign reason of the Enlightenment.

SCHOPENHAUER AS A BRIDGE TO FREUD

Schopenhauer romantically stressed man's kinship with all living things. In reviewing man's goals he saw the individual human life as of no importance and insisted that man was impelled from behind—not drawn from in front by rational goals. This concept explains many apparently irrational phenomena and is very important. It also presents a bridge to the fundamental ideas of Freud. Even Schopenhauer's contention that metaphysics is only possible because the intellect, though by nature the servant of the will, can develop to such an extent that it achieves surplus energy for objectivity, is reminiscent of current notions of the conflict-free sphere of the ego and of Alexander's notion (see chapter 13) of surplus energy. Though man's mind is in the first instance an instrument for satisfying his bodily needs, it can develop a kind of surplus energy which sets it free, at least temporarily, from the service of desire. Man can then adopt a creative contemplative attitude as in aesthetics and philosophy.

Freud acknowledged that Schopenhauer's Will is equivalent to the psychoanalytic concept of the instincts. As Schopenhauer wrote, "Consciousness is the mere surface of our mind, of which, as of the earth, we do not know the inside but only the crust" (1958). He described the Will as preventing the rise to consciousness of thoughts and desires that if known would arouse feelings of humiliation, embarrassment, or shame, and gave examples of instances of memory failure under powerful inducements because we feel them to be unendurable. He wrote that attempts to suppress events and experiences can lead in extreme cases to insanity, with fantasies and delusions replacing what has been extruded from consciousness.

Schopenhauer showed an uncanny prescience in his discussion of "madness," anticipating the essence of Bleuler's theory of the group of schizophrenias. He explains, "Now, from what we have stated, we see that the madman correctly knows the individual present as well as many particulars of the past, but that he fails to recognize the connexion, the relations, and therefore goes astray and talks nonsense" (1958, Vol. 1., p. 193). He adds, "Although the immediate present is correctly known, it is falsified through a fictitious connexion with an imaginary past" (p. 192). Furthermore, in his supplementary essay "On the Association of Ideas," he pinpoints the basically irrational Will as the source of the healthy or unhealthy association of ideas: "This drives its servant, the intellect, according to its powers to link one idea on to another, to recall the similar and the simultaneous, and to recognize grounds and consequents. . . . For that which rules the sensorium, and determines it to follow analogy or another association of ideas in this or that direction, is the will of the thinking subject" (1958, Vol. 2, p. 136).

In addition there are famous striking parallels between what Schopenhauer had to say about the sexual instinct and Freud's account of libido. Schopenhauer claimed that the sexual urge represents the "focus of the will" and is the most powerful motive of all except for the instinct to survive, and that it exercises a pervasive influence in every area of human life. Numerous autobiographical writings about sex left by Schopenhauer on his death were tragically burned by his executor, who judged them unsuitable for publication.

Surely many of Freud's formal conceptions, the cornerstones of psychoanalysis, were first given at least a poetic or visionary form through the intuition or introspection of Schopenhauer.

SCHOPENHAUER'S THEORY OF CHARACTER

Schopenhauer's remarkable theory of character bears a striking parallel to psychoanalytic theory. The metaphysical Will objectifies itself in the individual will and the individual will, considered in itself anteriorly to its acts, can be called the intelligible or noumenal character. The noumenal character manifests itself gradually in each individual by a series of successive acts which may be called the empirical character that one gradually becomes aware of in one's self. Thus the empirical character, which appears to consist of free behavior, is really the rigid and predetermined unfolding of noumenal character. Superficial conduct may change but motives remain the same. Such a totally deterministic theory of character Schopenhauer himself cannot accept and ends up insisting we deny Will by turning to an asceticism which culminates in nothing or extinction. Schopenhauer himself could not face this denial. In fact there is a self-contradiction in the theory that the Will can deny itself and denounce what the phenomena express, namely the will to live. Here Schopenhauer has to introduce an exception to the principle of determinism.

At any rate, a man comes to know his own character only gradually and imperfectly. He is in the same position as an outsider and conscious only of acts he has already done; since he cannot foresee his future acts from Will, it seems to himself that he is free, but each empirical act is really the unfolding of the noumenal character. It is Schopenhauer's contention that a man's noumenal character never changes but remains permanently the same throughout the whole course of his life. It may appear to undergo alterations and modifications but that is an illusion. Furthermore, it is impossible for anyone by some voluntary effort or resolution to advance himself into something different from what he is.

What he can do is discover, through the observation of his own behavior and reactions to situations, the nature and limitations of his personality and grow to an acceptance of these. The goal then is to attain what he calls an acquired character. A person who has come fully to understand his noumenal character as it has unfolded itself to him through experience is thereby enabled to carry out in a methodical manner the role which uniquely belongs to his own person—his acquired character—without being continually side-tracked or ensnared by delusive hopes and wishes or led astray by the impossible belief that he might by his own efforts become something other than he is.

STRUGGLE WITH THE
RELENTLESS FORCE OF WILL

According to Schopenhauer the three basic springs or motives of human behavior are egoism (self-love), which is the impulse to achieve one's own good regardless of the pain it causes others; malice, or the impulse to pain or hurt others and enjoy their woe; or compassion, which is behind the impulse toward helping other people. He considered egoism to be the clearest expression of the will to live and to be at the basis of most human behavior. He saw malice, as the basis of immorality, existing only in human nature and quite foreign to other living creatures. He also believed that sympathy or compassion existed rarely here and there and arose essentially out of the empathy certain tender souls feel at the suffering of others.

Taylor explains, "The evil of the world seemed to him its most salient, positive, and ineradicable feature, but the intellectual apprehension of this fact, however certain, does not by itself turn one away from the world and life, and it did not do so in Schopenhauer's own case. He lived it to the fullest, pursuing much the same ends that all men rush after—honor, recognition, comfort, and longevity—in the full conviction of his own folly and the vanity of life, never taking even the first step on that path to salvation that he had so carefully described. This indicates no hypocrisy however, for the explanation is implied in his own philosophy; namely, the strength of his own will, his bondage to it, and its complete independence from his thought and reason" (1964).

Other than the radical concept of asceticism which Schopenhauer advises as denial of Will and which seems to be a self-contradictory concept in his philosophy, is there any other escape from the endless striving of Will? Schopenhauer answers yes: there is a temporary escape in aesthetic contemplation. The appetite is stilled temporarily during certain aesthetic experiences. Music is the highest of all the arts, not only stilling the appetite but, according to Schopenhauer, providing a direct revelation of the Will. No other major philosopher has elevated art to a higher status. He yields to art a cognitive function in which aesthetic experience provides a more adequate vision of reality then does science and an ethical function in which the aesthetic attitude gives us temporary release from the striving of Will. The function of art is to tease us out of thought and to project us into a realm where pursuit is frozen and desire is stilled. This is the point of Keat's great "Ode to a Grecian Urn." Unfortunately this relief is only temporary and the pressure exerted by the Will is strong so we soon relapse again into the senseless round of passion and frustration.

Thus in the aesthetic experience a person may be said to lose himself in the object of his contemplation; he forgets his will and exists as pure subject; the notions of space and time seem to lose all their ordinary meaning, and we are temporarily outside of the force of Will. Furthermore, in listening to music a man receives a direct revelation, though not in conceptual form, of the reality which underlies phenomena. And he intuits this reality, revealed in the form of art, in an objective and disinterested manner, not as one caught in the grip of the Will's tyranny. If it were possible to express accurately in concepts all that music expresses without concepts, we should have the true philosophy, explains Schopenhauer.

In spite of the metaphysical weakness of Schopenhauer's notion of Will it afforded him an enormous plethora of insights into human life and human character, and made him the first philosopher to fundamentally break with the optimism of the Enlightenment, correctly predicting the previously unthinkable phenomena of twentieth century war. Freud (1925d, 1933) made repeated complimentary references to the emphasis which Schopenhauer had laid on the importance and power of sexuality, the supreme manifestation of the will to life.

In Schopenhauer's view a man appears to himself to be sharply separated from the people and things surrounding him, and yet each man is also impelled relentlessly and unceasingly forward by the fundamental drives of self–preservation and reproduction. "Thus he pursues his lonely and restless course, on the one hand seeking protection against the dangers that beset him on every side, on the other trying to fulfill his ever-pressing needs and to gratify his desires, and conscious all the time that in the end everything will be brought to a conclusion by 'the total, inevitable, and irremediable shipwreck' " (Gardiner 1971).

The focus of man's unhappiness, according to Schopenhauer, ought to be man himself; *homo homini lupus,* that is to say it is futile and useless to seek to throw the responsibility for the evil state of things upon systems or institutions, for life as we find it is nothing but the reflection of our own nature. As Schopenhauer puts it, "If men were in general not so worthless, their fate as a whole would not be so sad." Schopenhauer compared the life of a man to the journey of someone riding a raft upon swift turbulent rapids, struggling to avoid every shoal and rock throughout the whole course of the journey, only to reach the escarpment at the end, from which he is hurled down to an eternal nothingness.

OBJECTIONS TO SCHOPENHAUER'S METHOD

There are grave difficulties with Schopenhauer's fascinating viewpoints. The most obvious is based on the question of what knowledge can be gained through intuition. There has of course been increasing acceptance in recent years of the force of irrational influences in the formation of character, and the small role played by reason in this respect is now generally recognized. At the same time, to preach the denial of Will against such a deterministic theory is self-contradictory. His philosophy would have been more consistent had he simply denied the possibility of *any* release from the Will and accepted the fatalism that this implies. Apparently this was too pessimistic even for Schopenhauer, but in the light of twentieth century history it is no longer an untenable position.

Concepts, according to Schopenhauer, do not provide us with new knowledge. Intuition is fundamental, but intuition must be raised to the conceptual level if it is to become philosophy. Copleston points out that this argument puts Schopenhauer in a difficult position: "He does not wish to postulate as the basis of philosophy an exceptional intuition which will be something entirely different from perception on the one hand and abstract reasoning on the other. Hence the intuition of which he is speaking must be on the level of perceptive knowledge. But perception is concerned with individual objects, and so with phenomena. For individuality belongs to the phenomenal sphere. He is forced, therefore, to try to show that even on the level of perception there can be an intuitive awareness of the noumenon, an awareness which forms the basis for philosophical meditation" (1965, pp. 35-36).

Even Schopenhauer at times admits that the method of turning inward can only reveal phenomenal information: Gardiner explains, "On this view it is no longer the case that 'inner knowledge,' any more than direct perceptual awareness, give us actual direct cognizance of the will. What we come upon through both are no more than expressions of the will experienced at the level of idea; and, although it is implied that by way of the former we obtain a more vivid and immediate conception and realization of its true nature, because here 'the thing-in-itself has in great measure thrown off its veil,' the point remains that it still does not appear 'naked' " (1971).

We are here dealing with "something" that is literally unknown and unknowable if we are to be philosophically consistent. So how can it be thought to aid our comprehension of the sensible world in any conceivable way? What sense can there be in talking of such an entity at all?

Thus Bradley in his famous *Appearance and Reality* dismisses Schopenhauer's theory of Will as "an uncritical attempt to make play with the unknown," offering merely "the pretense of a ground or explanation, where the ground is not understood or the explanation discovered" (1951).

Only in the transition from Schopenhauer to Freud, whose similarly criticized idea of the unconscious mind is seen as a necessary scientific or heuristic concept (indispensible to explain otherwise inexplicable links in the chains of associations or in finding a meaning to apparently irrational phenomena) can we get around this basically metaphysical objection, by simply dropping arguments about the "reality" of the unconscious (Chessick 1961).

Taylor eloquently sums up the situation:

> If one were to step afresh into our world, having the faculties to appreciate what he found, he could contemplate one of nature's living works, whether it were a man or a contemptible fly, only with awesome admiration. It would appear to him so exquisitely designed, so painstakingly harmonized in all its parts, so delicately adjusted to its purposes, a work of artifice so elaborate, as to make it seem some sort of final end. Yet that individual thing is by Schopenhauer's philosophy nothing but an effortless expression of an infinite will, and counts in nature for nothing, being obliterated by the merest vagary. Innumerable creatures perish in the woodlands from a chance spark, and small animals play guilelessly among the ubiquitous threats that can extinguish them at a stroke. We are so accustomed to viewing animal life in this light that we no longer see anything incongruous in it; yet Schopenhauer claimed that it is no different with human life. If we declare human nature to have some special transcendent worth—to be, in Kant's terms, an 'end in itself'—it is from our own wishful thinking. It is not from the lessons of nature and history, for these contradict us daily. A man is often felled at the height of his powers by a bacterium; a civilization is robbed of one of its geniuses by the most trivial trick of fate; cities are abolished by earthquakes; millions are slaughtered at the caprice of a tyrant and their bodies piled into pits and burned like grasshoppers. (1964, pp. 371-372)

Chapter 10

Overcoming the Unbearable

The most general characteristic of the modern age: man has lost dignity incredibly in his own eyes. Long as center and tragic hero of existence in general; then at least struggling to prove himself related to the decisive and intrinsically valuable side of existence ... he has become an animal, animal without metaphor, abatement and reservation, he who in his previous faith was almost God ("child of God," "God-man") ... Since Copernicus man seems to have got upon an inclined plane—he is now rolling faster and faster away from the center—whither? into nothingness? into the "overwhelming feeling of his nothingness?"
Friedrich Nietzsche, *Ecce Homo*

Now I have my own study plan and behind it my own secret aim, to which the rest of my life is consecrated—it is too difficult for me to live unless I do it in the grandest style. I tell you this in confidence, my old comrade. Without an aim, which I thought to be indescribably important, I would not have kept myself up in the light and above the black torrents! This is actually my only excuse for the kind of things which I have been writing since 1876; it is my prescription and my home-brewed medicine against weariness with life. What years! What wearisome pain! What inner disturbances, revolutions, solitudes! Who has endured as much as I have? ... And if I now stand above all that, with the joyousness of a victor and

*fraught with difficult new plans—and, knowing myself, with the
prospect of new, more difficult, and even more inwardly profound
sufferings and tragedies and with the courage to face them!—then
nobody would be annoyed with me for having a good opinion of my
medicine. Mihi ipsi scripsi—and there it stands; and thus everyone
should do for himself his best in his own way—that is my morality,
the only remaining morality for me. If even my physical health
reappears, whom have I to thank for that? I was in all respects my
own doctor; and as a person in whom nothing stands separate, I
have had to treat soul, mind, and body all at once and with the same
remedies.*

Friedrich Nietzsche, *Letter of 1882*

NIETZSCHE AND FREUD

Nietzsche seems to have influenced many artists and thinkers of our
century more than any other individual. Heidegger, for example,
considers him to be "the last great metaphysician and the end point of a
development that began with Plato." There are two well known
quotations of Sigmund Freud expressing his views toward Nietzsche:
"The degree of introspection achieved by Nietzsche has never been
achieved by anyone, nor is it likely ever to be reached again" (Nunberg
1962), and "In my youth he signified a nobility to which I could not
attain" (Jones 1957). Ellenberger (1960) argues that it is "impossible to
overestimate Nietzsche's influence on dynamic psychiatry. . . .
Nietzsche may be considered the common source of Freud, Adler, and
Jung." Ellenberger describes an obvious similarity of the thought of
Nietzsche and Freud and adds, "There can be no question about the
former's influence over the latter." Freud himself admitted that
Nietzsche was a philosopher "whose guesses and intuitions often agree
in the most astonishing way with the laborious findings of
psychoanalysts," and states that for a long time he avoided reading
Nietzsche on that very account, in order to keep his mind free from
external influences. Ellenberger points out that at the time of Freud's
early maturity it was not necessary to have studied Nietzsche to be
permeated with his thought, since Nietzsche was quoted, reviewed, and
discussed in every circle, journal, or newspaper.

Waugaman (1973) answers this argument and lays to rest for once and for all the myth that Freud's great ideas came from Nietzsche. Freud's attitudes toward speculation in general and Nietzsche in particular were due in part to his great desire to establish psychoanalysis as a scientific discipline at a time when it was generally unaccepted by the scientific community. Thus though he greatly admired Nietzsche he vigorously denied any influence by him out of concern for the reputation of psychoanalysis. All of Nietzsche's fundamental philosophical concepts (if one is willing to call them philosophy rather than poetical vision) are profoundly different from Freud's principles of psychoanalysis. This difference is obscured by the fact that superficial reading, especially in the light of current psychoanalytic knowledge, makes Nietzsche's views appear to be similar.

Though the dynamic concept of mind, containing the system of drives that can collide with the ego and become fused into each other or transformed, is anticipated by Nietzsche, he gave prevalence not to the sexual drive but rather to aggressive and self-destructive drives. He did understand the processes that have been called "defense mechanisms" by Freud, especially sublimation, repression (Nietzsche calls it "inhibition"), and the turning of instincts toward one's self. However, Ellenberger's argument that so much more of Freud is anticipated by Nietzsche is difficult to substantiate.

First of all, "Nietzsche's ideas are particularly difficult to appraise, because of their lack of systematization and innumerable contradictions" (Ellenberger 1970). Morgan points out that like St. Paul, whom he so hated and admired, Nietzsche has been all things to all men. His work suffered more than that of any philosopher from the wildest sort of subjective interpretation and criticism. This is because the way he wrote makes it easy to mistake or twist his meaning, and the way he lived makes it still easier to explain his meaning away. Morgan feels that "only the most patient and self-critical effort, therefore, can hope to discover what Nietzsche meant" (1965).

First we run into the problem that, as Jaspers says, "all statements seem to be annulled by other statements. For nearly every single one of Nietzsche's judgments, one can also find an opposite. He gives the impression of having two opinions about everything. Consequently it is possible to quote Nietzsche at will in support of anything one happens to have in mind" (1935a).

Copleston in an incisive discussion of Nietzsche, makes the similar argument that "obviously Nietzsche's method of writing is partly responsible for the possibility of diverse interpretations." Copleston points out, "It is . . . possible for the commentator to depict Nietzsche either as a lover of war or as almost a pacifist. A judicious selection of texts is all that is required" (1965).

In addition to these contradictions, there is a definite vagueness in Nietzsche's style. This cannot be attributed to mediocrity on Nietzsche's part. He was a brilliant and penetrating thinker, a studious and learned man. The vagueness in his style is deliberate. It is just that he is not in the ordinary sense a philosopher and he has not left a systematic account of his views. Russell (1964) calls him "an aristocratic humanist in the liberal sense." It is a fair and honest appraisal to say that Nietzsche wrote in such a way that he has become all things to all men, and has been charged with anticipating all sorts and kinds of diverse and often conflicting psychological, philosophical, and political theories.

Nietzsche's aphoristic style further compounds the difficulty of finding in him a consistent philosophy. In some cases he jotted down and published thoughts as they came to him on his long solitary walks. Some of these are very brief and sometimes incomprehensible. Often ideas and important aphorisms are scattered all over his various books. The scattering of ideas and his aphoristic style are consequences of his method of thought which did not take place in an orderly fashion, but in fits and starts culminating in jotted down flashes of intuition.

Nietzsche himself discussed his style: "People find difficulty with the aphoristic form; this arises from the fact that the form is *not taken seriously enough.* An aphorism, properly stamped and molded, has not been 'deciphered' . . . when it has simply been read; rather, one has then to begin its *exegesis,* for which is required an art of exegesis" (Hollingdale 1965). These aphorisms assume on the part of the reader a serious intent of thinking about them over again and again, for the purpose of having the reader reproduce the set in his own mind that leads up to the magnificent, succinct, and highly polished aphorism. Nietzsche points out that he is "a teacher of slow reading. Now it suits my taste . . . no longer to write anything but that which will drive the sort of person who 'is in a hurry' to desperation" (Jaspers 1935a). This is certainly true, and it will be recalled that Nietzsche, a brilliant philologist, was extremely word conscious.

Nietzsche's doctrines themselves are very difficult and present a challenge even to the professional philosopher. In this chapter I will not make an effort to try to outline Nietzsche's fundamental philosophical ideas when they are not pertinent to clinical and theoretical psychotherapy. There are, however, certain aspects both of Nietzsche's life style and his basic thought which are extremely important to the practice of psychotherapy and which make Nietzsche a most pertinent thinker even down to the present day.

It must be understood that nothing short of reading all of Nietzsche's works would really give a balanced picture of Nietzsche's creative endeavor. The usual approach for the reader who obviously has not the time to go over the voluminous writings of this difficult thinker is the first three parts of *Thus Spoke Zarathustra* (Nietzsche 1968b). Kaufmann (1967), who is one of the leading exponents of Nietzsche's work, argues that the little one hundred page book entitled *The Twilight of the Idols* (Nietzsche 1968b) written in 1888 just before Nietzsche's mental collapse, contain a good summary of Nietzsche's work. The aphoristic style of *The Twilight of the Idols* is, however, extremely difficult and confusing for anyone who is not already thoroughly acquainted with much of Nietzsche's writing. Therefore, I have stayed with the first three books of *Zarathustra* in spite of their lyricism, and I will discuss this reading in greater detail later on.

One additional factor that makes Nietzsche so difficult and yet so important and pertinent, is that his life style itself can be understood as a form of philosophical communication. The essential question of Nietzsche's life is presented in *Zarathustra:* "Something unknown is around me and looks thoughtful. What! You are still alive, comments Zarathustra? Why? What for? By what? Wither? Where? How? Is it not folly still to be alive?" (1968b). As Kaufmann puts it: "Modern man finds that his values are worthless, that his ends do not give his life any purpose, and that his pleasures do not give him happiness. Nietzsche's basic problem is whether a new sanction can be found in this world for our values; whether a new goal can be found that will give an aim to human life; and what is happiness?" (1968). Jaspers actually considers the course of Nietzsche's life and thought as a sort of primal self analysis in which Nietzsche attempts to actually find his own self or to reach, in Jasper's terms, an authentic being. Nietzsche frequently quotes Pindar, who exhorts us, "Become what you are."

Nietzsche describes the periods or phases in the development of his life and thought as so many "masks." Copleston points out that, "For example, he asserted that the attitude of a free spirit, that is, of a critical, rationalistic, and skeptical observer of life, which he adopted in his second period, was an 'eccentric pose,' a second nature, as it were, which was assumed as a means whereby he might win through to his first or true nature. It had to be discarded as the snake sloughs its old skin" (1965). This conception of Nietzsche's life as representing a series of phases or masks toward which he attempted to realize some kind of authentic and perhaps mysterious "being" is used by some to explain the many changes and contradictions in his writings, and the deliberate vagueness of his style. Thus we are never sure when we read any aspect of Nietzsche's work whether we are encountering the "real" Nietzsche or being presented with yet another side of his complex personality as he struggles to reach his true identity.

Perhaps it is most ironic that when Nietzsche appears to reach what he considers his true identity in the year of 1888, his last phase, it reaches the frenzied pitch of insanity. Indeed the basic theme of the publications of that year, culminating in *Ecce Homo* (Nietzsche 1968a) can be understood by the psychotherapist as representing a psychotic self-fragmentation, followed by a confusional state with a megalomanic attempt at restitution. Thus the extreme cynic might even argue that Nietzsche's entire life and thought represented at base an attempt to ward off an inevitable impending mental collapse; whether this collapse was secondary to general paresis or schizophrenia is impossible to determine.

NIETZSCHE

Let us turn then to an actual examination of the phases or periods of Nietzsche's mental development. A good year-by-year chronological sketch of Nietzsche appears in Fuss and Shapiro (1971). This little volume is highly recommended as an introduction to Nietzsche and contains a self portrait taken from his letters.

Nietzsche was born in Prussia to one Lutheran minister and the daughter of another. His father died when he was about six years old, in 1850, and around that time his widowed mother also lost her youngest son. Nietzsche was raised in a household which consisted of his mother, his sister, his father's mother, and two maiden aunts. This—as well as his sister's horrible character—could explain Nietzsche's continuous imprecations against women. He was recognized as a brilliant student. It is a matter of debate whether or not in his student days he contracted syphillis; at any rate Nietzsche never thought he had the disease and most of his life he was sexually abstinent.

He certainly suffered from what we would call severe hypochondriasis, especially an enormous variety of headaches, sinus problems, and gastrointestinal complaints. He was recognized at twenty-four as already a remarkable philologist and was recommended by his professor with the comment, to the effect that he had never published contributions from another student nor seen a student like Nietzsche in thirty-nine years of teaching (for details see Kaufmann 1968, p. 7). He was conferred a doctoral degree without thesis or examination, and in 1869 became a Swiss object; in 1870, a full professor. At twenty-eight he seemed on the way to a brilliantly successful career as a professor of philology. In the eyes of the world, the remainder of his life was devoted to throwing all this away.

It must also be admitted that although Nietzsche has been reported a considerate and gentle person, he seems to have been extremely subject to morbid introspection and preoccupation with himself and utterly at a loss with women. In other words, from the point of view of the psychotherapist, he was a severely pathological man from the very beginning; it was only his great intellectual brilliance that made the difference between Nietzsche and millions of other unfortunate people.

The Birth of Tragedy (1968a) announced to the world in 1872 that Nietzsche was no ordinary philologist. The traditional professors found the book sensational and scandalous; most readers simply failed to understand it. In this beginning work Nietzsche distinguishes two tendencies—the "Apollinian" and the "Dionysian." These two tendencies appear again and again in his work, unfortunately with changing meanings. In *The Birth of Tragedy* the Apollinian represents the genius of restraint, harmony, and measure that found expression in Greek sculpture and architecture. The Dionysian could be understood as the longing to find an outlet in a drunken frenzy, such as in the famous Dionysian festivals (Chessick 1965). At the end of his intellectual career, Nietzsche identified himself with Dionysius, but saw Dionysius no longer as opposed to Apollo. At this point, he regarded Dionysius as a synthesis of both Apollo and Dionysius and contrasted him to the crucified Christ. This gives the reader a brief idea of the complexity and changing development of Nietzsche's thinking.

At the beginning Dionysius was for Nietzsche the symbol of the dynamic stream of life which knows no restraints or barriers and defies all limitations. Apollo, on the other hand, was the symbol of order, restraint, and form—the power to create beauty through art. The great contribution of *The Birth of Tragedy* was Nietzsche's realization that the Dionysian element has a rightful place in life and that as Nietzsche correctly saw, to attempt to repress the Dionysian element of life would lead at some later date to the inevitable explosion of vital forces. What disqualified religious faith in Nietzsche's mind was the denial and negativeness of Christian ethics with respect to the Dionysian elements of life.

Thus Nietzsche may be interpreted as foretelling the explosion in the twentieth century of the vital instinctual forces that were forcibly repressed in the nineteenth century. Or he may be interpreted as the forerunner of psychoanalysis in that he wishes to uncover and to sublimate the Dionysian instinctual forces in order to free man and recognizes that the repression of such forces actually leads to man's enslavement and the danger of breakdown.

His remarkable book, which was condemned by most academic scholars, was followed by four books of a rational and critical nature known as "Meditations" in which there was a gradual disillusionment with science and a break with his hero Wagner. This phase culminated in the writing of five "aphoristic" books published together in 1878 as *Human, All Too Human* (1968a). By this time his psychosomatic ailments made him so miserable that he had to resign from the university in 1879. He spent the rest of his life in solitude, wandering over Italy and devoting his remaining strength to the production of more and more writing. *Human, All Too Human* may be thought of as representing the second transitional period of Nietzsche's work, in which he begins to confront directly the problem of morality and the question of becoming a philosopher and finding answers to the basic issues of life. It represents a transition from professional philologist to maverick philosopher.

Thus Spoke Zarathustra (1968b) presents what Kaufmann (1967) calls, "The first comprehensive statement of Nietzsche's mature philosophy." Widely considered Nietzsche's greatest work, it was written in a frenzy. The first three books were written in ten days each in 1883 and in the winter of 1884. This time must have been a low point in Nietzsche's life. It was shortly after estrangement from a sado-masochistic relationship with Lou Salome and Paul Rée. His books, published at his own expense, were unread and ignored, and he was plagued night and day by psychosomatic ailments, severe insomnia, and repeated episodes of depression.

The fourth part of *Zarathustra,* written in the autumn and winter of 1884 and 1885, was intended as the first part of a second book of three parts. Hollingdale points out that "it is markedly inferior in style and contains no new ideas, and Nietzsche was wise to call a halt to the work: the glowing conclusion of the third part is the book's true climax and the seal upon what was by then a complete philosophical outlook on the world" (1965). Two major works *Beyond Good and Evil* in 1886 and the *Genealogy of Morals* in 1887 may be understood as enlargements and explanations of the poetical approach to Nietzsche's basic concepts as he presented them in *Thus Spoke Zarathustra.* Copleston (1965) believes that these three works taken together represent the main of Nietzsche's philosophical thought.

A final phase in 1888 was marked by the production of several small works which show a sharp stylistic change becoming frenzied and megalomanic. One might argue that Nietzsche *had* to write this way because it was clear that no one was paying any attention to him, or one might argue that these represent the outbreak of a psychosis which was marked by a total mental collapse in January, 1889, from which there was never even the smallest recovery. At forty Nietzsche completed part three of *Zarathustra,* and at forty-five he suffered a total collapse.

Although Nietzsche's decline into insanity took the form of an increasing feeling of euphoria, culminating at last in megalomania, the year 1888 was the first year of growing recognition by the world, and the works in this year should not be shrugged off lightly. *The Twilight of the Idols* (1968b) summarizes in aphoristic form his total philosophy. In *Ecce Homo* (1968a), he presents a rhetorical and polemical statement of his views, which Kaufmann compares to Voltaire's cry of *Écrasez l'infâme!* "This vehement polemic is not incompatible with the *amor fati* stressed in *Ecce Homo*" (1968). He considers these books of 1888 to be an excellent introduction to Nietzsche.

THUS SPOKE ZARATHUSTRA

It is best to turn directly to *Thus Spoke Zarathustra* in order to examine Nietzsche's basic ideas as they develop in this remarkable book. As an example of the fertility, complexity, and symbolism in this work Ellenberger (1970) mentions that Jung's courses on *Thus Spoke Zarathustra* are contained in ten unpublished typewritten volumes. We find Nietzsche, however, writing in 1888; "In Germany, though I am in my forty-fifth year and have published about fifteen books including a *non plus ultra, Zarathustra,* there has not yet been a *single* even moderately reputable review of any *one* of my books. People help themselves out now with the phrases 'eccentric,' 'pathological,' 'psychiatric.' There are plenty of bad and slanderous gestures in my direction; an unrestrainedly hostile tone is paramount in the periodicals—learned and unlearned—but how is it that nobody protests against this? that nobody even feels hurt when I am censured? And in all the years no solace, not a drop of humanity, not a breath of love" (1969).

In *Thus Spoke Zarathustra,* the work of an utterly lonely man, Part I introduces the concept of the will to power. This will to power is seen in *Zarathustra* as the basic force underlying all human activities. A monistic conception, which was transferred by Adler to psychology, it can easily be criticized in this era as being excessively simplistic. Kaufmann points out that it is "a striving that cannot be accurately described either as a will to affect others or as a will to "realize" oneself; it is essentially a striving to transcend and perfect oneself" (1968).

Even from this brief description, it should be clear that the will to power is intimately connected with Nietzsche's second basic concept, that of the overman or *Übermensch.* Both Parts I and II of *Zarathustra* concentrate considerably on the concept of the will to power, the overman, and what we would call today "sublimation."

Kaufmann writes: "The overman is the type approximated by Goethe—the human being . . . who has organized the chaos of his passions, given style to his character, and become creative. Aware of life's terrors, he affirms life without resentment" (1967). As this concept developed later in Nietzsche's thought, he began to think of the overman as a superior individual who has the courage to revalue all values and respond with freedom to his will to power. Stumpf points out that, "Such an overman is not to be confused with a totalitarian bully" (1966). The overman would have to possess a balanced unity with Dionysian and Apollinian elements, the passionate man who has his passions under control. The passions, or the Dionysian element, are not to be repressed but rather harnessed or sublimated in the service of creative work.

It is probably already clear to the discerning reader that little information is really given in detail on how to *become* the overman, and that the wider the application of concepts such as the will to power or the overman to human psychology, the more indefinite does the whole matter become. Copleston rather uncharitably describes the overman as, ". . . all that ailing, lonely, tormented, neglected Herr professor, Dr. Friedrich Nietzsche would like to be" (1965).

Nietzsche's psychological genius is revealed in his advice to the adolescent in Part I of *Zarathustra* where sublimation, self healing, self development, and overcoming are presented in poetic form.

The first two parts of *Zarathustra,* also have something to say to those who would teach and to those who would heal others. Nietzsche writes: "Physician help yourself! thus you help your patient too. Let this be his best help that he may behold with his eyes the man who heals himself." Nietzsche also points out "It is by invisible hands that we are bent and tortured worst," and he presents what ought to be the working slogan of every practicing psychotherapist: "But the worst enemy you can encounter will always be you, yourself; you lie in wait for yourself in caves and woods."

Zarathustra is sprinkled with psychological insights. The section on the "pale criminal" anticipates modern psychodynamics by a hundred years; as does the comment, "What was silent in the father speaks in the son; and often I find the son the unveiled secret of the father" (1968b). Kaufmann calls *Zarathustra* ". . . not only a mine of ideas but also a major work of literature and a personal triumph" (Nietzsche 1968b).

Part Three deals with Nietzsche's concept of the eternal recurrence, which is presented as an explosive discovery of the most important magnitude, and which to those trained in modern biology, evolutionary theory, and thermodynamics appears to be completely unintelligible and out of date. Yet the doctrine of eternal recurrence is absolutely necessary to Nietzsche's thinking and must be understood as central to his heroic attempt to overcome modern day nihilism, which, after all, is the whole point of his agony and philosophy.

Morgan (1965) presents as reasoned a discussion of the eternal recurrence as one can possibly expect, although others such as Danto (1965) have attempted to present it as a more formal philosophical theory. Stambaugh (1972) makes a brave attempt to rescue this muddled vision by distinguishing between "recurrence" and "return" to resolve the fantastic metaphysical and physical paradoxes it implies. Jaspers (1935a) points out that no one has taken this doctrine seriously since Nietzsche first proposed it—although it is the *decisive point* in his philosophizing! Attempts to explain or assimilate Nietzsche have usually sought to avoid it, and the reader can imagine the reaction that scientifically trained physicians have when they are confronted with it.

Jaspers writes: "Stated simply, the doctrine is to the effect that being is not an endless becoming of novelties, for everything recurs in extraordinarily great periods of time. . . . All that is has existed countless times and will return countless times" (1935a). As Nietzsche puts it in *Zarathustra:* "Everything goes, everything comes back; eternally rolls the wheel of being. Everything dies, everything blossoms again; eternally runs the year of being. Everything breaks, everything is joined anew; eternally the same house of being is built. Everything parts, everything greets every other thing again; eternally the ring of being remains faithful to itself. In every Now, being begins; round every Here rolls the sphere There. The center is everywhere. Bent is the path of eternity" (1968b). It should be noted that Zarathustra's immediate response to this doctrine as enunciated by his animals is to criticize them for turning the doctrine into a "hurdy-gurdy song." In other words this doctrine is to be taken in a somewhat mystical fashion: ". . . that all things recur eternally, and we ourselves too; and that we have already existed an eternal number of times, and all beings with us" (1968b).

What are we to make of this? The conception of the eternal recurrence was the "ultimate fruit of his study of the Greeks," according to Hollingdale (1965) and it is "the fundamental idea" of *Thus Spoke Zarathustra*. Later on in *Ecce Homo,* Nietzsche describes how it flashed into his consciousness and he regards the idea of the eternal recurrence as "the extremist formula of affirmation that can ever be attained." Morgan (1965) feels that this notion was developed by Nietzsche in order "to generate the greatest possible degree of energy." The purpose of generating this energy is to drive the individual *to live in such a way as he would be willing to have the life he has chosen recur again and again eternally*. It is Nietzsche's attempt to get the individual to overcome himself with the highest possible charge of energy—an exaltation of life—in which the individual attempts to become what he is to the fullest possible extent and which enables the individual to face the abyss and horror of the human predicament with "laughter" rather than despair, pessimism, and surrender. Thus Nietzsche introduces this important doctrine in an effort to stir the individual into a frenzy so as to aid him to affirm human life and live moment to moment.

This of course represents the starting point of much of existential philosophy and existentially oriented psychotherapy. It suffers as one might expect from a certain mysticism and vagueness, and really offers little in the way of guidance for the individual who wishes to find out *how* to achieve overcoming, authenticity, and the condition of the overman. For Nietzsche it presents a more powerful argument for his doctrine of the "revaluation of all values." Let us not forget that Nietzsche is tackling the question of what modern man must do in a situation where God is dead and, as Dostoevsky pointed out, thus anything is permitted. The revaluation of all values is Nietzsche's positive prescription for a critical analysis of modern man's ideals in order to develop a new approach to life that he may use, free of religious superstition, and leading to happiness, exultation, and a sense of the worthwhileness of existence.

ABSOLUTE INTEGRITY: NIETZSCHE AS A MODEL

The most impressive aspect of Nietzsche's life and thought has not been stressed yet in this chapter and that is his absolute integrity and sincere search for truth. It might be argued that such an integrity in our era almost *must* culminate in despair, since there are limits to truth beyond which humans cannot pass. Copleston (1965) suggests that what is really significant in Nietzsche "is not his proposed antidotes to nihilism but rather his existence and thought considered precisely as a dramatic expression of a lived spiritual crisis from which there is no issue in terms of his own philosophy." In fact it may be that the best

way to appreciate Nietzsche is to read Kaufmann's (1968) biography
and follow this up with Middleton's excellent collection of Nietzsche's
selected letters (1969). As we read about Nietzsche's life and hear him
speak in his letters, we can experience at least empathically the terrific
agony of a man tearing himself away from middle class values and a
secure professorship with a brilliant future and forcing himself to look
directly into the abyss of truth and nihilism in our time. He warns us in
Beyond Good and Evil "If you look upon monsters take care you do
not become one yourself; for, should you gaze down into the abyss, the
abyss may enter into you" (1968a). And indeed this is what happened
to Nietzsche.

Jaspers has described "the essential nature of the scholarly
investigator: his incorruptibility, his ceaseless critical struggle with his
own thinking, his simple and guileless passion" (1935a). During the
entire decade of Nietzsche's professorship, he lived in a state of tension,
ceaselessly striving to preserve as much energy as possible from his
rigorous professional duties to devote to the as yet indefinite calling
which attracted and agitated him. Following Nietzsche's life and works
as he attempts to become his authentic self and to pursue his
philosophical star is an experience intensely personal and vital to
anyone who sincerely wishes to live an honest life.

Morgan points out that the preponderant type of man in Nietzsche's
day was "the Philistine," the "flock animal," who permitted himself
occasional excursions into art or philosophy but was careful to
distinguish these amusements from the "serious business" of life, such
as making money. "Not so much his mediocrity as his shameless self-
satisfaction in mediocrity, as if he were rightly the measure of all things
aroused Nietzsche's ire" (1955). Perhaps when we recognize what
Nietzsche had worked through in his own mind in contrast to the
absolute indifference of the rest of the world to his writings, we can
understand better the shrill tone of his 1888 writings.

What is most essential in Nietzsche to the psychotherapist is his
unblinking honesty and personal integrity. His life depicts the abyss we
all face, to which there is as yet no solution (a situation that Clark
(1969) has called "the fallacy of hope"). Although personally he was a
dreadful and ironic failure, he was yet a man of great intellectual
honesty and courage.

Nietzsche's "lived spiritual crisis" reminds us intensely of his idea of living so that you want life repeated eternally. Thus it is Nietzsche's *agony* that has the great appeal, an agony which he compared to that of Christ's crucifixion. In psychotherapy, the agony of trying to reach or empathize with patients presenting the classical need/fear dilemma has a certain parallel to the agony of Nietzsche trying to overcome himself. Nietzsche is also attempting to reach us but our tendency, like that of such patients, is to not hear him.

Nietzsche himself anticipated this problem, for he wrote in *Beyond Good and Evil:* "Independence is for the very few; it is a privilege of the strong. And whoever attempts it even with the best right but without inner constraint proves that he is probably not only strong but also daring to the point of recklessness. He enters into a labyrinth, he multiplies a thousandfold the dangers which life brings with it in any case, not the least of which is that no one can see how and where he loses his way, becomes lonely, and is torn piecemeal by some minotaur of conscience. Supposing one like that comes to grief, this happens so far from the comprehension of men that they neither feel it nor sympathize. And he cannot go back any longer. Nor can he go back to the pity of men" (Nietzsche 1968a).

TEN COMMENTS ON NIETZSCHE

1. The number of irresponsible interpretations of Nietzsche is appalling. It is certainly true that reading a variety of commentators, one can hardly believe he is reading about the same philosopher. Much of this has been brought about by the distorted texts issued by Nietzsche's demoniacal sister and by the editorial stupidity and poor scholarship of translators. It is also a function of Nietzsche's vague style and thought as we have already discussed.

2. Nietzsche (1969) wrote to his sister: "Here the ways of men part: if you wish to strive for peace of soul and pleasure, then believe; if you wish to be devotee of truth, then inquire." Levi (1959) points out the parallel between Nietzsche's attempt to combat the pessimistic conclusions of Schopenhauer through solutions that offer optimism for the future (or at least the hope of some optimism), and the revisions of Freud by Rank, in which human potential and creativity are stressed in order to give a less pessimistic version of man than that based on Freud's mechanical concept of psychic function.

3. Muller sees Nietzsche's attack on "slave morality" as "the most devastating critique of the mediocrity of modern mass society . . . the shallow complacence, the slavish conformism, the slavish materialism, the rule of money values, the lack of real style, the devotion to a paltry kind of happiness and withal the hypocrisy of a society that calls itself Christian" (1971). In this way he argues that Nietzsche's basic ethic is not really new and really embodies "aristocratic virtues" that are incorporated in the Western tradition from Homer on down through the Renaissance.

4. Perhaps the best way to understand this is to have a look at Nietzsche's view of the role of a philosopher. He discriminates between "philosophical laborers" and "philosophers proper." The laborers present systems, which are nothing but sublimated wish fulfillments, as he points out in a famous and often quoted passage from *Beyond Good and Evil.* Morgan writes, "The real philosophers conquer the future: they create new values and scales of value, and are thereby the prime movers of history, men of the longest foresight, with responsibility for the destiny of man. They are not so much lovers of preexisting truth as creators of what shall be held true. These sovereign minds are 'commanders and law givers' " (1965).

5. Jaspers (who is never to be too much trusted in his interpretations of Nietzsche) spends considerable time describing the philosopher as he thinks Nietzsche conceives of him. Nietzsche sees the philosopher as an experimenter willing to involve his own self, and in this sense the fusion of Nietzsche's life style and works becomes apparent. Nietzsche is looking for what he calls "health." By health he means a plastic force available only for the strong who are able to make life worth living, who are able to overcome the diseases of modernity which Nietzsche sees as the great problem that presents itself to modern man. Thus Nietzsche attempts to tear down the values of Christianity which he views as repressive and dangerous because they will lead to an explosion in the twentieth century, and, at the same time he tears down the systems of the famous philosophers, he tries to refocus the role of the philosopher in modern times.

6. Blackham (1952) agrees that Nietzsche is important more because of the problems he poses than for their solution. Nietzsche was a profound and intuitive psychologist and one of the first to stress the importance of the irrational. For example, he writes: "How little

reason and how greatly chance rules over men is shown by the almost invariable disparity between their so-called profession and their evident unsuitability for them: the fortunate cases are exceptions . . . and even these are not brought about by reason. A man *chooses* a profession when he is not yet capable of choice: he does not know the various professions, he does not know himself" (Hollingdale 1965).

7. Barrett (1958) feels that *Ecce Homo* is the best of Nietzsche's work for the beginner, since it reveals him so completely and demonstrates Nietzsche's belief that the philosopher and his philosophy cannot be separated. Both Barrett and Bertrand Russell (1945) recognized the essential insecurity and madness that underlies megalomanic writing such as *Ecce Homo* and that haunt the entire Nietzschean solution. Barrett appreciates Nietzsche considerably more than Russell; at one point he even compares Nietzsche's tortured atheism with the "urbane atheism" of Russell, and in a way shows a better understanding of Nietzsche's madness as manifested in his philosophy than Kaufmann, the most important modern translator and Nietzsche scholar, who seems to have a need to present Nietzsche always being quite rational (see Kaufmann 1958, 1960, 1967, 1968).

8. Russell (1945) presents a most telling argument against Nietzsche by calling our attention to an utter lack of compassion for human suffering. This is strikingly presented as an imaginary dialogue between Nietzsche and Buddha and is a classical gem of Russell's magnificent writing style and lucid thought.

9. Roubiczek (1964) disagrees on many points with Kaufmann's commentary, and argues that Nietzsche's greatest contribution has been the passionate description of the starting point, nihilism in the twentieth century. The problem of nihilism, arising from the discovery that God is dead, eliminated the eternal realm of ideals in which man's high values had been traditionally located. If man has lost this anchor to which he has hitherto been moored, Nietzsche asks, will he not drift in an infinite void?

10. Nietzsche's work is filled with paradoxes and his life itself presents a remarkable series of ironies. Perhaps one of the most interesting of these paradoxes involves our field. Nietzsche in *Ecce Homo* describes himself as the greatest psychologist who ever lived. Yet in the *Great Psychologists from Aristotle to Freud* (Watson 1963), Nietzsche does not appear even in the index. What can we learn

from this about the relationship between academic philosophy and academic psychology? Is it not interesting that somehow this philosopher, because of his life or his style, has not managed to make explicit the enormous implicit influence he has had on modern day psychology and psychodynamics?

Chapter 11

Exploring the Unconscious

In psychoanalysis there is no choice for us but to assert that mental processes are in themselves unconscious, and to liken the perception of them by means of consciousness to the perception of the external world by means of the sense-organs. We can even hope to gain fresh knowledge from the comparison. The psychoanalytic assumption of unconscious mental activity appears to us, on the one hand, as a further expansion of the primitive animism which caused us to see copies of our own consciousness all around us, and, on the other hand, as an extension of the corrections undertaken by Kant of our views on external perception. Just as Kant warned us not to overlook the fact that our perceptions are subjectively conditioned and must not be regarded as identical with what is perceived though unknowable, so, psychoanalysis warns us not to equate perceptions by means of consciousness with the unconscious mental processes which are their object. Like the physical, the psychical is not necessarily in reality what it appears to us to be.

Freud, *The Unconscious*

FREUD AS MAN AND MODEL

Ellenberger points out that Freud inaugurated a new feature in the history of dynamic psychiatry by openly breaking with official medicine. "With Freud begins the era of the newer dynamic schools, with their official doctrine, their rigid organization, their specialized journals, their closed membership, and the prolonged initiation imposed upon their members" (1970). Ellenberger considers this development unique in Western philosophy since the philosophical "schools" of the Greeks.

The tremendous profusion of literature about Freud, and the many legends and distortions that have grown up about him make the task of an objective biographer exceedingly laborious and unrewarding. Roazen (1974) takes up these legends and distortions in exhaustive detail, but the subject is so acrimonious it is hard to determine where fact stops and legend begins. Behind the copious factual and apocryphal material there are some wide gaps in our knowledge of his life and personality.

Ellenberger feels that as time passes it will become more and more difficult to understand Freud because he belonged to a group of men like Kraeplin, Forel, Bleuler, and others who "had gone through long training in intellectual and emotional discipline; they were men of high culture, puritanical mores, boundless energy, and strong convictions, which they vigorously asserted." Their ascetic and idealistic type is becoming "increasingly foreign to our hedonistic and utilitarian generation" (1970).

Despite the difficulties of biography many aspects of Freud's personality still present us with a worthwhile model. He was capable of physical courage and amazing stoic endurance in his later years, as a recent book by his physician Schur (1971) illustrates. He was a man of tremendous energy and combined a boundless capacity for work with the ability to concentrate intensely on one goal. He allied physical courage with moral courage, and "his conviction of the truth of his theories was so complete that he did not admit contradiction. This was called intolerance by his opponents and passion for truth by his followers" (Ellenberger 1970).

Freud lived morally, socially, and professionally according to the highest standards of a man and physician of his time and status. He was a person of scrupulous honesty and professional dignity. He kept his appointments exactly and set all his activities to a time table. He was equally punctilious about his appearance; considerable dignity and decorum were expected of professional men in his day, and Freud lived up to these expectations. In many ways he may be said to have lived a life beyond reproach, and in his genuine and human interest in patients, his boundless capacity for work, and his passion to discover the truth, Freud makes a very fine model indeed for any one who is attempting to do psychotherapy.

Balogh gives a stirring picture of Freud at work:

> His time-table gives some idea of the fullness and the orderliness of his life during the first fourteen years of this century. His first patient arrived at eight and so he had to be roused at seven, which was not always easy, since he seldom went to bed before one or two in the morning. He saw each patient for fifty-five minutes, taking five minutes off between each to refresh himself with a visit into the main part of the family apartment, which was adjacent to the separate office flat. If you go to Vienna now you will see a plaque at 19 Berggasse indicating that Freud lived and worked there. The family always lived on the first floor, but Freud's first office was at street level, his chair facing towards the garden at the back.
>
> The main meal of the day was family lunch; at this he talked little. If a child were absent, Freud would point silently to the empty place and direct an inquiring look at his wife. She would then explain the reason why the child had not appeared. A visitor present at the meal would find that the conversation with the family rested almost entirely with him, Freud being, no doubt, immersed in thoughts about the morning's work.
>
> After lunch he would take a walk in the city, stopping daily to replenish his stock of cigars at a special *Tabak Trafik*. At 3 p.m. there would be consultations, and then further patients until 9 or even 10 p.m. He allowed himself no break before suppertime until he was 65, when he had a 5 o'clock cup of coffee. After a late supper, at which he would be more communicative, he would retire to his study to write his many letters (always by hand), correct proofs and see to new editions. (1971, pp. 70-71)

Freud was an extremely good writer. Almost all of his works are unfolded in a lucid and dramatic fashion; they may be taken as models of scientific exposition in our field. In this chapter, I shall deal directly with some of Freud's writings, in the hope that the student of psychotherapy will turn directly and repeatedly to Freud's writing and immerse himself in the development of Freud's thought.

FREUD'S GREAT IDEAS

The discussion in this chapter will be confined to the great ideas pertinent to the practice of long-term, intensive psychotherapy. Actually Freud went through four phases in his work: first, a search for methodology, culminating in the method of free association; second, a delving into the many ramifications of the unconscious, the preconscious, and the conscious—that is to say the workings of the mind according to the topographical theory; third, an unfinished development of modern structural metapsychology and ego-psychology; and finally, a preoccupation with matters of life and death and the general issues of sociology, anthropology, and philosophy.

As everybody knows, the founder of long-term, intensive psychotherapy was Freud, and in this sense *all* of Freud is worth reading for its historical interest as well as for the innumerable clinical pearls scattered throughout his writings. In my experience, the emphasis on actually reading the works of Freud is diminishing at an accelerated pace. This is *very* unfortunate not only for the loss of clinical knowledge and historical perspective it entails but also for the loss of an outstanding model of scientific writing.

What were Freud's great ideas? Actually in the briefest summary they fall into three categories: The first, depth psychology, forms the basic science of psychotherapy and demands a study of Freud's original work. The validity of these concepts remains open to question by many experimental psychologists and epistemologists (for example, see Ricoeur 1970 and Chessick 1969a, 1974g). Nevertheless his conceptual framework to date remains the only thorough-going and useful one for the practice of intensive psychotherapy besides that of Sullivan (see chapter 12). The second is the psychoanalytic method itself—the whole structure of the psychoanalytic situation including the basic rule of free association and the analysis of resistances and transferences. This is certainly Freud's incontestible discovery and with modifications is the methodological backbone of intensive psychotherapy. The third is the concept of a "school" of psychotherapists. Unfortunately, the present day approach to psychotherapy and the question of who should or should not do psychotherapy and what kind of training they should receive is in a dismal state indeed.

FOUNDATION OF DEPTH PSYCHOLOGY

In my judgment, if Freud had died before 1897 or before the age of forty, he would have achieved at most perhaps a page or two in books on the history of psychiatry. Up to then his work for less than ten years on a theory of the neuroses had culminated with his paper, *The Etiology of Hysteria,* published in 1896. His basic thesis was that hysteria is determined by traumatic experience in childhood, whose memory unconsciously reappears in a symbolic way in the symptoms of the illness. The illness, in turn, can be cured by recalling the memory into consciousness and discharging the associated affect. The sexual aspects of these traumata are stressed and Freud finds, with amazing frequency, that patients have been seduced by adults in their immediate environment and that this is often followed by sexual experience with children of the same age. Though Freud proclaimed this theory as a great discovery, a year later he realized he had been misled by patient fantasies.

Had Freud died at this point, he would have received credit for developing, with the help of Breuer and of his patient Emmy Von N., a method for investigating hysterical symptoms. The method of free association replaced hypnosis. The concepts of resistance and transference which it utilized were known also to hypnotists but poorly understood.

At this point in 1897 at forty-one, Freud took one of those rare and incredible turns in life that might be called a turn towards genius. Perhaps the discovery that his whole theory of hysteria was based on a misleading conception, or the death of his father in 1896, or the midlife crisis (on the midlife crisis see Jacques 1964) led Freud in 1897 to begin his self-analysis through the use of dreams. This courageous step enabled Freud to overcome what Ellenberger (1970) calls his "creative illness" and put depth psychology on a much more solid foundation.

The main tenets of depth psychology are Freud's dream theory and his theory of errors, which represent the first two generalizations of the pattern he had worked out for hysteria. These theories were elaborated simultaneously and presented in two of his best known books, *The Interpretation of Dreams* in 1900 and the *Psychopathology of Everyday Life* in 1901.

It is tempting but not pertinent to this book to discuss further Freud's self analysis. Perhaps he was thinking of St. Augustine's famous dictum: "Seek not abroad, turn back into thyself, for in the inner man dwells the truth" (see chapter 6).

THE INTERPRETATION OF DREAMS

Some biographers insist that *The Interpretation of Dreams,* which appeared when Freud was forty-four, was a failure; others argue it was not. At any rate the writing of this work coincides with Freud's self-analysis. I advise the beginning student to originate his study of Freud with selected chapters of *The Interpretation of Dreams* and with its logical sequel, the famous case of Dora (1905) who was actually analyzed in 1900.

In chapter two of *The Interpretation of Dreams,* Freud demonstrates that a dream fits consistently into the general mental content of an individual and can be interpreted and given meaning. The procedure for doing this, essentially the method of free association, had been developed during his therapeutic work with cases of hysteria and other neuroses.

Chapter three demonstrates the dream as wish fulfillment. Chapter four launches into the concept of distortion in dreams and develops the key principles that follow logically if one accepts the basic premise that every dream fulfills a wish. Thus the concepts of the latent dream and manifest dream, of things being represented by their opposites, and of multiple meanings to dream material are presented. The notion of defense and the idea that ". . . dreams are given their shape in individual human beings by the operation of two psychical forces (or we may describe them as currents or systems); and that one of these forces constructs the wish which is expressed by the dream, while the other exercises a censorship upon this dream-wish and, by the use of that censorship, forcibly brings about a distortion in the expression of the wish" (1900, p. 144). This leads to conclusions regarding the structure of the mental apparatus and forms the connecting link between the formation of a neurosis and the formation of a dream, thereby implying that the procedures involved in the formation of a neurosis also take place in normal people.

In chapter six, Freud introduces the concepts of condensation, multiple meanings, over determination, displacement (both of emphasis or through elements related by association), and plastic representation (the transposition of thoughts into imagery, as in the plastic arts). The whole purpose of chapter six is to help the student translate the manifest dream into the latent dream content just as Freud attempts to translate neurotic symptoms into the repressed infantile wishes. The methodology for investigation and the manner of disguise which is used by the "censor" is identical in both conditions.

Wollheim summarizes the dream theory as follows: "There is a persisting repressed wish, which forms the motive behind the dream. In the course of the day, this wish comes into contact, or forms an association, with a thought or train of thought. This thought has some energy attached to it, independently of this contact, through not having as yet been 'worked over': hence the phrase, the 'residues of the day.' The upshot is that the thought—or an association to it—is revived in sleep, as the proxy of the wish.

The question that remains to be asked about this alliance is Why should it assert itself while we are asleep? The answer is not that sleep is peculiarly well-disposed to the alliance, but that it prefers it to any more naked version of the same forces. If the wish did not express itself in the disguise of the dream, it would disturb sleep. And so we come to the overall function of dreams: they are *the guardians of sleep*" (1971, pp. 70-71).

THE TOPOGRAPHIC THEORY

Chapter seven of *The Interpretation of Dreams* and Freud's paper on "The Unconscious" (1915), written fifteen years later summarize, in an almost too condensed form, the basic concepts of depth psychology. These basic concepts as developed by 1915, are today called the topographic theory (Arlow and Brenner 1964). They are:

1. The system unconscious pertains to the infantile part of the mind; the system preconscious, the adult part.

2. The system unconscious mainly contains wishes and seeks to re-experience the sensations of previous gratifications.

3. The unpleasure principle, later called the pleasure principle by Freud, governs the system unconscious. Accumulated mental energy according to the pleasure principle must be discharged as quickly and fully as possible to bring the system back to the previous resting state. The system preconscious is guided by what Freud eventually calls the reality principle.

4. The system unconscious is oblivious to reality and operates essentially by condensation and displacement of mental energies; mutually contradictory tendencies can exist side by side.

5. In the system unconscious, mental energies are freely mobile.

6. A dynamic interplay exists between the unconscious and the preconscious, so that if a preconscious idea becomes associated with and cathected by an unpleasurable unconscious wish, the preconscious cathexes will be withdrawn, a process known as repression. When the preconscious fails ever to cathect an unconscious wish, Freud called this primal repression; where a preconscious idea, because of its association with a repudiated wish, is decathected, this is called repression. Thus primal repression is a pulling into the unconscious; repression proper is a pushing out from the system preconscious.

7. The topographic theory is not to be thought of as a special theory but as a functional theory.

8. Consciousness is like a sense organ for the perception of psychic qualities. This Kantian notion will be discussed later on when we evaluate the position of Freud in the history of philosophy.

THE SYSTEM UNCONSCIOUS

The famous diagrams in chapter seven of *The Intepretation of Dreams* are worthy of careful study. The idea that psychotherapy can bring the unconscious under the domination of the preconscious is first presented. Other early concepts central to Freud's later philosophical thought are presented. For example, in denoting primary and secondary process thinking, Freud points out that "the primary processes are present in the mental apparatus from the first, while it is only during the course of life that the secondary processes unfold, and come to inhibit and overlay the primary ones; it may even be that their complete domination is not attained until the prime of life. In consequence of the belated appearance of the secondary processes, the core of our being, consisting of unconscious wishful impulses, remains inaccessible to the understanding and inhibition of the preconscious; the part played by the latter is restricted once and for all to directing along the most expedient paths the wishful impulses that arise from the unconscious. These unconscious wishes exercise a compelling force upon all later mental trends, a force which those trends are obliged to fall in with or which they may perhaps endeavor to divert and direct to higher aims" (1900, pp. 603-604).

Thus the *system unconscious* plays the same role in Freud as the *noumena* did in Kant (see chapter 8 and the quotation at beginning of this chapter). Freud writes, "The unconscious is the true psychical reality; in its innermost nature it is as much unknown to us as the reality of the external world, and it is as incompletely presented by the data of consciousness as is the external world by the communications of our sense organs" (1900, p. 613). So in this chapter of *The Interpretation of Dreams,* the whole notion of dynamic psychiatry is set down: the explanation of the symptoms of mental illness on a dynamic basis, as a result of the strengthening and weakening of the various components in the interplay of inner forces, so many of whose effects are hidden from view even while ordinary mental functions are apparently normal. It is the unique brilliance and creative genius of this book that often led Freud to insist that it was, of everything he wrote, his greatest work.

The Psychopathology of Everyday Life (1901) makes a similar extension of Freud's concept of mental functioning to ordinary parapraxes. The famous *Three Essays on the Theory of Sexuality* (1905b) and the case of Little Hans (1909a) which represents a natural extension of these three essays, lay down the basis of Freud's libido theory, which (with modification) became a cornerstone of depth psychology and also formed the basic point of contention with most of the other schools of psychoanalysis that split away from Freud. I will not deal with the details of this theory at any length here as it can be read in summary form (Stafford-Clark 1965) and studied in the original; I have summarized these ideas in *The Technique and Practice of Intensive Psychotherapy* (1974g).

TRANSFERENCE: THE CASE OF DORA

Freud treated an hysterical eighteen-year-old girl named Dora in 1900. He wrote the case up immediately as *A Case of Hysteria* (1905a) after she broke off therapy, making numerous mistakes and some contradictions in the paper about dates and times. This case report, a logical extension of *The Interpretation of Dreams* because it was extensively written in part to demonstrate the use and importance of dream analysis in psychoanalytic work, is worthy of very careful study by the psychotherapist. It presents the first detailed consideration of transference, perhaps Freud's most important discovery.

The case broke up essentially because of the countertransference flounderings of the therapist. Dora was a very vengeful girl. She had sought revenge on her father, on Herr K., and now on Freud for stirring her up sexually. An erotic transference had developed which Freud himself should have foreseen, as he later admitted. This made her angry and resulted in her leaving treatment. In fact, it may be argued against Freud's forced interpretation that the long second dream is probably a resistance dream and is characterized by the desire to dominate the therapy hour. Because of its great importance and because it presents Freud's application of his methods and concepts at the time I will consider this case in some detail.

Dora, an eighteen-year-old girl, was the second in a family of two. She had an older brother nineteen and a half. She could not get along well at all with her mother who was described as having a "hausfrau psychosis" which means that she spent most of her time cooking and cleaning mainly in an effort to get away from any sexual or spontaneous libidinal relationships with her family.

The father is described as being in his late forties, a businessman, rather well-to-do. He had a brother who was a hypochondriacal bachelor and a sister who died of marasmus, seemingly some sort of melancholia. When Dora was six years old, her father became ill with tuberculosis and at that time began an affair with a Frau K. who began the work of nursing him at the sanitorium or resort area where he stayed. Frau K. was married and had two children.

When the patient was eight years old she developed chronic dyspnea. It is noteworthy that she had been suffering from bed wetting previous to the chronic dyspnea attacks, and when the attacks of chronic dyspnea occurred the bed wetting stopped. Some attention had been paid to the bed wetting by the father who had apparently hovered over her bed and made efforts to keep her clean. When the patient was ten years old, the father developed impairment of vision due to a retinal detachment. The etiology of this became apparent when the patient was twelve and the father had a confusional attack which was seen by Freud and diagnosed as a case of taboparesis. There was no question about the luetic origin of the father's symptoms.

At this time, the patient developed two types of symptoms; migraine headaches which disappeared by the time she was sixteen and attacks of nervous coughs which would last from three to five weeks and which continued until the onset of her treatment with Freud. Two years earlier at the age of sixteen the patient was first seen by Freud because these nervous coughs had developed into an aphonia. He proposed psychoanalytic treatment which was refused. When the patient was seventeen, she developed a feverish disorder. Over the next year she steadily worsened. She developed a rather unsociable personality and low spirits and wrote a letter about suicide. She was unable to concentrate and suffered from fainting spells and amnesia episodes in addition to previous symptoms of aphonia and nervous cough. At this point she was brought in for treatment to Freud. Study of the case revolves mainly around the analysis of the major symptoms, namely the nervous cough and the associated aphonia.

In the psychological history, we find that the patient became quite friendly with Frau K., who was carrying on an affair with Dora's father. There was quite an intimate relationship between them which continued until the patient was sixteen when she accused Herr K. of making a sexual advance toward her. She slapped Herr K. in the face and ran off but did not tell anyone of the sexual advance for two days. It was nine months later after this accusation (whether the episode actually occurred is not too clear) that she was put to bed with the feverish disorder.

Deeper in the psychological history, one finds that, at the age of fourteen, Herr K. had passionately kissed Dora on the lips. She reacted to this with a sensation of disgust and a feeling of pressure on the thorax. She formed a phobia and had to avoid walking past any man who she thought was in any kind of state of sexual excitement or affectionate conversation.

Freud writes "It is worth remarking that we have here three symptoms—the disgust, the sensation of pressure on the upper part of the body, and the avoidance of men engaged in affectionate conversation—all of them derived from a single experience. . . . The disgust is the symptom of repression in the erotogenic oral zone, which, as we shall hear, had been overindulged in Dora's infancy by the habit of sensual sucking [Dora was a passionate thumb sucker]. The pressure of the erect member probably led to an analogous change in the corresponding female organ, the clitoris; and the excitation of this second erotogenic zone was referred by a process of displacement to the simultaneous pressure against the thorax and became fixed there. Her avoidance of men who might possibly be in the state of sexual excitement follows the mechanism of a phobia, its purpose being to safeguard her against any revival of the repressed perception" (1905a, pp. 30-31). Thus, all three of the symptoms serve as defenses against sexual wishes.

Another aspect of the case touched upon is the so-called "homosexual" relationship between Dora and Frau K. Dora often spoke of Frau K.'s "adorable white body," and they spent much time talking about sexual matters in an intimate way. Although Freud was not aware of it at the time, we might understand this as really being a defense against Dora's deeper infantile wishes to suck at the white breast of Frau K. Both the phobia and the "homosexual" relationship illustrate the oral aspects of the unconscious polymorphous perverse sexual wishes of the patient who develops hysteria.

The actual analysis of the case hinges around the interpretation of the dream in the second part of Freud's paper. The dynamics of the case were this: Dora was confronted with frank sexuality by Herr K., and she definitely responded to this with feelings of sexual love towards Herr K. However, at the same time, Dora was a girl who was very vengeful and angry at all men, considering them evil and undependable. Because of this, she could not give in to her love impulses towards Herr K. She had an incapacity for meeting real erotic demands which Freud explains is one of the most essential features of a neurosis, especially of hysteria.

The confrontation with real erotic feelings therefore caused a conflict in this girl, which led to a regression. The specific type of regression made sense in terms of the conflict and it appeared in the dream. The dream represented an appeal in an infantile way to the father to help her repress her erotic impulses just as he had helped her once before when she was an infant to keep from bed wetting. She appeals to the father in her fantasies to save her from Herr K. who had aroused her sexual feelings directly.

We see therefore how a present conflict has caused the patient (a) to regress back to an earlier level of satisfaction where she did get some pleasure out of her relationship with her father and (b) to call upon him to help her repress her sexual impulses in the present situation toward the man and thus solve the conflict. The price of such regression is the revival of oedipal love for the father and incestuous guilt. So now the patient is forced to erect defenses against the oedipal love. These defenses, in the case of Dora, are many. For example, there is the compromise formation of identification with Frau K. Whenever Frau K. has intercourse with her father, the patient identifies with this and gains a vicarious gratification of her love impulses toward her father which lessen the energy cathexis on these impulses. One also sees projection in Dora's constant rumination that her father and all men are bad and that she hates them because of their sexual interest in her. The defensive meaning of this projection is that it is not she who has sexual impulses toward her father but it is her father and all men who are bad because they have sexual interest in women.

The major defense that Dora used against her infantile sexual longings toward her father was conversion. In order to understand why she used this defense we have to understand Dora's infantile sexual fantasy about intercourse. Intercourse was seen as an oral act, namely fellatio, and the fantasy was that babies are born when the mother sucks the father's penis.

The actual analysis of the conversion shows the meaning of the symptoms. Dora's attacks of aphonia are traced to the absence of Herr K. They turn out to be just the reverse of Frau K.'s behavior. Whenever Herr K. was home, Frau K. would be sick as a way of avoiding having to have sexual relations with him. Dora's sickness or aphonia on the surface level meant, "If I were his wife I should love him in quite a different way; I should be ill from longing when he is away and well from joy when he was home again." The deeper meaning of the aphonia, which is connected to the attacks of nervous cough which began around the time the patient's father had his attack of lues, lies in the fantasy of fellatio with her father. Freud explains, "The conclusion was inevitable that with her spasmodic cough—which, as is usual, was referred for its exciting stimulus to a tickling in her throat—she pictured to herself a scene of sexual gratification *per os* between the two people whose love affair occupied her mind so incessantly. A very short time after she had passively accepted this explanation, her cough vanished—which fitted in very well with my view, but I do not wish to lay too much stress upon this development, since her cough had so often before disappeared spontaneously" (1905a, p. 48). Freud also notes both the identification here with mother and Frau K. that Dora is in the passive situation i.e., sucking. Whether this sucking refers to deeper homosexual strivings or oral strivings or not is a matter of controversy. Certainly it is not hard to go from Dora sucking on the penis to Dora sucking on the white breast.

In summary, Dora, confronted with actual sexuality by Herr K., was unable to respond with erotic feelings. She summoned up help for the repression of her sexual impulses by fleeing from the conflict through a regression to infantile situations. She regressed to the infantile oedipal conflict summoning up her love for her father to help her repress her love for a mature man. She gained secondary gratification by developing a serious illness which forced her father to separate from Frau K. who really stood for the mother. At the same time, she paid for this regression by having to erect defenses against unacceptable oedipal longings. The main defense was conversion. The conversion symptoms, a nervous cough and aphonia, represented a substitute gratification through the tickling of the throat and through the need for care. They also represented a punishment: the unpleasant nature of cough and hoarseness is apparent. Conversion was accompanied by the fantasy gratification of fellatio with father, and by oedipal identification with the mother which provided homosexual gratification at a deeper level, perhaps at a deepest level fantasying sucking on the breast. Through the conversion symptom, the psychological conflict was converted into a physical conflict thus lessening anxiety about unacceptable oedipal wishes and giving in distorted, symbolized form some gratification to these wishes. It alleviated the guilt about the wishes by the punishment of having the symptoms.

A follow-up on the case of Dora was published by Deutsch, who described for us one of the most repulsive hysterics he ever met:

In the first interview where the patient was seen about twenty years after she had broken off treatment with Freud, she continued to complain of ear noises, dizziness, and attacks of migraine. She then started a tirade about her husband's indifference, about her sufferings, and how unfortunate her marital life had been. She felt her only son had begun to neglect her. He often stayed out late at night and she suspected he had become interested in girls. She always waited listening until he came home. She expressed a great amount of hostile feelings toward her husband especially her disgust with marital sex life. Dora's fate took the course that Freud had predicted twenty-four years earlier after the three months analysis with her. She clung to her son with the same reproachful demands she made on her husband who had died tortured by her vengeful behavior. (1957, pp. 159-167)

THE OTHER FAMOUS CASE HISTORIES

The model for all psychoanalytic therapy of phobias in children is "Analysis of Phobia in a Five-Year-Old Boy" (1909a). Guided by the material produced by the boy, although Freud actually directly observed him only once, the analysis followed definite steps as it proceeded from one level to another.

A five-year-old boy suddenly refused to go on the street because he was afraid of horses. His unwillingness to leave the house, where he seemed contented, happy, and fear-free, either alone or accompanied, was an attempt to avoid his feelings of fear.

The fear of horses consisted of two parts: a fear that a horse might fall down and a fear that a horse might bite him. The boy recognized and could discuss the former with greater clarity and ease than he could the latter which indicates that the latter was the more important nucleus of the phobia. It should be noted that there is a reality element to the fear that a horse might bite him. Horses do bite, but such occurrences are so infrequent that a child usually does not consider them.

These two fears were projected expressions of the boy's conflict in his feelings about his father. He was jealous and hostile toward the father and toward his younger sister and wished that he could bite them both and that they would both fall down or die. This aggressive hostility was the result of his strong attachment to his mother, which made him desire to possess her wholly himself, without having to share her with anyone, and to obtain from her not only all the physical manifestations of love and tenderness which he already had but also all that she gave to his two rivals.

Hans feared these hostile feelings for two reasons. He was afraid that if his father knew about these hostile wishes, he would become angry. Being bigger and stronger, he would then inflict on Hans by way of punishment the same misfortune as the boy wished on him. He loved his father and knew that if he injured or killed him, he would not have any father to love him. In the face of the fear of injury at his father's hands and loss of his loving care, he attempted to repress his hostile feelings and was successful in that they did not seem to exist toward the father but only in a confused fantasy about horses.

Freud calls attention to three important points. First, Hans' anxiety dared show itself boldly in a phobia because he had been brought up by understanding parents, and so the anxiety situation was not too severely complicated by a guilty conscience or a fear of punishment. Second, the turning point of the case—the beginning of the entrance of unconscious material into consciousness—came with the interpretation to the boy that he was afraid of his father because he cherished jealous and hostile wishes against him. The boy's realization that the father knew and yet was not angry allowed him to produce his unconscious thoughts and fantasies. Third, the motive for the illness, the gain the boy obtained by being ill, was that his illness allowed him to stay with his mother and thus gave him an excuse whereby he could avoid the conflict between his affection for and his hostility toward his father. This point is highly important, Freud says, because it often forms a marked resistance to treatment and may necessitate lengthy discussion with the child at some point during the course of treatment.

The case of the Rat Man (1909b) was used by Freud to present a great deal of material on the obsessive compulsive neurosis, but also contains a remarkable transference to Freud, and at times may confuse the reader. Some have argued that Freud's acting out in the countertransference rather than Freud's interpretations provided a corrective emotional experience which was crucial in the case of the Rat Man. There was a definite contrast between Freud's behavior and that of the Rat Man's rather kind but hot-tempered father. Symbolic and intellectual material is much emphasized in the exposition, whereas actually the transference and countertransference aspects are the key to the treatment.

The Case of Schreber (1911a) is not a clinical case history at all, but the analysis of Schreber's diary in which Freud presents his well-known theory of paranoia. It is skillfully written although the theory of paranoia presented remains controversial.

The case of the Wolf Man (1918) is perhaps the most interesting of the cases from the human interest point of view. A recent volume edited by M. Gardiner (1971) presents the whole fascinating story of the Wolf Man, who became a kind of lay critic and mascot for the entire psychoanalytic movement. This volume is well worth reading for its human interest about Freud and the psychoanalytic movement as well as giving some insight into the sociologic conditions under which this movement flowered. The case itself was written to illustrate the crucial importance of the castration complex, early seduction, primal scene, and various phases of infantile sexuality in the development of neurosis. It is a superb example of Freud's literary style but the case interpretation itself is subject to considerable argument. The human kindness of Freud for this patient as he suffered the vicissitudes of the catastrophic historical changes going on in Europe is very moving. Here again Freud's behavior serves as a model for the psychotherapist.

THE STRUCTURAL THEORY

By 1913 it would have seemed that the psychoanalytic theory of depth psychology had achieved its completion. However, even to the surprise of Freud's followers, a great metamorphosis was still to occur. This time the new teaching was not contained in a single book but in a series of articles and short monographs published by Freud over a period of ten years. I have dealt at length with the topographic theory because it tends to be somewhat neglected in some reviews of Freud's work, whereas the structural theory developed after 1913 is in essence the theory that is still used today. A comparison of the structural and topographic theories, very well written and most worthwhile, is to be found in Arlow and Brenner (1964).

Freud's great new creative surge begins in the 1914 paper *On Narcissism*. This is the first paper following the *Three Essays on*

Sexuality where he modifies his instinct theory. (Freud's instinct theory actually went through four phases and caused him a great deal of difficulty and heavy thinking, but there is not much point in summarizing these phases in this book. The reader is referred to Bibring 1963). The difficult paper on narcissism and the series of five papers that followed it were written essentially to present Freud's notion of metapsychology. In fact, the five papers were conceived of as chapters in a book entitled *Introduction to Metapsychology,* and they were written with an amazing burst of creative energy in six weeks during the spring of 1915. Perhaps even more remarkably, he wrote five *more* essays in the next six weeks, which he subsequently destroyed. Again in *Beyond the Pleasure Principle,* an attempt is made to give metapsychology its final shape. The notion of the *repetition compulsion,* of the utmost importance to psychotherapists, is here presented and this is the most original practical contribution in the book. From it Freud also derives his concepts of the death instinct and primary masochism which are still controversial.

It is best to begin study of this phase of Freud's work with one of his great masterpieces *The Ego and the Id* (1923), which describes the "three harsh masters" that the ego has to deal with—reality, the id, and the superego. The concept of the id was borrowed from Groddeck (1961) and the concept of the superego seems closest to Nietzsche in *The Geneology of Morals* (see chapter 10) but this is a matter of dispute. Freud did not acknowledge a debt to Nietzsche although he did acknowledge his debt to Groddeck. With the publication of *The Ego and the Id,* ego psychology became the predominant interest of depth psychology. The final touches were put on this theory in 1926 with the publication of *Inhibitions, Symptoms, and Anxiety* (1926). This work, which some have called one of Freud's most difficult books, was written partly to be a refutation of Rank's birth trauma theory and contains the famous signal theory of anxiety.

As a consequence of all this, the focus in long-term, intensive psychotherapy shifted permanently from the analysis of the instinctual forces to the analysis of the ego. Ellenberger writes, "Analysis of defenses would necessarily uncover anxiety, and the task of the analyst was now to dispel the excess of anxiety and to strengthen the ego, so that it could face reality and control the pressure of drives and superego" (1970).

THE TECHNIQUE OF
PSYCHOANALYTIC PSYCHOTHERAPY

I have already characterized Freud's second category of great ideas as the development of the technique of psychotherapy. This development involves such matters as the method of free association, already described in his early book with Breuer (1893–1895), the use of dream interpretation, and the phenomenon of countertransference as illustrated on *On the Future Prospects of Psychoanalytic Therapy* (Freud 1910a) and *Wild Analysis* (Freud 1910c). This led to his early ideas on the training of therapists and to his insistence on setting up an organization to teach analysis and qualify analysts. The famous specific *Papers on Technique* (1911-1915) require a thorough and meticulous study. Here the dynamics of transference, the notion of free floating attention, the debatable concept of the therapist as neutral mirror, the analogy of the therapist to a surgeon, as well as the focus of therapy on the transference neurosis is presented. I will not review these concepts in detail as I have already done so in two previous books (1969a, 1974c).

In *Beyond the Pleasure Principle* (1920) mentioned above, Freud reinterpreted the meaning of transference as being a manifestation of the repetition compulsion; this book should be reviewed for the light it throws on psychotherapeutic technique, especially in section three. All in all, *Beyond the Pleasure Principle* is a monumental book, in which the various trends of Freud's metapsychological, philosophical, and practical methodological thinking all come into confluence. This book is more intelligible *after* the other works in depth psychology and the papers on technique have been reviewed.

A few other later papers are masterpieces and have important ramifications for the technique and practice of intensive psychotherapy. "Some Character Types Met With in Psychoanalytic Work" (Freud 1916) discusses such cases as those wrecked by success and criminals suffering from a sense of guilt. "A Child is Being Beaten" (Freud 1919a) introduces a common kind of fantasy in many patients. "Lines of Advance in Psychoanalytic Therapy" (Freud 1919b) deals with the subject of the state of abstinence during psychotherapy. Freud disavowed Ferenczi's innovation of the active role of the analyst; he protested against the idea of the analyst trying to shovel out emotional gratifications to the patient. Here he writes that analysis should be conducted in an atmosphere of abstinence, and he started off a controversy and debate that is still going on. This has been summarized in previous publications (Chessick 1969a, 1974g).

To understand Freud's methodology, one must also review carefully certain papers of his old age. There are to be found in Vol. 23 of the *Standard Edition* and include the pessimistic paper "Analysis Terminable and Interminable" (Freud 1937a), "Constructions in Analysis" (Freud 1937b), and the second part of the unfinished *Outline of Psychoanalysis* (Freud 1940).

FREUD'S PHILOSOPHICAL FOUNDATIONS

"A Note Upon the Mystic Writing Pad" (Freud 1925c) and "Negation" (Freud 1925b), show the important relationship of Freud's thought to Kantian philosophy. The two foundations upon which Freud's scientific philosophy rests, according to Levi (1959) are: "(1) a theory of representative perception, and (2) a determinism so pervasive as to encompass all mental phenomena (including those previously considered universally as both 'meaningless' and 'irrational'). Freud never doubts the assumptions of realistic epistemology concerning the world. Reality is objective. It is that which exists outside us and independently of us, and the adequacy of scientific knowledge is measurable by the degree to which it corresponds to reality."

In the course of his lifetime Freud imperceptibly passed from the epistemology of Locke to the epistemology of Kant. Beginning with a representative theory of perception as described above, he is, in his investigations of man's inner life, led toward the postulation of a psychical apparatus which is not accessible to direct perception. Levi writes: "For what is the unconscious but a kind of psychological *ding-an-sich,* a thing-in-itself, metaphysically ultimate and causally efficacious, but beyond the reach of immediate perceptual knowledge? At the end of his life Freud arrives at a Kantian phenomenalism, a distinction between "appearance" and "reality" somewhat at variance with the naive realism and easy scientific optimism of his youth."

As Freud (1920) admits, he was unwillingly steering his course into the harbor of Schopenhauer's philosophy but insists he quickly steered it out again. Although there is a similarity of the sombre realism in the two men, Freud sticks implacably with a dualism that Schopenhauer does not present. Levi points out that the second chapter of *Civilization and Its Discontents* (Freud 1930) appears like a condensed version of the last two books of the *World as Will and Idea,* but Freud offers us no metaphysical explanation like Schopenhauer's. There is a remarkable parallel between the intuitive insights of Nietzsche and the more well developed insights of Freud. Freud's duality of the primary and the secondary processes is closely related to Nietzsche's Dionysian and Apollinian concepts. Nietzsche's famous writing on the pale criminal echoes Freud's paper mentioned above on some character types met in psychoanalytic work. Many other aspects of the superego and the ego at work are described in flashes by Nietzsche. Finally, we return to Plato's ancient insight that sickness in the mind is the result of conflict, and harmony and integration are the health of the soul.

Chapter 12

Mental Illness as
Human Interpersonal Process

Philosophers of science have repeatedly demonstrated that more than one theoretical construction can always be placed upon a given collection of data. History of science indicates that, particularly in the early developmental stages of a new paradigm, it is not even very difficult to invent such alternates. . . . So long as the tools a paradigm supplies continue to be capable of solving the problems it defines, science moves fastest and penetrates most deeply through confident employment of those tools.

The act of judgment that leads scientists to reject a previously accepted theory is always based upon more than a comparison of that theory with the world. The decision to reject one paradigm is always simultaneously the decision to accept another, and the judgment leading to that decision involves the comparison of both paradigms with nature and with each other.

Thomas Kuhn, *The Structure of Scientific Revolutions*

H. S. SULLIVAN

Harry Stack Sullivan (1892-1949), who died prematurely at the age of fifty-seven, offered the first and so far the only comprehensive and possibly viable alternative paradigm of mental illness to that of Freud. The question of whether to abandon the Freudian paradigm and accept Sullivan's remains unsettled. In this chapter, I will delineate some of the crucial points of Sullivan's theoretical system, indicate his great ideas, and offer a certain comparison to the Freudian paradigm. It must be made clear from the beginning that because of the basic difference in the orientation of the observer, *no compromise* is possible between the two paradigms as their originators conceived of them. They are profoundly opposed, and although it is possible to keep both in mind and to shift back and forth in one's thinking about patients from one to the other, it is not possible to adhere consistently to both at the same time.

Sullivan was unquestionably the greatest American psychiatrist. Born in Norwich, N.Y., of Irish parents, he belonged to a Roman Catholic family, the only people of that faith in a Yankee, protestant community. Sullivan was the only surviving child (two other children died in infancy) and he has been repeatedly described as a lonely and rather isolated person from his earliest childhood. His mother was a complaining semi-invalid with chronic resentment at the humble family situation. Sullivan apparently got little warmth from her. According to Clara Thompson, he was only able to establish rapport with his father after his mother died.

Sullivan's theories arose from a profound study of the schizoid and schizophrenic. At first he tried to adhere to the classical Freudian model but soon decided it was gravely defective. At Saint Elizabeths Hospital in Washington D.C., he came under the influence of William A. White. Simultaneously, during staff conferences at Johns Hopkins University's Phipps Clinic, he became familiar with Adolph Meyer's psychiatry, especially his approach to schizophrenia. Sullivan became the director of clinical research at Sheppard and Enoch Pratt Hospital in Baltimore in 1925, and his papers from 1924 onwards demonstrate his new ideas, in which interpersonal affairs came to be regarded as paramount in the etiology of mental illness. Mullahy writes: "Intrapsychic processes were not, and could not be, separated from the social history and actual, current living of the individual. To claim otherwise, Sullivan thought, is as erroneous—and therapeutically disastrous—as to claim that one can walk without a ground to walk upon. Of course, Freud never did—and never could—completely ignore interpersonal relations. But his study always focuses on intrapsychic occurrences as if they had a life of their own" (1970).

His major work with schizophrenics was during the period at Sheppard and Enoch Pratt Hospital. Although he left in 1930 for private practice, he continued to lecture there until 1933. During that time he set up his famous experimental ward for the treatment of schizophrenia.

He moved to New York in 1931 and entered private practice, working primarily with obsessional patients, who suffered from a pathological condition that long intrigued him because of a possible relationship to schizophrenic disorders. In 1938 he left New York and returned to Washington, becoming a consulting psychiatrist and supervisor for many psychiatrists and clinical psychologists in the New York, Washington, and Baltimore areas. He was one of the founders of the William Alanson White Psychiatric Foundation, established in Washington in 1933 by several former associates of Dr. White. The Foundation led to the Washington School for Psychiatry in 1936 and the journal *Psychiatry* in 1937 of which he eventually became the editor. The Washington School of Psychiatry became known as an important center for training in Sullivanian theory, but according to Mullahy, it has generally reverted back to orthodox psychoanalysis since his death.

Sullivan became increasingly interested in international affairs, and at the time of his death in Paris in 1949, he was participating in the UNESCO project studying tensions affecting international understanding and war.

Sullivan was a brilliant yet difficult and very complex individual, and he presents many special problems to the student. One of the most striking of these is that Sullivan actually never wrote a book aside from *Personal Psychopathology*—a manuscript with a curious, ambiguous title that was never published in his lifetime. The various books published under his name after his death are essentially compendiums of his lecture tapes and notes, and I will indicate as I go along in this chapter the relative strength and weaknesses of these volumes. In addition, Sullivan *continuously and rapidly changed* his theories, and he had a need (arising from complex motivations) to completely reformulate the language of Freudian psychodynamics.

The major popular expositor of Sullivan's theories has been Patrick Mullahy. In *Oedipus Myth and Complex* he presents a worthwhile summary of Sullivan's views; in a very long later book, *Psychoanalysis and Interpersonal Psychiatry* he gives a detailed exposition of Sullivan's views. In my opinion the brief review is best for the beginner, and then the works of Sullivan should be read directly. Elkind (1972) and Salzman (Freedman and Kaplan 1972) present useful brief reviews of Sullivan's theories.

Sullivan's first personal analytic experience, in 1916, consisted of about seventy-five hours with a Chicago psychoanalyst, whose identity is not known for certain. In 1930, he began formal psychoanalytical training in New York City with Clara Thompson, a student of Ferenczi.

The first ten years of his psychiatric career, from about 1920 to 1930, were spent in studying schizophrenic conditions. This study convinced Sullivan of the interpersonal nature of the psychiatric field. The next ten years (1931-1940) spent in office practice with the "closely related substitutive states, obsessional and other," enabled him to refine and consolidate his earlier insights. His last eight years, Sullivan spent largely teaching and supervising and in consultations with colleagues. At the time of his death, he was still actively elaborating and refining his theoretical views. Sullivan's attitude toward his work is revealed in *The Psychiatric Interview:*

> As I shall presently suggest, there is no fun in psychiatry. If you try to get fun out of it, you pay a considerable price for your unjustifiable optimism. If you do not feel equal to the headaches that psychiatry induces, you are in the wrong business. It is work—work the like of which I do not know. True, it ordinarily does not require vast physical exertion, but it does require a high degree of alertness to a sometimes very rapidly shifting field of signs which are remarkably complex in themselves and in their relations. And the necessity for promptness of response to what happens proves in the course of a long day to be very tiring indeed. It is curious, but there are data that suggest that the more complicated the field to which one must attend, the more rapidly fatigue sets in. (1954, p. 10)

Another example of his inimitable personal style comes from *Personal Psychopathology:*

> It has been said that from those who cannot forget the religion of their adolescence there comes two classes of beings; those who are able to follow the olden ways—the priests, who know; and those who are not content—the philosophers, who seek. The philo-

sopher who finds, or who grow weary of searching becomes a priest. . . . I know that many a student of personality has grown weary of searching, and has made a religion of what little or nothing he has found. The quest for certainty in the world of personality is an adventure on which all adolescents embark, from which but few travelers return with that contentment born of achievement, and in the course of which many reach the Isle of Circe, and remain. (1972, p. 327)

Only reading Sullivan himself reveals the quality, subtlety, and complexity of his thinking. He was less interested in goals than in human process; less interested in developing a system and solving high order abstractions than in developing testable hypotheses. He credited Freud, Meyer, and W. A. White as the important influences on his intellectual life. The contributions of Freud and Meyer are obvious. It was his association with White that encouraged him to do clinical research with schizophrenics and to develop his own ideas. White emphasized the nonmedical aspects of psychiatric problems and Sullivan credits him with envisioning the synthesis of medicine with other disciplines having to do with understanding the social situations in which man has always found himself. This lead to Sullivan's effort to produce a multi-disciplinary science of man or, as some have called it, a fusion of psychiatry with social science (Sullivan 1964).

In addition, Mullahy has correctly pointed out that Sullivan was possibly influenced by Dewey, the great philosopher of interpersonal or social relations. He writes: "I surmise that Sullivan read some of Dewey's work though I cannot recall a single reference to him. When I broached this matter to Sullivan, in 1945, he became evasive and would not let me pin him down" (1970). Since Sullivan did not openly acknowledge any debt to Dewey, I will not go further into the matter in this chapter (see chapter 19). Suffice it to say that there *are* obvious parallels.

SULLIVAN'S ATTEMPT TO
MAKE PSYCHIATRY "SCIENTIFIC"

I would introduce the beginner to Sullivan's ideas through chapter 4 of *Schizophrenia as a Human Process,* (1962) "The Common Field of Research and Clinical Psychiatry." This is one of the truly great classic papers of psychiatric literature, and it defines the starting point for Sullivan's dissatisfaction with Freud. He objects that Freud's conceptions cannot be regarded as true scientific hypotheses regardless of their therapeutic utility because it is impossible to construct crucial experiments to test them. He points out that after "discovering" the truth of some basic generalization, the enthusiast sees no evidence but that of Freud's correctness from then on: "His disciples rediscover and rediscover his genius; they amass 'evidence' in support of his theory. But if you sift the whole business you find that there is nothing. You must begin all over from the beginning. The most elementary canon of science has been ignored: his data are wholly subjective or so tainted with his preconceptions as to be useless" (1962). It is tempting to quote this chapter at great length; in quick summary it represents Sullivan's insistence on beginning at the beginning with the meticulous observation of schizophrenic patients in a clinical setting, and it may be fairly said that from 1925 to 1930 this is precisely what Sullivan set out to do.

In order to keep psychiatry "scientific," Sullivan insisted that although we were greatly interested in what transpired on the inside of an individual we could only study the individual in terms of his interaction with others. Thus the main focus for Sullivan's study was the field of interpersonal relations—how one person behaved toward another, how each person's behavior was affected by the behavior (both overt and covert) of the other, and the reported subjective experiences of each. The process was greatly enhanced when the therapist was one of the participants in the field for then the science of psychotherapy became a transaction between the therapist who was a participant-observer and a patient who was demonstrating in the therapy situation his typical interpersonal relationships. Sullivan argued that our sticking strictly with these observable phenomena could lead to theories and concepts that would be more operational and verifiable and thus more valid as tools for scientific investigation.

Salzman (Freedman and Kaplan 1972) points out that Sullivan's theories were congenial to social scientists because they stayed close to the traditional scientific methodology and because he emphasized the social and cultural context in which personality develops. Salzman feels this makes Sullivan the paradigm of the ego psychologist, and that one of his greatest contributions was to focus the direction of psychiatric research and thought on the ego. Eldred puts it more formally: "His concept of the interpersonal field as a source of solid evidence provided a generation of psychiatrists and behavioral scientists with the promise of testing psychological and sociological theories against behavioral and clinical observations. In short, he provided a methodological basis for the subsequent growth of ego-psychology, social psychology, and cultural anthropology. His methodological concepts had intellectual impact upon behavioral science, which is perhaps as important in retrospect as his making the understanding of schizophrenia a respectable pursuit for psychiatrists" (1972).

For almost every psychological concept Sullivan introduces new terms to guard the reader against misunderstandings based on preconceptions carried over from different usage in other schools of thought. Unfortunately, such a plethora of idiosyncratic terms makes it difficult for the reader to call upon his past psychological knowledge in a positive understanding of the new position. Munroe's reaction is not unusual: "I am not alone in feeling—when reading Sullivan—as if I were floundering not in a morass but on the precarious summit of a brilliant display of fireworks" (1955). Sullivan's fundamental concept of *dynamism* is illustrative. He describes the dynamisms "of interest to the psychiatrist" as "the relatively enduring patterns of energy transformation which recurrently characterize the interpersonal rela-tions—the functional interplay of persons and personifications, personal signs, personal abstractions, and personal attributions—which make up the distinctively human sort of being" (1953). These relatively enduring dynamisms arise out of the interaction in interpersonal situations, and they are continually modified by interpersonal relations. For example, the extremely important self dynamism is a construct built out of the child's interpersonal experience: "The self is said to be made up of reflected appraisals" (1947). For a detailed description of the self dynamism or the self system see *The Technique and Practice of Intensive Psychotherapy* (Chessick 1974g). One of the most important aspects of Sullivan's concept of dynamism is the corollary that rather than emphasizing a certain fixed and immutable set of dynamisms formed by the first few years of life, Sullivan sees the personality as continuously showing changing manifestations in reaction to the various interpersonal situations in which it is found.

The interpersonal field is made up of the interaction of a variety of dynamisms of two or more organisms. Some of these dynamisms are *conjunctive* (for example, the need for intimacy) and lead to an integration of the situation, with the resolution or the reduction of tension. Others, which involve anxiety, are *disjunctive* and lead to disintegration of the situation. The self dynamism is essentially an anti-anxiety system according to Sullivan. It maintains felt interpersonal security and contains "sub-dynamisms" many of which overlap, such as the oral dynamism or dynamism of lust which manifests "concomitant activity."

Thus Sullivan felt that the concept of a unique personal individuality is a pernicious illusion, because it must always escape the methods of science. Sullivan did *not* deny either that each person is a unique individual, or the uniquely felt experience of being an individual. He denied that these conceptions have any usefulness for the study of psychiatry and the science of man. The personality studied by the science of man, according to Sullivan, is the series of dynamisms in which persons become personal only through relationships with other people and not by the way of their unique individuality.

SULLIVAN'S FOUNDATION IN KANT

The parallel with Kant is quite obvious here. Thus for example Kant argues that we can know and study only phenomena but never the real *noumena* which lie behind them; we can deal publicly only with the manifestations of the noumena as they present themselves to us in the phenomena of the sensory manifold. Similarly, Sullivan argues that the unique inner self can never be the subject matter of science and he insists that we can study publicly only the personality as it manifests itself in the human behavior of interpersonal situations. He writes: "Psychiatry, instead, is the study of processes that involve or go on between people. The field of psychiatry is the field of interpersonal relations, under any and all circumstances in which these relations exist. It was seen that *a personality* can never be isolated from the complex of interpersonal relations in which the person lives and has his being" (1947). The unique individual personality that a person feels is what Sullivan calls the private mode of being, which cannot be a matter for the method of science. Thus the science of psychiatry is interested in the public mode of being or the individual's "relative adequacy and appropriateness of action in interpersonal relations, which constitute extraordinary success, average living, or mental disorder" (1947). Sullivan in some sense may be said to be amending and expanding Kant's theory. He begins with the sensory manifold as contained in Spearman's concept of "sentience." But he points out that this primary data of sensation is experienced by human beings not in one but in three modes which are primarily inner elaborations of events.

The prototaxic mode is characteristic of infancy and some psychotic states. In this mode, the infant barely distinguishes between himself and the outer world and external events are perceived in a primitive dim manner. There is no organization and no differentiation.

The parataxic mode is founded on the development of the self dynamism and the developing capacity to become aware of essential differences between the infant and the world around him. Experiences are differentiated, and they exist side by side without being logically distinguished, reflected upon, or compared. This seems to resemble Freud's notion of primary process thought. The parataxic mode of experience is autistic, magical, arbitrary and not checked or tested against reality.

The syntaxic mode is characterized by full appreciation of the logical interrelatedness of experience and seems to be the same as Freud's secondary process mature thought.

These distinctions are very important to clinicians. For example, the psychotic is thought to regress to the prototaxic mode of experience. Freud's notion of transference is renamed, expanded, and changed to the phrase parataxic distortion. Parataxic distortions are not, as transference reactions, repetitions of earlier one-to-one relationships, although they may include these, but are manifestations of the total interpersonal relationships of the person. They are not primarily of sexual etiology but rather the result of anxiety-laden experiences with significant people, and these parataxic distortions come not only from early childhood, but also from experiences with people later in life.

HEALING THROUGH PSYCHOTHERAPY

Sullivan's whole notion of cure consists basically of the therapist's participating in an interpersonal relationship with the patient, observing the parataxic distortions, and helping the patient to dissolve them. This leads to "an *expanding of the self* to such final effect that the patient as known to himself is much the same person as the patient behaving with others. This is *psychiatric cure"* (1947).

Conceptions of Modern Psychiatry, which represents a series of lectures presented in 1939 and published in 1940 in the journal *Psychiatry,* is probably the best basic presentation of Sullivan's ideas, but it must be read quite closely. In this book Sullivan specifically denies the existence of the death instinct and introduces one of his most important ideas. He writes: ". . . personality tends toward the state that we call mental health or interpersonal adjustive success, handicaps by way of acculturation notwithstanding. The basic direction of the organism is forward. Regardless of the warp incorporated in the self, the psychiatrist, given sufficient insight and skill may expect favorable changes to ensue from his study of the patient's situation" (1947).

The Psychiatric Interview consists of two lecture series which Sullivan gave in 1944 and again in 1945. It has perhaps the most immediate appeal to the beginner. It contains a clear statement of Sullivan's notion of therapy: "The brute fact is that man is so extraordinarily adaptive that, given any chance of making a reasonably adequate analysis of the situation, he is quite likely to stumble into a series of experiments which will gradually approximate more successful living, . . . work toward uncovering those factors which are concerned in the person's recurrent mistakes, and which lead to his taking ineffective and inappropriate action. There is no necessity to do more."

The Interpersonal Theory of Psychiatry (1953) represents Sullivan's last complete statement of his views. They are based on a series of lectures in the Washington School of Psychiatry in 1946 and 1947. This very difficult text emphasizes certain basic postulates as the foundation for all experience, and it refers to the central role of anxiety in human development. Briefly the postulates are (1) that man is basically biological but distinguished from plants and animals by the fact that human life requires interchange with an environment which includes culture, (2) that everyone is much more simply human than otherwise, and anomalous interpersonal situations are a function of differences in the relative maturity of the persons concerned, (3) that there are various human developmental "epochs" or "eras" (see Chessick 1974g), and the basic emphasis is on *anxiety* in the formation of the self system and its subsequent functioning and modifications.

EMPATHY AND LOVE

In *Conceptions of Modern Psychiatry* he introduces the crucial notion of empathic linkage: "Long before there are signs of any understanding of emotional expression there is evidence of this emotional contagion or communion. This feature of the infant-mother configuration is of great importance for an understanding of acculturation or cultural conditioning to which I have referred" (1947). Due to the empathic linkage, for example, the reaction of the parent to the satisfaction-response of the infant communicates good feelings to the infant, and thus he learns this response has power.

The whole theory of the self dynamism and interpersonal relations hinges on the disruptive effect of anxiety, which is also communicated through empathic linkage. The tension of anxiety, when present in the mothering one, induces anxiety in the infant although Sullivan writes that it is "thoroughly obscure" how this happens.

The tension called out in the mothering one by the manifest needs of the infant Sullivan labels tenderness; furthermore, "a generic group of tensions in the infant, the relief of which requires cooperation by the person who acts in the mothering role, can be called need for tenderness" (1953). That the vicissitudes of tenderness and anxiety in the mothering one form the basic influence on the earliest pre-verbal development of the self system is one of Sullivan's greatest contributions.

Also vital to the discussion of anxiety and tenderness is the appearance of the capacity to love, which "ordinarily first involves one of one's own sex. The boy finds a chum who is a boy, the girl finds a chum who is a girl. When this has happened, there follows in its wake a great increase in the consensual validation of symbols, of symbol operations, and of information, data about life and the world" (1947).

When the satisfaction or the security of another person becomes as significant to one as is one's own satisfaction or security, then the state of love exists. Consensual validation—a comparing of notes, a checking and counterchecking, is greatly facilitated by love, and therefore the capacity to exchange love becomes a vital aspect in the development of success in interpersonal relations.

Love thus has its roots in tenderness. The mother responds to the infant's needs with tenderness, and the growing child continually needs the nourishment of tenderness and intimacy particularly from his parents. In the juvenile era the child finds a chum, and there emerges a new capacity to be concerned with the welfare of another human being. In contrast to Freud's emphasis throughout his theories on the problems based on sexuality. Sullivan emphasizes some of the other significant problems of modern man—loneliness, isolation, loss of self esteem, and unrelatedness.

MALEVOLENT TRANSFORMATION

One further great concept of Sullivan's, which is so vital in this era of troubled adolescents, is the notion of the malevolent transformation, as presented in *The Interpersonal Theory of Psychiatry*. It is too long to quote in detail, but it basically represents a miscarriage of the need for tenderness, in which a child discovers that manifesting the need for for tenderness toward the potent figures around him leads basically to anxiety rather than relief. Under these circumstances the child learns that it is highly disadvantageous to show any need for tender cooperation from authority in which case "he shows something else; and that something else is the basic malevolent attitude, the attitude that one really lives among enemies—that is about what it amounts to. And on that basis, there comes about remarkable developments which are seen later in life, when the juvenile makes it practically impossible for anyone to feel tenderly for him or to treat him kindly; he beats them to it so to speak, by the display of his attitude. And this is the development of the earlier discovery that the manifestation of any need for tenderness, and so on would bring anxiety or pain. . . . Thus there can occur this very serious distortion of what might be called the fundamental interpersonal attitude; and this distortion, this malevolence, as it is encountered in life, runs something like this: Once upon a time everything was lovely, but that was before I had to deal with people" (1953, pp. 214-216). Sullivan did not regard the capacity for interpersonal relations as completed during any point of development—another very important disagreement from basic Freudian concepts.

PSYCHOTHERAPY OF SCHIZOPHRENIC PATIENTS

One of Sullivan's greatest contributions was showing that schizophrenia could be treated through psychotherapy, just like any other mental illness. Sullivan developed a psychological explanation for the causes of schizophrenic disorder and demonstrated that schizophrenic processes were never very far from the normal processes of living. In contrast to prevailing theories, Sullivan showed that schizophrenia can develop as direct outgrowth of psychological issues and that it can occur in any individual. He saw schizophrenia as a personality distortion growing out of a complicated and warped series of interpersonal relations, and he documented this in innumerable case histories and studies.

By demonstrating the origins of schizophrenia in the distortions of personality development, he greatly stimulated the hope of a possible psychotherapeutic resolution of this disorder. He said, "The most peculiar behavior of the acutely schizophrenic patient, I hope to demonstrate, is made up of interpersonal processes with which each of us is or historically has been familiar. Far the greater part of the performances, the interpersonal processes, of the psychotic patient are exactly of a piece with processes which we manifest some time every twenty-four hours" (1947). The essence of the schizophrenic state is defined by Sullivan as a failure of the self-system, and the schizophrenic change is due to an inability to maintain dissociation. The best detailed discussion of this is to be found in *Clinical Studies in Psychiatry* (1956) which consists of material contained in lectures given in 1943.

For the purpose of our study, suffice it to say that Sullivan's view of schizophrenia is still not generally shared because only a mere handful of schizophrenic people receive intensive psychotherapy today. As Eldred points out: "There are but a few training centers that provide training for such treatment and actually encourage it. In my more gloomy moments, I compare such training centers to the isolated Irish monasteries of the Dark Ages that preserved the written language. More modest goals of symptom relief are applied to ninety-nine per cent of the severely disturbed patients. Less than one per cent are exposed to an opportunity to achieve characterological change through intensive psychoanalytically oriented psychotherapy" (1972). I believe the main reason for this is not so much theoretical argument about the meaning of schizophrenia as it is the lack of financial resources in our country to maintain long term intensive psychotherapy of schizophrenics over many years. One of my deepest hopes is that a foundation will be set up to sponsor this type of therapy. I am certain that a vast unexplored area of research and therapeutic help is waiting as a reward for such a sponsorship.

SULLIVAN AS A MASTER CLINICIAN

The discussion of schizophrenia brings us to the issue of why Sullivan is entitled to close attention from anyone who would practice psychotherapy, whereas certain other famous theorists can be ignored selectively depending on the wishes or interests of the therapists. This is primarily because Sullivan was a masterful clinician capable of tremendous intuitive insight and infinite patience. Certain basic sections of Sullivan's writing illustrate his clinical acumen and are replete with clinical pearls for anyone who would do psychotherapy. An outstanding example is chapter 6 of *Clinical Studies in Psychiatry* entitled "Envy and Jealousy as Precipitating Factors in the Major Mental Disorders." The entire second part of the same book, on "Therapeutic Approaches to Patterns of Difficulty" represents Sullivan the clinician at his very best, and is mandatory reading. Part III of the Sullivan book on *The Interpersonal Theory of Psychiatry* (1953) is the most excellent description of the development of schizophrenia as explained by his general theory. I would recommend chaper 6 and Part II of *Clinical Studies in Psychiatry* and Part III of the *Interpersonal Theory of Psychiatry* as classic demonstrations of Sullivan's clinical excellence in psychiatric treatment.

A number of fine psychiatrists have been deeply influenced by Sullivan. Most notable of these were Fromm-Reichmann (see chapter 13) and a variety of others, as represented in a collection edited by

Mullahy (1949). This collection of papers includes one by Sullivan on the education of the psychotherapist, "Notes on Investigation, Therapy, and Education in Psychiatry and Their Relations to Schizophrenia," which is one of the classic papers on the subject. Thompson (1964) applied Sullivan's theoretical position to a detailed study of feminine psychology, another area in which Freud's theories are notoriously weak (see chapter 14). Her work on the problems of womanhood are most vital to anyone who is convinced the Sullivanian position is the one to employ.

COMPARISON OF SULLIVAN AND FREUD

Let us turn more specifically now to the great differences between Sullivan and Freud. Crowley writes that Sullivan's thinking was quite different from that of Freud's in that it avoided seeing man and his culture as opposed to one another: "Freud's instinct theory saw culture as inimical to the expression of man's instincts and therefore to the free development of man. Sullivan avoided this dichotomy. He saw culture as the matrix which made it possible for people to grow up to be human, as well as being the source of their anxieties" (1971). Sullivan emphasized the importance of cultural transmission in communication, and in this aspect of his work, he called attention to the value of the study of ego operations (in Freudian terms). These operations have also been emphasized by numerous psychoanalysts that followed Freud, beginning with Anna Freud (see chapter 13).

Already in *Personal Psychopathology* written between 1929 and 1933, Sullivan arrives at a more or less systematic theory that diverges radically from Freud's. He no longer thought that it is sound theory or practice to see manifestations of sexual impulses in the individual from birth onward, and so he largely abandoned Freud's fundamental theory of psychosexuality. The entire central role of the Oedipus complex is dropped, and sexuality only appears with any important emphasis during adolescence at the appearance of what Sullivan calls the lust dynamism.

For example, as Salzman points out, Freud viewed obsessive symptoms as a compromise attempt to deal with ambivalent feelings and to prevent the expression of unacceptable aggressive or sexual impulses. "The symptom, as he saw it, was not only a displaced substitute for impulse but also a partial satisfaction of it. Sullivan, on the other hand, viewed the obsessional process as one in which the individual attempts to exert maximal control over himself and the universe in order to guarantee and protect himself against deep feelings of uncertainty and insecurity. He attempts to do this by the personal magic of compulsive ritual or obsessive, ruminative, omniscient thinking. And he strives to achieve perfection, omnipotence, and omniscience so that he may be beyond criticism, rejection, or danger. He avoids commitment and involvement, since these contain emotional elements that cannot be controlled" (Freedman and Kaplan 1972).

Thus Freud is accused by Sullivan in *Clinical Studies in Psychiatry* of making "the flat mistake of assuming that the unconscious is largely the habitation of the primitive, the infantile, the undeveloped, and so on." For Sullivan the unconscious is "quite clearly that which cannot be experienced directly, which fills all the gaps in the mental life" (1956). And thus only the study of each individual can unearth what is in their unconscious according to Sullivan. No generalizations can be made.

By under-emphasizing infantile sexuality as his reaction against Freud and his insistence on what he called "the illusion of personal individuality" (which may be a reaction against Fromm), Sullivan loses a great deal. He underplays the role of the biological demands of the organism and seems to underplay certain organized aspects of the self. For example, Munroe (1955) notes that although Sullivan writes of "the development of an internal critic of some importance" this critic seems "a very pallid homologue of Freud's *superego,* not well studied in origin or function."

These very serious omissions do not take away from the importance of Sullivan's emphasis on what happens to the growing child in the nonsexual area. Here Sullivan becomes a bridge to the work of Erikson (discussed in chapter 17). Erikson and Sullivan in different ways point out that the nonsexual capacities of the child in gradual maturation are played upon by, and play into, interpersonal relations. Thus it is not correct to insist that the personality is solidly formed in the first few years of life. Erikson is the boldest in stating that ego development autonomously goes through definable specific stages all through life. Sullivan's point is that new relationships to people are made possible by the maturation of new capacities in the child *plus* reciprocal shifts in attitudes toward the child by his associates.

This invites a careful cross cultural study of precisely how the child fits into its changing interpersonal situations and what reciprocal influences these have upon the subsequent development of the child's personality. I think Sullivan pointed out an important area of weakness in Freudian theory here.

It has to be frankly admitted that Sullivan intended his theoretical conceptions to be a complete replacement for Freudian psychology. It is pointless to debate why Sullivan tried to do this, but I think there is sufficient evidence already today that he failed; the Sullivanian paradigm is not going to replace the Freudian paradigm in psychiatry. Sullivan was using a rather obsolete notion of the philosophy of scientific methodology when he insisted that all the conceptions of scientific theory must be testable by crucial experiments (see chapter 16). There are many fields of science today, most notably physics, where the crucial experiments are either very rare or actually impossible to perform. It is possible to get around this problem by thinking of our theoretical preconceptions as heuristic principles for the purpose of explanations or as-if hypotheses (Chessick 1961). We would then be less concerned with the absolute validity of these conceptions and more concerned with their utility in our psychotherapeutic work.

Chapter 13

Psychoanalytic Psychotherapy

The most universal source of inner helplessness in adults, I believe, stems from their unresolved fixations to the emotional entanglements with significant persons of their early lives. . . . The result of these fixations is that people compulsively appraise other people in terms of their ancient childhood patterns of living, judgments, and expectations. They act upon and respond to people in line with these misconceptions. Many times people are half-aware of their erroneous judgments, expectations, and behavior, yet are helpless in their attempt to change. This is due to their lack of awareness of the unconscious roots of their compulsive need to repeat old patterns of relatedness and living. . . . This powerlessness in the face of repetition compulsion versus change and in the presence of its concomitant uncontrollable hatred produces deep emotional insecurity in people.

Frieda Fromm-Reichmann, *Psychoanalysis and Psychotherapy*

FOCUS ON THE EGO: ANNA FREUD

The three outstanding pioneers discussed in this chapter have been instrumental in applying the theories of Freud and Sullivan to the modern clinical practice of individual psychotherapy and have had leading roles in the development of the main stream of psychoanalytic psychotherapy, that is to say, the application of insights gained from classical and formal psychoanalysis to the treatment of a variety of patients by various modified techniques. The question whether major, alternative modifications are necessary remains moot to this day, and I shall not debate this subject here. I have, therefore, left out the proponents of major and incompatible modifications such as Jung and Adler and remained within the field of generally accepted psychoanalytic psychotherapy.

Anna Freud extended the theories of Freud to the psychoanalysis of children, Frieda Fromm-Reichmann played a crucial role in the burgeoning field of the psychoanalytic psychotherapy of schizophrenia, and Franz Alexander applied the theories of Freud to patients with character disorders and psychosomatic problems. All three of these pioneers were gifted teachers who accumulated large followings, and were thus responsible for the training of many outstanding clinicians. Practicing clinicians themselves, they developed an active discipline now known as psychoanalytic psychotherapy.

Anna Freud has passed seventy-five years of age. As Sigmund Freud's famous daughter, she shared his later life intimately. Her own contributions began essentially in the 1920's, and the seven volumes of her *Collected Works* (A. Freud 1972) have recently been published. During the Second World War, she came with her father to England from Austria and started there the Hampstead War Nurseries for children who had suffered through bombing, shelter sleeping, indiscriminate evacuation and billeting. After the war she founded a child therapy clinic, the largest center in the world for the treatment of children and training of child analysts.

She has lectured innumerable times to teachers, social workers, nurses, pediatricians, hospital authorities—always with the purpose of elucidating the problems of understanding children. She is a woman of enormous energy. For example, in one six week period, she flew to Topeka to lecture to psychiatric residents at the Menninger Foundation and to preside over the meeting of the Association for Child Psychoanalysis. She then went to New Haven to work at the Yale Law School and to hold seminars at the Yale Child Study Center. Ending her trip in New York she delivered the Freud Anniversary lectures under the auspices of the New York Psychoanalytic Institute.

Although she has become almost a living legend in psychoanalytic circles, she has still preserved a considerable modesty and genuine desire to stay out of the political and popular limelight. At the same time, she shows inexhaustible patience in her work with children, and to her colleagues she has given all manner of attention, often at the expense of her own productivity.

Since the death of Freud, the theoretical focus in psychoanalysis has shifted simultaneously from the study of the adult to the study of the child and from the exploration of the unconscious (the exploration of the id) to the exploration of the ego. The psychoanalyst who more than any other stands at the center of these new developments is Anna Freud. Her most famous work, *The Ego and the Mechanisms of Defense* (1946) constitutes a milestone in the development of psychoanalytic psychotherapy. Essentially this book represents an elaboration and development of Freud's short book- *The Ego and the Id* (1923), which was itself a vital milestone and turning point in the development of psychoanalysis.

Anna Freud's book not only elaborates in detail on the ego and the mechanisms of defense, but it also extends the study of the ego to the study of adolescence and, by implication, to the study of children. For the purposes of the present book, I will not take the time to review here Anna Freud's discoveries and viewpoints on the psychoanalytic treatment of children or elaborate on the controversy between the followers of Anna Freud and those of Melanie Klein on this subject. The idea of interest to us here is the sharp focus on understanding the ego and the mechanisms of defense which Anna Freud precipitated from the general atmosphere of treatment at the time.

Anna Freud pointed out that the ego could be studied through examination of the resistances presented during psychoanalytic treatment. She reviewed such mechanisms of defense as regression, repression, reaction–formation, isolation, undoing, projection, introjection, turning–against–the–self, reversal, and sublimation or displacement of instinctual aims. She wrote: "So far as we know at present, the ego has these ten different methods at its disposal in its conflicts with instinctual representatives and affects. It is the task of the practicing analyst to discover how far these methods prove effective in the processes of ego resistance and symptom formation which he has the opportunity of observing in individuals" (1946). The purpose of psychoanalysis is shifted to the study of the ego in which the defenses are made conscious, permitting the impulses to come through, so that the patient can deal with them in a more adult way. Thus in wild analysis, point blank interpretations usually just bounce off the patient. A correct therapist must wait until the patient is ready to know and understand the defenses against the impulses; otherwise the patient is not ready to give up these defenses and develop new ego adaptive techniques.

Much of her book is devoted to elucidating hitherto poorly understood and rather vague concepts of the mechanisms of defense. Preliminary stages of the defense mechanisms are discussed—defenses against objective anxiety. Examples given are denial in fantasy, denial in word and act, and ego restriction. Two important types of defenses are investigated at length: identification with the aggressor (crucial in superego formation) and "a form of altruism" (the altruistic surrender of one's own instinctual impulses in favor of other people). Finally, defenses motivated by fear of the strength of the instincts are illustrated by focusing on the phenomena of puberty, in which a relatively strong id confronts a relatively weak ego. The battle of puberty is resolved depending on the strength of the id (which is seen as a physiologic aspects of the individual), the ego's tolerance or intolerance of instincts (which depends on the character formed by latency period), and the nature and efficacy of the defense mechanisms at the ego's command. This last group of factors is decisive. Certain characteristic adolescent defense mechanisms are discussed in detail, such as asceticism, intellectuality, adolescent object love, and identification. The ego is seen as victorious when its defensive measures effectively avoid anxiety and transform instincts so that even in difficult circumstances some gratification is secured. Thus a harmonious relation between the id, superego, and outer world is established.

Much of this material sounds almost banal today because it forms the backbone of psychoanalytic psychotherapy, but in the forties it represented a vital and concise contribution to our understanding of treatment through the psychoanalytic method. The subsequent work on ego psychology which has developed at great length in psychoanalytic circles takes its starting point with Anna Freud's book.

LIMITATIONS OF PSYCHOANALYTIC TECHNIQUE

A lesser known, but very worthwhile contribution of Anna Freud is to be found in her little monograph *Difficulties in the Path of Psychoanalysis* (1969). This work again takes as its starting point Sigmund Freud's "Analysis Terminable and Interminable" (1937a). It also draws on an outstanding paper by Lampl–de Groot (1967) on the obstacles standing in the way of psychoanalytic cure. Anna Freud's monograph, read along with these two papers, presents in concise form one of the most timely problems for all psychoanalytic psychothera-pists today. In outline form, these papers summarize the various obstacles and difficulties in the path effecting psychotherapeutic change by the psychoanalytic method, whether it be a formal psychoanalysis or a psychoanalytically oriented psychotherapy.

Anna Freud begins with Freud's suggestion that therapeutic alteration of the ego must be accomplished by the psychotherapist, while on the other hand, the ego distortions which hinder analysis are acquired by the individual in his earliest defensive struggles against unpleasure. The importance of a therapeutic normalization of the ego is focused upon by Anna Freud, but it is left open as to how and in what way this can be accomplished. Anna Freud writes: "A considerable cross section of the psychoanalytic community today pins their faith on the analysis of the first year of life, with the purpose of therapeutically modifying the impact of the earliest happenings. Freud's discovery that every neurosis of the adult is preceeded by an infantile neurosis and that the latter has to be analyzed before the former can be reached, is paraphrased by them as follows: every infantile neurosis in the oedipal period is preceeded by fateful interactions between infant and mother in the very first days and months of life, and it is this archaic, preverbal phase which has to be revived in the transference and analyzed before the later infantile neurosis can be approached effectively" (1969).

Lampl–de Groot (1967) reviews the list of difficulties which Freud cites as in the way of psychoanalytic cure, and refers each back to some happening during the earliest mother-infant interaction:

1. The (masochistic) *negative therapeutic reaction* of some patients who have a need for self punishment, referred back to "the primitive

fear of their own aggressive drives and the destruction of their omnipotent fantasies," directed against the mother.

2. The *incapacity to tame the instinctual drives,* referred back to the modes of drive discharge initiated when the ego is helpless vis-à-vis the drives and "strongly dependent on the mother's support."

3. *Irregular and distorted ego development,* referred back to failures in the original dyad between infant and mother.

4. *Bisexual problems,* referred back to the infant's fear of merging with the dominating mother, or fear of passivity which later, in the phallic phase, acquires sexual meaning.

Anna Freud points out that, "Any attempt to carry analysis from the verbal to the preverbal period of development brings with it practical and technical innovations as well as theoretical implications, many of which are controversial" (1969). There is no doubt that this issue is just as pertinent and controversial today. As Anna Freud explains, "The new technical proposals aimed at the beginning of life imply the assumption that whatever is acquired is reversible. This is by no means proved" (1969). We must leave the question of whether or not a basic therapeutic alteration of the ego is possible or not to technical writings on the practice and technique of psychoanalytically oriented psychotherapy.

This emphasis on the first years of life also has important implications for training as Lampl–de Groot points out, "In training analyses, where we aim at liberating the future analyst's capacity to form empathy, our effort cannot be confined to a mere attempt—its success is a prerequisite of our profession" (1967). In other words getting at the basic early mother-child symbiosis is not only vital in the treatment of many patients but is vital in the training of the psychotherapist in order to liberate the capacity for empathy, which, of course, is fundamentally based on the earliest mother-child symbiotic experiences.

EMPATHY AS THE CRUCIAL TOOL
OF THE PSYCHOTHERAPIST: FROMM-REICHMANN

The subject of empathy leads directly to the work of Frieda Fromm-Reichmann, who puts it at the very center of the psychoanalytic psychotherapy of schizophrenia. As Anna Freud shifted attention from the understanding of the id to the understanding of the ego, so Frieda Fromm-Reichmann shifted attention from the understanding of the patient to the understanding of the psychotherapist in attempting to clear away the obstacles to psychoanalytic cure and extend the theoretical knowledge of psychoanalysis to the treatment of schizophrenia. Her great textbook on *The Principles of Intensive Psychotherapy* (1950) still remains one of the outstanding fundamental texts on the subject, and every other book written on the subject since that time refers extensively back to her textbook. She sees psychoanalytic therapy as offered in a "spirit of collaborative guidance." Basing her work on Sullivan's writings, she conceives of treatment as aimed at the solution of difficulties in the living, growth, maturation, and independence of the patient in order to develop the capacity for mature love—a self realization in which the patient becomes able to use his talents, skills, and powers to his satisfaction within a realistic, freely established set of values.

Although it is tempting to quote from this text at length, I have done so in other books (1969a, 1971c) and will not repeat myself here, except to remind the reader of the most important cornerstone of Fromm-Reichmann's notion of therapy: "The success or failure of psychotherapy depends greatly on whether there is an empathic quality between the psychiatrist and patient" (Fromm-Reichmann 1950).

> The psychotherapist is expected to be stable and secure enough to be constantly aware of and in control of that which he conveys to his patients in words and mindful of that which he may convey in empathy; that his need for operations aimed at his own security and satisfaction should not interfere with his ability to listen consistently to patients, with full alertness to their communications per se and, if possible, to the unworded implications of their verbalized communications; that he should never feel called upon to be anything more or less than the participant-observer of the emotional experiences which are conveyed to him by his patients. . . . On the surface, these rules seem obvious and easy to follow; yet they are not. . . . In actuality, none of us will be able to live up to all of them. We have to bear in mind that no amount of inner security and self respect protects the psychiatrist from being as much a subject of and vulnerable to the inevitable vicissitudes of life as is everyone else. (1959, p. 86)

Fromm-Reichmann graduated from medical school in Prussia in 1914, and during World War I, she took care of brain-injured soldiers as a member of the staff of Kurt Goldstein. Under his leadership, she gained a solid foundation in the physiology and pathology of brain function and acquired insights into Goldstein's notion of the "catastrophic reaction" of brain injured patients that prepared her for an understanding of psychotic panic states. During the 1920's she worked in a sanatorium at Dresden and became a visiting physician at Kraeplin's Psychiatric Clinic in Munich. Her discovery of Freud's writings led to a turning point in her professional career. Here she found many of her burning questions answered. She undertook psychoanalytic training and practiced in Heidelberg, establishing a private psychoanalytic sanatorium there; together with Erich Fromm she founded the Psychoanalytic Training Institute of Southwest Germany. Georg Groddeck, who offered the first understanding of the term "id," became an important influence in the group of Heidelberg psychoanalysts to which Fromm-Reichmann belonged. Groddeck's approach to psychosomatic diseases through psychoanalytic understanding is well known to the psychiatric profession. When the Nazis over-ran Germany, Fromm-Reichmann fled to Alsace Loraine, Palestine, and finally the United States. An opportunity to test the psychoanalytic treatment of functional psychoses was offered to her at Chestnut Lodge, a sanatorium in Rockwell, Maryland. There, in an atmosphere of open–minded and enthusiastic understanding, her ingenuity blossomed, and she achieved, in the course of the years, surprising results in the treatment of psychoses. At Chestnut Lodge, she became a close friend of Harry Stack Sullivan.

The four outstanding teachers of her life—Sigmund Freud, Kurt Goldstein, Georg Groddeck, and Harry Stack Sullivan—suggest the wide range of human potentialities which Frieda Fromm-Reichmann's mind was able to encompass. At the same time she welcomed the modern development of ego analysis which stressed the integrated aspects of the ego functions; it agreed with her own growing understanding of the integrative processes of the total personality.

Thus Weigert writes: "Primarily this understanding was directed less toward the content of the patient's productions than toward the phenomenon of his resistance. She worked, in particular, to elucidate all those defenses that delayed and distorted his ego development, while protecting his acute sensitivity from experiencing massive anxieties. . . . She was even reluctant to offer interpretations herself and preferred to listen, without theoretical prejudice, to the schizophrenic patient, who is more surprisingly original and removed from conventional lines of thought than the neurotic. She was ready to learn from her patient" (Fromm-Reichmann 1959).

The selected papers of Fromm-Reichmann entitled *Psychoanalysis and Psychotherapy* have not received sufficient attention from practicing therapists. Several of the papers in this volume deserve to become classics in the psychiatric literature and demand study by anyone who does psychotherapy. For example, her paper on the "Philosophy of the Problem" contains an outstanding definition of intensive psychoanalytically oriented psychotherapy: "Communications between two people through spoken words, gesture, and attitude, the psychiatrist and psychiatric patient, with the goal that both may learn to understand the troublesome aspects of the patient's life and bring them and their hidden causes to the patient's awareness, so that his living may be facilitated and his difficulties in living may be alleviated, if not eliminated." This is based on the notion that in order to accomplish this goal the patient must verbalize his problems and investigate them with another trained and experienced person, the psychotherapist. "As he does so, he may be freed from his difficulties in living to the extent to which he will be able to become aware of, and therefore capable of handling, his interpersonal relationships" (1959).

This definition is based in turn on the premise that there is a tendency toward health in every human being regardless of how seriously mentally disturbed they are. Fromm-Reichmann was fully convinced of this idea taken from Harry Stack Sullivan. In her (1950) textbook, sometimes the patient is even asked to operate for the time being on the therapist's belief that it might be worthwhile to recover. The presence or lack of presence of this inherent tendency toward health and the capacity of the ego to become altered in psychotherapy remains one of the most important and controversial issues facing modern psychoanalytic psychotherapists. One of the most interesting facets of this issue is that the older and more experienced therapists tend in general to be more pessimistic about the extent to which the ego can be basically altered, whereas the younger and more enthusiastic therapists tend to be more optimistic about how thoroughly basic changes can take place. This was not true about Fromm-Reichmann, who remained optimistic to the end of her life and wrote beautifully about it.

The final paper, unfinished, in Fromm-Reichmann's selected papers is entitled "On Loneliness." It stands apart from her other productions because it combines important psychoanalytic insight with an extraordinary aesthetic effect. It exists only as a rough draft found in her desk and should not be missed.

In summary, Fromm-Reichmann's great contribution consisted first of all, in applying the principles of psychoanalysis and the findings of Harry Stack Sullivan to the clinical practice of intensive psychotherapy with schizophrenics. In addition to this she focused more accurately on the meaning of maturity in terms of the capacity to exchange love and success in interpersonal relationships which—in psychoanalytic language—represents shifts and alterations in basic ego functions, and she put the responsibility for the success or failure of psychotherapy more heavily upon the psychic field offered to the patient by the psychotherapist. At the essence of the psychic field is the therapist's capacity for empathy and his ability to listen, which in turn depends on his own treatment, his own innate abilities, and the kind of education he has had. I have tried to enlarge and elaborate on the development of an optimal psychic field for the psychotherapist in previous books (1971c, 1974g).

I have only had the privilege of personally knowing two of all the various experts and thinkers mentioned in this book, Frieda Fromm-Reichmann and Franz Alexander. In reviewing what I have written on Fromm-Reichmann, I realize I have not sufficiently done justice to her because, although she wrote beautifully about her concepts, part of her real greatness arose only out of interpersonal experience with her, and it is impossible to describe this.

STIMULATION AND CHALLENGE:
LIFE AND WORK OF FRANZ ALEXANDER

Franz Alexander was an equally extraordinary teacher, who inspired his students in a somewhat different manner—by the incisive capacity of his brilliant mind to penetrate quickly through masses of clinical material and develop an understanding of the nuclear core of a given patient's neurotic difficulties. It was an unforgettable experience to attend clinical case seminars presided over by Alexander and to watch his gifted mind at work in unravelling the mystery. One can see this brilliant tendency at work in his writings on psychosomatic medicine (1950) where he leads a group of psychoanalysts in attempting to develop nuclear constellations of emotional conflict at the basis of various classical psychosomatic disorders. This kind of work has fallen considerably into disrepute today, although it is by no means given up. It certainly illustrates Alexander's capacities as a teacher, clinician, and research investigator, which remain an ever present inspiration to all those who were fortunate enough to be trained under his influence.

It is not necessary to present much of a biography of Franz Alexander here, as he has already written an excellent autobiography, Part I of *The Western Mind in Transition* (1960). Born in Budapest, Hungary, in 1891 to a father who was an outstanding philosopher and educator, Alexander grew up in a world of artists, philosophers, scientific theorists, and people dedicated to the humanistic tradition. He studied medicine at the universities of Budapest and Gottingen, receiving his medical degree in 1912. He began research in brain physiology as physician to the military during World War I. His research led him to an interest in psychiatry and from there to the works of Freud, which represented a turning point for him. He travelled to Berlin to study at the Berlin Psychoanalytic Institute and later became a permanent teacher and training analyst on its staff. In 1930 he came to the United States, and at the University of Chicago held the first psychoanalytic professorship at a university. He received many honors and held many posts after that. Most prominently, he was the director and founder (in 1932) of the Chicago Institute for Psychoanalysis, which under his guidance for twenty-five years became an important center for training and research in psychoanalysis and psychosomatic medicine.

In 1956 he became head of the department of Psychiatry at Mount Sinai Hospital in Los Angeles where he died in 1961, leaving his last book *The History of Psychiatry* unfinished. A retrospective review of all of Alexander's books and papers reveals a difference from the previous pioneers mentioned here in that no one remarkable idea of Alexander has become established as an enduring contribution to psychotherapy; perhaps the closest is his extremely controversial concept of the corrective emotional experience. In my judgment the really great contribution of Alexander was in his capacity to stir up our entire field, which seems to have an inherent tendency to become ossified and even petrified, and to constantly attempt to enlarge the horizon and boundaries of that field and stimulate continuing research in all directions. The driving force of Alexander as an educator and stimulator of ideas during his sojourn at the Chicago Institute for Psychoanalysis is demonstrated in a series of papers by his students and colleagues, *Dynamic Psychiatry*. It is hard to sufficiently catch the spirit of Alexander's probing, searching, and stimulating intellect.

The death of Franz Alexander was felt most keenly, I think, in the loss of his tremendous and fertile imagination and stimulative mind, which perpetually presented new controversies, new challenges, and new conceptualizations to a field in which a certain rigid and conservative "old guard" tends to dominate and impede change, progress, and innovation. This controversy continues today, and even the formal psychoanalytical associations remain split into two major groups.

I would suggest that the student approach Alexander's thought through his selected papers *The Scope of Psychoanalysis* rather than attempting to read any other of his many books, except his autobiography. Although his books are easy reading and brilliant in style, they suffer from a certain lack of organization, they give the impression of a certain hurriedness in preparation, and some of their conceptions are dated or controversial and may mislead the student. For the advanced reader, Alexander's most timely book is *Psychoanalysis and Psychotherapy* and the sociologists will be most interested in *Our Age of Unreason* and *The Western Mind in Transition*.

Alexander's earliest interest seemed to have evolved around problems of criminality, punishment, and masochism in general, beginning with an early book *Psychoanalysis of the Total Personality* and culminating in two other volumes *The Criminal, the Judge and the Public* and *Roots of Crime*. In these studies Alexander is much impressed by a type of criminal whom he suspects is a social consequence of the blocking of opportunities for pioneer adventure by the closing of the frontiers in America—youthful criminals whose need is to prove themselves tough in order to deny their dependent needs. Criminality arising out of inferiority feelings and guilt feelings was also of special interest to him.

Another interest was in the field of psychosomatic medicine (1950). I will not review this in the present volume because of the controversial nature of his speculations, but pause only to again point out how fertile and vital many of Alexander's ideas were in establishing the entire discipline of psychosomatic medicine and stimulating a whole series of studies on a variety of poorly understood disorders. Marmor explains, "To grasp the importance of Alexander's contribution, it must be understood that most psychoanalytic formulations concerning vegetative psychophysiological disorders prior to this time endeavored to explain them as symbolic representations of unconscious content. Thus, peptic ulcers were interpreted as efforts to devour the introjected mother, diarrhea might mean weeping from the colon or expelling the hated mother-introject, hypertension could be a symbolic substitute for phallic erection, etc. Alexander felt that such symbolic interpretations were justified only in conversion hysteria where sense organs and functions under voluntary control were affected but that efforts to explain disturbances of vegetative functions in this way were misleading and unwarranted" (1973).

Perhaps more pertinent to our interests here is a somewhat simultaneous phase of study in which Alexander began some revisions of basic psychoanalytic theory, based on his so called vector theory of the life processes. In his book *Fundamentals of Psychoanalysis* he recapitulated his "surplus energy theory" of sexuality. After first postulating pleasure in stimulation or activity *for its own sake* as a criterion for distinguishing erotic behavior from other behavior, he continues, "Ferenczi maintained in his ingenious biological speculations that the organism expresses sexually all tensions which it cannot or need not coordinate for useful purposes. This is essentially equivalent to the view I later elaborated—that sexuality discharges any surplus excitation, regardless of its quality. . . . Propagation results from surplus energy generated by growth. The psychological equivalent of propagation is love" (1948).

Alexander also regards the spontaneous play of children as an overflow of surplus energy: "The child plays and exercises its voluntary body functions merely for the sake of the pleasure he derives from these activities. . . . The Greek god Eros was the god of both love and play and was represented appropriately by a child" (1948).

Turning to the selected papers *The Scope of Psychoanalysis,* "Three Fundamental Principles of the Mental Apparatus and of the Behavior of Living Organisms" summarizes his concept of the principles of surplus energy together with that of two other principles, the principle of stability and the principle of economy or inertia, which are basic to his concept of the dynamics of behavior. A later theoretical paper "Unexplored Areas of Psychoanalytic Theory and Treatment" (Part I) attempts a more far-reaching generalization, bringing his theory of surplus energy into relation with the physical concept of entropy and with communication theory. These papers are recommended to the reader but the general theoretical position of Alexander does not seem to have been widely accepted in the field and perhaps serves better as a provocative starting point to basic thinking on the part of the reader.

THE CORRECTIVE EMOTIONAL EXPERIENCE

What must be counted as the most important and the most provocative contribution of Alexander to the field of psychotherapy is his concept of the corrective emotional experience. Alexander has written about this in many places, the most basic being the paper "Analysis of the Therapeutic Factors in Psychoanalytic Treatment." Alexander insists that the fundamental aspect of psychoanalytic therapy is the corrective emotional experience which the patient obtains in the transference. It is significant not only that the patient relives his original conflicts in his relationship with the analyst, but that the analyst does not react as the parents did. His reactions should correct the pathogenic effects of the parental attitude. The objective understanding attitude of the analyst itself is so different than that of the parents that this alone necessitates a change in the patient's original attitudes.

In *Psychoanalytic Therapy* (with T. French), Alexander reports that he attempted to shorten the length of psychoanalytic treatment; he emphasized the importance of the corrective emotional experience by urging the therapist to actually deliberately provide certain corrective emotional experiences for patients based on a thorough knowledge of the psychodynamics involved. This book was not well received and Alexander had to point out, "This does not consist of artificial play acting but in creating an emotional atmosphere which is conducive to undoing the traumatic effects of early traumatic influences" (1961).

Alexander continued to insist that "the corrective emotional experience is the most powerful factor in making the patient's original ego defenses unnecessary and thus allowing the mobilization and emergence into consciousness of repressed material. It helps the patient's ego to assume a modified attitude toward hitherto repressed or inhibited impulses" (1961).

In a later book, *Psychoanalysis and Psychotherapy,* he insists that the corrective emotional experience is "the central therapeutic agent in the original and now standardized psychoanalytic procedure. . . . The course of the treatment consists of a long series of corrective emotional experiences, which follow one another as the transference situation changes its emotional content and different repressed childhood situations are revived and reexperienced in the relationship to the therapist" (1956b). This conception remains highly controversial even today especially in the area of formal or classical analysis.

Most importantly Alexander's concept of corrective emotional experience called attention to the fact that the therapist has a personality too and that his personality has a vital role in the therapeutic process. Alexander was constantly interested in this role and actually a deep disagreement still remains in our field regarding the importance of the role of the therapist and the extent to which emotional involvement by the therapist with the patient is desirable or undesirable in the treatment process. It is to Alexander's credit that he brought this controversy into the open and made it an issue which every therapist must face and resolve to some extent in his own therapeutic style.

An immediate caution must be added that when Alexander discusses corrective emotional experience or involvement he is not talking about countertransference. He insists repeatedly that it must be based on a thorough understanding of the patient's psychodynamic situation at the moment. French points out: "The flexibility that Alexander and his colleagues advocate is indicated only when it is guided by real understanding of the patient, only when the analyst knows exactly what he is trying to accomplish" (Alexander 1961).

REGRESSION AND FIXATION

Alexander's interest in what happens when the ego is confronted with a conflict it cannot master, led him to be concerned with regression and fixation. In working out the implication of two forms of regression and their therapeutic implications, Alexander shows how this distinction is important in the handling of a transference in psychoanalytic therapy. Thus although the commonly observed dependent transference of a patient may be based on a fixation in the pregenital phase of development, it perhaps more frequently involves an evasion of a later oedipal conflict and is really a regressive flight.

These considerations about dependency, flight, and evasion are generalized by Alexander in his long-standing interest in social and political studies. His most important book on this subject is *Our Age of Unreason,* a work organized in three sections—"From Reason to Unreason," "The Fundamentals of Human Behavior," and "From Unreason to Reason." In the first section Alexander emphasizes the unleashing of the unconscious and the forces of irrationality upon the world. The second section provides an excellent review of Alexander's conceptions of the fundamentals of both the regressive and progressive aspects of human behavior. The third section optimistically attempts to apply his principles to the solution of social and cultural difficulties. Alexander writes, "It must have become clear by now that the type of society that serves the individual best and allows him the full expression of his creative abilities is threatened by the present increased need for security. For the sake of greater security, man appears to be inclined to sacrifice all those specifically human values which make life worth living. The most paradoxical of all these developments is the fact that science, by increasing insecurity, has created conditions which counteract its own further development. This condition calls for extreme governmental controls which are incompatible with the free advancement of knowledge." He concludes, "Neurosis is a sign of succumbing to inertia and of vainly trying to evade novel and necessary adaptations by adhering or regressing to older behavior patterns. In social life the appearance of the cultural lag has the same significance: adherence to outworn social attitudes in a changed order" (1951, pp. 295, 315). These outworn social attitudes involve political nationalism, war as a means of settling conflicting interests, and an outworn hierarchy of values in which economic gain derived from producing goods is supreme.

THE RELENTLESS ATTEMPT TO IMPROVE TECHNIQUES

In "Unexplored Areas in Psychoanalytic Theory and Treatment," Part II, Alexander illustrates his outstanding capacity to organize principles and presents a lengthy series of unanswered main questions about the psychotherapeutic process. He leaves us with what may be considered his final plea to prevent stagnation in our field: "Therefore it appears to me not too exaggerated a hope that the mere fact that analysts are willing to expose their activities to the direct observation of their confreres will give opportunity to learn more about the therapeutic process." He points out that an impressive accomplishment was made in our field at its beginning when all our psychodynamic knowledge was acquired through private practitioners making scattered observations which never could be fully reproduced, studied, and precisely communicated to others: "At the same time it is equally impressive that since the discovery of the role of transference and resistance as proposed in Freud's technical papers between 1912 and 1915, no great technical advances have been made" (1961).

It is difficult to know whether the therapeutic effectiveness of treatment has increased at all in these years, and Alexander sadly compares this stagnation with the great advances in organic medicine during the same period of time. He believes the explanation to be that we continue to use the same methods of observation and are adverse to try out new avenues of approach. It is in his persistent efforts to stimulate new ideas and new avenues of approach that Alexander approaches greatness as a clinician and pioneer.

He understood perhaps better than any other author the extreme difficulties involved in drawing fine distinctions in our field such as that between the "pure gold" of psychoanalysis and the "copper" of direct suggestion or the differences between supportive and uncovering therapy which I have discussed elsewhere (1969a). He concludes "Even today when we do possess a reasonable and well established theory of personality and of treatment, psychotherapy, in all its forms, including psychoanalysis, is more an art than a science. Aptitudes—intuition and empathy—although not always reliable, are possibly more important for competence in therapy than is theoretical knowledge. The therapist's personality, his intangible suitability to certain types of patients and refractoriness to others cannot be disregarded" (1956b).

There is a certain pathos in a review of Alexander's writings, because one gets the impression that as he became older he became increasingly frustrated in his hopes for change, reform, and research. In the preface of his collected papers he concludes about himself: "What the author considers the most consistent feature in his writings is the conviction that psychoanalysis is in dire need of critical re-evaluation and further development of its theory and method of treatment. Because psychoanalysis originally represented an extraordinary advancement in the understanding of personality functions and dysfunctions, and therefore revitalized an at the time primarily descriptive and custodial psychiatry, it developed an inordinately conservative tendency to preserve its original formulations and methods and to rest on the laurels of past accomplishments" (1961). Yet at the same time, Alexander was not easily taken in by fancy sounding modifications and rhetorical appeals. For example, his criticism of existential psychiatry in "Impressions from the Fourth International Congress of Psychotherapy" (1961) is the best short critical challenge to existential psychiatry that I have read anywhere.

Chapter 14

The Unsolved Problem
of Feminine Psychology

I cannot evade the notion . . . that for women the level of what is ethically normal is different from what it is in men . . . Character-traits which critics of every epoch have brought up against women—that they show less sense of justice than men, that they are less ready to submit to the great exigencies of life, that they are more often influenced in their judgments by feelings of affection or hostility—all these would be amply accounted for by the modification in the formation of their superego which we have inferred above. We must not allow ourselves to be deflected from such conclusions by the denials of the feminists, who are anxious to force us to regard the two sexes as completely equal in position and worth.

Freud, *Some Psychological Consequences of*
the Anatomical Distinction Between the Sexes

The great question that has never been answered and which I have not yet been able to answer, despite my thirty years of research into the feminine soul is, "What does a woman want?"

Freud, quoted by Jones,
The Life and Work of Sigmund Freud

EXPERIMENTUM CRUCIS FOR FREUD'S THEORY

The riddle of feminine psychology is rapidly becoming the Michelson-Morley experiment of psychoanalysis. The Michelson-Morley experiment was designed to test one of the fundamental underpinnings of Newtonian or classical physics, namely the theory of the luminiferous ether. The fact that the Michelson-Morley experiment yielded completely negative results, although it was repeated again and again, indicated that something was basically wrong with the paradigm of Newtonian physics and led to a complete restructuring of physical theory and eventually to Einstein's theory of relativity.

In the area of classical psychoanalytic theory, no set of concepts has come under so much question from the clinical and experimental point of view as the psychoanalytic view of feminine psychology. It has been attacked from all sides. It is very important for the modern practicing psychotherapist to have a thorough understanding of the issues that are involved if he or she works at all with female patients.

Let us begin by reviewing the psychoanalytic view of feminine psychology. According to the classical Freudian theory, the divergence between the psychosexual development of the boy and the girl appears early in the phallic phase. Before that phase the girl shares with the boy the passive position in relation to her mother. With the development of motility and locomotion they both enter an increasingly active phase with the emphasis on autonomy and mastery of the object world. At this point a basic diversion takes place.

Although Freud assumed in his early formulations that sexual development in boys and girls was similar, in his later formulations he maintained the Oedipus complex in the girl to be a much more complicated process. In 1935 for example, he remarked on the fact that the little girl not only has to change her sexual object from the woman or mother to the man or father, but her leading genital zone as well—from the clitoris to the vagina. This stands in sharp contradiction to the little boy, whose sexual development remains simpler in that his leading genital zone remains the phallus and the sexual object remains a woman.

For many years it was assumed that the vagina was virtually non-existent and possibly did not produce sensations until puberty. The sexual life of women is now regularly divided, according to classical psychoanalytic theory, into two phases of which the first has a masculine character and only the second is specifically feminine. In female development there is a process of transition from one phase to the other to which there is nothing analogous in the male. The matter is further complicated because the clitoris continues to function in later female sexual life in a manner which is quite variable and not satisfactorily understood. Parallel with this great difference in genital zones there is another great difference concerned with the finding of the object. The girl has her mother as first object just like the boy, but at the end of her development, her father, a man, becomes the new love object. According to Freud, *"Whereas in boys the Oedipus complex is destroyed by the castration complex, in girls it is made possible and led up to by the castration complex"* (1925e). Thus the castration complex inhibits and limits masculinity and encourages femininity.

This is further elaborated in classical theory, where it is postulated that the narcissistic wound in the girl from her discovery of the lack of a penis tends to bring about the giving up of clitoral sexuality for the development of "femininity." The girl's libido slips into a new position and at this point the Oedipus complex begins to play its part. The basic equation is that penis-equals-child, and for the purpose of getting a child, she now takes her father as love object and the mother becomes the object of her jealousy. She turns to her father but this attraction to him is secondary to her wish to obtain a baby from him. Thus whereas in boys the Oedipus complex is destroyed, in girls it escapes this fate because the girl is already castrated. The Oedipus complex may be slowly abandoned or dealt with by repression, or its effects may persist far into a woman's normal mental life.

Carrying these considerations one step further, we speak about the girl as having an early identification with the active mother that is an initial active (negative) oedipal position. Then the girl turns with the passive aim to the oedipal love object, the father, which forms the passive (positive) oedipal position; this occurs relatively late compared to the boy's active (positive) oedipal position. Thus in turning from the mother to the father, according to this theory, the girl turns from an active to a passive sexual position. Passivity then becomes the normal sexual orientation for the girl. Furthermore, the very recognition of castration which in the boy brings on the destruction of the Oedipus complex, in the girl brings the Oedipus complex into existence, and no force or circumstance similar to the one which makes the boy renounce his oedipal wishes exists in the situation of the girl.

Blos explains, "Only the limitations of physical immaturity, incestuous guilt feelings, and the persistent narcissistic injury experienced in masturbatory activity combine to bring about a decline of her Oedipal phantasies and facilitate her entrance into the latency period" (1962). Thus the resolution of the girl's Oedipus complex may not come about until her adolescence, perhaps even later with the birth of a child, or perhaps never at all in any complete fashion.

This led with superficial logic to some of Freud's deprecative remarks about the superego in woman. Here is a clinical concept that bears testing and that throws scientific light on the postulates. Muslin (1971) reviews carefully the entire matter of the superego in women and Freud's concept that the woman has an insufficient internal cathexis of the mother and father to make for the usual autonomous superego system. Muslin saves the theory by pointing out that it is *not* necessary to reach any conclusions about any kind of inferiority of superego function in women from the basic psychoanalytic theory about the Oedipus complex. Thus although the superego in women may have different specific contents than in men, and the superego of a woman may be unique as compared to the superego of a man, superego functioning is similar and effective in both sexes.

It may be possible to argue that there is or is not a specifically female or masculine superego, but at any rate it does not follow, as Freud thought from his concept of feminine sexuality, that women have an inferior conscience, and it is time to lay that kind of argument to rest for once and for all.

The final group of conclusions from Freud's basic postulates about female sexuality involve the three final pathways that feminine sexuality may take: (1) a general revulsion from sexuality, (2) a defiant self-assertiveness in which the girl clings to her threatened masculinity in the hope of getting a penis and to the fantasy of being a man (the so called phallic woman), and (3) a circuitous development in which she takes her father as her object and finds her way to the feminine form of the Oedipus complex.

ADDITIONS TO THE CLASSICAL THEORY

Only the third path according to Freud leads to the final normal female attitude. Certain additions were made to Freud's basic postulates, some of them even in Freud's lifetime and with his approval. For example, Ruth Mack-Brunswick (Fliess 1948), one of the early female classical psychoanalysts, stresses the anger at the mother that the oedipal girl feels when she discovers that she does not have a penis. Thus the girl abandons the mother as love object with far more embitterment and finality than the boy, and this tremendous anger at the mother is also expressed in feminine masochism. Thus masochism is seen as a normal part of femininity and a consequence of the defense against the anger of the mother.

Probably the most complete exposition of the classical psychoanalytic position on feminine sexuality is to be found in the various works of Helene Deutsch. Several of her papers are reprinted in Fliess's *Psychoanalytic Reader* (1948) while her expanded views are in the two volume *Psychology of Women* (1944). Deutsch played an interesting role in the history of the psychoanalytic movement. She explains in her autobiography that "three of Freud's women pupils achieved a certain degree of prominence as 'pioneers in feminine psychology' (that was the phrase Freud used in his writings). These were Ruth Mack-Brunswick, Jeanne Lampl–de Groot, and myself" (1973). These pioneers and their special relationship to Freud are discussed in detail by Roazen (1974).

Deutsch maintains that parturition constitutes for women the termination of a sexual act which was only inaugurated by coitus. The ultimate gratification of the erotic instinct in women takes place at the point of giving birth. Thus femininity for Deutsch means the feminine, placid, masochistic disposition in the mental life of women and the basic feminine fantasy, according to Deutsch is, "I want to be castrated and raped by my father and to have a child by him," a threefold wish of plainly masochistic character. Castration, rape, and parturition are mixed together as basic elements in feminine psychology. The masochistic fantasies and wish for a child are permeated by pleasure tendencies of a masochistic nature. This masochism is a defensive consequence of the bitterness toward the mother generated by the little girl's discovery that she has no penis. This wish for castration, rape, and parturition is termed by some authors the masochistic triad in the female.

Recently Blos (1970) studied the preadolescent girl and emphasized that preadolescence in a girl is quite different from that in a boy. The emotional vulnerability of the preadolescent girl is twofold—(1) the regressive pull to the preoedipal mother, reinstituting the ambivalence of early object relations, and (2) the bisexual identity that is typical of this stage. Thus the task of normal female preadolescence is the successful resistance to the regressive pull toward the preoedipal mother and the renunciation of pregenital drive identifications.

OBJECTION TO "FEMININE MASOCHISM"

A whole series of clinical objections has been made to these basic theoretical conceptions about feminine psychology. The first objection is well reviewed for example by Gardiner (1955), who discusses in detail the whole subject of feminine masochism and passivity. Is this need, or culturally enforced tendency, in women to repress their aggressiveness more than men do a real link between the masochistic and the feminine? That is to say, is it really true that femininity and masochism are inextricably connected? According to Deutsch, they are inextricably connected. This turning in the direction of masochism is part of the woman's anatomical destiny marked out for her by biological and constitutional factors, and it lays the first foundation of the ultimate development of femininity.

Gardiner asks whether the masochistic wish to be castrated by the father is really a normal wish to be found in all women. For example, one could think that when the girl begins to accept the fact that her clitoris is an inferior organ and incapable of actively penetrating, the wish then develops passively to receive caresses and stimulation from the love object and eventually, by way of the father's penis, a child instead of the penis which has been taken away from her or denied her. But this is hardly a wish for pain or suffering. Gardiner points out that it seems rather a wish for libidinal pleasure which can be achieved passively, and indeed the child experiences receiving pleasure passively in the mother's physical care and caresses during the preoedipal phase. It also seems an instinctual wish for a child, which is then reinforced by the equation penis-equals-child or child-equals-penis. Thus there is no substantial proof clinically of the theory that the little girl in her normal development wishes the pain and suffering of being castrated by the father. Her acceptance of the fact that she has no penis is forced upon her by reality, and this might be thought of, according to Gardiner, perhaps as making the best of things. Gardiner insists that the wish to suffer pain from the father is a regression from normal feminine psychology to an earlier stage of development, the anal-sadistic stage, and certainly the wish to be beaten by the father, as Freud says, is a regressive distortion of the wish to have sexual relations.

Gardiner also questions Deutsch's concept that "in actual fact, parturition is for the woman an orgy of masochistic pleasure, and the dread and premonition of death which preceed this act are clearly due to a perception of the menace of the destructive instincts about to be liberated" (Fliess 1948). Gardiner cannot agree that the wish to have a child is a pleasure in pain or a desire for pain as an end in itself. When pain occurs in pregnancy or giving birth, this is a reality and must be suffered for the sake of the result, but it is normally not enjoyed for itself. Gardiner asks, "What normal woman would voluntarily undergo or far less enjoy pregnancy and parturition if these were not for producing a child?" (1955). The same is to be said about sexual intercourse itself. Gardiner points out that the pleasure in the sexual act is direct and immediate and except perhaps at defloration and for a short time thereafter, intercourse for the normal woman is without pain. Here the pleasure principle pure and simple is at work. Woman does not require the hope of a child to tolerate intercourse. Thus when a normal Oedipus complex develops and there is no regression to the anal-sadistic or oral stage, Gardiner feels we should not expect to find more than a trace of masochism or sadism. "Feminine masochism" grows out of a passive attachment to the father which is a normal feminine attitude, but masochism is not normal except within well defined and narrow limits (as any component instinct may be) and serious masochism is a regression from the genital to an earlier stage and *not* an essential part of feminine sexual fulfillment. I doubt very much if clinicians today hold that parturition is a masochistic orgy, and I think most today would agree with Gardiner's correction of the basic theory.

OBJECTION TO "FEMININE PASSIVITY"

A second major objection to the basic postulates is raised, for example, by Ash (1971). She focuses especially on the Freudian concepts of penis envy, masculinity and femininity equated to activity and passivity, and the achievement of feminine identity. The objection that she discusses specifically is to the concept that femininity implies passivity. Thus she takes the objections to basic psychoanalytic concepts one important step further than Gardiner. The eventual logical conclusion of her view leads to the arguments of women's liberation, which I will discuss later.

Ash argues that Freud's concept, femininity implies passivity, was simply a cultural prejudice and nothing more. As a matter of fact, already in the *New Introductory Lectures on Psychoanalysis* Freud expressed reservations about equating femininity with passivity. In that work his struggle with inner contradictions in the theory becomes especially evident. After enumerating many reasons for regarding the femininity-passivity equation as inadequate Freud states, "There is one particularly constant relation between femininity and instinctual life which we do not want to overlook. The suppression of women's aggressiveness which is prescribed for them constitutionally and imposed on them socially favors the development of powerful masochistic impulses. . . . Thus masochism, as people say, is truly feminine" (1933).

THE FEMALE ORGASM AND SEX RESEARCH

I have presented the classical psychoanalytic viewpoint about feminine psychology and two major objections to it: (1) femininity does not have to imply masochism or the wish for masochistic orgy and (2) femininity does not necessarily have to imply passivity. These are objections based on clinical and social observations but they are objections that do not threaten the basic theory itself but merely require modifications. Over the past fifteen years, however, objections have arisen that threaten the whole structure of the analytic concepts of feminine psychology. Perhaps the most striking and dramatic of these objections arose from the work of Masters and Johnson. This objection is that the entire concept of the female orgasm is misunderstood. Sherfey (1973) makes an extreme attack on the whole psychoanalytic concept of female sexuality. Her position consists of three major theses: (1) the early embryo of all human beings is female; (2) by the nature of their physiological structure, women are sexually insatiable; and (3) civilization arose as a means of suppressing the inordinate demands of female sexuality that result from an inherent insatiability. The first thesis challenges the Freudian belief in an embryo that is sexually undifferentiated and therefore bisexual. This is of course vital in analytic theory, because Freud assumed that the clitoris served as a residual organ of the masculine element in women. The second and third theses are based on the work of Masters and Johnson. Sherfey discusses what is known as the clitoral-vaginal transfer theory: the little girl turns from the clitoris as the zone of genital excitation to the vaginal zone. Masters and Johnson's work indicates that there is no such thing as a basic vaginal orgasm. Sherfey also takes their work to mean that, from the standpoint of normal physiologic functioning, the more orgasms a woman has the more she will continue to have, unless inhibited by fatigue or external repression. Leaning on Masters and Johnson's work, she throws out the whole concept that the transfer from clitoris to vagina takes place in a normal female sexual development and contends that the forceful suppression of women's inordinate sexual demands has led to the development of civilization.

Fisher presents a much less spectacular argument and a more mundane and scientific type of study. Through a series of question-naires and studies, he could discover no correlation between the consistency with which women achieved orgasm to their degree of psychological maladjustment, to the extent to which their mother and father may or may not have been permissive in sexual matters, to their sexual information prior to marriage, to their femininity as conventionally defined, or to their aggressiveness, passivity, religiosity or even preference for clitoral versus vaginal stimulation. Further-more, the length of foreplay, the duration of coitus, and so on, have no consistent correlation with a woman's ability to achieve orgasms regularly. As a matter of fact, Fisher attacks the Freudians for thinking that the woman who prefers vaginal stimulation is more normal or more mature than others, and he emphasizes the importance of male dependability as a determining factor in the woman's orgasmic responses. Fisher's study can only be seen as a preliminary study on a question requiring further work and it is open to considerable argument from a methodological point of view.

Important for us is that clinical study brings the whole clitoral-vaginal transfer theory into serious question. In the July 1968 issue of *The Journal of the American Psychoanalytic Association* a whole variety of studies are presented on this subject which the reader interested in the details of feminine psychology can have a look at. New discoveries in embryology, physiology, and even ethology seems to be involved in trying to understand the enigma of female sexuality. Freud admitted that psychoanalysis has not solved the riddle of femininity and what constitutes masculinity and femininity. This remains an unresolved riddle and it is very difficult to reach any conclusion on the matter at this time.

Stoller (1973) reviews the whole area of sex research and the methodological problems that it involves, and these are many. The concept of the primacy of the penis has come into doubt. There is no question that male chauvinism is connected to Freud's enthusiasm for the position that men are emotionally and intellectually and morally superior to women and fitted anatomically with something superior. The observations of Masters and Johnson have had much vogue in diminishing Freud's ideas about femininity. Stoller, however, does not feel that the clitoris-vaginal transfer theory is refuted by Masters and Johnson. Masters and Johnson found that all female orgasms orginate in the clitoris and did not observe vaginal orgasms, but innumerable women have sensed that they had two sorts of orgasms, one clitoral and the other vaginal, and they don't have trouble distinguishing between the two. So just because gross vaginal changes at the moment of orgasm are not visible to the laboratory observer does not prove the absence of vaginal orgasm. On the other hand, many feminine women have been known who do not have vaginal orgasms, while too many who do—schizophrenics, neurotics, and grossly masculine women— cannot by Freud's definition of maturity be feminine. The matter remains for further investigation. The present clinical data do not yet either prove or disprove the clitoral-vaginal transfer theory, and thus sex research does not at the present time either prove or disprove the basic psychoanalytic postulates about feminine psychology.

WOMEN'S LIBERATION

A fourth objection currently in vogue may be loosely termed the women's liberation movement. In turning to this movement, one has to sharply differentiate between its social and political aspects and its fundamental objections to psychoanalytic psychology. In this discussion, I will assume that the movement is absolutely justified in demanding equal social and economic conditions for women and will confine my discussion *only* to its objections to the psychoanalytic concept of feminine psychology. The basic point this group makes, at least in its extreme form, is that penis envy and *all* differences postulated psychologically between males and females is nothing but a totally social myth engendered and cultivated by male chauvinists for the purpose of keeping women in subjugation.

The women's liberation movement and a variety of feminists have served a useful function in challenging some of the basic early psychoanalytic tenets about feminine sexual development. Even the less extreme advocates have brought under serious question certain basic postulations that were more or less taken for granted until the 1960s, after which, under pressure from feminists and the women's liberation movement, there has been an increasing reassessment of the entire subject. Let us turn specifically to some of the objections and contentions that have been raised by various feminists against the developmental theories of Freud and his "pioneers," and discuss them briefly.

1. The contention that psychoanalysis places motherhood near the center of female psychology for the purpose of severely limiting women and helping men to dominate them. Whether or not motherhood is or is not at the center of female psychology is a clinical question. If it is not, then the whole psychoanalytic theory of feminine development and feminine psychology must be wrong.

2. The claim that penis envy is nothing but a reassurance created by frightened males and is only symbolic of realistic justified envy of man's dominant social advantages. The issue of penis envy is probably blown somewhat out of proportion. It is possible to fudge on this issue, for example, by arguing that penis envy is only one of several constituent forces at work on the girl that cause her to turn to the father. This is a question that *can* be resolved clinically. In my clinical

experience, it is the narcissistic blow to the little girl, partly a function of her environment, that is crucial. So penis envy is probably closely related to recent formulations on the vicissitudes of narcissism (Kohut 1971).

3. The contention that analysts find biological and anatomical differences to be important contributants to the gender personality traits, but these psychological distinctions are *solely* the products of a male dominated culture. If it is true that anatomical and biological differences do not make important contributions to gender personality traits, then the whole analytic approach to female psychology must be wrong. This again is a clinical issue.

4. Finally, the recitation over and over again of Freud's various snide and demeaning comments about women, implying that since Freud had a prejudice or blind spot against women the entire psychoanalytic theory of the psychology of women is wrong. This is an *ad hominem* rather than a clinical argument.

The final basic objection to current psychoanalytic thinking about feminine psychology is founded on the methodology in use. Salzman (1967) points out that a tremendous variety of factors go into the formation of character, and the concept that anatomy is destiny is probably too simplistic a view of character formation. There is no question that Freud's libido theory was male centered and the psychology of the female was forced to fit the model by introducing a number of hypotheses (see chapter 16) to cover up the discrepancies. Historical and cultural prejudices were given scientific status in Freud's theory, and a far-reaching reappraisal of the theory is certainly in order. Salzman points out that the attempt to link character and gender overlooks the multicausal basis for character and the crucial significance of the role of the individual at a particular time and place. This is the view of post-Freudian ego psychologists and cultural analysts, who see character structure as a result of cultural pressures interacting with libidinal development (see chapter 17).

Freud's view was almost entirely the result of superficial observation and speculation, and the evidence used to support his original hypotheses was derived from interpretations that grew from the original assumptions. There is an absolutely unsatisfactory ambience about his theory, in that the woman is viewed as an embittered castrated male rather than a healthy female in her own right (see also

Schafer 1974). Furthermore, the complex problem of gender role has been studied in a number of physiologic, biochemical, and chromosomal ways in recent years. Thus we see that although the whole matter requires review and restudy there is no evidence at this time that the basic tenets of female psychology have been disproven by any form of evidence. The entire debate over feminine psychology has unfortunately been very muddled and confused by the issue of who is for or against psychoanalysis as a whole, and by such political issues as women's liberation and radicalism.

HORNEY VERSUS FREUD ON FEMININE PSYCHOLOGY

It is of great interest to note that the whole issue has been raised before. This is pointed out in an excellent article by Fliegel (1973) on the debate between Deutsch, Lampl–de Groot, and Freud on the one side, and Horney and Jones on the other. It is well worthwhile reviewing the history of this debate.

Freud's later writing on the subject began with his paper on "The Dissolution of the Oedipus Complex" (1924), and was answered in a 1924 paper "On the Genesis of the Castration Complex in Women" by Horney (1967). Her basic contention was that the little girl's oedipal attachment develops out of her intrinsic innate femininity undergoing its own maturational processes. Thus a fundamental disagreement was established about the importance of penis envy as a determining factor in the genesis of the girl's Oedipus complex.

The notion of the maturation of intrinsic, innate, internal femininity was not accepted by Freud, and in his next paper "Some Psychical Consequences of the Anatomical Distinction Between the Sexes" (1925e), he stuck to his original concept of the importance of penis envy in setting the little girl off on the pathway of the Oedipus complex.

Fliegel (1973) suggests that Horney's thesis of an intrinsic, pleasure-oriented feminine sexuality that undergoes its own vicissitudes of development is practically a mirror-image of Freud's (1925e) paper. Freud's paper also contains some criticism of Horney which she did not accept, and she responded in 1926 in a second paper entitled "The Flight from Womanhood: the Masculinity Complex in Women as Viewed by Men and Women" (1967). This is a frankly polemical paper by Horney which actually stresses the importance of motherhood envy in men. This paper, which may be thought of as the inception of the women's liberation movement, led to a complete separation between Horney and Freud.

Freud's final word on the subject is presented in the *New Introductory Lectures on Psychoanalysis* (1933), which also contains some very disparaging antifemale remarks, and in his paper "Female Sexuality" (1931) that simply recapitulates his theories. Freud still essentially saw the little girl beginning as a little man, whereas Horney would argue that there is such a thing as feminine oedipal feeling developing spontaneously in the girl, who then temporarily takes flight in the phallic position. This issue still cries out for clinical clarification.

These opposing views carry important theoretical implications. The result of Freud's view is reached by Freud in his paper "Analysis Terminable and Interminable": "We often have the impression that with the wish for a penis and the masculine protest we have penetrated all the psychological strata and reached bedrock, and that thus our activities are at an end. This is probably true, since, for the psychical field, the biological field does in fact play the part of the underlying bedrock. The repudiation of femininity can be nothing else than a biological fact, a part of the great riddle of sex" (1937a). Thus since women can never really gain a penis, it is implied in this paper that a woman never really gets what she wants and no amount of psychotherapeutic work can ever disguise this fact. In this sense all psychotherapeutic work with females must be regarded as unfinished and unsatisfied.

In contrast to this, Horney argues that it is not correct that activities are at an end by reaching penis envy, nor can penis envy be accepted with resignation as the end point of treatment. Penis envy, according to Horney, could be found to screen other early losses and privations or deeper feminine wishes and developmental failures in other areas. This is an extremely important clinical debate.

KAREN HORNEY

Horney's conception of intrinsic femininity that develops in its own way analogous to the development of sexuality in the boy could in the end turn out to be a great idea in psychotherapy and could save psychoanalytic theory from destruction. The clinical issue of whether penis envy is the most important aspect of feminine sexuality, or whether there exists an intrinsic development of feminine sexuality forced Horney—in the tradition of an *experimentum crucis*—to completely revise psychoanalytic theory. Let us review where Horney went next in her development after this unpleasant disagreement with Freud.

In general Karen Horney is probably insufficiently appreciated today. She presented at least two ideas which may turn out to be important in psychotherapy; her ideas, however, still remain extremely controversial and cannot yet be judged in perspective. *First,* she contended that Freud was wrong in his postulates about feminine psychology as I have already discussed, and *second,* she emphasized the subject of self realization. This concept of course, is closely related to the whole field of current existential psychotherapy. For example, Medard Boss, author of the famous existential work on *Daseinanalysis* writes: "Perhaps it would be possible to add editorially that during the years of 1931-32 I was in training at the Berlin Psychoanalytic Institute and there I did supervised analytic work with Karen Horney. From her I received my first impulses which led me to overcome mechanistic thinking and to replace it with a holistic view which since has developed into my *Dasein-analysis* concept" (Kelman 1971). Kelman explains: "The influence of phenomenological and existential thought is evident throughout Horney's early papers on *Feminine Psychology*. Her original formulation of basic anxiety has existential roots. Nietzsche's *Lebensneid*—feelings of bitter, begrudging envy and of being excluded from life—and Scheler's *Ressentiment* are sources for her ideas on sadistic trends. References to Kierkegaard appear frequently. His *Diary of the Seducer* is quoted for its insights on sadistic trends; and *Sickness Unto Death* is used to improve our understanding of hopelessness, despair, and the fear of nothingness. She relies on Kierkegaard and more particularly on William James as sources for her concept of the real self. Horney also valued Paul Tillich's exposition of non-being" (1971).

Kelman and many others give a detailed exposition of Horney's life, including a number of rather unpleasant episodes. I will not do more here than to summarize her life story. She was born in Germany near Hamburg in 1885. Her father was a sea-captain, a Norwegian who had become a German citizen and her mother was Dutch, seventeen years younger than her husband and of a different temperament. Father was morose and devoutly Protestant, given to long silences and bouts of Bible reading, while mother was attractive with a taste for worldly living. Karen Horney and her elder brother remembered as children seeing many parental explosions. Her father was away much of the time on ocean voyages, and she both admired and feared him; she felt her mother favored her good looking older brother.

She decided on medicine as her future profession at the age of twelve and was supported in this by her mother, who helped her through schooling, even though her father adamantly opposed his daughter's career plans. The family turmoil ended with both mother and daughter leaving home; when Horney began medical school, her mother stayed with her.

She married and had two daughters in 1911 and 1913, the same year she received her medical degree; a third daughter was born in 1915. She began as a Berlin neurologist and soon under the influence of Karl Abraham she became involved with the Berlin Psychoanalytic Institute. Her first psychoanalytic paper was published in 1917 and already showed some disagreement with Freud. She acquired a reputation for outspokenness, a trait that did not endear her to most of her colleagues, although she rose steadily at the Berlin Institute. She traveled frequently leaving her husband, a lawyer, behind at home.

Her husband began to drink and gamble and the marriage ended in 1926. In 1932 on the invitation of Franz Alexander, she became the assistant director of the Chicago Institute for Psychoanalysis, but they did not get along very well, and in 1934 she moved to the New York Psychoanalytic Institute.

She was very impressed with the differences in culture between the United States and Germany and, as Cherry explains, "She was particularly appalled by the emphasis on success in American society and noted its costly toll on the emotional lives of the members of the culture. Success, she pointed out, is a concept that necessarily implies failure, and she found many Americans who felt life basically centered on 'winning' or 'losing.' But by the very nature of the competition, Horney said, the losers must predominate and must be tormented by envy and self-loathing. Even the winners in American life, she said, feel insecure because they are aware of the mixed admiration and hostility directed at them" (1973). Horney's ideas were presented in 1937 in her first and most popular book *The Neurotic Personality of Our Time*.

The appearance in 1939 of Horney's *New Ways in Psychoanalysis* led to the ugly episode of a complete break between herself together with four others who supported her and the rest of the New York Psychoanalytic Institute. She went on to form the Association for the Advancement of Psychoanalysis and, a year later, a training institute, The American Institute of Psychoanalysis. There were further administrative clashes which in 1943 resulted in the departure of Harry Stack Sullivan, Erich Fromm, and Clara Thompson for the William Alanson White Psychiatric Foundation in New York. She remained at the head of her institute with a busy schedule, and died in 1952.

I make no effort here to review Horney's work in any detail but concentrate on what is pertinent to great ideas in psychotherapy. Horney, like Adler, resisted compartmentalization of the personality into instincts and forces and thus basically rejected both the Freudian instinct theory and the Freudian structural approach. For her the purpose of psychotherapy is definitely *not* release from repression of specific infantile material of continuing dynamic importance. In her major book, *The Neurotic Personality of Our Time* (1937) she lays down the principles of her approach, attempting to explain neurotic phenomena *not* primarily in terms of the Oedipus complex but in terms of what she called basic anxiety.

BASIC ANXIETY

Basic anxiety is characterized roughly as "a feeling of being small, insignificant, helpless, endangered, in a world that is out to abuse, cheat, attack, humiliate, betray, envy." She briefly explains the origin of basic anxiety:

The basic evil is invariably a lack of genuine warmth and affection. A child can stand a great deal of what is often regarded as traumatic—such as sudden weaning, occasional beating, sex experiences—as long as inwardly he feels wanted and loved. Needless to say a child feels keenly whether the love is genuine, and cannot be fooled by any faked demonstrations. The main reason why a child does not receive enough warmth and affection lies in the parent's incapacity to give it on account of their own neuroses. More frequently than not, in my experience, the essential lack of warmth is camouflaged, and the parents claim to have in mind the child's best interest. Educational theories, oversolicitude or the self-sacrificing attitude of an 'ideal' mother are the basic factors contributing to an atmosphere that more than anything else lays the cornerstone for future feelings of immense insecurity. (1937, p. 80)

Although Horney writes in an excellent style and in a language easily understandable to the educated lay reader and what she says is almost invariably a correct description, these descriptions remain on a superficial level. As a matter of fact, they are most useful to the psychotherapist who wishes to talk with the patient in a language that the patient can understand, but as a metapsychological theory or a basic structural or dynamic approach to understanding psychopathology and normal personality dynamics, they remain on the level of superficial ego psychology. Thus the reader is in the mixed position of often agreeing with what Horney has to say but at the same time feeling that she remains irritatingly on the surface of the phenomena.

She outlines four main ways in our culture for escaping anxiety—to rationalize it, to deny it, to narcotize it, and to avoid thoughts, feelings, impulses and situations which might arouse it. According to Horney, *"Hostile impulses of various kinds form the main source from which neurotic anxiety springs."* The hostility in turn springs from lack of genuine warmth and affection. Munroe explains, "Lacking the early warmth, love, appreciation, and security which allow the real self to develop soundly with flexible, realistic responsiveness to later social events, the child of the neurotic home is over-sensitive both to the neurotic social values of its parents and to the later impacts of social groups. 'Normal' self-esteem and feeling for others and for the realistic contours of life situations are hampered" (1955). Horney is less elaborate in describing the specific conditions of the family group that are likely to produce certain kinds of character development, although she often uses sibling rivalries and the like for understanding individual cases. The infantile experiences are never wholly without importance, but they are viewed as really determining "only for the more inflexible and deeply neurotic patients" (1937). The basic evil in the home is lack of warmth and affection, almost always a consequence of the neuroses of the parents.

Thus already in *The Neurotic Personality of Our Time* (1937) a fundamental difference is presented from Freud, which goes far deeper than merely the substitution of a need for superiority or safety for the

Freudian emphasis on sexuality. The essential point is that man is considered as a social being from the very beginning rather than a biological specimen that learns sociability. In the neuroses, according to Horney, the craving for affection and the craving for power and control are set to play the greatest roles.

HORNEY'S DIRECT REJECTION OF FREUD'S THEORIES

New Ways in Psychoanalysis (1939) must be viewed as a direct polemical assault on Freud. It was her declaration of independence from the Freudian movement and is directly in disagreement with Freud's major doctrines, including a biting attack on Freud's feminine psychology, which—Horney claims repeatedly—first motivated her to dissent from Freud and to review the whole of Freudian theory. Munroe writes, "For her, the fundamental error of the Freudian formulation is the derivation of conflict from the pressure of instinctual needs against the inhibitions opposed by society. Hence the inevitable pessimism of the doctrine" (1955). According to Horney's summary of the main of Freudian doctrine, man for Freud is born for conflict and can at best only mitigate and sublimate its effects. One of the major objections to Horney's *New Ways in Psychoanalysis* is that the summary and explanations of Freudian doctrine are not always accurate. Nevertheless this book is excellent for inclusion in seminars on Freudian psychoanalysis because it contains a well-written critique of his doctrine from another point of view and invariably stimulates the reader to think about these matters for himself.

Munroe explains, "Horney believes that man is born a potentially harmonious organism, capable of expanding his own capacities normally, in happy relationship with his surroundings. Conflict appears only as a consequence of social mishandling which institutes exaggerated impulses and fears in contradictory directions. 'Normally,' the child is confident of help from his parents, because he has experienced it regularly. The neurotic child believes he must fight for everything he wants in a hostile world, because he has experienced deprivation. Yet open aggression in a creature as helpless as the human infant brings swift and overwhelming counteraggression. Thus aggression and the fear of being aggressive *both* develop to an exaggerated degree" (1955).

In her introduction to *New Ways in Psychoanalysis* Horney claims that "the system of theories which Freud has gradually developed is so consistent that when one is once entrenched in them it is difficult to make observations unbiased by his way of thinking. It is only through recognizing the debatable premises on which this system is built that one acquires a clearer vision as to the sources of error contained in the individual theories." Anticipating her later concept of self-realization she explains, "The aim of therapy is then not to help the patient to gain mastery over his instincts but to lessen his anxiety to such an extent that he can dispense with his 'neurotic trends.' Beyond this aim there looms an entirely new therapeutic goal, which is to restore the individual to himself, to help him regain his spontaneity and find his center of gravity in himself" (1939). She throws out the entire sexual manifestations of the Oedipus complex, and although she admits that such a complex appears she interprets the dynamic structure of these attachments as already an early manifestation of neurotic conflicts—much in the way she originally objected to Freud's formulation of penis envy in women, as a secondary formation.

In *Our Inner Conflicts* she continues, "Freud's pessimism as regards neuroses and their treatment arose from the depths of his disbelief in human goodness and human growth. Man, he postulated, is doomed to suffer or to destroy. The instincts which drive him can only be controlled, or at best "sublimated." My own belief is that man has the capacity as well as the desire to develop his potentialities and become a decent human being, and that these deteriorate if his relationship to others and hence to himself is, and continues to be, disturbed. I believe that man can change and go on changing as long as he lives" (1945).

The polemic that she sets up between herself and Freud is actually a false polarization. Many classical Freudian psychoanalysts could agree with some of her conclusions and would not have to do so by throwing out the basic tenets of Freud at all.

THE BASIC CONFLICT

In *Our Inner Conflicts* Horney moves farther and farther toward a reductionistic and simplistic theory of human psychopathology. She begins writing of a *basic conflict* which is found in the personality of *all* neurotics. The basic conflict stems from basic anxiety and from the neurotic's attempt to cope with pathogenic factors in his world, even as a child. Horney's description of this basic conflict sounds very much like some of the writings of the existentialists: "Because of his fear of being split apart on the one hand and the necessity to function as a unity on the other, the neurotic makes a desperate attempt at a solution. While he can succeed in this way in creating a kind of artificial equilibrium, new conflicts are constantly generated and further remedies are continually required to blot them out. Every step in this struggle for unity makes the neurotic more hostile, more helpless, more fearful, more alienated from himself and others, with the result that the difficulties responsible for the conflicts become more acute and their real resolution less and less attainable" (1945).

She carries this further by introducing her important concept of the idealized image of the self. In the neurotic the sense of self is idealized at the expense of true appreciation of one's potentialities, authentic goals, and genuine interpersonal relationships. The idealized image becomes a dictator—she calls it "the tyranny of the should"—which demands rigid fulfillment of its rules regardless of the cost in personal satisfaction or to other people. The real self becomes lost in an effort to preserve the unrealistic exaggerated image of the self and is even hated for its limitations. The idealized image offers a major stumbling block to therapy, since recognition of trends in himself that the patient could readily forgive in others means for him a collapse of his own integrity as a person. In her last book, *Neurosis and Human Growth* (1950), Horney presents the tension between the idealized image of the self and the real self as the *central* conflict in all neuroses.

Before we turn in detail to this, it should be pointed out that chapter two of *Our Inner Conflicts* (1945) contains an excellent description of Horney's notion of the basic conflict, a conflict born of incompatible attitudes which she insists constitutes the core of neurosis. This concept was first presented in 1937 in *The Neurotic Personality of Our Time,* her earliest book, and grows in importance throughout her writings. A child can move toward people, against them, or away from them, but in neuroses there are several reasons why these attitudes and solutions are irreconcilable: "The neurotic is not flexible; he is driven to comply, to fight, to be aloof, regardless of whether the move is appropriate in the particular circumstance, and he is thrown into a panic if he behaves otherwise. Hence when all three attitudes are present in any strong degree, he is bound to be caught in a severe conflict" (1945).

THE STRUGGLE TOWARD SELF-REALIZATION

In *Neuroses and Human Growth* (1950) Horney presents the end point or crystallization of her theoretical position. The neurotic's attempt to solve the basic conflict gives only a false unity and results in self idealization. The attempt sets in motion a new neurotic development called by Horney "the search for glory," representing essentially an attempt to actualize the ideal self. The conflict between the real self, and the proud investment and attempt to actualize the ideal self, is what Horney finally decides is the central inner conflict in all neuroses.

This conflict becomes increasingly central in her thinking. At first it is an important but limited aspect of human adjustment, but the later theoretical development places the tension between the idealized image and the real self at the very center of her psychological theory. According to Munroe (1955), this seems "an error almost as serious as the reductionist trend of Adler. To my mind it obscures the value of Horney's clinical observations concerning the idealized image by overextending the concept of the self to the point at which it is used as a 'general principle,' as an abstraction which seems quite unwarranted no matter how well it seems to 'work' in our culture."

The purpose of therapy for Horney now becomes to help the person lose the neurotic obsession with his idealized self. It will be most instructive for the reader at this point to compare Horney's *Neurosis and Human Growth* (1950) with Kohut's *Analysis of the Self* (1971), an important book that I have reviewed in *The Technique and Practice of Intensive Psychotherapy*. The difference in depth and understanding between these two authors who are in some ways describing the same clinical phenomena speaks for itself.

There is no question that *Neurosis and Human Growth* leads directly to existential psychiatry and to the whole area of so-called third force psychology. This interesting and provocative third force psychology, as presented for example by Maslow (1968, 1971) and reviewed by Goble (1970), is the next rather mystical step after *Neurosis and Human Growth*. I will not make any effort to review it here, since it is essentially a mystical extension of Horney's concept of self-realization and the later existentialist authors.

Horney's theoretical position is almost as reductive as Adler's, since the need for security becomes a kind of universal which supplies the dynamic theme upon which the variations of personality development are constructed. This reductionism and oversimplification, although it makes for easy and popular reading, for example her book *Self-Analysis* (1942), leads to serious and insurmountable theoretical problems. Horney's modes of operation are much better thought of as ego subsystems and superego substructures than as really constituting a new theory in themselves. She is importnat for her emphasis on the current adaptation of the person as a whole, the retaining of early anxiety as an important basic determinant of behavior, and a consequent refocusing on the pregenital relationship with the parent. I cannot avoid the impression that Horney's need to reject and quarrel with first the Freudians and then many of her own followers and peers led her into an untenable theoretical rejection of the whole structure of psychoanalytic theory. Without this problem, Horney might have been considered the honored and remembered founder of ego psychology.

It is extremely important in reviewing this chapter to recognize the central position of Freud's doctrines on feminine psychology as constituting the Michelson-Morley experiment of psychoanalytic theory. The shakiness of these doctrines forms a weakness in psychoanalytic theory that tends to repel certain individuals who have the need to reject the theory altogether. Out of the weakness that they detect in this basic doctrine, they attempt a scientific revolution and seek an entirely new paradigm (Kuhn 1962). Basically this is an acceptable way for science to make progress, and we cannot ignore the fact that if classic psychoanalytic theory is to maintain its present central position in our understanding of psychodynamics and psychopathology, considerable work will have to be done to improve and explicate the basic tenets of feminine psychology. The riddle remains: What does a woman want?

Chapter 15

Language and Language Games

What is your aim in philosophy? - To show the fly the way out of the fly-bottle.
Ludwig Wittgenstein, *Philosophical Investigations* (1962)

Dear Dr. Chessick,

It is 3:15 A.M., between Saturday and Sunday and I have eaten a sandwich. That is not monumental. It's factual. These words I'm using and how I'm using them remind me of when I am making a collage and there is some problem I'm having getting the basic structure of the collage and I find myself altering the paper as soon as I have put it down. I've wrecked a lot of collages that way and some have turned out. Also I have done this writing poetry and writing papers—the same about turning out. Always I am trying to make something perfect when I work this way. But the sandwich is no monument and these words writing to you are me wanting to speak clearly.

I am like a Rube Goldberg machine signifying nothing. I use words like building blocks trying to get them to balance as one piece. But I try to make the most unusual piece possible. And so on the outside they look like a very exotic but unified whole. And then you look at them and you see that the words really do not mean anything. It *looks* nice and it *looks* interesting. Only now and then do I say what I really mean. Up there when I said that I ate a sandwich—now I meant that, I meant to say that only I don't

know what it means and maybe that's why I started talking about
the collage and it seems that I do that a lot—meaning that if
there's something somebody says to me that I don't really
understand or that frightens me, and by the way the somebody
could be me or it could be also something I'm reading or even a
place, then my response if it's verbal gets real complicated and
looks intriguing and sometimes it looks even a little related to
what was said, but, more often than not, has very little to do with
what was said. Large complicated roof houses of words and me
big as life hiding in these words saying try and guess. Right now I
am trying to talk only to tell you something 1) that I ate a
sandwich at 3:30 and maybe it has something to do with a
puzzling (to me) incident with my father and 2) that I have this
problem with words. They can be symbols or meaning and it
seems I use them, exploit them maybe, to hide behind and
confound people. And I think I do this in therapy and sometimes
it frightens me because really I don't want to do that at all. But I,
me, Mary, I lose control over me and it is almost as if the
compulsion is speaking.

You're a good person Dr. Chessick and in some way I trust you.

Mary

THE SEMIOTIC APPROACH TO PSYCHOTHERAPY

Harley Shands suggests an approach to psychiatry based on
philosophy, that he calls a semiotic approach. This approach is based
on the term *semiotic* introduced by Locke at the end of *An Essay
Concerning Human Understanding* (1969): "The third branch may be
called *semiotike* or the *doctrine of signs;* . . . the business whereof is to
consider the nature of signs the mind makes use of for the
understanding of things, or conveying its knowledge to others. . . . The
consideration, then, of *ideas* and *words* as the great instruments of
knowledge makes no despicable part of their contemplation who
would take a view of human knowledge in the whole extent of it. And
perhaps if they were distinctly weighted, and duly considered, they
would afford us another sort of logic and critic, than what we have
been hitherto acquainted with."

In the analysis of language, *semantics* refers to that discipline in
which we study the relation between *words* and what is *meant* by

words. When we raise questions about the rules which prescribe how a language is to be used, this is known as *syntactics*. Both semantics and syntactics are today considered as part of the general discipline of *semiotic*. According to the professional philosopher Brennan, "The name of this study was introduced into general usage by Charles Morris. Semiotic is defined as the general theory of signs and languages" (1967). The reader who wishes a deeper understanding of semiotic itself, which is somewhat peripheral to the purposes of this book, is referred to Morris (1946). He should also review the work of Piaget, who describes "the appearance of the semiotic function" (Evans 1973) as part of normal development.

Shands is determined to make psychiatry a branch of "natural philosophy" and remove it from the "hard sciences," as he calls them. He is particularly interested in the communicative process and believes "human beings are primarily occupants of a universe of meaning rather than a universe of physical being" (1970). He is inclined to doubt that the outside world exists in the form we usually assume and worries at length over its nature, feeling that reality is based primarily in the mind. This immediately takes him somewhat away from Locke's position and toward later developments in philosophy. Because the world of objects is much less than we tend to assume, Shands believes that true reality for all of us is the world of ideas, conveyed primarily through language and conceptualized by Shands in terms of information or communication theory.

Thus Shands emphasizes that psychiatric problems are largely problems of communication and that dynamic psychiatric issues come down basically to problems of language use. Spence emphasizes the great danger in this kind of discipline hopping from philosophy, communication theory, and other theories back and forth to clinical psychiatry. He explains, "The computer and the brain have obvious similarities, for example, but we are gradually coming to learn that they also contain large differences in that one is a misleading model for the other. An ambiguous concept from one discipline may seem similar to a linguistically comparable concept from another, but the ideas represented by the two concepts may be quite different and possibly antagonistic. Only a detailed study of each set of concepts would reveal these discrepancies; they cannot be seen by remaining at the conceptual level. Working with a broad brush, Shands gives us a dazzling series of aphorisms that may or may not prove true" (1972).

PSYCHOTHERAPY AS TRAINING
IN THE USE OF WORDS

For Shands, "Psychiatric disorders are simply disorders of communicative method; the 'patient' is unable to share meaning with his fellows in ways we normatively expect human beings to be able to share such meanings" (1970). He contends that the psychiatrist is most like a language coach, working with patients to improve the degree to which they construe the world in the manner in which their fellows see it. Thus he proposes that the goal of psychotherapy is to "diminish deviance" especially in the manner in which the patient uses language to describe his experience. This must be done in the context of a meaningful and intense relation with a preceptor, in which the primary method is that of encouraging the patient to identify with or model his own behavior upon that of the "preceptor-therapist" (1960). This is clearly a major difference from psychoanalytic methodology and theory, and falls more in the category of inspirational therapy brought to a peak in *War With Words* (1971).

Shands sees psychotherapy as intensive training in the use of words to contain and convey the universe, i.e., as training in a very complex skill. "The psychotherapeutic situation comes to an end when the descriptions of the two participants are reasonably similar. The patient in the psychotherapeutic situation becomes free of the situation when he has accepted it. In the usual terms, we say that he has 'worked through his resistances'; that is, he has ceased to resist. He ceases to be a patient when he consistently formulates his experience in agreement with the therapist" (1960).

The process of psychotherapy according to Shands, is one of *changing descriptions.* This changing of descriptions, which involves the processing of data in a new way, is invariably unpleasant and the mechanisms of defense are seen by Shands as processes which tend to maintain constant routine methods of processing data. Thus Shands here is immersed in information and communication theory and lays the groundwork for his later books. The psychotherapy situation is designed "to facilitate data processing into patterns of description, both in terms of an examination of previously undescribed aspects of the series of events and in terms of the alternative description from a different point of view." The end process of working-through in psychotherapy is found when the therapist and patient agree substantially on their descriptions.

Psychotherapy tries to provide the patient with a better instrument to adapt to the demands of the external world and the demands or restrictions coming from internal drives, conscience, and the like. The test of therapy becomes a test of whether the patient's adaptation or emotional maturity has improved. Changing the descriptions of the patient so that they come into substantial agreement with the descriptions of the therapist improves the patient's adaptational capacity, for the descriptions of the therapist are better power instruments—that is, they explain and predict more accurately and consistently. The question then becomes not one of the "truth" of a given description set, but of its adaptational value. The various schools of psychiatry represent a variety of description sets which have been found to have considerable adaptational value as power instruments and so have attracted adherents. To search for the single absolutely "true" description set is futile and impossible. Thus Shands sees psychiatry as more a branch of natural philosophy, primarily oriented toward the understanding of communicative process and secondarily oriented toward epistemology, rather than as a branch of standard medical science.

Shands insists that in spite of much conscious disagreement among the schools of psychotherapy, there is "a surprisingly wide area of *unconscious* operational agreement upon method and attitude." This is because "It is characteristic of human beings not only to have a language but also to be intolerant of the language of their neighbors" (1960). The question constantly arises as to how one knows which descriptions are true and which are false, bringing us the analogy with Wittgenstein. A description is like a language game. Just as there is no one true language game with one set of true rules, there is no one true description.

The parallel between this approach and the philosophy of Wittgenstein is even deeper. Descriptions, just like language games, have a multiplicity of uses. Sometimes these uses conflict, and one must sacrifice the use of a language game or description for one purpose in order to use it for another purpose in a given situation. An excellent example is what Sullivan (1953) calls the "paranoid crystallization" in a marvelously accurate portrayal of the development of the paranoid delusional system. Unbearable anxiety is reduced by the paranoid crystallization, which is a description set as defined above and adopted for that specific purpose. Unfortunately, however, in adopting a paranoid description set, one must sacrifice alternative description sets that would have much greater power as instruments for adaptation. The result is the paranoid patient sitting on the back ward of the state hospital in a totally unadapted state but clinging tenaciously to his description set for the purpose of reducing unbearable anxiety.

WITTGENSTEIN:
LANGUAGE PROBLEMS AND PSYCHOTHERAPY

By this time it should be clear that we are in "troubled and uncharted waters" and "bumping up against the limits of language" as an introduction to the spectacular and seminal thinker Ludwig Wittgenstein. Levi points out that "despite its fragmentary appearance certain themes keep recurring in Wittgenstein's work: the contrasting nature of the series of 'language games'; an attempt to discover or suggest how language is related to inner experience; the attack upon the primacy of a private language which seems to be presupposed in every attempt to 'infer' philosophically the existence of other minds or of an external world; the intimate connection between the language of sensation and the forms of behavior which are its expression; the relation of "form of life' to linguistic usage and the natural context of experience which surrounds the words with which we express our natures; the limitations of a merely labelling or reportorial theory of language; analyses of such crucial logical and epistemological expressions as 'seeing,' 'imagining,' 'thinking,' 'understanding,' 'naming,' 'intending,' and the like" (1959, pp. 467-468).

A simpler exposition of Wittgenstein is offered by Fann (1971) and a more difficult but still readable and accurate one is presented by Pears (1970).

There is no doubt that all Wittgenstein's philosophy expresses his strong feeling that the great danger to which modern thought is exposed is domination by science, and the consequent distortion of the mind's view of itself. Pears explains, "Wittgenstein's defenses of religion and morality are cryptic, inhibited, possibly unhappy, and certainly for the most part not original" (1970). It is clear that Wittgenstein would have strongly supported moving psychiatry away from "hard science." In his later life he came to view psychoanalysis as a form of mythology.

Wittgenstein began by mastering the mechanics of Hertz and the thermodynamics of Boltzmann. In his twenties he played a part in the development of symbolic logic. He abandoned philosophy at the age of thirty and found himself at fifty urging his hearers to reflect more carefully on the ways in which children learn the standard patterns of behavior within which our language has a practical function, and on the metaphysical confusions that can flow from any failure to keep these practical functions clearly in mind. Janik and Toulmin proclaim, "Yet, for all its seeming changes, his intellectual Odyssey had been directed along a single, constant compass bearing. A man could obey the Socratic injunction, *Know Thyself,* only if he came to understand the scope and limits of his own understanding; and this meant, first and foremost, recognizing the precise scope and limits of language, which is the prime instrument of human understanding" (1973).

Wittgenstein was a passionate thinker for whom philosophical problems appeared as tormenting personal problems. Philosophy was an obsession for Wittgenstein; being a philosopher meant worrying about problems in such a concentrated way that one might at any moment go mad. It was no accident that Wittgenstein's favorite philosophers were St. Augustine, Kierkegaard, and Tolstoy. Opinions of him range from his being utterly crazy to his being the greatest genius of the twentieth century. There are an endless variety of interpretations and misinterpretations of his work, and he is one of the unique philosophers who produced not one but two entirely different and original philosophical systems in one lifetime.

LIFE OF WITTGENSTEIN

Wittgenstein (1889-1951) was born in Vienna, the youngest of eight children. Janik and Toulmin (1973) describe the background of the Vienna in which Wittgenstein was raised. They claim that his family situation placed him at the focus of the Austrian quandaries and paradoxes of the time. Ludwig was the youngest child of a millionaire industrialist, whose home was one of the most important musical salons in Vienna. His father was convinced that the only genuine educational foundation for life was a rigorously disciplined form of private tutoring, and his youngest son Ludwig was educated at home until the age of fourteen. Thus there was an idiosyncratic atmosphere to the Wittgenstein family and household, which as the psychotherapist might predict, led to a great deal of tragedy.

All the children were amazingly talented. The second youngest son, Paul Wittgenstein, lost his right arm but went on to become a successful concert pianist, commissioning a piano work for one hand by Richard Strauss as well as Maurice Ravel's famous Concerto for the Left Hand. "The determination and discipline so required of him, as well as his steadfast and single minded devotion to perfection of technique, were integral elements in the heritage of stern Protestant morality characteristic of the world-view which Karl Wittgenstein transmitted to his entire family" (Janik and Toulmin 1973). The oldest of the children, Hermine, was a painter of ability; the second child, Rudi, was inclined to the theatre. Margaret, the youngest of the three daughters, was the rebel of the family and its brightest intellectual light. She became a close friend of Freud and helped Marie Bonaparte to arrange his escape from Austria. It was likely that Margaret put the writings of Schopenhauer and Kierkegaard into the hands of her brother Ludwig.

There were important conflicts of religious loyalty in the family. Although Karl Wittgenstein's children adopted his Protestant outlook on life, they thought of themselves as entirely Jewish. Father Karl did not wish to allow his sons any choice in deciding on their life's work. He insisted that Hans' extraordinary musical talents be sacrificed to a career in finance and industry, and even as a youth forbade him to play upon the family musical instruments. Hans escaped to North America and committed suicide. This had no apparent effect on the father, and his second son Rudi committed suicide in similar circumstances. Father died in 1913 and did not live to hear of the suicide in 1918 of his third son, who killed himself rather than permit himself to be captured on the Russian front.

Ludwig Wittgenstein could show musical ability, gaiety, and sparkling intelligence, at least before the First World War. From 1919 on, he became a lonely and introverted figure. "He had admitted to having been impressed by Oswald Spengler's *Decline of the West,* and he retreated more and more into ethical attitudes of extreme individualism and austerity. For Wittgenstein as for Tolstoy, the demands of personal integrity were associated with a theoretical commitment to an absolute egalitarianism and an over-riding concern with his brother men. Yet this commitment remained largely theoretical. His normal habit of life was that of a recluse, and it was only during the Second World War that his convictions had a chance to express themselves practically, in his decision to take up war work in the most menial of occupations, as a hospital porter and orderly" (Janik and Toulmin 1973). A great deal of Wittgenstein's depression and seclusion can be explained as the result of a substantial conflict over homosexuality (Bartley 1973).

Ludwig was an indifferent student at home, and his original interest was in machinery. He was trained as a mechanical engineer after fourteen, and his interest began to shift to pure mathematics and then to the philosophical foundations of mathematics. He began to study with Bertrand Russell at Cambridge in 1912 and 1913 and was soon engaged in the research that culminated in his first great work, the *Tractatus Logico-Philosophicus.*

Malcolm gives us a glimpse of Wittgenstein's gaiety at that time. In 1912 he became friends with a fellow student, Pinsent. They were united by strong musical interests. Malcolm explains, "They had a repertoire of forty of Schubert's songs, whose melodies Wittgenstein would whistle while Pinsent accompanied him on the piano. Wittgenstein could play the clarinet and had an excellent memory for music and an unusual gift for sight-reading. He retained a deep interest in music throughout his life; in his philosophical writings there are many allusions to the nature of musical understanding" (1961). Pinsent described Wittgenstein as a difficult companion—nervously sensitive, irritable, often depressed.

When his father died in 1913, Wittgenstein inherited a large fortune. He gave this away partly because of his inclination for the simple and frugal life and partly because he felt it was not right for a philosopher to have money. He worked with fierce energy at his logical ideas, and in 1913 lived alone in a hut in Norway in complete seclusion working at the *Tractatus* until the outbreak of World War One. Strangely, he believed that no one would understand the *Tractatus* only by reading it, but that some day some person might independently think those same thoughts and would derive pleasure in finding the exact expression of them in his book. When war broke out Wittgenstein entered the Austrian army as a volunteer. While serving on the Eastern front he continued to work at his book, writing down his philosophical thoughts in notebooks that he carried in his knapsack. He completed the *Tractatus* in August 1918 and was taken prisoner by the Italians two months later in November. From prison camp he sent the manuscript of the book to Bertrand Russell. During his time in the prison camp in Italy, he read a standard version of the Gospels and was much disturbed by it, coming more and more under the influence of Tolstoy's unique interpretation of religion.

There was considerable struggle in getting his book published and a lot of argument with Russell, whom he claimed did not understand the book, but it finally appeared in an English translation in 1922. See Russell's description of this interaction and the letters of Wittgenstein to Russell (1968). A new and improved translation appeared in 1961. Some of the notebooks used in preparing the *Tractatus* were preserved and were also published in the same year. They present a vivid picture of the intensity of Wittgenstein's struggles with the problems of the *Tractatus*.

Returning to civilian life, Wittgenstein decided to become a school teacher since he felt that in the *Tractatus* he had solved all the problems of philosophy. In 1920, after completing a teacher's training course, he began teaching classes of children of ages nine and ten in Austria. He was an exacting teacher, did not get on with his colleagues, and was often depressed. He taught school for six years and prepared a dictionary published in 1926 of six or seven thousand words for the use of pupils in the elementary schools of the Austrian villages.

In 1926 he resigned as a school teacher and thought of becoming a monk but instead worked as a gardener's assistant at a monastery. One of his sisters commissioned a mansion in Vienna, and Wittgenstein at her invitation worked on it's design for two years, also doing some sculpture at the same time. When Moritz Schlick, a Vienna professor of philosophy who was deeply impressed by the *Tractatus,* managed to prevail upon Wittgenstein to attend one or two meetings of the famous Vienna Circle of logical positivists, they were horrified to discover that instead of discussing philosophy with them he insisted on reading poetry.

In 1929 he suddenly returned to Cambridge to devote himself again to philosophy, for reasons that are not clear. He began to lecture at Cambridge in 1930 and remained there for six years; in 1936 he went again to live in his hut in Norway and began writing the *Philosophical Investigations*. In 1937 he returned to Cambridge, and two years later succeeded G. E. Moore at the Chair of Philosophy. Malcolm explains, "Wittgenstein's lectures made a powerful impression on his auditors. They were given without notes or preparation. Each lecture was a new philosophical work. Wittgenstein's ideas did not come easily. He carried on a visible struggle with his thoughts. At times there were long silences, during which his gaze was concentrated, his face intensely alive, and his expression stern, and his hands made arresting movements. His hearers knew that they were in the presence of extreme seriousness, absorption, and force of intellect. . . . His lectures moved over a wide range of topics and were marked by great richness of illustration and comparison" (1967). Others have not been so praising of Wittgenstein's lectures, in that he was apparently quite sarcastic and insisted on personally attacking his listeners.

Although at times he could put on a light-hearted mood, most of the time he was dismayed by the insincerity, vanity, and coldness of the human heart. He was always troubled about his own life and often close to despair and suicide. In World War II, he could not remain a spectator but worked as a lowly porter in a London hospital and later as a "lab boy" in a clinical research laboratory until 1944. In 1944 he resumed his lectures at Cambridge but became increasingly dissatisfied with his role as a teacher and felt an increasing need to live alone. In 1947 he resigned his chair and sought a secluded life in isolated cottages in Ireland. He worked hard on the *Philosophical Investigations* but after a three month trip to the United States in 1949 discovered that he had cancer. He visited his remaining family for the last time and moved to the home of a physician in Cambridge in 1951 in order to spend his last days away from the hospital. He continued hard at work and died in 1951.

Janik and Toulmin insist that the two most important facts about Wittgenstein are that he was a Viennese and that he was trained as an engineer. Their hypothesis is that in *fin-de-siècle* Vienna one had to

"Face the problem of the *nature and limits of language, expression and communication.* . . . by the year 1900, the linked problems of communication, authenticity and symbolic expression had been faced in parallel in all the major fields of thought and art. . . . So the stage was set for a *philosophical* critique of language given in completely general terms" (1973).

Stegmuller explains, "It is this union of metaphysical brooder and technical expert in the one person of the author or the *Tractatus* that constitutes a further reason for the difficulties we experience in understanding this work" (1970). In turning to the *Tractatus* it is important to remind the reader that only those aspects of it that are vital for great ideas in psychotherapy are to be reviewed here.

THE TRACTATUS LOGICO-PHILOSOPHICUS

The *Tractatus,* a very difficult and controversial work, deviates in at least four significant respects from Kant's philosophy: (1) it brings back an ontological conception that Kant rejected; (2) The picture theory of sentence meaning and thinking in the *Tractatus* is suitable only to a *realistic* system, not to intellectual structure that holds the world to be in part the product of mental constructions; (3) it adopts the position of Hume rather than Kant with respect to the notion of causality; and (4) it rejects the synthetic *a priori* entirely (see chapter 8).

The *Tractatus* is a thoroughly metaphysical work in which the ultimate purpose seems to be to demonstrate what cannot be said or even talked about. "The principal theme of the book is the connection between language, or thought, and reality" (Anscombe 1967). Language shows us something we cannot think and the function of philosophy is to indicate what *cannot* be said by presenting clearly what *can* be said. According to the *Tractatus,* there is a realm of the unthinkable which far from being unimportant is actually the foundation of all language and all thought. In some way we grasp this foundation of thought; it is mirrored in our thoughts, but it cannot be an object of thought. It is interesting that this thoroughly metaphysical work was once widely regarded as being the foundation of positivism in its outlook. Wittgenstein did not reject the metaphysical; he rejected the possibility of talking about the metaphysical or stating it.

Fann summarizes the *Tractatus* as follows: "Language consists of propositions. All propositions can be analyzed into elementary propositions and are truth-functions of elementary propositions. The elementary propositions are immediate combinations of names, which directly refer to objects; and elementary propositions are logical pictures of atomic facts, which are immediate combinations of objects. Atomic facts combine to form facts of whatever complexity which constitute the world. Thus language is truth-functionally structured and its essential function is to describe the world. Here we have the limits of language and what amounts to the same, the limits of the world" (1971). Thus Wittgenstein contends that the really important things such as moral and aesthetic values, the meaning of life, and so on are "mystical" (1969c, proposition 6.522). In fact he considered the cardinal problem of philosophy to be the delineation of what can be said and what cannot be said but only shown.

Wittgenstein's attitude toward the mystical is abundantly substantiated by the publication of his *Lectures on Ethics*. He describes the effort to talk about ethics and religion as a "running against the walls of our cage," which he sees as perfectly and absolutely hopeless. He writes, "Ethics, so far as it springs from the desire to say something about the ultimate meaning of life, the absolute good, the absolute valuable, can be no science. What it says does not add to our knowledge in any sense. But it is a document of a tendency of human mind which I personally cannot help respecting deeply and I would not for my life ridicule it" (1965).

Just as Kant maintained that thought necessarily ceases in the rarefied atmosphere beyond the boundary which he plotted, so too Wittgenstein maintained language necessarily ceases at his line of demarcation, and that beyond it there can only be silence. Pears explains, "Kant's boundary enclosed factual knowledge, and Wittgenstein's enclosed factual discourse. In each case the withdrawal from speculative metaphysics left religion and morality in an exposed position. Wittgenstein's solution to this problem, though not the same as Kant's, was very like it; he placed the truths of religion and morality not outside factual discourse, but in some mysterious way inside it without being part of it" (1970).

After over seventy pages apparently devoted to nothing but logic, theory of language, philosophy of mathematics, and natural science we are suddenly faced by the five concluding pages of the *Tractatus* (proposition 6.4 on) in which our heads are seemingly wrenched around, and we are presented with a string of dogmatic theses about solipsism and "The sense of the world must lie outside the world." There has been tremendous debate as to whether these last few reflections about ethics and values are mere after-thoughts or of integral importance.

Positivism argues that what we can speak of is all that matters in life, whereas Wittgenstein passionately believed that all that really matters in human life is precisely what we must be silent about. *Right feeling*—the capacity to respond to the suffering of another—is more important than the facts of science. This is the Tolstoyan view and in the *Tractatus,* scientific knowledge is relegated to a secondary role. The vehicle for conveying feeling, Wittgenstein agrees with Kierkegaard, is in poems, aphorisms, fables, or such stories as Tolstoy's tales. These fables reach to a man in his *Innerlichkeit* and so are the means of touching the fantasy, which is the fountainhead of value. Thus subjective truth for Kierkegaard is communicable only indirectly through fables, polemics, irony, and satire. This is the only way that one can come to "see the world aright." Ethics is taught not by arguments but by providing examples of behavior, and this is the task of art. It explains why Wittgenstein read poetry to the members of the Vienna Circle. Where the Vienna Positivists had equated the important as the verifiable and dismissed all unverifiable propositions as unimportant because unsayable, the concluding section of the *Tractatus* insisted that the unsayable alone had genuine value.

THE PHILOSOPHICAL INVESTIGATIONS

In 1929 he returned to Cambridge following an absence of more than fifteen years. From then until his death, Wittgenstein did a huge amount of writing. None of this was carefully organized. In 1933-1934 Wittgenstein dictated a set of notes to his students that constitute *The Blue Book*. It is a comparatively superficial work, although it is clear and lively and some say the beginner's best introduction to Wittgenstein. He also wrote *The Brown Book* which for a short time he regarded as a draft for an important manuscript but gave it up in 1936 when he began to write the *Philosophical Investigations*.

The *Philosophical Investigations* was first published in 1953, posthumously at Wittgenstein's request. It is divided into two parts, Part One written in 1936-1945, and Part Two written in 1947-1949. There are also extensive other writings of Wittgenstein from 1937-1944, which have been published in various places and parts. All of them are disorganized and aphoristic in style.

Malcolm explains that "Wittgenstein believed that the *Investigations* could be better understood if one saw it against the background of the *Tractatus*. A considerable part of the *Investigations* is an attack, either explicit or implicit, on the earlier work. This development is probably unique in the history of philosophy—a thinker producing at different periods of his life, two highly original systems of thought, each system the result of many years of intensive labors, each expressed in an elegant and powerful style, each greatly influencing contemporary philosophy, and the second being a criticism and rejection of the first" (1967).

There are two main changes in Wittgenstein's doctrine from his early to later periods. First he abandoned the idea that the structure of reality determines the structure of language. He suggested that it is really the other way around—our language determines our view of reality because we see things through it. So he no longer believed it possible to deduce the pre-existing structure of reality from the premise that all languages have a certain common structure. The second change is in his theory of language. In the *Tractatus* he argues that all languages have a uniform logical structure which can be disclosed by philosophical analysis. He came around to the diametrically opposite view in *Philosophical Investigations*. The *diversification* of linguistic forms, he now thought, actually reveals the deep structure of language, which has *no* common essence, or at least if it has one it is a minimal one. The various languages are connected with one another in a more elusive way, like games, or like the faces of people belonging to the same family. Thus, "a sophisticated anthropocentric relativism, a kind of comparative anthropology of linguistic systems whose meaning was determined by their usage, replaced the objective realism of the *Tractatus*" (Bartley 1973).

This new theory of language is the key to the understanding of Wittgenstein's later philosophy, because it also led to a radical change in his method. The *Tractatus* is a continuous treatise, with a clear aim and a clear way of achieving it. But in *Philosophical Investigations* it is easy to get lost, because it is a series of remarks selected from notebooks and arranged according to their subject matter and has no master plan. The result is a new kind of philosophical work which contains no sweeping generalization and is full instead of ordinary detailed descriptions of language, which we are invited—almost forced—to take part in. Pears writes, "In the *Tractatus* the limit of language was drawn with one great sweeping stroke, and he was evidently confident that it was a barrier which would be felt from the inside to be insurmountable. In his later work there has been a change of mind on both these points. He has come to think that the only way to understand the limit of language is to try to cross it and to return to language in its ordinary human setting only after a genuine and of course necessarily unsuccessful attempt of this kind. So the limit is now to be plotted by a kind of oscillation and not by a single well-defined movement" (1970).

In *Philosophical Investigations,* Wittgenstein argued that the problems of philosophy are all due to confusion in the use of language and that philosophy was a form of therapy to clear up these confusions. He contended that everyday language was good enough for everyday purposes, and that we get into difficulty only when we look for something in language that is not there. To dissolve the problems of philosophy, we need to understand how everyday language actually functions; it is our misunderstanding of how it functions that has created the problems of philosophy. Philosophy thus becomes "A battle of the bewitchment of our intelligence by means of language." The trouble comes when philosophers use words like "knowledge," "being," "object," and so on, and try to grasp the essence of what these words refer to. The answer is that there is no such essence, and the way to discover this is to ask oneself, "Is the word actually used in this way in the language game which is its original home?" Thus what philosophers do or should do is "bring words back from their metaphysical to their everyday use" (1962).

There is nothing in common to what we call language or linguistic usages; they are merely related to one another in many different ways in the sense of a family resemblance. There is no mysterious essence. Wittgenstein focused his attention on language as behavior, concentrating his analysis on the rules that govern the use of different expressions, and the language in which those rules are operative, and on the forms of life that gives those language games their significance. This may be an *a posteriori* method of investigating the actual phenomena of language and seems to be based on the years Wittgenstein spent in teaching elementary school children. In order to find out whether a child knows the meaning of a word or not, one must observe how the child uses the word. The explanation of the meaning of the word consists in teaching the child the *use* of the word.

Fann explains, "The *Investigations* is completely unsystematic in both its form and content. Unlike most earlier or later philosophical writings in the Western tradition, it consists of loosely connected remarks, unanswered questions, unamplified hints, imaginary dialogues, vague parables, metaphors, and epigrams. This as Wittgenstein points out in the Preface, is 'connected with the very nature of the investigation.' If we ask, 'What is Wittgenstein *saying?* What kind of theory is he advancing?' as we usually do upon reading a philosophical book, we would be on the wrong track. I wish to suggest a way of looking at the *Investigations* which may reveal something of the 'nature' of his investigation. I recommend asking instead, 'What is Wittgenstein *doing?*' The answer is: confession and persuasion" (1971, p. 105).

Followers of Wittgenstein have attempted to systematize and explicate his philosophy, in spite of his warnings. Thus he is credited by Quinton with breaking "wholly new ground" with a theory of mind that interprets our descriptions of mental acts and states "not as referring to something private within our streams of interior consciousness but as governed by criteria that mention the circumstances, behavior, and propensities to behave of the persons described" (Pitcher 1966). This was carried further by the Oxford philosophers in Britain after World War II, culminating in Ryle's *The Concept of Mind* (1949; see also Chessick 1971c). This notion of *philosophical* behaviorism has not led to any major alterations in psychotherapy and will not be developed here; some day it may prove to have interesting implications, but so far it is rather disappointing as a meeting-place for philosophers and psychotherapists (For details see Wisdom 1952, 1953, and Hartnack 1965.)

It is clear that *Philosophical Investigations* is one of the most difficult works in the history of philosophy and represents a constant struggle against man's natural tendency to misunderstand his own language. As many ways as there are of describing the world, just so many ways are there of analyzing it into individual states of affairs. Thus the world is not in itself organized in such and such a way and cannot as organization be described truly or falsely by language. On the contrary, the possibilities of its organization *first* arise through linguistic articulation, argues Wittgenstein.

LANGUAGE GAMES

Employment of the expression "language games" is not accidental, for Wittgenstein leads us necessarily to comparison with a complicated game such as chess. What stands in the foreground is the operative aspect common to games and language. Stegmuller writes,

> To realize a game is to *operate with playing pieces* in a particular way, to actualize a language as a language game is to *operate with words and sentences.* And just as operating with playing pieces is governed by *rules,* so too is *operating with linguistic expressions.* . . . As we understand the 'meaning' of the individual chessmen only when we know the rules of chess and thus know the rules governing the moves of the individual chessmen only when we know the rules of chess and thus know the rules governing the moves of the individual pieces, so we grasp the meanings of linguistic expressions only after we have learned the rules according to which we may operate with these expressions in individual language games. . . . The analogy perceived by Wittgenstein is such a strong one that we might term his new conception, figuratively, a 'chess theory of language' in contrast to the 'mosaic theory of language' championed in the *Tractatus,* according to which linguistic signs are combined into mosaic pictures of the state of affairs which are themselves built of individual and attributive elements." (1970, pp. 444-445)

Some of the basic themes of *Philosophical Investigations* may be summarized as follows:

1. The speaking of language is in itself a form of life. The actual use of language is like a game, let us say like chess. It has certain rules that must be observed by those who play the game, and there are certain

restrictions on the moves that are allowed. Since we use language in a multiplicity of ways, we speak of each of these ways as a "language game."

2. "Our language can be seen as an ancient city: a maze of little streets and squares, of old and new houses, and houses with additions from various periods; and this surrounded by a multitude of new boroughs with straight regular streets and uniform houses" (1962).

3. Language is much more complex than previously believed and is used in a variety of related ways. "Language games" form a "family" in that when we look for similarities between the various "language games" we "see a complicated network of similarities, overlapping and criss-crossing" (1962).

4. According to Bertrand Russell on Wittgenstein: "By learning to play a variety of language games, we acquire the meaning of words through and in their use. . . . The raising of metaphysical problems would then be the result of a defective grasp of the 'grammar of words" (1959). Philosophy, for Wittgenstein, would consist of clearing up confusions in our use of language. If we could obtain complete clarity in our use of language, it follows that philosophy would disappear, for philosophical questions only arise when we "don't know our way about" in linguistic usage.

5. There is a philosophical prejudice in favor of the "primacy of the private," that is, first we have private experiences and then we label them with words. Words can be behavior. For example, adults can teach a child new pain-behavior so that the verbal expression of pain rather than *describing* pain *replaces* such primitive expressions of it as crying.

6. Thus language is learned as a series of language games, many of which have important utility and are *instruments* for various purposes. As Levi puts it: "This is to pass far beyond a theory of meaning which identifies meaning with the connotation and denotation of names. The significance of an expression is like the *power* and the *functions* of a knight or rook in chess; to understand the piece you must understand its utility for the game. It follows that there are plural pieces with plural utilities" (1959).

An aside is now in order regarding the complexity and difficulty of this material. The lack of a clear and simple presentation of the language game is not a function of poor writing; it is because of the multiplicity of language games. In fact, the search for one clear and simple set of rules is responsible for serious and hopeless paradoxes in philosophy. This insight is Wittgenstein's basic and brilliant contribution.

THE PARALLEL TASKS OF
PHILOSOPHY AND PSYCHOTHERAPY

Ambrose points out, "Anyone who reads the post-Tractatus writings of Wittgenstein cannot fail to be struck by the psychoanalytic atmosphere with which he surrounds a good deal of his philosophical work. It is therefore interesting to learn that Wittgenstein once described himself as 'a disciple of Freud,' that his first reaction to reading Freud, presumably sometime after 1919, was one of admiration. . . . 'I sat up in surprise,' he said, 'here was someone who had something to say.' It is known that he later rejected psychoanalysis, its theory, and what he took to be its practice" (Hanly and Lazerowitz 1970). He continued to admire Freud for his observations and suggestions, and apparently psychoanalytic theory kept sufficient hold on his mind to prompt him to discuss it in the course of several lectures at Cambridge University (1967). By 1946 he rejected psychoanalysis as imposing upon one a mythology. Ambrose argues that despite his rejection of Freudian theory. "What was most original about Wittgenstein's conception of philosophical problems derives in part from certain likenesses between psychoanalytic insight into the workings of the mind and his understanding of philosophy." It should already be obvious to the reader of this chapter that the description by Wittgenstein of his conception of his task in *Philosophical Investigations* is reminiscent of psychoanalytic descriptions of the treatment of neurotic symptoms. Just as insight into their determinants effects their cure, so insight into the linguistic structure of a philosophical problem eliminates the pathological entanglement with words. Ambrose develops this theme at length and the reader is referred to her chapter for details (Hanly and Lazerowitz 1970).

Philosophy resembles psychoanalytic psychotherapy in that to the extent that it is successful, it simply disappears. Even in the *Tractatus* Wittgenstein explains that when one has climbed out through them, on them, and over them, then Wittgenstein's views are no longer needed and the problems of philosophy are dissolved: "He must, so to speak, throw away the ladder after he has climbed it" (1969c). Anyone who has fully understood the nature of the ladder that Wittgenstein has offered him no longer needs the ladder. He has escaped from philosophy which Wittgenstein, the reader will remember, sees as a painful obsession and a sickness to be cured.

In *Philosophical Investigations* the same idea is presented—to show the fly a way out of the fly bottle, and thus dissolve the problems philosophy presents. It is indeed a remarkable parallel to psychoanalytic psychotherapy. Philosophical questions are tormenting questions arising from our misuse of language; they are "vexations" into "intellectual discomfort" comparable to some kind of mental disease. Fann explains, "The metaphorical description of philosophical problems in psychological terms—such as 'mental cramp,' 'mental torment,' etc—is not accidental. For one thing, it is an expression of Wittgenstein's *personal* involvement with them, for another, it is an appropriate characterization of Wittgenstein's own methods and aim of philosophy. 'The philosopher's treatment of a question is like the treatment of an illness' (P.I. Par. 255). Just as there is not *one* conclusive therapy for all mental illness; there is not *a* 'philosophical method, though there are indeed methods, like different therapies' (P.I. Par. 133). Which therapy should be used would depend on the illness and the person who is afflicted by it. . . . However philosophy is never trivial or unimportant just as treatment by psycho-analysis should not be regarded as trivial on the ground that it merely restores a man's sanity" (1971, pp. 87-88).

Wittgenstein's work is open to many criticisms. Why should linguistic philosophy not be systematic? What is wrong with the suggestion that philosophy ought to theorize about language in a way that would reveal the general nature of the material to which language is applied? It is arguable that Wittgenstein's later philosophy does not really avoid implicit generalizations. Wittgenstein never really solved the questions that tormented him and as a result "paradox haunts the pages of the *Investigations*" (Jones 1969). There is no question that in conceiving of philosophy as a therapeutic rather than a cognitive enterprise, Wittgenstein, like Nietzsche, made a profound shift in orientation. For such thinkers the existential problems come to the fore. In this way and in his passionate, almost obsessional commitment to philosophy, Wittgenstein has a definite affinity to existentialist thought. However, the problems he aimed to dissolve have obstinately refused to stay dead.

APPLICATIONS TO THE CONCEPTS OF WORKING THROUGH AND INSIGHT

It should be clear by now that the great ideas implicit in this chapter remain to be elucidated and resolved in the future. The use and limits of language in everyday life and in psychotherapy require considerable study, as a thorough conception of the notions of working-through and of insights from psychotherapeutic interaction rests upon such usage. For example, Wittgenstein states "When he suddenly knew how to go on, when he understood the principle, then possibly he had a special experience—and if he is asked: 'What was it? What took place when you suddenly grasped the principle?' perhaps he will describe it much as we described it above—but for us it is the *circumstances* under which he had such an experience that justify him in saying in such a case that he understands, that he knows how to go on. . . . 'What happens when a man suddenly understands?'—The question is badly framed. If it is a question about the meaning of the expression 'sudden understanding,' the answer is not to point to a process that we give this name to. The question might mean: what are the tokens of sudden understanding; what are its characteristic psychical accompaniments?" (1962, pp. 61, 81).

Controversy between so-called "schools" of psychotherapy at times rests on linguistic confusion (Chessick 1971c). Honesty about the language games he chooses also ties the psychotherapist more completely to an epistemological position of one sort or another—which in turn will determine the approach he will take to the notions of insight and working-through. Recognizing the importance of description sets and language games and understanding that the one truth is that there is no Truth can be a vital starting point in resolving some of the emotional differences between schools of psychotherapy. Wittgenstein fully recognizes this difficult problem when he writes in *Philosophical Investigations*.

"How does it come about that this arrow >>>—> *points?* Doesn't it seem to carry in it something besides itself? - 'No, not the dead line on paper; only the psychical thing, the meaning, can do that.'—That is both true and false. The arrow points only in the application that a living being makes of it.

This pointing is not a hocus-pocus which can be performed only by the soul.

We want to say: 'When we mean something, it's like going up to someone, it's not having a dead picture (of any kind).' We go up to the thing we mean." (1962, pp. 132)

In previous publications reviewed in Chapter 8 (1971c, 1974d, 1974e, 1974f, 1974g, 1975), I pointed out how two competing languages, grounded on different nuclear operations of the mind, are used by psychotherapists for the description of psychotherapeutic interaction. These are the language of scientific understanding and the language of the humanistic imagination. Psychotherapists must be educated in both, or their understanding and interpretative capacities will be seriously impaired. Furthermore, processes describing by these languages are not chronologically equivalent in psychotherapy, and serious amateur errors occur if this is not clearly comprehended.

The language of science stresses true and false propositions, error, causality, law, prediction, fact, and equilibrium of systems. The language of the humanistic imagination focuses on destiny and human purpose, fate and fortune, tragedy, and illusion. Depending on which nuclear critical faculty of the mind—imagination or understanding—is being employed, a different map of what appears to be reality will emerge. One map of psychotherapeutic interaction will be sober and factual, claiming to be the custodian of literal truth, mechanistic and objective. The second will be mythical, teleological, and dramatic, dealing more with concepts like creativity, destiny, and human purpose. The need to construct objective, factual, mechanistic chains of causal explanation as well as the need to construct heuristic often dramatic and anthropomorphic, explanatory fictions are both fundamental human cognitive needs based on different nuclear operations of human critical mental functioning as first delineated by Kant (1965).

This discussion leads directly to the next chapter and the problems of metapsychiatry. As Popper eloquently concludes, "All scientific descriptions of facts are highly selective, that they always depend upon theories. The situation can be best described by comparison with a searchlight. What the searchlight makes visible will depend upon its position, upon our way of directing it, and upon its intensity, colour, etc; although it will, of course, also depend very largely upon the things illuminated by it. Similarly, a scientific description will depend, largely, upon our point of view, our interests, which are as a rule connected with the theory or hypothesis we wish to test; although it will also depend upon the facts described. Indeed, the theory or hypothesis could be described as the crystallization of a point of view" (1966).

Chapter 16

Philosophy of Science
and Metapsychiatry

A work that aspires, however humbly, to the condition of art should carry its justification in every line. And art itself may be defined as a single-minded attempt to render the highest kind of justice to the visible universe, by bringing to light the truth, manifold and one, underlying its every aspect. It is an attempt to find in its forms, in its colors, in its light, in its shadows, in the aspects of matter and in the facts of life, what of each is fundamental, what is enduring and essential—their one illuminating and convincing quality—the very truth of their existence. The artist, then, like the thinker or the scientist, seeks the truth and makes his appeal. Impressed by the aspect of the world the thinker plunges into ideas, the scientist into facts—whence, presently, emerging they make their appeal to those qualities of our being that fit us best for the hazardous enterprise of living. They speak authoritatively to our common sense, to our intelligence, to our desire of peace or to our desire of unrest; not seldom to our prejudices, sometimes to our fears, often to our egoism—but always to our credulity. And their words are heard with reverence, for their concern is with weighty matters: with the cultivation of our minds and the proper care of our bodies, with the attainment of our ambitions, with the perfection of the means and the glorification of our precious aims.

It is otherwise with the artist.

Confronted by the same enigmatical spectacle the artist descends within himself, and in that lonely region of stress and strife, if he be deserving and fortunate, he finds the terms of his appeal. His appeal is made to our less obvious capacities: to the part of our nature which, because of the warlike conditions of existence, is necessarily kept out of sight within the more resisting and hard qualities—like the vulnerable body within a steel armor. His appeal is less loud, more profound, less distinct, more stirring—and sooner forgotten. Yet its effect endures forever. The changing wisdom of successive generations discards ideas, questions facts, demolishes theories. But the artist appeals to that part of our being which is not dependent on wisdom: to that in us which is a gift and not an acquisition—and, therefore, more permanently enduring. He speaks to our capacity for delight and wonder, to the sense of mystery surrounding our lives; to our sense of pity, and beauty, and pain; to the latent feeling of fellowship with all creation—to the subtle but invincible conviction of solidarity that knits together the loneliness of innumerable hearts, to the solidarity in dreams, in joy, in sorrow, in aspirations, in illusions, in hope, in fear, which binds men to each other, which binds together all humanity—the dead to the living and the living to the unborn.

Joseph Conrad, *The Nigger of the "Narcissus"*

METAPSYCHIATRY DEFINED

The subject matter of metapsychiatry (Chessick 1969a) is the investigation of whether the "knowledge" gained through psychotherapy such as the "principles of psychodynamics" is knowledge at all, and, if so, in what sense. The scientific, artistic, and philosophical aspects of psychotherapy all need to be clarified under the study of metapsychiatry. In metapsychiatry we try to determine (a) the position of psychotherapy in Western philosophical tradition, (b) to what extent psychotherapy can be said to be a "science" and to yield "scientific knowledge," and (c) to what extent it is philosophy or art. Clarification of these issues could save much needless rhetoric and argument.

The great physicist Niels Bohr (Heisenberg 1971) distinguished the language of religion, science, and art as *complementary descriptions* which, though they exclude one another, are needed to convey the rich possibilities flowing from man's relationship with the central order. Thus the language of the humanistic imagination and the language of the scientific understanding represent different complementary ways of looking at the same sensory manifold.

This notion of complementary perspectives does not *have* to imply either equality in kind or the presence of a linguistic continuum between scientific and humanistic descriptions as Jones (1967) would have us accept in his provocative notion of "meta-metaphysics." To insist that it does would involve us in controversial philosophical issues beyond the scope of this book and unnecessary for our purposes as psychotherapists.

THE PRINCIPLE OF COMPLEMENTARITY

The conception of complementary descriptions of psychotherapeutic interaction is consistent with Bohr's great idea—the controversial *principle of complementarity* to which we will refer again and again in this chapter. In 1927 during the International Congress of Physics, Niels Bohr introduced in a public lecture his formulation of complementarity. What Bohr was pointing to in 1927 was the curious realization that in the atomic particle domain, the only way the observer (including his equipment) can be uninvolved is if he observes nothing at all. Holton explains, "As soon as he sets up the observation tools on his workbench, the system he has chosen to put under observation and his measuring instruments for doing the job form one inseparable whole. Therefore, the results depend heavily on the apparatus" (1973).

Bohr was able to show that any apparatus designed to measure position at the level of atomic particles with ideal precision cannot provide any information about momentum, and vice versa. Two mutually exclusive experiments are needed to obtain full information about the mechanical state, each complementing the other. He expressed this conclusion as a general principle of complementarity, and in developing this particle he asserted that it is neither possible nor necessary to make a choice between waves and particles and that indeed *both* are essential for complete comprehension of reality.

The uncertainty principle of Heisenberg has sometimes been misconstrued to imply that a particle actually *has* both a precise position and momentum until it is disturbed by the experimenter and that the act of observing the position precisely "destroys" the precise momentum; in other words, that nature is involved in a bizarre conspiracy to prevent the discovery of something that had real existence. Guillemin points out that "it is nearer to the truth to assert that a particle of itself has neither a position nor a momentum and that the act of observation *creates* its mechanical state. This conclusion followed directly from the general principle of quantum-mechanics that all the circumstances of the particle's position and momentum are contained in its accompanying matter waves" (1968).

This point of view was criticized because it seems to treat particles and waves as equal when as a matter of fact, particles are a mode of existence, while waves are a mode of behavior. The choice is a matter of temperament and taste. The conflict between describing psychotherapeutic interaction either in terms of *Existenzphilosophie* (see chapter 18) or in terms of intrapsychic (or interpersonal) psychodynamics presents an identical dilemma to the participant-observer. Thus some choose to characterize the interaction as an investigation of and intrusion into the patient's mode of existence, whereas others are more comfortable in using Freud's or Sullivan's psychodynamics. The point is that *both* are essential for a complete comprehension of reality and it is not a matter of one descriptive language being "right" and one descriptive language being "wrong."

Indeed, Bohr (1958) hoped that the principle of complementarity would come to be applied to many other areas of knowledge beside atomic physics. Thus Bohr's real ambition for the complementarity conception went far beyond dealing with the paradox of the physics of the 1920's. "From this point of view we realize that Bohr's proposal of the complementarity principle was nothing less than an attempt to make it the cornerstone of a new epistemology. . . . It was the *universal* significance of the role of complementarity which Bohr came to emphasize" (Holton 1973).

Many ways of characterizing this principle, none completely satisfactory, are possible (see Bohr 1963). At any rate, in place of a precisely definable conceptual mode, *the principle of complementarity states that we are restricted to complementary pairs of inherently imprecisely defined concepts, and the maximum degree of precision of either member of such a pair is reciprocally related to that of the opposite number.* Bohr explains, "The specific experimental conditions then determine how precisely each member of a complementary pair of concepts should be defined in any given case. But no single overall concept is supposed ever to be possible, which would represent *all* significant aspects of the behaviour of an individual system precisely" (1971). This renounces the notion of unique and precisely defined conceptual models in favor of that of complementary pairs of imprecisely defined models, and this represents an absolute and final limitation on our investigation and understanding of every domain of knowledge.

APPLICATION OF THE PRINCIPLE OF COMPLEMENTARITY TO PROBLEMS IN PSYCHOTHERAPY

The debate in the Western world today is intense between the proponents of the Freudian deterministic metapsychology and the proponents of the existentialist and phenomenological approach. To see these as complementary descriptions related to whatever nuclear critical aspect of the psychotherapist's mind is being employed on the data at the time is a way out of the dilemma.

The apparent paradox between a Freudian psychodynamic description of a given psychotherapeutic interaction and an existential one can be resolved by applying Bohr's principle of complementarity and recognizing that a choice between these descriptions is not necessary in terms of one being wrong but that *both* are essential for a complete comprehension of the reality of the situation. Furthermore, the kind of approach, attitude, and personality that the psychotherapist brings into the interaction will determine the kind of description set or language that he uses to describe the process and its results. Thus for example, Freud, who was extremely concerned to make psychoanalysis 'scientific' describes all psychotherapeutic interaction in strict, scientific, classical terminology; Buber, who bordered on the existential mystique, uses an entirely different language in describing the same kind of confrontation that takes place in a meaningful, therapeutic interaction. The principle of complementarity explains that it is not a question of who is right and who is wrong, but rather a question of the aims and the tastes of the psychotherapist.

This also explains why there is actually not much difference in the practical technique of psychotherapy employed by the Freudian or the existential psychoanalyst; the enormous difference appears far more in the language employed to describe the phenomena. This difference in turn depends on which nuclear critical aspect of human mental functioning is chosen by the psychotherapist for emphasis in his conceptualization of psychotherapeutic interaction. The type of the experimental apparatus used will determine either position or momentum of a particle but never both at the same time. Similarly in psychotherapeutic interaction, we can experience the rigid determinism of the repetition compulsion in understanding our patient's behavior if we approach the psychotherapeutic interaction by employing one set of nuclear mental functions, *or* we can experience the patient's freedom for existential choices and leaps into life styles if we approach the psychotherapeutic interaction from an entirely different standpoint.

The complementary approach is supported by recent advances in the philosophy of science. Thus Magee writes, "If Popper is right, there are not two cultures—one scientific and the other aesthetic, or one rational and the other irrational—but one. The scientist and the artist, far from being engaged in opposed and incompatible activities, are both trying to expand our understanding of experience by the use of creative imagination subjected to critical control, and so both are using irrational as well as rational faculties. Both are exploring the unknown and trying to articulate the search and its findings. Both are seekers after truth who make indispensable use of intuition" (1973).

KARL POPPER

Karl Popper was born in Vienna in 1902. In his early and middle teens, he was a Marxist and then became an enthusiastic social democrat. He had considerable contact with Alfred Adler, and also was very interested in music, which remains to this day one of his greatest preoccupations. He earned his living as a secondary school teacher in mathematics and physics, but he became absorbed in many areas of human scholastics. He was a peripheral member of the famous

"Vienna circle" of philosophers. He debated continuously with them and was nicknamed "the official opposition."

He had great difficulty publishing his early books. It was necessary for him to leave Austria, which, as he accurately foresaw, would become dominated by the Nazis. Although his childhood was Protestant, he would have been considered a Jew by Hitler because of his Jewish parents. From 1937 to 1945, he taught philosophy at the University of New Zealand, where he apparently had difficulties with his contemporaries. After the Second World War, he came to England where he has lived ever since. He spent the next twenty-three years of his university career at the London School of Economics as Professor of Logic and Scientific Method. He reports that a great many of his manuscripts are as yet unpublished so any discussion of Popper must be based primarily on what *is* published, with an eye on what is yet to come.

Popper's writing style is clear, but he is an extraordinary scholar of immense erudition who wanders all over the fields of knowledge. Magee's brief book (1973) is a good introduction to Popper which suffers only because it is too laudatory and uncritical. The psychotherapist who is interested in the social sciences and such historical theories as those of Marx, Spengler, and Toynbee should read Popper's *The Poverty of Historicism.* Those psychotherapists who are familiar with Plato and Marx and are more interested and immersed in the discipline of the social sciences will gain most from Popper's two volume *The Open Society and Its Enemies.* His most famous technical book, *The Logic of Scientific Discovery,* is today included in all formal courses on philosophy of science. My personal favorite starting point for Popper is his book of essays entitled *Conjectures and Refutations* (1965) which includes the best general introduction to his basic philosophy of science plus some of his more highly speculative notions which read almost like science fiction.

Popper assails his opponents with arguments of all kinds and sometimes with ridicule and abuse as well; in addition, he can also be tediously repetitious and irritatingly egotistical. Popper, the biting critic of petty scholastic wrangling, now has to admit that his own work has become the subject of the same wrangling (see Schilpp 1974). In fact Popper complains so frequently of being misunderstood that one begins to suspect the fault may lie with the author as much as with the critic.

Popper as a philosopher of science is *a passionate scholar*. This passion comes from the notion that the history of philosophy is not simply seen as a record of past errors "but as a running argument, a chain of linked problems and their tentative solutions, with us in the present walking forward if we are lucky, holding one end." This approach leads to *a sense of personal involvement* in the history of ideas.

Magee continues, "A consequence of always proceeding from problems which really are problems—problems which one actually has, and has grappled with—is, for oneself, that one will be existentially committed to one's work; and for the work itself, that it will have what Existentialists call 'authenticity.' It will be not only an intellectual interest but an emotional involvement, the meeting of a felt human need. Another consequence will be an unconcern for conventional distinctions between subjects: all that matters is that one should have an interesting problem and be genuinely trying to solve it" (1973). Popper characterizes his own work as being basically for provocation and indeed no one can come away from his writings, which range over an enormous variety of subjects, without being mentally provoked to think for himself. This is exactly what Popper wants. For our purposes the most important aspects of his writings deal with his ideas about the progress of human knowledge and of scientific knowledge in particular rather than with his celebrated criterion of demarcation between science and pseudoscience. The application of some of his thinking to therapeutic process can be important to a clearer understanding of the proper technique of psychotherapy.

The historical turning point of Popper's thought seems to have been his decision about whether to accept or reject Marxism and psychoanalysis. He insists the theories of Freud or Adler cannot be put to test since no conceivable observations contradict them. They invariably explained whatever occurred (though differently). "Popper saw that their ability to explain everything which so convinced and excite their adherents, was precisely what was most wrong with them" (Magee 1973). Popper explains that the problem with such theories is: "Once your eyes were opened you saw confirming instances everywhere: the world was full of *verifications* of the theory. Whatever happened always confirmed it. Thus its truth appeared manifest; and unbelievers were clearly people who did not want to see the manifest truth; who refused to see it, either because it was against their class interest, or because of their repressions which were still 'unanalyzed' and crying aloud for treatment" (1965).

Popper never dismissed such theories as *valueless* or nonsense as the logical positivists attempted to do. His point is only that *falsifiability* is the criterion of demarcation between science and non-science. If all possible states of affairs fit in with a theory, then no actual state of affairs, no observations, no experimental results, can be claimed as supporting evidence for it. There is no observable difference between its being true and its being false, so it conveys no scientific information. Only if some imaginable observation would refute it is it testible, and only if it is testible is it scientific.

HOW DO SCIENTISTS WORK?

In the tradition of Francis Bacon, science proceeds from the open-minded accumulation of observations. When the scientist accumulates enough data, he will notice a pattern beginning to emerge and will hypothesize that this indicates some natural law. He then tries to confirm this law by finding further evidence to support it. If he succeeds he has verified his hypothesis and discovered another law of nature. Popper *completely disagrees* with this view, and this is his basic contribution to the philosophy of science. He says it is wrong to begin by accumulating observations and it is wrong to seek confirming instances of a theory. Instead we should advance bold conjectures— derived from intuition, or creative genius, or any way we like—and attempt to refute them. Of any competing theories, the one that runs the greater risk of falsification but has not been falsified is the better corroborated theory. This does not mean that it is *true* since it *may* be falsified in the future, but it is likely to be a closer approximation to the truth than other theories. Thus we can never in science feel comfortable that we have finally discovered the truth.

Kuhn (1962) and others object to this because it is always possible to *deny* that a theory has been falsified by an observation that at first seems to have falsified it. Popper's reply is that we should avoid immunizing our theories by trying to explain away an observation that seems to contradict or falsify it but there *is* a vagueness in his writing about how to decide at what time we should change the theory and at what time we should deny the observation. He attempts to cling carefully to the central point: an asymmetry of verification and falsification.

I will not deal with the primarily philosophical issue of whether or not Popper has solved Hume's famous problem of the impossibility of induction; Popper, of course, claims that he has decisively done so, but many philosophers disagree. This remains a matter for technical philosophy.

Popper still believes it possible to examine even irrefutable theories at least rationally, although this cannot be called science. For example, even if it is a non-empirical and irrefutable theory we can ask, Does it solve the problem? Does it solve it better than other theories? Has it perhaps merely shifted the problem? Is the solution simple? Is it fruitful? Does it perhaps contradict other philosophical theories needed for solving other problems?

In his philosophy of science, Popper follows Tarski's theory of truth, which defines truth essentially as correspondence with the facts. We are guided by the idea of truth as a regulative principle, as Kant might have said. Thus we have what Popper calls a *metascientific* idea of what science ought to be doing and of how it ought to proceed which is also an inborn or *a priori* expectation.

Popper attempts to define a greater or lesser correspondence to truth which he calls the idea or degree of verisimilitude. He distinguishes this notion from probability theory. In this task of getting nearer to the truth, the search for theories which better agree with the facts, there are three requirements which each allegedly more valid new theory must meet. First, the new theory must be capable of explaining the same experimental facts the earlier theories explained, others they could not explain, and some by which the earlier theories were actually falsified. The new theory should also resolve if possible, such theoretical difficulties as how to dispense with certain *ad hoc* hypotheses. Second, the new theory should proceed from some simple, new, and powerful unifying idea about some connection or relation between hitherto unconnected things or facts, and should be independently testable. It must lead to the prediction of phenomena which have not been so far observed. Thus it will be fruitful as an instrument of exploration and suggest new experiments. Even if these new experiments should lead at once to the refutation of the new theory, our factual knowledge would have grown through the unexpected results of the new experiments. Third, the theory should pass some new and severe empirical tests, crucial experiments.

In place of the principle of verification, Popper proposed his own principle of falsifiability as a means of separating scientific theories from various kinds of pseudo-science. By failing to make claims that might be shown false, pseudo-sciences evade refutation at the cost of their scientific status.

These arguments occur in Popper's basic work, *The Logic of Scientific Discovery,* published in German two years before A. J. Ayer's opposed and famous book *Language, Truth and Logic* (1952). Here he explained:

> Science is not a system of certain, or well-established statements; nor is it a system that steadily advances towards a state of finality. Our science is not knowledge *(epistēmē):* it can never claim to have attained truth, or even a substitute for it, such as probability.
>
> *We do not know: we can only guess.* And our guesses are guided by the unscientific, the metaphysical (though biologically explicable) faith in laws, in regularities which we can uncover— discover. (1968, p. 278)

For clarity the relationship between epistemology and the disciplines of science, psychology, psychiatry, and ethics has been presented in the diagram at the end of Chapter 8.

Magee summarizes the difference between Popper and the traditional view: "The traditional view of scientific method had the following stages in the following order, each giving rise to the next: (1) observation and experiment; (2) inductive generalization; (3) hypothesis; (4) attempted verification of hypothesis; (5) proof or disproof, (6) knowledge. Popper replaced this with: (1) problem (usually rebuff to existing theory or expectation); (2) proposed solution—in other words, a new theory; (3) deduction of testable propositions from new theory; (4) tests, i.e., attempted refutations by among other things (but only among other things), observation and experiment; (5) preference established between competing theories" (1973).

APPLICATION TO
INTERPRETATIONS IN PSYCHOTHERAPY

In *Conjectures and Refutations* Popper presents six types of cases in which we should be inclined to say of theory T_1 that it is superceeded by T_2, "in the sense that T_2 seems . . . to correspond better to the facts than T_1 in some sense or other" (1965). These criteria are quite useful in attempting to choose between alternative interpretations during the actual process of psychotherapy, and may be summarized as follows:

1. T_2 makes more precise assertions than T_1, and these more precise assertions stand up to more precise tests

2. T_2 takes account of and explains more facts than T_1

3. T_2 describes or explains facts in more detail than T_1

4. T_2 has passed tests which T_1 has failed to pass

5. T_2 has suggested new experimental tests (or hypotheses or interpretations) not considered before T_2 was designed, and T_2 has passed these tests

6. T_2 has unified or connected various hitherto unrelated problems

Popper will probably *not* agree that his theory of scientific progress should be applied to the process of evaluating interpretations in psychotherapy. He *will* agree that science begins with myths and the criticisms of myths, not with the collection of observations or the invention of experiments. Science is not indubitable knowledge *(epistēmē, scientia),* it is also not *technē* (technique or technology), but rather consists of *doxa,* that is of opinions and conjectures controlled by critical discussion as well as by experiments.

The underlying pattern of the continuous development of knowledge takes place when the process of error elimination is applied to the trial solution of the initial problem resulting in new problems. It is essentially a feed-back process. It is not cyclic, for the new problem is always different from the initial one. Furthermore, even complete failure to solve a problem teaches us something new about where its difficulties lie, and what the conditions are which any solutions for it must meet—and therefore alter the problem situation.

Popper continues, "But these marvelously imaginative and bold conjectures or 'anticipations' of ours are carefully and soberly controlled by systematic tests. Once put forward none of our 'anticipations' are dogmatically upheld. Our method of research is not to defend them, in order to prove how right we were. On the contrary, we try to overthrow them. Using all the weapons of our logical, mathematical, and technical armory, we try to prove that our anticipations were false—in order to put forward, in their stead, new unjustified and unjustifiable anticipations, new 'rash and premature prejudices,' as Bacon derisively called them" (1968). I believe that this is (unintentionally) an *excellent characterization* of the process of interpretation and subsequent rejection or confirmation that goes on in the everyday work of psychoanalytically informed uncovering psychotherapy.

Magee quotes the psychiatrist Storr, "When we enter a new situation in life and are confronted by a new person, we bring with us the prejudices of the past and our previous experiences of people. These prejudices we project upon the new person. Indeed, getting to know a person is largely a matter of withdrawing projections; of dispelling the smoke-screen of what we imagine he is like and replacing it with the reality of what he is actually like" (1973).

In his autobiography Popper gives what would be a fine characterization of the attitude in the psychotherapist that generates successful interpretations: "But it seems to me that what is essential to "creative" or "inventive" thinking is a combination of intense interest in some problem (and thus a readiness to try and try again) with highly critical thinking; with a readiness to attack even those presuppositions which for less critical thought determine the limits of the range from which trials (conjectures) are selected; with an imaginative freedom that allows us to so far unsuspected sources of error: possible prejudices in need of critical examination" (Schilpp 1974).

THE PSYCHOTHERAPIST AS
A PUZZLE-SOLVER

The correct application of Popper's methods to the use of interpretations in psychotherapy and to the notion of the psychotherapist in intensive uncovering psychotherapy as primarily a *puzzle solver* (in this sense functioning as an accessory ego to the patient's observing ego) is central to the crucial conception of the analytically oriented psychotherapist, even as delineated by Freud himself. Possible disagreement with Popper comes primarily at a level he correctly calls metascientific, at which he attempts to apply his theories in a rather dogmatic fashion to the accumulation of *all* knowledge. For the purposes of the practicing psychotherapist this issue is of secondary relevance.

The point is that Popper's basic schemata are uniquely applicable to understanding the progress of knowledge in the individual patient's psychotherapy. In this process the creative intuition of the therapist comes up with hypotheses about psychodynamic explanations, which are then subjected to testing by presenting them to the patient and observing the patient's reaction which either corroborates or tends to refute or falsify the hypotheses. This leads to an elimination of error and the formulation of new hypotheses that, although they may incorporate some aspects of the early hypotheses, are closer to the truth and approach a deeper level of understanding.

Thus the new and correct interpretations permit us to move deeper into an approximation of the basic truth about the patient, and even a failure of an earlier hypothesis or interpretation teaches us something new about where the difficulties lie and helps us formulate a more active and deeper interpretation or hypothesis. Obviously the process of error elimination in psychotherapy also leads to unexpected new problems.

The *formulation* of initial and new problems in psychotherapy is creative but limited by (a) the reality of the patient's situation and (b) the principle of complementarity (Chessick 1975). Thus interpretation formation *and* problem formulation are *both* creative steps in psychotherapy and are interrelated.

This extremely valuable theoretical understanding of the psychotherapy process entirely sidesteps the issue of whether or not psychoanalytic psychotherapy is or is not a science. It also brings into congruence the issue of science versus art, because the processes involved in the formulation of the interpretations or hypotheses (that Popper labels "conjectures") represent a combination of *all* the human mental faculties of the therapist, whether they involve creative intuition or careful logical reasoning. So all these faculties, whether artistic or scientific, by definition are involved in this basic creative process that the therapist repeatedly goes through during every hour with every patient.

It is not even necessary in this chapter to review the well known responses from patients which serve the practicing psychotherapist as either corroborations or refutations of his interpretations (or conjectures) since these are presented in any standard textbook (see Langs 1974, vol. 2). The experienced psychotherapist who has a thorough knowledge of his countertransference usually has little difficulty in deciding whether a given interpretation has correctly made its mark, or for some reason is incorrect and is being rejected by the patient. Only the most inexperienced neophyte attempts to force an interpretation on a patient without accepting the possibility that the interpretation may simply be wrong. This is a matter for the personal treatment and training of the therapist but again need not concern us here since we are talking about psychotherapy as practiced by an experienced therapist.

CRITICISMS OF POPPER'S APPROACH

It is this approximation process, if it is clearly understood, that forms the basis of understanding a patient and works consistently with Freud's notion of psychotherapy as peeling off the layers of an onion. Popper's thought gives us a chance to formulate this in a specific and exact terminology.

On the other hand, such formulations run us into the difficulty presented by Bohr's principle of complementarity, in which this neat procedure breaks down at a certain level because of alternative ways of looking at the same data. Thus some data is lost depending on the approach the therapist takes, and to minimize the loss of data the therapist has to be prepared to take at least two approaches—that of the scientific understanding and that of the humanistic imagination.

Innumerable criticisms can be leveled against Popper without throwing out his basic concepts. For example, Kneale (Schilpp 1974) points out that various activities are carried on under the name of scientific research, and various theses may be advanced by scientists in their professional capacity. It is perhaps unwise to be dogmatic about the logical form of scientific theories as Popper insists by saying that they are *all* unverifiable propositions of unrestricted universality.

Skolimowski (Schilpp 1974) explains that Popper's philosophy was formulated in two periods, a methodological period lasting until 1960 and a metaphysical period. The methodological conceptions of Popper were worked out and formulated in conscious opposition to the positivistic philosophy of the Vienna Circle, whereas thirty years later, Popper acquired new opponents who went too far in subjectivizing science—such opponents as for example, Michael Polanyi in *Personal Knowledge* and *Scientific Thought and Social Reality* and above all by Kuhn in *The Structure of Scientific Revolutions*.

KUHN'S CRUCIAL IDEA: THE PARADIGM

The heart of Kuhn's account is the notion of paradigm. A paradigm is simply "a scientific theory together with an example of a successful and striking application" (Putnam in Schilpp 1974). This application must be *striking* because if it is sufficiently impressive the scientists will take the new paradigm in exchange for the old. This is the progress of science according to Kuhn's more-or-less sociological theory. Kuhn maintains that the paradigm is highly immune to falsification—in contrast to Popper—and as a matter of fact it can only be overthrown by a new paradigm. Once a paradigm has been set up and a scientific field has grown up around that paradigm, there occurs an interval of what Kuhn calls "normal science." The activities of scientists during such an interval are described by Kuhn as *puzzle solving,* and this is *very* important and sharply differentiates Kuhn and Popper. So Kuhn describes "normal science" as consisting of elaborating existing knowledge in the nature of puzzle solving. It is at the breakdown of puzzle solving that the epochal problem arises, for this produces a crisis which can then lead to the overthrow of an entire paradigm. Popper retorts that Kuhn's concept of paradigm is dangerously near to Hegel's *zeitgeist* (spirit of a period).

Kuhn's most controversial notion has to do with the process whereby a new paradigm supplants an old paradigm. Data in the usual fashion do not establish the superiority of one paradigm over another, because the data themselves are perceived through the spectacles of one paradigm or another. Changing from one paradigm to another requires what Kuhn calls a "Gestalt switch."

During their tenure of office, paradigms are highly immune to falsification and their tenure of office is ended by the appearance on the scene of a better theory. Thus falsifiability is *not* the *sine qua non* to a scientific theory. Popper himself recognizes that the derivation of a prediction from a theory may require also the use of "auxiliary hypotheses," and an attempt to save a theory from a contrary experimental result is often done by making what is called an *ad hoc* change implicit in the auxiliary hypothesis. Popper insists that this should be avoided but actually it is very common in the practice of science.

Thus there are many arguments that science is not a homogenous enterprise and many dissimilar enterprises exist within the discipline of science. In fact, Kuhn argues, "to rely on testing as the mark of science is to miss what scientists mostly do and, with it, the most characteristic feature of their enterprise." This is because, "All experiments can be challenged, either as to their relevance or their accuracy. All theories can be modified by a variety of *ad hoc* adjustments without ceasing to be in their main lines, the same theories. It is important, furthermore, that this should be so; for it is often by challenging observations or adjusting theories that scientific knowledge grows" (Schilpp 1974). Kuhn claims that Popper has erred by transferring selective characteristics of everyday research to the occasional revolutionary episodes in which scientific advance is most obvious, and thereafter ignoring the everyday scientific enterprise entirely.

Popper is worried about Kuhn's characterization of normal science as "puzzle solving." He does not accept Kuhn's basic distinction between "normal science" and extraordinary periods. He agrees there are different periods but does not see them as *fundamentally* different from the scientific point of view. He argues that, "from the amoeba to Einstein we learn from our mistakes" and adds that, "from the amoeba to Einstein there is just one step," and "the new step is the conscious and critical search for one's errors." This fundamental disagreement about what is "normal science" remains the irreconcilable dividing point between Kuhn's and Popper's point of view. Lakatos and Musgrave (1970) present a complete review of this controversy.

THE VITAL QUESTION OF INNATE DISPOSITIONS

Popper is willing to accept the resemblance of his theories to Chomsky with respect to "innatism." He writes, "I conjecture that animals and men have what can be called 'inborn knowledge,' or more especially, 'inborn expectations' and 'inborn dispositions.' I should not greatly relish speaking of 'inborn ideas,' . . . but this is a minor and largely terminological issue. The learning by a human child of an articulate, descriptive and argumentative language is, I conjecture, based upon innate dispositions; it has a genetic basis. The genetic basis comprises dispositions to state, to describe, to agree or disagree with a description; to argue, to be critical of a statement; and countless more" (Schilpp 1974).

It is clear that if we accept the arguments of Popper and Chomsky on the issue of genetic *a priori* dispositions, it is possible to develop a thorough and modern correction of Kant's philosophy and to refute once and for all any simplistic behavioristic theories of learning, motivation, and change. If we don't accept this concept of innate dispositions, a whole variety of phenomena remains unexplained and there is no competing conjecture that can explain them. Thus as far as the state of knowledge has advanced today, the most useful conjecture which has withstood the most empirical testing, and also which explains the most phenomena, is the theory of some sort of innate disposition or expectations. I have already discussed this at length in the final chapter of *The Technique and Practice of Intensive Psychotherapy* (1974g).

Popper agrees with Chomsky in that (in Popper's language) every organism has inborn reactions or responses and among them responses adapted to impending events. Just because these responses are expectations we do *not* imply that such expectations are conscious: Popper writes, "Thus we are born with expectations; with 'knowledge' which, although not *valid a priori,* is *psychologically or genetically a priori,* i.e. prior to all observational experience. One of the most important of these expectations is the expectation of finding a regularity. It is connected with an inborn propensity to look out for regularities, or with a *need to find* regularities, as we may see of the pleasure of the child who satisfies this need. . . . When Kant said, 'Our intellect does not draw its laws from nature but imposes its laws upon nature,' he was right. But in thinking that these laws are necessarily true, or that we necessarily succeed in imposing them upon nature, he was wrong." Kant believed that Newton's dynamics was *a priori* valid. Now we know that Newton's theory is no more than a marvellous conjecture, an astonishingly good approximation; unique indeed, but not as divine truth. As Popper points out, "With this Kant's problem 'How is pure natural science possible,' collapses, and the most disturbing of his perplexities disappears" (1965, pp. 47-48, 94).

Popper replaces this with an *a priori* expectation propensity, due to which we search and attempt to understand and invent. Because we have this inborn, we invent various conjectures which we can then put to the test. As we falsify these conjectures and make new ones, we approach the truth but we never reach pure fixed *epistēmē*. He believes this has a genetic basis which comprises dispositions to state, to describe, to agree or disagree with a description, to argue, to be critical, and so on. "All this has to be learned by the child in the course of its development, but the possibility of learning it is inborn, in the shape of inborn dispositions and inborn expectations" (1965).

LIMITATIONS OF SCIENCE AND PSYCHOTHERAPY

If the reader has followed my discussion of Popper it will not be hard to see that his view is a kind of modified essentialism in which he formulates the idea that scientific theories are *genuine conjectures*— "highly informative guesses about the world which although not verifiable (i.e. capable of being shown to be true) can be submitted to severe critical tests. They are serious attempts to discover the truth . . . even though *we do not know, and will perhaps never know, whether it is true or not"* (1965, p. 115). Thus we attempt to approach the truth by producing theories which are harder and harder to falsify, but we never know what the truth is and we never produce a theory which is essentially true or certainly true, only a series of hypotheses which are more or less falsifiable. The latest and best theory is always an attempt to incorporate all the falsifications ever found in the field by explaining them in the simplest way. If we do not know how to test the theory there is no way of approaching the truth value for the theory. "Testible conjectures or guesses are thus conjectures or guesses about reality; from their uncertain or conjectural character it only follows that our knowledge concerning the reality they describe is uncertain or conjectural" (1965, p. 117). Thus science is capable of real discoveries and can approach the truth, but can never reach certain permanent and irrefutable truth.

The basic complaint of Popper against Bohr's principle of complementarity is that this principle approaches instrumentalism, for it gives up all hope on a theoretical basis of explaining certain phenomena in an unambiguous way. What Bohr is saying is that at a certain level, the basic rules of cause and effect or our basic asymptotic approach to "truth" in scientific progress break down because of the nature of things itself. Thus reality in certain situations forbids us to go further in the progress of scientific explanation.

There is an inherent limitation in nature or reality beyond which we cannot go *in principle*. This is because in certain types of situations the experimental approach itself determines the kind of data we will get, and rules out the discovery of other kinds of data. If on the other hand, we change the experimental approach we reverse the situation and the original data are lost for the sake of discovering the new data. The principle of complementarity views this as *inherent in the nature of reality itself*.

Bohr is certainly approaching this instrumentalist view because he claims that the kind of experiment we set up will determine the kind of data that we receive, and will exclude other data that could be obtained by a different type of approach to the situation. It is not fair, however, to accuse Bohr of pure instrumentalism. The only fair statement that can be made on the subject is that in certain situations, when dealing with certain kinds of problems, there is a limitation to the discoveries that we can make that is built in to the nature of reality itself. It does not follow from this that *all* scientific progress and discovery is limited by simple instrumentalism. Thus we have a form of modified instrumentalism that is forced upon us by our scientific work in certain areas such as microphysics or the investigation of psychotherapeutic interaction.

Chapter 17

Identity and Inner Sustainment

When the child must be weaned, the mother blackens her breast, it would indeed be a shame that the breast should look delicious when the child must not have it. So the child believes that the breast has changed, but the mother is the same, her glance is as loving and tender as ever.

When the child has grown big and must be weaned, the mother virginally hides her breast, so the child has no more a mother. Happy the child which did not in another way lose its mother.

When the child must be weaned, the mother too is not without sorrow at the thought that she and the child are separated more and more, that the child which first lay under her heart and later reposed upon her breast will be so near to her no more. So they mourn together for the brief period of mourning. Happy the person who has kept the child as near and needed not to sorrow any more!

Kierkegaard, Fear and Trembling

So then, the fact that the man in despair is unaware that his condition is despair, has nothing to do with the case, he is in despair all the same. If despair is bewilderment, then the fact that one is unconscious of it is the additional aggravation of being at the same time under a delusion. Unconsciousness of despair is like unconsciousness of dread: the dread characteristic of

spiritlessness is recognizable precisely by the spiritless sense of
security; but nevertheless dread is at the bottom of it, and when
the enchantment of illusion is broken, when existence begins to
totter, then too does despair manifest itself as that which was at
the bottom.

Kierkegaard, Sickness Unto Death

KIERKEGAARD

The life of Kierkegaard can be viewed as revolving around a series of personal crises, as certain authors prefer to do (Kahn 1963). Or the famous crises can be viewed as high points in Kierkegaard's chronic externalization, in which the crises are like an iceberg—sticking above the water but really having a large contiguous mass beneath. The most well-known crises are first, the discovery of his father's infidelity (before 1836) and their subsequent reunion shortly before the death of his father (1838) and second, the breaking of his engagement to Regina Olsen in 1841. Other crises of less dramatic import also occurred, such as the affair of the *Corsair* in 1846, in which he precipitated his own persecution in the media—a classical example of externalization (Chessick 1972)—and the attack on organized Christianity near the end of his life that precipitated a near-riot at his burial.

Kierkegaard's father was a relatively old man (fifty-six) when Kierkegaard was born, a successful business man who rose from the peasantry by a combination of good luck and hard work. Soren Kierkegaard (1813-1855) was the youngest of seven children from his father's second marriage to his housekeeper. He was frail and stooped in appearance, physically weak, and very sensitive. A very good scholar and debater he was nicknamed by his fellow-students "the fork" and described as "the most polemical of men" by his contemporaries. He wrote that he was never a child and had always been old. The father was quite intelligent but a depressed, morose, and guilt-ridden man, who reared his children in a stuffy religious atmosphere. Kierkegaard claims to have adored him like a god, and they spent much time together in his childhood.

Only once in his voluminous writtings does Kierkegaard ever mention his mother who was forty-four when he was born. Kahn points out, "He certainly had observed that his father treated the mother more like a servant than like the lady of the house" (1963). In spite of this obvious fact, Kierkegaard claimed to have been shaken as if by an earthquake by the revelation that his father had not been faithful to his mother. Around 1836, probably related to this confession, Kierkegaard became seriously immersed in suicidal thoughts and dissolute living. Shortly before his father's death they became emotionally reunited. When his father died Kierkegaard experienced a religious conversion which was accompanied by "indescribably joy." He also inherited a fortune.

Sometimes the confession from his father and the death of his father are considered as precipitating separate "crises," since the one led to melancholy and delinquency and the other to religious restoration. At any rate Kahn (1963) claims that his early crisis (or two crises) clearly interrupted his way of life or career-line, and allowed him to come back to the father and to God in new adoration. Wiegert (1960) offers a psychoanalytic view of the relationship of his inner struggle with his father to his creative work.

Kierkegaard clearly was suffering from a considerable problem with respect to his mother as well as his difficulties with his father. The absence of writing about his mother must be regarded as extremely significant and "ominous" (Lowrie 1971). The difficulties regarding women surfaced again in the crisis of his betrothal to Regina Olsen, a teen-age girl. After considerable internal rumination Kierkegaard broke his engagement to her, which he regarded as a matter of fantastic importance. Imagine his chagrin when Regina promptly married the suitor whom Kierkegaard had replaced.

His inner struggle continued and, beginning in 1843 with the remarkable *Either/Or*, led to the creation of an important body of essentially religious or quasi-philosophical works which take as their starting point his concepts of existential dread and existential despair. In fact, the combined arguments of Kierkegaard's two "psychological" works, *The Concept of Dread* and *Sickness Unto Death*, "add up to a dismaying conclusion: that a human life consists generally in a series of failed projects, each doomed from the outset by its own inherent contradictions or by the incapacity of creatures who are themselves bundles of contradictions to sustain them" (Thompson 1972). Thus arises the peculiar situation of human life that every project begins in dread and ends in despair.

Kierkegaard embarked on a grandiose campaign to awaken the sleeping human race. His strategy (critics disagree as to whether it was deliberate) was to present his theme through publishing a series of works, each of which had its place in a master plan known to the author but not the reader. The publications are attributed to an assortment of authors, such as Johannes Climacus, Anti-Climacus, Virgilius Hofniensis, Johannes de Silentio, Victor Erimeta, and also finally Soren Kierkegaard. Each alleged author has his point of view, attitudes toward life and his purpose; often several authors are thrown together in one book. The incredible complexity of all this and the deliberately paradoxical and ironic style resembling a Chinese puzzle box is well reviewed by Thompson (1973).

Popkin in discussing these authorial persons explains:

> The lowest group are the so-called aesthetic authors, whose function it is to awaken interest in man's plight, in the emptiness and sordidness of ordinary human existence. On this level, Kierkegaard's authors are masters of human psychology. And his story from *Either/Or,* "The Diary of a Seducer" is a magnificent presentation of human tragedy, of a life lived on the surface, solely for the pursuit of pleasure. No message is advanced. Just a picture painted of how the world ordinarily goes on.
>
> The second level of "authors" are the philosophical ones, those who explore the possibility of understanding the human world, and of developing a theory of knowledge, and a system of values. And philosophically, their achievement turns out to be almost entirely negative. . . . The philosophical authors develop the bankruptcy of intellectual endeavor, and point out the irrationality of the solution Kierkegaard will propose—a religious solution. (Thompson 1972, p. 363)

Of course, Kierkegaard emerges as one of the principal members of the third group of "authors," some of whom are fanatical and some of whom are groping. "He rhapsodizes on religious themes, he preaches, he prophesises. He rants and raves against philosophers and philosophy. And finally, in his last work, he unleashes a tirade against the Christian world, in his *Attack on Christendom,* one of the most virulent denunciations of accepted religious practices ever written" (Popkin in Thompson 1972).

Out of his powerful skepticism, Kierkegaard builds a case for the acceptance of Christianity on faith alone, by a "leap." Jones points out: "He was persuaded—again by personal experience—that no rational, scientific, or economic procedure could heal the break within the self and between the self and its world; only a leap of faith could accomplish that. And God—this was his faith—had helped him, Soren Kierkegaard, to make the leap that had brought his life into 'focus' and given it a 'center' " (1969).

CURE FOR THE AGONY

Jones discusses "the cure for the agony," which according to Kierkegaard is to become passionately committed to one of the options that life offers. Jones writes: "It is a psychological fact that, to the extent that we commit ourselves utterly and passionately to one option (from the psychological point of view, it does not matter which one), we no longer care about the others. At this moment the agony of decision obviously disappears. Passion alone may be satisfactory psychologically, but it is hardly satisfactory ethically. . . . This is why Kierkegaard emphasizes commitment as well as passion. His point was that the act to which one becomes passionately committed must be deliberately chosen" (1969).

Jones tries to contrast Kierkegaard's position with that of a psychiatrist who wishes to help a patient agonizing over a decision: "If the psychiatrist adopted Kierkegaard's psychological theory, he would aim at getting his patient to interpenetrate consciousness with passion. If the patient's agony was thereby alleviated, he would be satisfied" (1969). However, Kierkegaard was not a psychiatrist, but a Christian advocate.

In *Sickness Unto Death* written in 1849, Kierkegaard reminds us of three general ways of coping with existential despair. He labels these the unsuccessful, the demoniacal, and the religious. There is a marvelous discussion of boredom and despair, especially in what Kierkegaard has labeled the esthetic life, marked by hedonism and childish behavior. For Kierkegaard the leap from esthetic life to the ethical life—the latter marked by immersion in marriage, family, and object relations—is not sufficient. He advocates a further leap to the Christian God in which one breaks the ordinary moral code in a way similar to Kierkegaard's renunciation of Regina. One can easily argue that this is a rationalization or a need on the part of Kierkegaard to externalize and produce a failure in his relationship with a woman, based on a repetition compulsion of the defective holding that he experienced from his mother.

A careful study of the lives and writings of Kierkegaard and Nietzsche brings these problems into very sharp focus, and presents dramatic expositions of the struggle of a superior mind with deep feelings that must be almost compulsively written about, ruminated on, and that force some kind of resolution out of the troubled psyche of the victim. Jaspers (See chapter 18) presented a remarkable nonpsychoanalytic approach to the life of Nietzsche, trying to explain the agony of his life pattern as representing and illustrating the same intellectual problems of existential anguish and despair that he was writing about as a philosopher and poet. There is no question that the best way to approach Kierkegaard also is through the study of his life, since his life story is inextricably bound up with his writings and thoughts. Start with Lowrie's *Short Life of Kierkegaard* (1971) or Thompson's *Kierkegaard* (1973).

There is an interesting introduction to one of Kierkegaard's famous books, *Concluding Unscientific Postscript* written in 1846, in which he describes his point of departure as a thinker. While he sat one Sunday afternoon in the Fredriksberg Garden in Copenhagen smoking a cigar and turning over a great many things in his mind, he reflected that as yet he had made no career for himself, whereas everywhere around him he saw the men of his age becoming celebrated, establishing themselves as reknown benefactors of mankind. They were benefactors because all their efforts were directed at making life easier for the rest of mankind either materially constructing railroads, steamboats, or telegraph lines or intellectually by publishing compendiums of universal knowledge or even spiritually by showing how thought itself could make spiritual existence easier. His cigar burned down and he paused to light another but the train of reflection held him. It occurred to him, since everyone everywhere else was engaged in making things easy perhaps someone might be needed to make things hard again; that life might become so easy that people would want the difficult back again; and this might be a career and destiny for him. This passage is typical of Kierkegaard's famous irony.

OBJECTIVITY AND COMMITMENT

In his journals, for example, on January 17th, 1837 he writes, "There are many people who reach their conclusions about life like schoolboys; they cheat their master by copying the answer out of a book without having worked out the sum themselves" (1959). Kierkegaard has exercised influence on many people who would not call themselves existentialists, professional philosophers, or theologians. He gets men to see their existential situation and the alternatives with which they are faced and he calls on them to choose, to commit one's self, to become "an existing individual." This basically represents a protest in the name of the free individual or person against submergence in the social collectivity. Kierkegaard exaggerates tremendously in his writing and this exaggeration often serves to draw attention to what he is saying—and what is well worth saying even more appropriately in the present day.

Kierkegaard draws a highly questionable distinction between objective and subjective truth. Philosophers up to Kierkegaard accepted the ideal of impartiality and merely disagreed about whether it is actually attainable or whether men can only approximate to it. Therefore they regarded words like *impartial, disinterested,* or *dispassionate* as ideal. For Kierkegaard, however, they are pejorative and impossible, and there is no such thing as an impartial observer, for all truth in varying degrees is not disinterested. This theme is developed at length in his most famous philosophical work, *Concluding Unscientific Postscript.*

He argues that pursuit of impartiality is doomed to failure and is a distraction insofar as it draws our energies away from what ought to be our sole concern—becoming a Christian. Furthermore, pursuit of impartiality, according to Kierkegaard, is a form of escapism. In direct contrast to Hume's argument (an approach which today we would consider to be a sign of health) that the solution to existential dread is a cheerful concern with the affairs of the world, Kierkegaard maintains that cheerful concern with the affairs of the world is a desperate escape from boredom and despair.

His published works in English alone now comprise thirty books and ten anthologies and it would be heroic to expect anyone except a

Kierkegaard scholar to be familiar with all of them. He is of
fundamental importance to psychotherapists basically because of his
concentration on the development of the self (the stages on life's way)
and his concept of a leap emphasizing the importance of what he calls a
criterionless choice in moving from one stage on life's way to another.
He maintains there are no objective standards where human existence
is involved, and a jump from one stage on life's way to the next must
take place primarily on the basis of nonrational considerations.

STAGES ON LIFE'S WAY

Turning to *Either/Or* his first important book in 1843, the doctrine
of choice is first put to work in relation to a distinction between two
ways of life, the ethical and the esthetic. The esthetic point of view is
that of a sophisticated and romantic hedonism, but in the end the
search for novelty in this form of life leads to boredom and to the
threshold of despair. By contrast, the ethical constitutes the sphere of
duty, rules, demands, and tasks. The chief thing for the ethical man is
to feel the intensity of duty in such a way that the consciousness of it is
for him an assurance of authentic life.

The esthetic stage or sphere is characterized by the level of the senses,
impulses, and emotions, but not necessarily by being simply and solely
a grossly sensual man. The esthetic stage can also be exemplified by the
poet who transmutes the world into an imaginative realm and a
romantic place or the idealistic philosopher. The ethical stage is typical
of the man who renounces the satisfaction of the sexual impulses
according to passing attraction and enters into the state of marriage,
accepting all its obligations.

The description of the two alternatives is actually heavily weighted
in favor of the ethical, and the difficulty is that Kierkegaard wished
both to maintain that there could be no objective criterion for the
decision between the two alternatives and to show that the ethical was
superior to the esthetic. This leads to an impossible inconsistency that
runs all through Kierkegaard's thought.

In *Fear and Trembling* written also in 1843, a further stage is
delineated entitled the religious stage, in which one makes the leap into
Christianity and renounces even the ethical stage by a process of

"suspension." The first major psychological work of Kierkegaard, *The Concept of Dread*, published in 1844, completes this basic doctrine. In this he describes dread or anxiety as preceeding a qualitative leap from one of these stages to the next and as produced by the agony prior to the decision. This is the basic notion of existential anxiety. (See Chessick 1969a).

The emphasis on the leap as irrational is underscored by Copleston: "As Kierkegaard's dialectic is one of discontinuity, in the sense that the transition from one stage to another is made by choice, by self-commitment, and not through a continuous process of conceptual meditation, he not unnaturally plays down the role of reason and emphasizes that of will when he is treating religious faith. In his view faith is a leap. That is to say, it is an adventure, a risk, a self commitment to an objective uncertainty" (1965).

The two major quasi-philosophical works of Kierkegaard are *Philosophical Fragments* in 1844 and *Concluding Unscientific Postscript to the Philosophical Fragments* published in 1846. These are generally considered Kierkegaard's deepest philosophical and theological speculations, especially the latter. Another important book entitled *Stages on Life's Way* (1967) reviews the three stages previously discussed, but adds little to the conceptualizations; it appeared in 1845, two years after *Either/Or,* and was written for the purpose of developing the religious stage in the perspective of the esthetic and ethical stages presented in *Either/Or.*

The year of 1848, was exceptionally productive for Kierkegaard, as he himself recognized in his journals. It produced the final work of importance to us, entitled *Sickness Unto Death*, published in 1849. Bretall claims, "It is clear that Kierkegaard understood the 'death instinct' fifty years before Freud. Indeed, the whole murky realm of the subconscious is here opened up in so illuminating a fashion as to prove Kierkegaard one of the fathers of 'depth psychology,' even though his interest in this realm is always a religious and more specifically a Christian one" (Kierkegaard 1947). This work seemed to follow an important religious experience and produced what Barrett (1958) calls "the most powerful of Kierkegaard's distinctly psychological trea-tises." *Sickness Unto Death*, as mentioned above, is a study of the various modalities of despair; the sickness in which we long to die but cannot. It is the extreme emotion in which we seek to escape from ourselves, and it is universal in nature, according to Kierkegaard. Despair is never ultimately over the external object, but always over ourselves and it involves in its center, according to Kierkegaard, a certain form of sinfulness. Today we tend to label people who are preoccupied with despair as sick or neurotic, but according to Kierkegaard, the closer we get to any neurotic the more we are assailed by the sheer human perverseness, the willfulness of his attitude. Despair and dread point in the same direction, for the experience of each forces the individual to realize that he confronts a void and that he is responsible for his own condition. Kierkegaard sees this as the starting point of a leap into the next stage on life's way.

CRITICISM OF KIERKEGAARD

Kaufmann (1960) distinguishes two major faults of Kierkegaard as a psychologist and four major faults as a philosopher. As a psychologist, a serious defect is in his tendency to self-projection coupled with a range of experience that is far too narrow to permit significant generalizations. The second important defect is self deception. Kaufmann points out that *Fear and Trembling,* for example, was clearly prompted by his own broken engagement to which it alludes constantly. He refers to Kierkegaard's failure to search his heart as to whether he was not also afraid of marriage.

Kierkegaard neither was nor wanted to be a philosopher, and he reverses the whole trend of modern philosophy by going back to the authority of Scripture, citing verses and even a single word to establish points. He dogmatizes about original sin like a theologian rather than a philosopher, and his psychological observations add spice but no more. Kaufmann further charges that Kierkegaard accepts Christian and Hegelian categories and modes of thinking without examining them, and juggles around many such phrases as dialectical, spirit, the eternal, nothing, infinite reflection, potentiate, the posited sin, self, freedom, and many others without seeking clarity about their meaning.

Finally, the kind of dialectic in which he excells could easily be used to prove anything at all. Kaufmann writes, "Although he constantly invokes Socrates, he fails to understand the central point of Socrates' mission: the relentless questioning of convention, prompted by the evident conviction that even holy and respectable ends do not justify unanalyzed concepts, murky arguments, and the lack of a sensitive intellectual conscience" (1960).

IDENTITY AS PREDETERMINED: D. W. WINNICOTT

In contrast to Kierkegaard's strong stress on the role of will, leaps, and choice in moving from one stage on life's way to another, the important British school of psychoanalysis in the present century has stressed extreme determinism in any life situation. Here the early mother-infant symbiosis predetermines all the subsequent development of the individual. As a moderate representative of this great idea in psychotherapy—which still remains controversial and a matter for research—let us have a look at the work of the great pediatrician-turned-psychoanalyst, Donald W. Winnicott (1897-1971). In addition to being one of the clearer and more readable of this group of authors, Winnicott is an admirable individual as a human being and a model for the psychotherapist to follow (see Guntrip 1975).

At the beginning of this century, Freud established the ubiquity of the role of unconscious instinctual wishes and conflicts in the development of the human individual, and he also invented a therapeutic setting and process, which he named psychoanalysis, where these conflicts could be discovered, explored, and resolved. The emphasis was upon knowing and insight. Winnicott, from his deep involvement with infants and their caretaking mothers, took the next logical step and enlarged the scope of the psychotherapeutic task to include realization of and meeting the need of the patient as a person. His researches in this area have had a momentous impact on the whole nature of the therapeutic undertaking, in which according to Winnicott the therapist patiently waits for the patient's own creative unfolding from formlessness to reintegration. He was undaunted by the criticism and misgivings of his colleagues. Kahn (1971) points out that "Winnicott modeled his clinical orientation to the patient largely on an 'ordinary and devoted mother's' holding care of her infant."

Winnicott had a long and distinguished career as a Fellow of the Royal College of Physicians, a Fellow of the British Psychological Society, President of the British Psychoanalytical Society, and

President of the pediatric section of the Royal Society of Medicine; he was awarded the James Spence medal for pediatrics in 1968. He did not write a great deal, and there are only four books especially pertinent to psychotherapists of adults. Most important to us are his *Collected Papers* and *The Maturational Processes and the Facilitating Environment,* which collects his later papers and which with the first collection forms the basis of his thought.

The Family and Individual Development is a somewhat popularized but well written version of his thought. *Playing and Reality* develops his important contribution about transitional objects and transitional phenomena. *The Maturational Processes and the Facilitating Environment* is carefully reviewed by Widlocher (1970) and a scholarly review of *The Family and Individual Development* is presented by Geleerd (1967).

THE MATURATIONAL PROCESSES AND THE FACILITATING ENVIRONMENT

For our purposes his work may be divided into three general categories. The first of these deals with the gradual crystallization of separate psychobiological existence out of the matrix of the union of the mother and child. The second is on psychotherapy of patients who have experienced what Balint (1968) calls the basic fault—serious defects in the early interaction with the mother. Finally, certain classical papers and other contributions, such as those to pediatrics and child psychiatry, which I will discuss only in passing.

Winnicott writes of the "average expectable environment" as essential to the growth of the health and personality in the child, and the important element in it is the "good enough mother." Guntrip explains that "Winnicott implies a continuously healthy, fostering, nursing environment, accepting the infant's immature dependence while supporting his tentative adventures into independence, individuality, and finding a life of his own in and through personal relationships. . . . Winnicott saw how profoundly the struggles of the infant and child to grow a real self determine the nature and state of every problem the adult experiences" (1971). Compare this with Kierkegaard's concept of criterionless free choice at every stage in development.

The capacity of the secure mother to provide security for her baby is described by Winnicott as "primary maternal preoccupation." For example, he writes, "We notice in the expectant mother an increasing identification with the infant . . . and a willingness as well as an ability on the part of the mother to drain interest from her own self onto the baby. . . . She knows what the baby could be feeling like. No one else knows" (1966).

Winnicott introduces his important concept of "basic ego-relatedness." This conceptualizes what a good-enough mother-infant relationship does for the child in terms both of an experience that lasts for a lifetime and as a foundation upon which all the child's later growth can take place. One of his famous papers on "The Capacity To Be Alone" (1966) discusses this subject at length. The sense of belonging, of being securely in touch that grows in the baby from the mother's loving reliability, becomes an established property of his psyche.

Thus Winnicott believes that apart from interpersonal relations, an ego or true self never develops at all. Winnicott concentrates on the beginnings of the ego and argues that the differentiation of subject and object out of the state of primary identification stimulates the beginning of specific ego development. The growth of the experience of basic ego relatedness, and therefore of the capacity both to enter into object relations and also to be alone without anxiety and insecurity, is based on the early relationship between the mother and the infant— "the nursing couple" as Winnicott puts it in "The Relationship of a Mother to Her Baby At the Beginning" (1968).

This is presented in a formal fashion in chapter 3 of *The Maturational Processes and the Facilitating Environment* in which Winnicott presents his theory of the parent-infant relationship. He argues that infant development is facilitated by good-enough maternal care and is distorted by maternal care that is not good enough. The infant ego can be said to be weak, but "in fact it is strong because of the ego support of maternal care. Where maternal care fails the weakness of the infant ego becomes apparent" (1966). Processes in the mother and the father bring about a special state in which the parent is oriented to the infant and thus in a position to meet the infant's dependence.

Great attention must be paid to Winnicott's concept of "holding." This is defined as a protection from physiologic insult which takes account of the infant's skin sensitivity and includes the whole routine of care throughout the day and night. It is not the same with any two infants because it is part of the infant and no two infants are alike. Also it follows the minute day to day changes belonging to the infant's growth and development, both physical and psychological. Winnicott writes, "Holding includes especially the physical holding of the infant, which is a form of loving. It is perhaps the only way in which a mother can show the infant her love. There are those who can hold an infant and those who cannot; the latter quickly produce in the infant a sense of insecurity, and distressed crying. All this leads right up to, includes, and co-exists with the establishment of the infant's first object relationships and his first experiences of instinctual gratification" (1966).

A discussion of Winnicott's contributions to the developmental processes would not be complete without a description of his concept of the true self and the false self. Thus for example, in *The Family and Individual Development* he explains how if the environment is not reliable there is a hidden true self and all we can see is a false self engaged in the double task of hiding the true self and of complying with the demands that the world makes from moment to moment. The development of drive is a basic element in normality and the maturational process proceeds as a result of an internal force. The true self is the manifestation of such a development. The false self is characterized, as Widlocher points out, "by its artificiality, its submission to the environment, without relating to the maturational process. It is the result of reactions to the external world, which, by a process of introjection, becomes the internal world" (1970). When there is very early failure in the holding stage of infancy, the tremendous anxiety provoked by this experience is followed by the building up of a false self in order to save the infant from total disintegration. In other cases, the false self disguises the true self which exists only as a potential and is allowed a secret life. In health the false self is represented by the whole organization of the polite and mannered social attitude, something which is adaptable.

"GOOD ENOUGH HOLDING" AND PSYCHOTHERAPY

Winnicott's view of the basic psychotherapeutic relationship rests squarely upon his concept of the maturational processes and the facilitating environment. Only the mother who is capable of primary maternal preoccupation and identification with her baby is capable of giving it a sound start in ego development. This view plants human personality squarely in the soil of personal object relationships as the starting point of all human living. It is clear then that the earlier the cause of trouble in the patient, the more fundamental his ego weakness, the more profoundly important does the quality of the therapeutic personal relationship become.

Thus Winnicott distinguished between psychoanalysis for Oedipal cases and "management" for preoedipal cases, where initial good-enough mothering cannot be taken for granted. For these sicker patients Winnicott takes the mother-infant relationship as the model for and the basis of psychotherapy. Our personal knowing of the patient which is emotionally perceptive, working by empathy and intuition, seems to be the essence of the therapy or as Winnicott puts it, "In our *Therapeutic* work over and over again we become involved with the patient. . . . What we do in therapy is to attempt to imitate the natural process that characterizes the behavior of any mother with her own infant" (Guntrip 1968).

This leads to Winnicott's concept of the "unfreezing" of destructive introjects (see also Chessick 1974g). Winnicott's great idea in psychotherapy is that patients who have suffered serious disturbances of the mother-child symbiosis early in life will not get well unless the therapist "behaves" himself. (Of course, this concept of the therapist behaving himself is a shibboleth and covers a great deal of the patient-therapist interaction, as described at length by Winnicott in chapters 22 and 23 of the *Collected Papers*). To explain, Winnicott divides Freud's classical psychoanalysis into two parts. First there is the technique as it is gradually developed and in which the material presented by the patient is to be understood and to be interpreted. Second, there is the *setting* in which this work is carried through. He enumerates in some detail certain points which seem obvious but tend to be overlooked about the setting. In this description of a favorable and correct setting for successful psychoanalytic psychotherapy he writes, "The whole thing adds up to the fact that the analyst behaves himself or herself, and behaves without too much cost simply because he is a relatively mature person. If Freud had not behaved well he could not have developed the psychoanalytic technique or theory to which the use of his technique led him. . . . The setting of analysis reproduces the early and earliest mothering techniques. It invites regression by reason of its reliability" (1958). The value of this from Winnicott's point of view is that such regression eventually permits the true self to meet environmental situations without organization of the defenses that invoke a false self protecting the true self. Thus a new progression of individual processes may take place which have stopped, and an unfreezing of an environmental failure situation occurs.

Later on he writes, "When a psychoanalyst is working with schizoid persons (call it psycho-analysis or not) the insightful interpretation becomes less important, and the maintenance of an ego-adaptive setting is essential. The reliability of the setting is a primary experience, not something remembered and re-enacted in the analyst's technique. . . . You will see that the analyst is *holding* the patient, and this often takes the form of conveying in words at the appropriate moment something that shows that the analyst knows and understands the deepest anxiety that is being experienced, or that is waiting to be experienced" (1966).

It is not possible in the present book to go into detail about this extremely complicated and rather mysterious subject and many readers find it difficult to understand exactly what "attitude" is being talked about. At any rate Winnicott and others of the British school of psychoanalysts deserve credit for careful investigation of the therapeutic role of the setting in psychoanalytic psychotherapy. In future years every effort will have to be made toward understanding this setting better and arranging it to suit the needs of the patient in an optimal fashion. This can only be done if the importance of such a setting is accepted (see Chessick 1971b).

Three other papers have vital implications for the therapeutic relationship. The importance of hate in the countertransference, and the countertransference itself, are discussed in detail in two classic papers by Winnicott (*The Maturational Processes and the Facilitating Environment* chapter 14 and *Collected Papers* chapter 15). Winnicott's most famous paper is "Transitional Objects and Transitional Phenomena" the *Collected Papers* chapter 18. I will not review these papers in detail here; they are all short and should be read and studied carefully.

THE PROBLEM OF ORIGINOLOGY

So far in this chapter we have oscillated from the pole of a rather naive psychology stressing the importance of free choice at every stage in development to the pole of a highly deterministic psychology stressing the importance of the earliest stages of infancy and the deterministic influence of the facilitating environment on all further maturational processes. Obviously, both extremes are highly controversial and each has adherents who more or less follow the general line but add different innovations of their own.

It is no accident that Coles begins his biography of Erik Erikson with a discussion of Kierkegaard. The reader of the present book will understand Coles' statement that "what Saint Augustine did through autobiography, Kierkegaard did as a solitary observer of others. He was a step removed from himself" (1970). Coles agrees with me in that he feels, "perhaps Kierkegaard's phrase 'stages on life's way' summarizes what Erikson wanted to study." Coles sees Erikson in the existentialist tradition: "Certainly, like Kierkegaard, he saw life as far more than the sum of any or all descriptions" (1970).

As much as there is a modern parallel between Erikson and Kierkegaard at least in discussing stages on life's way, so there is a strong opposition between the British School of psychoanalysts and Erikson. The former are totally absorbed in the first years of the life-cycle and tend to see life unwinding or unravelling itself from some intricate nuclear core that is rather quickly constructed in the first few years.

Is life a series of steps, each one before it and after, and each person's set of steps very much beside and connected to those that belong to others? Are we essentially what we are by the time we start asking questions like these, or are we so many things that it is impossible from moment to moment to say what we are because the nature of the moment itself "determines" or conspires to bring out the "inside" of us, that always lurks as "potential" or "possible"? Erikson coined the term *originology* which he explains and defines as follows: "In its determination to be sparing with teleological assumption, psychoanalysis has gone to the opposite extreme and developed a kind of *originology*—a term which I hope is sufficiently awkward to make a point without suggesting itself for general use. I mean by it a habit of thinking which reduces every human situation to an analogy with an earlier one, and most of all to that earliest, simplest and most infantile precursor which is presumed to be its "origin" (1958).

ERIK ERIKSON

Erikson certainly in his life story illustrates the enormous problem of finding identity, as he himself has recognized. Coles claims that he actually had two identity crises: first, as a youth coming to terms with himself and with the Danish-German world in which he grew up, and second, as an American psychoanalyst in the decade from 1950 to 1960, after the writing of *Childhood and Society*. Let us look in greater detail at Erikson's life story. Erikson himself in the "Fragments of an Autobiography" acknowledges that as a youth he experienced "identity confusion" resulting in pathological disturbances which analysts today would locate on the "borderline between neuroses and psychoses" (1970).

He was born in Frankfurt, Germany, in 1902 and never knew his father, a Dane, who abandoned his mother before his birth. This was kept from him for some time after his mother had remarried her Jewish pediatrician, Dr. Theodore Homburger in Germany. In signing his first psychoanalytic papers he used his stepfather's surname as his own; today he is Erik Homburger Erikson.

Erikson's stepfather urged him to become a physician, but he became an artist instead—an artist who did portraits of children. He left home after finishing high-school to travel across Europe, hiking and sketching. In 1927 an unexpected invitation from Peter Blos brought Erikson to Vienna, where he worked as a tutor in a family friendly with the Freuds. He met Freud on informal occasions when the family went on outings together. He became enormously influenced by psychoanalysis and undertook and completed psycho-analytic training in the late 1920s with Anna Freud and August Aichorn. His major interest at the time was in psychoanalysis and education and he became trained and certified as a Montessori teacher. He also met and married an American artist of Canadian descent.

They came to America in 1933 when Erikson was invited to practice and teach at Harvard and he became one of the first child analysts in the Boston area, although he had no formal degree. He was well received in Boston.

In 1938 he moved to California in order to test some of his theories by studying the Dakota Sioux Indians and the Hurok Indians in Northern California. From both these cross cultural experiences he attempted to correlate parental and communal values with personality growth. By 1942, Erikson was a professor of psychology at the University of California in Berkeley.

His first major paper "Ego Development and Historical Change" appeared originally in 1946 and has been reprinted several times. In 1950, over a quarrel involving the loyalty oath, Erikson resigned from Berkeley and moved to Stockbridge, Mass., where for the next ten years he worked with borderline youths at the experimental Austin Riggs Center. From a preoccupation with childhood and society his interest shifted to the larger questions of youth and its relation to history. His major book *Childhood and Society* appeared in 1950, at which time Erikson was already forty-eight years old.

Then occurred a period of rethinking in Erikson's life. It resulted in the publication of *Young Man Luther* in 1958, which marked a major shift away from classical psychoanalytic preoccupations. By 1960 Erikson returned to Harvard and became a revered teacher and very popular member of the academic world. Later he visited India and became preoccupied with a major study of Ghandi, culminating in the publication of *Ghandi's Truth* in 1969. At present he is retired.

Erikson's work has received little in the way of full length critical study, explication, or polemic from his fellow psychoanalysts, although he has achieved a remarkable prestige and popularity in the academic world of sociology. His books, beginning with *Young Man Luther*, represent a tense interdisciplinary study which has received wide praise from nonpsychoanalysts as having a genuinely sophisticated theory and methodology. As his published work proceeded from *Young Man Luther*, questions were raised about his style and language, his increasing moralizing, the markedly abstract level of discourse in his later essays, and the distance of his concerns from those of clinical practice. Most critics seem to feel that he goes to the edge of a full theoretical break with psychoanalysis—moving from deterministic psychoanalytic reductionism to existential structures of meaning and self realization—but then discreetly draws back.

PSYCHOSOCIAL STAGES OF EGO DEVELOPMENT

Erikson's contributions can be divided into those before and after the publication of *Young Man Luther*. The great ideas, as far as psychotherapy is concerned, reside in the former and may be further subdivided into his contributions to ego psychology in general, and his catchy descriptions of the eight stages of man and the accompanying crises of each stage. It is the simplest to begin with Erikson's eight stages of man which has survived as a schematization mainly because of its clever and brilliant wording rather than because of any profound analysis of human development. To my knowledge Erikson's famous chart of stages and crises has not been much utilized in clinical practice.

The description of the eight stages of man and indeed Erikson's fundamental contributions to ego psychology in general may be found in the famous monograph *Identity and the Life Cycle* (1959) and in *Childhood and Society* (1950). These two works are mandatory reading for any psychotherapist.

Erikson posits that side by side with the stages of psychosexual development described by Freud, are psychosocial stages of ego development, "in which the individual has to establish new basic orientations to himself and his social world." He argues that personality development continues throughout the entire life cycle, that each stage has a positive as well as a negative component, and that each stage builds upon the last—a process known as Erikson's *epigenetic* point of view (1968). Epigenetic development, the emergence of each stage of the life cycle from all the earlier ones, and profoundly shaped by them, would seem essentially a deterministic theory, emphasizing the life-long influence of early experiences on the structure and functioning of the later personality. Glynn writes, "Yet Erikson simultaneously insists that 'identity' begins where 'identifications' leave off, that each stage offers a chance for a new configuration, that 'the person is constituted anew at each stage of development.' From adolescence on, freedom, choice, self determination, are crucial, at least in the healthy. . . . Can Erikson have his cake and eat it too?" (1971).

Erikson frequently said he is not a theoretician at all but is only offering a point of view, so it is debatable whether his description of the eight stages of man, which has become so popular in scholastic circles, is a theory at all.

The first stage, corresponding to Freud's oral stage, extending through the first year of life, involves basic trust at one extreme and mistrust at the other. Stage two spans the second and third years of life, the period which Freud's theory calls the anal stage; Erikson emphasizes the emergence of autonomy. This autonomy dimension is built upon the child's developing motor and mental ability; the psychosocial conflict is between autonomy versus shame and doubt. In the next stage, the child aged four to five develops enough to initiate various motor activities on his own, and no longer merely responds to or imitates actions of other children. Erikson argues that the social dimension that appears at this stage has initiative at one of its poles and guilt at the other. Of course, this corresponds to Freud's oedipal phase. Stage four is the age period from six to eleven, the latency phase of Freud, and is marked by a psychosocial dimension having a sense of industry at one extreme and a sense of inferiority at the other. The dominant theme of this period is the concern with how things are made, how they work, and what they do.

When the child moves into adolescence between twelve and eighteen, the new interpersonal dimension which emerges has to do with a sense of ego identity at the positive end and a sense of role confusion at the negative end. Delineating this problem of ego identity was a major contribution by Erikson, especially to an understanding of adolescence. I will discuss it in detail later. Elkind points out, "Erikson, perhaps more than any other personality theorist, has emphasized that life is constant change and that confronting problems at one stage in life is not a guarantee against the reappearance of these problems at later stages, or against the finding of new solutions to them" (1973).

Stage six in the life cycle is young adulthood, the period of courtship and early family life that lasts until middle age, and for Erikson the new interpersonal dimension is that of intimacy at one extreme and isolation at the other. Erikson seems to use the concept of intimacy similarly to Sullivan—the ability to share with and care about another person without fear of losing one's self in the process. According to Erikson, in the case of intimacy, success or failure depends only indirectly upon the parents as they have contributed to the individual success or failure at the earlier stages and more directly on the stages that the individual has gone through and how he has resolved them in terms of forming ego identity of his own.

Middle age brings with it either generativity or self-absorption and stagnation. If there is generativity the person begins to be concerned with others beyond his immediate family, with future generations and the nature of the society and world in which those generations will live. Erikson's description of middle age is rather brief, and a series of papers have appeared which attempt to add further light on the period of middle age. For example, Gould (1972) attempted a detailed observational study of the phases of adult life and tried to develop subdivisions.

It is easy to see the contrasts between Erikson's approach and the classical psychoanalytic approach by looking at two other excellent papers on middle age by Jaques (1964) and by Prosen (1972). Prosen explains some of the crises of middle age as a denial of the aging process and an attempt to find a woman who more closely resembles the faintly remembered fantasized mother of youth. The image of the wife becomes split in these situations; she becomes both a degraded ugly object and an idealized woman. There is an accompanying idealization and hypersexualization of the self. Middle age, according to Prosen, is a period with its own stages of psychological development and its own particular crises.

Perhaps the most profound paper on the subject is by Jaques, who sees mid-life as a crisis calling for a reworking of the infantile depression: "It is this fact, the entry upon the psychological scene of the reality and inevitability of one's own eventual personal death, that is the central and crucial feature of the mid-life phase—the feature which precipitates the critical nature of the period. Death—at the conscious level—instead of being a general conception, or an event experienced in terms of the loss of someone else, becomes a personal matter, one's own death, one's own real and actual mortality" (1964).

Erikson's final stage, when as an individual's major efforts are nearing completion there is time for reflection, is characterized by a psychosocial dimension of either integrity on the one hand, or despair and disgust on the other. Despair expresses the feeling that the time is short, too short for the attempt to start another life and to try out alternate roads to integrity: "Such despair is often hidden behind the show of disgust, a misanthrope, or a chronic contemptuous displeasure with particular institutions and particular people" (1959).

Rapaport, in his introduction to the Erikson monograph (1959), reviews the whole field of psychoanalytic ego psychology and places Erikson in perspective. He sees the ego states of Erikson's epigenesis as related to a particularizing of Hartmann's concept of autonomous ego development. Each phase of the life cycle, according to Erikson, is characterized by a phase-specific developmental task which must be solved in it. His concept of mutuality specifies that a crucial coordination occurs between the developing individual and his human environment. Thus Rapaport considers Erikson and Hartmann to have made major and not contradictory contributions to the study of ego psychology. All Erikson's major work centers on the social and historical forces that make for the ego's weakness and its strength.

If one thinks of a psychic apparatus essentially and solidly made by the time a child is five to ten, then life becomes an environment able only to exert pressure on that apparatus, modify it, or elicit one or another quality from it. If one follows Erikson, the mind is really never developed, but *always developing in its essence*. According to Coles, this would lead the clinician to approach the later phases of life after adolescence "with the same clinical interest and theoretical devotion, the same mixture of bewilderment, surprise, and unyielding attention that the oedipal drama ("family romance") obtains from me, the psychiatrist. That is, I can think of life as progressively unfolding, with its direction essentially fixed in the first few years by what happens between the child and his parents, or I can think of life as a series of steps, with plateaus and precipices that do far more than reveal the direction set by the first few steps—in which case only when a person's last breath has been taken can his biographer draw psychological conclusions" (1970).

THE PROBLEM OF EGO IDENTITY

Another important idea of Erikson related to ego psychology is his emphasis on the problem of ego identity, which appeared in a paper in 1956 (1959). At this point, Erikson began moving farther away from psychoanalytic metapsychology and increasingly toward the fields of social anthropology and comparative education. From this shift of interest came his extremely popular concepts of identity crisis and identity diffusion—conceptions developed during his work at the Austin Riggs Center. He saw the problems of the borderline adolescents at this center as being based on acute identity confusion—a split of self images, a loss of centrality, a sense of dispersion and confusion, and fear of dissolution. His movement away from metapsychological formulations becomes much more apparent at this point.

Jacobson points out that originally Erikson did not overlook the genetic approach—that is the dynamic-genetic formulation of classical psychoanalytic metapsychology though he seemed "increasingly to remove himself from it" (1964). His studies on identity focused mainly on the adolescent and preadolescent period as his use of the terms ego identity and identity formation suggests. The term *ego identity* as Erikson employs it retains ambiguity even by Erikson's own admission, and Jacobson agrees. He first equates it with "a more realistic self esteem which grows to be a conviction that the ego is learning effective steps toward a tangible collective future, that it is developing into a fine ego within a social reality." Ego identity is defined as "the awareness of the fact that there is a self sameness and continuity to the ego's synthesizing methods" and explicitly distinguished from the feeling of "personal identity", because it conveys not only "the mere fact of existence" but the "ego quality of this existence" (1959).

Jacobson writes, "No doubt the term *ego identity* in this sense lends itself readily to a psychosociological study which relates individual identity to group identity. But I find it very difficult to distinguish personal identity from ego identity, all the more since Erikson links up the latter with 'realistic self esteem' and relates the individual superego to the value systems of the society in which the individual is reared" (1964). Thus Erikson uses the term ego identity in a broad and confused manner. He does not distinguish between the person's identity as it develops and can objectively be described and the subject's experienced identity or the striving for it.

Erikson's concepts shift the emphasis from the infantile stage to the adolescent and post-adolescent period as is evidenced by his drastic statement "Identity formation ... begins where the usefulness of identification ends" (1959). To complete this criticism of Erikson, Jacobson writes, "His formulations, unfortunately, do not clarify the continual and close interrelations between the infantile (and also the adolescent and postadolescent) processes of identification and the concomittant process of identity formation. His statement that identification as a mechanism is of limited usefulness is questionable, because identifications cannot be regarded as mechanisms and their usefulness for ego development is almost boundless. Combined with his further remarks, his comments show a regrettable misunderstanding of these processes, of the vicissitudes of identifications, and their contribution to ego and superego formation and to the autonomy of these systems" (1964).

Erikson in his further writings made the transition from clinical work to psychohistorical research. Two of his last three books are collections of essays—*Insight and Responsibility* and *Identity, Youth and Crisis*, but they are not focussed on clinical problems in psychotherapy. In *Young Man Luther,* Erikson began to emphasize what he called the "identity crisis"—that crucial moment which occurs in all men of some self awareness, and with a special force in great ones. He is fascinated by its importance especially in men who have shaped history. The concept of identity crisis lured Erikson into speculations about the psychic attributes of greatness and enabled him to attempt a new biographical genre resting on a fusion of psychoanalysis and history. It marks his gradual and unacknowledged movement away from the psychoanalytic clinician.

Erikson emphasizes the inherent strengths of the human personality by showing how individuals can use their neurotic symtpoms and conflicts for creative and constructive social purposes while healing themselves in the process. Erikson moved more and more from cross-cultural observations to psychohistorical analysis, a field which he himself established.

In summary, Ross claims, "Erikson presents the profession of psychoanalysis with a synthesis of an individual, psychosocial, historical, political, and ethical phenomena, which far transcends the narrow confines of the room with the couch" (1966). In reviewing *Insight and Responsibility,* Ross underscores Erikson's emphasis on our excessive addiction to the study of psychopathology, our dread of social commitment, our fear of studying value systems, and our failure to recognize the nature of psychoanalytic evidence as different from that of the natural sciences.

APPLICATION TO THE IDENTITY PROBLEM
OF THE PSYCHOTHERAPIST

As a postscript to this chapter it is worthwhile to consider Coles' remark, "For that matter, all too many psychiatrists fail to consider the issue of their own identity—and how their own training, their own analytic experience affects the view they have of themselves" (1970). Coles' remark is based on the end of Erikson's paper "The Problem of Ego Identity" (1959). A discussion of this matter by Modlin shows an interesting extension of Erikson's approach. "The awareness of personal professional identity and worth divorced from any single supporting and restricting unitary frame of reference is the surest base for relatively comfortable ventures into community psychiatry" (Usdin 1973). Modlin opens his brief paper quoting the challenge of an internist as to whether psychiatrists can justify their existence and attempts to establish what he calls "the realization of his psychiatric identity." Modlin bases this identity on the following:

1. Psychodynamics—the trained professional, understanding the critical influence of the irrational in human affairs, listens with a third ear. He is aware of the importance of separating conscious from unconscious motivational processes.

2. The professional has cultivated a sense of the longitudinal life-history and is alert to the possibilities for awakening and challenging latent growth potentials.

3. The professional has a sense of timing and process in interpersonal relations—an awareness that a relationship proceeds through sequential phases of development; he has knowledge of how to guide that development as the quality of the relationship changes with changing circumstances over a span of time.

4. The professional comprehends the difference between empathy and sympathy, and his trained capacity to maintain the relative uninvolvement of his own emotional vulnerabilities in the disabilities and misfortunes of his clients is an asset. (This is in part the notion of "professional objectivity").

5. Professional interviewing includes more than friendly conversation, information gathering, and even the establishment of rapport; it involves diagnostic and therapeutic dimensions and if done inexpertly, it can create serious obstacles to subsequent communication.

6. Experience with countertransference phenomena and knowledge of how to recognize them and deal with them is an essential part of the identity of psychiatrist or mental health professional. This approach to helping ourselves as professionals would be unthinkable without the contributions of Erik Erikson.

Chapter 18

Self-Realization and Transcendence

We have no objective picture of what the contemporary psychotherapist in fact is like. He has to be a philosopher, *consciously or no, methodically or haphazardly, in earnest or not, spontaneously or following contemporary fashions. It is not theory, but his example which teaches us what manner of man he may be. The art of therapy, of relationship, gesture and attitude cannot be reduced to a few simple rules. We can never anticipate how reason and compassion, presence of mind and frankness, will show themselves in the given moment nor what will be their effect. The greatest possibility of all has been expressed in the Hippocratic sentence:* iatros philosophos isotheos.

Karl Jaspers, *The Nature of Psychotherapy*

How in the world is the reality of philosophizing to prevail over the usual scarcity of men who are themselves, over the impact of egotistical passions and violent drives, over the will to power? How can it prevail over the positive evils of refusing to listen, dismissing arguments, and breaking off communication, of constant concealment, nonrecognition of truth, and the use of speech itself as a medium of suggestive magic and deception—the positive evils which at the crucial moment enable men to invent or obediently execute any crime?

The work of philosophy consists in the individual's inner

*dealings with himself. It is to him that the thinker appeals, to his
will to share and to communicate, to hear and to pass on what he
has heard—in the ineradicable belief that true philosophizing
works and will keep working, though how, where, and through
whom can be neither forecast nor planned.*

Karl Jaspers, *Philosophy*

EXISTENTIALISM IN
PHILOSOPHY AND PSYCHOTHERAPY

Existentialism represents a muddled half step further in the
evolution of psychotherapy. It accelerates with the phenomenology of
Husserl but originates from a variety of unclassifiable predecessors—
famous authors such as St. Augustine (chapter 6), Pascal, Dostoevsky,
Nietzsche (chapter 10), and Kierkegaard (chapter 17) who concentrated on their own experience to obtain knowledge.

The existentialist movement itself divides into two major groups of
authors, the agnostic or atheistic existentialists such as Sartre, Camus,
and Ortega y Gasset and the Christian existentialists such as Marcel,
Tillich, and Unamuno. Jaspers is usually classified as a Christian
existentialist although his concept of religion is not anywhere as
formed as Christian theology.

In many ways these authors take Kant as their starting point. The
philosophy of the enlightenment reached its apogee in Kant, but his
work already mirrors the growing dissatisfaction with eighteenth
century rationalism and the industrial revolution. After Kant a great
variety of schools developed as a reaction to the increasingly obvious
limits of what can be known through the use of reason and science.
There was also a great upsurge of scientific specialization, in which
many workers spent their lives working within the limits of narrow
scientific investigation without bothering themselves with what was
beyond.

According to Jaspers, the existential movement is *primarily* the
result of themes developed by Kierkegaard and Nietzsche. The entire
movement was popularized by Sartre, who borrowed his terminology
from Heidegger. He spoke of the "beings-of-thing" (être-en-soi) as
being complete, but the "being of humans" (être-pour-soi) as open,
because the future of humans is open, unmade and depends on *choices*.

Confronting the emptiness of the future we feel what Sartre called nausea, and Kierkegaard called *angst*.

Sartre popularized the notion of the absurd and the meaninglessness of our existence. He described the ordinary attempts to escape this by following the customary roles and runways of life, which he called "bad faith." He posed the question, "How does one escape from nausea without recourse to bad faith?" and tried to resolve the problem by blaming the entire situation on bourgeois capitalism and embracing Marxism as a system where man makes his own history. This remains a foggy generalization, and also contradicts his earlier contention that nausea is *inherent* in the "being of humans," by making it now contingent on the political life of man. Simone DeBeauvoir pointed out most tellingly the ironical contrast between Sartre, leading an eager and meaningful life with many friends and projects, and the figure Roquentin in his novel *Nausea* (Sartre 1963) whose existence is meaningless and empty. Thus in his own behavior Sartre contradicts his own philosophy, a striking example of "bad faith."

The entire existentialist movement proposes the exact reverse of Freud's philosophy. Existentialist philosophers generally claim that we are *not* determined in our life style or behavior either by any underlying neurophysiology or by forces in the unconscious mind. Emotions are seen as "intentional" and must be explained teleologically by bringing in the object of the emotions each time. Existentialists postulate an *inherent freedom in human nature,* sometimes linked with political freedom, and in which all moral principles are based on choice.

Sartre's voluminous works, especially his efforts to develop what he calls an existential psychoanalysis, lead down a blind alley, mainly because they have little relevance or clinical application for the practicing psychotherapist who is trying to deal with emotional illness. For this reason, I have not chosen Sartre as a representative of the great ideas in this chapter, although his vocabulary is often filled with psychiatric sounding terminology.

There is a movement that calls itself "existential psychotherapy." This school tries to assimilate and employ a variety of ideas and terminology from many existentialist authors. There is little agreement among the members of this school as to the meanings and definitions of these terms, and each author tends to use his terminology in a fashion unique to himself. Although some serious efforts exist in the literature to explain what existential psychotherapy is all about (May 1958; Havens 1974), in practice there seems to be little agreement and not much effect on actual clinical psychotherapy. Unfortunately, the phrase existential psychotherapy is sometimes used as an excuse to engage in a variety of bizarre maneuvers with a patient or group of patients under the guise of drawing out from them something uniquely human or that of engaging with them in some kind of meaningful experience.

Most legitimate existential authors agree that the major problems in their philosophy arise from ultimate or extreme human situations (boundary situations, as Jaspers calls them), and it is on the crucial issue of how people deal with these extreme or boundary situations that the various existential philosophers can be sorted out. We have already discussed Kierkegaard's concept of a leap to faith (chapter 17) and Nietzsche's concept of overcoming and laughing at the abyss (chapter 10). Let us turn now to the psychiatrist and philosopher Karl Jaspers, for a careful examination of this crucial human problem of boundary situations, and see how he embodies in his philosophy some important ideas for the field of psychotherapy.

KARL JASPERS

Karl Jaspers is a philosopher of our time. He suffered in the prime of his life through the Second World War and experienced the horrors of our current day to the utmost. His voluminous philosophical writings illustrate and combine a great many of the themes that have been developing in Western philosophy since the time of the Greeks. In previous chapters on Kierkegaard and Nietzsche as well as the elucidation of the philosophy of Kant, I have already touched on many of the themes that appear in Jaspers, but they are always adopted by him for his own purposes. Jaspers even rejects the term existentialist because he insists on a philosophy of his very own style. Although he utilizes themes from many authors, he utilizes them in a unique and individual way.

His writing style is usually turgid and is deliberately ambiguous, as I will discuss soon. There is little reason however, for his voluminous repetition in his writing, which includes some changes in terminology that are not clearly explained. Kaufmann, who is especially uncharitable toward Jaspers, reports that Jaspers kept his ideas on a series of index cards and wrote book after book around them in a repetitious fashion.

I have chosen Jaspers because of his unusual evolution from famous psychiatrist to famous philosopher and because he has breathed life into philosophy in a way that no one else in our time except Heidegger has been able to so effectively accomplish. The reason for this vitality is grounded in his view that philosophy must be lived and experienced. The major point for the psychotherapist is that Jaspers has fused philosophy and psychotherapy in a remarkable way and called attention to the fact that the psychotherapist must be a practicing philosopher, whether he likes it or not.

Jaspers was born in 1883 in Oldenberg, Germany. His father, descended from generations of farmers and merchants, was a lawyer and later a bank director. His mother came from a family of farmers. At the age of eighteen he was diagnosed as having bronchiectasis with secondary cardiac insufficiency and was told by his school director, "With such chronic illnesses, you will never become anything." He learned from Virchow that most such patients died in their thirties from generalized infection (Jaspers died at the age of eighty-six in 1969).

The recognition that he was a chronic invalid caused Jaspers to reorganize his daily life and use the leisure time other students employed in militaristic and social activities to thoroughly ground himself in the fields of medicine and psychiatry.

Perhaps the most important turning point of his life was his marriage in 1907 to Gertrude Mayer, a Jewish philosophy student, who remained his close companion for the rest of his life and who was the only one who could decipher his unreadable handwriting for the typist and the printer. She apparently submerged herself to become his full time assistant and secretary so that he could write with a minimum of disturbance.

He obtained his medical degree in 1908 and for four years worked in the psychiatric clinic in Heidelberg, which was headed by the famous neuropathologist, Nissl. Although Nissl correctly considered Jaspers to be out of the main stream of science and psychiatry, he was kindly toward him, and apparently forgave him because of his physical incapacities and anticipated early demise. He had to work as voluntary assistant because his illness would not permit him to undertake full clinical and hospital duties and fully participate in the communal life of the clinic staff.

Because he did not have so many clinical duties, he used the time available to apply himself more and more thoroughly to understanding the psychiatric literature of the nineteenth century. He produced some interesting papers, which led to an invitation by a publisher to produce a general work on psychopathology. This in turn led in 1913 to his major psychiatric book, entitled *General Psychopathology*. This book has undergone frequent and numerous revisions since its first appearance and Jaspers regarded it by 1959 as an almost entirely new book.

Although it has many weaknesses, *General Psychopathology* (1913) may be regarded as Jaspers' first major contribution to psychotherapy. It applies Jaspers' version of the phenomenological method to psychopathology. He attempts to produce an empirical method that will define experienced mental states or subjective mental phenomena within the narrowest possible confines, to distinguish between them, and to separate them terminologically. It may be thought of as an effort to fuse the subject and object of the investigation, or in other words, to form an empathic linkage between the felt mental state of the patient and the observing mental state of the doctor.

THE NATURE OF PSYCHOTHERAPY

Taylor and Heiser underscore the main tenet of Jaspers' approach to patient material: "Jaspers emphasizes that it is not necessary for the experiences and behavior analyzed to be logical or goal-oriented toward any particular social, personal, ethical or economic value system. The total person is experienced in an intuitive holistic psychological way. . . . Jaspers classified knowledge into 'empathic understanding' at one extreme and rational knowledge at the other. One acquires or communicates rational knowledge when he observes, describes, collects data, notes correlations, or reduces these to testable hypotheses that may become 'laws.' Jaspers placed the bulk of human understanding between these two extremes of empathy and rational knowledge, calling it 'interpretive understanding.' Interpretive understanding is a variable mixture of fact, fantasy, hunch, speculation, myth, metaphor, and hypothesis. All psychological theories belong to this hybrid group of interpretive understanding" (1971).

An extract from *General Psychopathology* published separately as *The Nature of Psychotherapy* illustrates in a more concise fashion some of Jaspers' subsequent applications of philosophy to psychiatry. Even if one cannot accept his phenomenological approach one cannot help being influenced by his description of what goes on between the therapist and patient. Jaspers is extremely preoccupied throughout his philosophy with the subject of communication. He emphasizes communication as a way of reaching the true nature of man and he feels that the ultimate factor in the doctor-patient relationship is existential communication, which goes far beyond the therapy itself. In existential communication both the doctor and the therapist are touched and both gain a fleeting glimpse of their true being, according to Jaspers. Only in this process can growth occur in an individual. It follows from this that, "We cannot rid ourselves entirely of some basic philosophical viewpoint when formulating our psychotherapeutic goals. This may get obscured or undergo chaotic changes but we cannot develop any psychotherapy that is purely medical, self-contained and appears to be its own justification" (1963).

Not only must the therapist have some philosophical underpinnings to his life and his work, he must, if we accept Jaspers' viewpoint, live a philosophical life. In his insistence on the psychotherapist living a philosophical life, Jaspers presents another genuine new idea to the psychotherapist. The philosophical life is implicitly described in his early work through his enumeration of the qualifications of the psychotherapist and is made explicit and emphasized in his later work, especially the *Way to Wisdom*.

In *The Nature of Psychotherapy* Jaspers writes:

Where I to try and characterize *a type* of psychiatrist who *in this scientific age* manages to remain balanced between the paradoxes of all his various functions, yet touches all the psychic dimensions with undoubted success, the following picture seems to take shape: He is a man who has a solid background of somatic medicine, physiology and the natural sciences. His attitude with his patients is preeminently one of empirical observation, of factual assessment and generally one that understands and appreciates reality. He will not easily find himself deceived nor will he readily agree to any dogmas, fanaticisms or absolutisms.

If we are looking for the prototype of the *ideal psychiatrist*, the one who will combine scientific attitudes of the skeptic with a powerful impressive personality and a profound existential faith, Nietzsche's words are not altogether inept: 'No profession can be developed to such great heights as that of the physician, especially since the "spiritual doctors," the so-called "custodians of the soul" are no longer permitted to practice magic arts and most educated people tend to avoid them.'

The individual needs a lifetime to found himself successfully upon that traditional practical wisdom of mankind from Plato to Nietzsche, which is the characteristic feature of psychotherapy as distinct from medical therapy in the narrower sense. (1963, pp. 30-32, 40)

For Jaspers philosophy is an activity, a becoming, not a state of being or a body of facts. Philosophy is philosophizing. To appreciate philosophic insights we must arrive at them ourselves. We must live philosophy, since we cannot meaningfully paraphrase its conclusions. Genuine philosophy arises directly out of problems confronting the individual philosopher in his unique existential or historical situation.

The most striking example of this attitude is to be found in volume 1 of *Philosophy* (1932), in which Jaspers describes a medical treatment from his point of view, emphasizing existential communication. He points out that the doctor himself has been called the patient's fate— his fate in a sense being brought upon himself and partly the result of the kind of doctor he will find. How the patient relates to his doctor and what he expects of him will mark the way of their developing communication.

JASPERS AND FREUD COMPARED

Jaspers' attitude toward the patient in psychotherapy in some ways is the diametric opposite of Freud. Jaspers insists that we must have philosophic faith *(philosophische Glaube)*, a conviction that man has a certain freedom and an infinity of possibilities. Jaspers calls this the

Existenz of man, the true nature of the self, which can never be reached but only illuminated or circumscribed. This is the real, the valuable, and the authentic in man, the genuine unique self, in contrast to the *dasein,* which represents the superficial self in Jaspers' philosophy (not to be confused with Heidegger's entirely different notion of *Dasein).* The key shibboleth from Jaspers that illustrates this attitude and appears repeatedly in his writings is: "For the totality of man lies way beyond any conceivable objectifiability. He is incomplete both as a being-for-himself and as an object of cognition. He remains, so to speak, 'open.' Man is always more than what he knows, or can know, about himself" (Schilpp 1967).

Jaspers repeatedly attacks Freud and cannot accept Freud's notion of infantile sexuality being the key to human neuroses. Kaufmann presents Jaspers' attitude toward Freud in summary form in an article reprinted in his book *From Shakespeare to Existentialism.* It is not necessary to belabor this issue here. Jaspers clearly does not understand Freud and has gone off in an entirely different direction.

Most important is the difference in the attitude toward man that Jaspers and Freud represent. Jaspers cannot accept any scientific theory which claims to completely understand man and his behavior, and he argues that the psychotherapist must decide for himself whether he will have philosophical faith in the infinite potential of man, or whether he will try to understand man from a strictly scientific point of view in terms of cause and effect. This is an issue on which the psychotherapist *must* take a philosophical position and it will substantially affect his therapeutic work.

The great idea of Jaspers, in my opinion, is to point out that the psychotherapist is *forced,* whether he likes it or not, to deal with essential philosophical questions in the actual practice of his clinical work. If he refuses to face these questions then he is working without insight as to what he is doing and as such cannot help but do an inferior job.

FROM PSYCHOLOGY TO PHILOSOPHY

From his psychiatric work and from his realization that the psychotherapist *must* trouble himself with philosophical questions, Jaspers became increasingly involved in philosophy. In 1919, he published what might be called a transitional work, *Psychology of World Views,* which to my knowledge has unfortunately not been translated into English. Three years later he became a full professor of philosophy in Heidelberg. He wrote a minor pathography on Strindberg and Van Gogh in the same year, but a long silence followed, during which there was a general rumor that Jaspers' works had been a flash in the pan and now that he had his professorship he would publish nothing further.

However during that time Jaspers decided to review all of philosophy from the beginning to the present. He produced a short book, *Man in the Modern Age* in 1931 in which he brilliantly summed up some of the difficulties of the current culture from the existential point of view and which contains some of his uncomprehending attacks on Freud, but the real essence of his work was contained in his three volume *Philosophy,* which appeared in 1932.

If one reads the *General Psychopathology* and the *Philosophy* along with Jasper's *Philosophical Autobiography* (Schilpp 1957) one can grasp the evolution of his thought in an unusually clear manner. He describes how he spent about seven years in reviewing other philosophers and thinking about the subject but giving no definitive shape nor direction to his own work. In a beautiful passage in the autobiography he writes: "Such work is, to be sure, work which requires planning and direction. It can, however, be successful only if something else is constantly effective: namely, dreaming. Often I gazed out on the scenery, up at the sky, the clouds; often I would sit or recline without doing anything. Only the calmness of meditation in the unconstrained flow of the imagination allows those impulses to be effective without which all work becomes endless, nonessential, and empty. It seems to me that for the man, who does not daily dream a while, his star will grow dark, that star by which all our work and everyday existence may be guided" (Schilpp 1957).

It appears that two major themes guided the evolution of Jaspers from psychology to philosophy. The first of these was his conviction that man could not ever be known in a total or scientific way. Because of this he developed the concept of *Existenz* and indeed called his philosophy *Existenzphilosophie.* This philosophy represents a reaction to academic philosophy at the time. Jaspers argued that the academic philosophers in writing their textbooks were attempting to make philosophy into a branch of science or a sciencelike discipline, and he felt that this was fundamentally wrong. He insisted that philosophy must be lived and that no set of definitions or sciencelike propositions could give for once and for all solutions to the problems of philosophy. Thus *Existenz* can only be illuminated and circumscribed, and the most effective way to do this is in the communication between man and man. However, in the writing of philosophy we can only approach this concept. There is a necessary ambiguity in all philosophical writing and definitions according to Jaspers; such concepts simply cannot be pinned down into words, and when one tries to do so, one automatically loses part of their potential.

Thus all expressions in *Existenzphilosophie* are ambiguous in principle. The best way to approach *Existenz* is through the illumination of *Existenz* by what Jaspers calls boundary situations. These ultimate situations require the facing of the existential questions and also require crucial choices in a person's life. The finest example of a boundary situation comes from Tolstoy's (1951) magnificent story, *The Death of Ivan Ilitch.*

BOUNDARY SITUATIONS, *EXISTENZ,* TRANSCENDENCE

Boundary situations represent the crises in human existence in which conflict and its meaning become poignantly and tragically clear. Jaspers emphasizes death, suffering, and struggle or "death, chance, guilt, and the uncertainty of the world," and two more general boundary situations—that of the particular historical determination of my particular existence, and that of the relativity of all that is real—its self-contradictory character as being always somehow what it is not.

Jaspers' three volumes of *Philosophy* (1932a, b, c) develop an increasingly mystical set of themes, beginning with science and the limits of our scientific knowledge as leading to the necessity for philosophy and philosophizing. Boundary situations such as the knowledge of our impending death brings us to illumination of our *Existenz* (if we let them). Jaspers arrives finally at *transcendence,* which is known only indirectly by what Jaspers calls "ciphers" such as myths or religions. The key point for psychotherapists is that man is unknowable and always more unknowable and indescribable than can be known.

Grene differentiates Jaspers from other existentialists by his emphasis on communication and transcendence: "By *communication* he means not, of course, the unreal gregariousness of the social conventions but the direct togetherness of two human beings struggling jointly to realize, always precariously, yet absolutely, the fulfillment of their deepest personal reality" (1970). Jaspers believes that the individual can free himself from the deluding snares of external demands to become genuinely himself, but only in union with another self.

When one reaches the concept of transcendence and ciphers, one has made the shift from psychiatry to philosophy (or perhaps theology). The arguments for transcendence, a concept which seems to be related to the notion of God even as it was for Aristotle (see chapter 2), preoccupied Jaspers in volume 3 of Philosophy (1932c). He claims that we can never really know transcendence, but through ciphers such as myths and religion we can illuminate transcendence, just as through boundary situations we can illuminate *Existenz*. If we have achieved this illumination we have gained strength by our experience of transcendence (see Chessick 1974g). His philosophy was carried to its major final point by the publication of *Reason and Existenz* (1935b) introducing the notion of the *encompassing*.

Most of the remainder of Jaspers' writing revolves around attempts to circumscribe, illuminate, and defend these basic philosophical concepts. Jaspers points out in *Reason and Existenz,* "Philosophical faith is the fundamental source of that work by which man makes himself in an inner act as an individual before his Transcendence, stimulated by tradition, but without any rationally definable bond to any particular form. For all philosophizing is unique and unrepeatable, although it is all rooted in one source making every philosophy akin to every other in its form" (1935b).

Jaspers argues very well for "philosophical faith," especially from the point of view of what there would be left *without it.* As he points out, if one is unwilling to accept this concept, then one must hold that the immediate world is all there is, that man's destiny is fully determined, that man is imperfectible and alone, and that the world is self-supporting. He tries to illustrate again and again through the use of the lives of the great philosophers how they have dramatically struggled with these existential questions and boundary situations, and how by their actual lives and active philosophizing they have illuminated the various concepts which he is trying to get across. There can in the ultimate be no rational justification for the final leap of philosophical faith, and transcendence must be discovered through doubt rather than reassurance. A good starting point to study these notions is in Jaspers' book *The Way to Wisdom.*

JASPERS ON
EDUCATION OF THE PSYCHOTHERAPIST

Jaspers' thought reaches a logical end point that demonstrates the importance of becoming immersed in the ideas of the great philosophers rather than studying a textbook. He writes, "Philosophy can only be approached with the most concrete comprehension. A great philosopher demands unrelenting penetration into his texts. This necessitates both the realization of a whole philosophy in its entirety, and taking pains with every single sentence in order to become conscious of its every nuance. Comprehensive perception and accurate observation are the basis of our understanding" (1941).

Here Jaspers brings up a point of great interest to the student of psychotherapy. There is a tendency to quickly slide over papers, books, and even whole areas of a man's work. Jaspers challenges the tradition of rapid review by insisting that a thorough understanding of the idea of *one* thinker, as the result of a total immersion in his work and from a careful study of everything he has to say, will bring greater rewards than a superficial textbook knowledge of a variety of thinkers, *for it will bring the great thinker to life in his active philosophizing.*

Jasper's insistence on comprehensive study is best illustrated by his remarkable book on *Nietzsche* which deserves separate consideration. No one else has used the subject of Nietzsche in this way, for Jaspers uses the life and work of Nietzsche as an illustration of *Existenzphilosophie* rather than presenting a standard approach to his life and work. For example, he uses the book to introduce his concept of philosophical truth as contrasted to scientific knowledge. He eloquently describes what he calls the self analysis of Nietzsche, immediately bringing forth the parallel to Freud's *Interpretation of Dreams.* He sees the self-analysis and the various phases in the works and life style itself as illustrating Nietzsche's attempt to reach beyond the limits of science, to aspire to the life of authentic creation. He reminds us of Nietzsche's use of Pindar's demand: *become what you are*. He describes his book on Nietzsche as "An introduction to the shaking up of thought from which *Existenzphilosophie* must spring" (1935).

CRITICISM OF JASPERS

Kolle (Schilpp 1957) points out that Jaspers actually demands too much of the ordinary man. Not many men have the courage and determination of Jaspers, and he probably overrates the capacities of the average individual. Kolle speaks from the point of view of "a thoughtful and experienced physician, who is well on in years." He mentions that a good many human beings are simply incapable of interpreting their *Existenz* transcendentally or being-in-the-world in relation to the encompassing. Thus they really cannot become themselves in Jaspers' sense, so that his philosophical faith can animate only those few who are capable of it. The mass of people are in need of the "little remedies" among which we reckon ordinary psychotherapy, and indeed there is a certain grandiosity to Jaspers' design, which perhaps we could forgive if we think of it as a distant goal for the human spirit rather than as having any immediate application to the practice of psychotherapy.

More serious criticisms confront Jaspers. Grene points out that Jaspers' philosophy is "a morass of abstractions presumably dealing with the most concrete and vivid of problems, neatly organized under heads and subheads, but carrying no conviction as philosophical argument, no vividness as the expression of an individual life. . . . There is a spread-out, swamplike placidity in Jaspers' writing that obscures its truth as well, perhaps, as cloaking its errors" (1970).

The most serious of all criticism from the point of view of the psychotherapist is also leveled at Jaspers by Grene. She points out that it is not clear *in what way* the achievement of freedom or authentic existence by the individual depends on communication with another individual: "Nor is it at all apparent in what sense the freedom of the individual involves transcendence, or how transcendence is achieved in communication. Jaspers asserts that all these dependencies hold"

(1970). This represents the most difficult and controversial aspect of the entire problem of applying existential philosophy to psychotherapy. There is simply *no clarity* on how the authentic self is to be reached and in *what way* the encounter between the therapist and the patient can help the patient to reach his authentic self.

The criticism becomes increasingly severe when we turn to Kaufmann who is an authority of erudition equal to that of Jaspers. Kaufmann (1960) takes apart Jaspers' book on Nietzsche and presents a towering argument against Jaspers' misreading of Freud.

The criticism of Jaspers is brought to a final extreme by MacIntyre who insists that Jaspers' solutions are simply empty of content. MacIntyre points out that Jaspers "sees a mediocre, scientistic frame of mind overwhelming the West; the solution is a spiritual aristocracy that has assimilated inwardly the truths which the external social world has rejected. But what is the content of *this* inwardness? Kierkegaard's hidden faith loses all its particularity. Even with Kierkegaard it is difficult to grasp what the sense of being before God consists in, but to try to secularize and to generalize this sense is to see it evaporate. In Kierkegaard we may suspect a final lack of content in the solution, particularly if we are not ourselves Christians; in Jaspers the lack of content is there for all to see" (O'Connor 1964). MacIntyre feels that Jaspers has engaged in a vulgarization of the important themes of Kierkegaard.

The obscurity in Jaspers hides a certain lack of content in the entire existential concept of authentic existence. In the boundary situations where *Existenz* is illuminated and where choice must be made, there are certain "mysteries and antimonies." From this we are told in a rather dogmatic fashion that in these situations we just inauthentically fall or we can authentically choose. Psychoanalysis is attacked because it moves in a contrary direction, seeing man as lived by his unconscious.

The only way that Jaspers really proposes to escape from this deterministic viewpoint is again to make a great leap to accepting a philosophical faith, in which we posit concepts like *Existenz,* that are illuminated by the boundary situations, but cannot actually be described or defined. Jaspers' work is not gripping like the poetic work of Heidegger, and reads in many ways like another watered down form of German mysticism. At times it seems to hide little matter beneath a plethora of words. Heidegger reasons more cogently and has a certain fascinating inner consistency, but Jaspers writes more like a theologian and is sometimes frankly irrational as in his attacks on psychoanalysis. What is fundamental in Jaspers has already been said either more cogently or dramatically by Nietzsche, Kierkegaard and Heidegger.

As a reply to Jaspers' book on Nietzsche, one may ask if we don't simply *wish* there were such a thing as *Existenz*. The only way to get information or right opinion about any subject is to approximate the method of science as much as possible. The intuitive, poetic, mystical search for authentic being or *Existenz* in order to get away from mundane living is poetry and has great esthetic appeal. In its most vulgar forms, we have an excuse for all sorts of drug abuse and escapism.

Jaspers in many ways is correct about trying to lead philosophy back to the important questions and away from science and technical epistemology, and Nietzsche was right about this too. Is the leap from the second level to the highest level of Kierkegaard's hierarchy really representative of going forward or is it a regression? I think if Freud were asked to answer the claims of Jaspers he would simply refer the reader to his book *The Future of an Illusion*.

BASIC QUALITIES OF THE PSYCHOTHERAPIST

The great idea of Jaspers for the psychotherapist has to do with living the philosophical life. Philosophizing as mere thinking and reading textbook summaries of thoughts of philosophers does not bring one to face one's self. Active philosophizing must be the goal of philosophy: the great philosophers are fine models of self elucidation who live their philosophy. Thus philosophy for Jaspers is a sort of mystical self-therapy using the great philosophers as models. The individual must bring himself to authentic being, or at least approach it, for the possibilities are unbounded. The great point is that philosophical thinking brings the choices leading to action and the philosophical life.

For Jaspers philosophizing is daily self examination and philosophizing deals with both the great shocks and with everyday life. Jaspers describes what he calls "man as a philosopher" which could serve very well for a description of the basic human qualities of the psychotherapist; never have these basic human qualities been spelled out more dramatically than in *Philosophy*.

> The poise that protects me from myself lies in the reserved gesture, in confining expressions to the situation; it does not permit me to waste myself on the random public and on every-day life. . . . It is courage and composure. It lets me tackle concrete tasks without fanaticism but with vigor, keeping calm if I do not succeed.
>
> *Humanitas* is open mindedness: putting myself into every other man's place, listening to reason, entering into the rationality of the case, and boundlessly expanding myself in ideas. It is resistance to sophisms, to the pressures of willful self-interest, and to accidental sensitivities. . . .
>
> Passion is the threat of unclarified ferocity erupting into chaos. It is the untamed force that does not turn into a motor of diurnal energy but looms menacingly in the background of humane reality. . . .
>
> Absolutized poise ossifies and deadens. Absolutized *humanitas* avoid decisions; it is erudition as the universal mode of knowing everything and understandingly, contemplatively dealing with everything. Unleashed passion leads man to destroy his world and himself. . . .
>
> These are, so to speak, the fields of existence into which the philosopher enters. He does not become identical with them, and neither is he without them. His own being lies in becoming; it is imperfectible in temporal existence. (1932b, pp. 358-359)

Chapter 19

A Quintet on the Foundations
of Four Fundamental
Psychological Systems

To this nobler purpose the man of understanding will devote the energies of his life. And in the first place, he will honour studies which impress these qualities on his soul, and will disregard others.

Clearly, he said.

In the next place, he will regulate his bodily habit and training, and so far will he be from yielding to brutal and irrational pleasures, that he will regard even health as quite a secondary matter; his first object will be not that he may be fair or strong or well, unless he is likely thereby to gain temperance, but he will always desire so to attemper the body as to preserve the harmony of the soul?

Certainly he will, if he has true music in him.

And in the acquisition of wealth there is a principle of order and harmony which he will also observe; he will not allow himself to be dazzled by the foolish applause of the world, and heap up riches to his own infinite harm?

Certainly not, he said.

He will look at the city which is within him, and take heed that no disorder occur in it, such as might arise either from superfluity or from want; and upon this principle he will regulate his property and gain or spend according to his means.

Very true.

And, for the same reason, he will gladly accept and enjoy such honours as he deems likely to make him a better man; but those, whether private or public, which are likely to disorder his life, he will avoid?

Then, if that is his motive, he will not be a statesman.

Plato, *Republic*

I.

In April 1973 I went down to the Piraeus with my wife so that I might sail forth and experience the beauty and magnificence of *Magna Graecia*. The road from Athens to the Piraeus was crowded—jammed with little taxicabs, ramshackle trucks and rusty cars—and surrounded on all sides by disintegrating industrial buildings and warehouses. Smoke and dirt blew everywhere in the air. It was a hot, dusty day, and as we travelled from Athens to Piraeus I found myself becoming increasingly depressed. It reminded me of a trip to the United States Steel mills in Gary, Indiana, except that the factories and buildings were far smaller and obviously less productive. Was this the end product of the civilization that began with the Golden Age of Greece? Is this form of government and this kind of environment the result of the explosion of Western science, which had its roots in the great thinkers of distant time?

After winding through a tangle of dirty streets and waiting interminably for a long string of freight cars to rattle by, we finally arrived at the port itself. Our driver went up and down the wharves, attempting to find our ship, a small one and very modest compared to the fancy pleasure yachts and de-luxe cruisers tied up in port. Finally we found it—a little Greek ship obviously quite old. I climbed aboard with my wife, each carrying our bags and checked in with the ship's Purser. We went up on deck at once in an attempt to get the smell out of our nostrils, the dust out of our lungs, and the industrial irritants out of our eyes. Sitting on the deck in the brilliant Grecian sun my wife soon fell asleep, and I began looking around at the magnificent blue water. We were quite early and other passengers for the shipt had not arrived, so we were alone on the deck. The ship rocked gently to and fro as it was tied in the harbor and the entire scene with the panorama of the

Aegean sea spreading out from the port was most conducive to reflection, if one could shake off the irritation of modern industrial society that lay over everything like a fog of yellow smoke.

Watching the birds I thought to myself of the line from *Jonathan Livingston Seagull:* "The gull sees farthest who flies highest," and just as I was beginning to associate to this I felt a tug at my jacket. Behind me I heard a voice saying: Polemarchus desires you to wait.

I turned around but saw nothing and said aloud, "Where is Polemarchus?" The voice replied, There he is coming after you if you only wait. I glanced over at my wife, but she was fast asleep, for which I was grateful. She knows things like this happen to me but simply attributes them to the feverish brain of an overworked psychiatrist.

I moved my chair a little away from hers, and in a few minutes I was astonished to see four life-sized spectres moving sedately, in the manner of patricians, over the azure water. They were an assortment of sizes and shapes, dressed in what I could only say was typical of the fashion of Athenian citizens of the Golden Age. Having heard the name Polemarchus I knew at once who they probably were, since I have spent many hours immersed in Plato's *Republic.* When they arrived, one stepped forward who seemed rather more stately and elevated above the others and said to me: I perceive Richard, that you and your wife are soon about to put to sea.

You are not far wrong, I said.

But do you see, he rejoined, how many we are?

Of course.

And are you stronger than all these? For if not you will have to remain where you are.

May there not be the alternative, I said, that I may persuade you to let us go?

But can you persuade us, if we refuse to listen to you? he said. Stay then and do not be stubborn, and we will have a good talk.

I said, Since you insist, I suppose that I must. Of course I made it appear as if they were overwhelming me, but really I was eager to stay.

I assume, I said to the leading spirit, that you are Polemarchus, and I think I have read of you and your companions before.

Yes, replied Polemarchus, drawing himself up. I am indeed the son of Cephalus and these are my companions, Glaucon, Adeimantus, his brother, and a little behind us, Thrasymachus. All but Thrasymachus smiled and looked benignly on me.

But why are you here, I asked, and where is Cephalus the wise and gentle father of Polemarchus whose appearance at the beginning of the *Republic* foreshadows Plato's description of a mature man at the end of Book IX, and above all, where is Socrates?

Polemarchus replied, My father and Socrates have gone beyond; we the mediocrities, are still striving to transcend. We feel a similar striving in you, with your one foot in the past and one foot in the present, and we have been waiting for you to visit the Piraeus and join us, since you too belong to the mediocrities. As my father said to Socrates, you should come oftener to the Piraeus. For let me tell you, that the more the pleasures of the body fade away, the greater is to me the pleasure and charm of conversation. If you will follow us to your cabin you will find yourself in our home; keep company with us as we are old friends and you will be quite at home with us.

I replied, There is nothing I should like better, lead on and I will follow. The spirits moved in procession down into the empty boat and passed into a cabin. Imagine my surprise when I opened the door and closed it behind me, to discover that we were in the setting of an old Greek ruin. There was nothing distinctive about it. Typical of most Greek ruins, it was very ruined indeed—a collection of stones of odd sizes and shapes, old columns, and some lovely trees among rolling hills. It was, of course, the house of Cephalus as it stood today in the country near the Piraeus.

Polemarchus wasted no time; when we were seated he commenced We wish to carry on the discussion of 400 B.C. in modern terms, and for this we need someone like you, not as smart as Socrates who demolished us all and in so doing left us without action and confused. You remember in the *Republic* that I was the heir of my father's argument, and I contended that justice is to give each man his due—an art which gives good to friends and evil to enemies?

I remember, I replied.

Polemarchus continued, Socrates twisted me around quite a bit in Book I of the *Republic,* but I still maintain that the focus of all human behavior must be on the freedom of the individual man, getting what he deserves through his choices. Man can never be thoroughly understood; he always transcends any attempts to completely explain him. Thus each man must have his due, and he has the freedom to earn whatever kind of a life he lives for himself. Only the meaninglessness, absurdity, and sheer horror of human existence can form the proper starting point for any philosophy of life. The original data of man's experience is always being-in-the-world, and a phenomenological approach to understanding man is the best.

I am astonished, I said, how you have kept up with the philosophical and psychological developments since your day. Let us reflect about this. If I remember correctly the phenomenological approach began with the descriptive psychology of Franz Brentano [1838-1917], who stressed *the intentionality of consciousness*. Thus consciousness does not consist of "mental states" but is always directed towards an object. It discloses or displays but does not construct the object, and all consciousness is consciousness *of* an object and towards it: to think is to think of something and to desire something.

Yes, replied Polemarchus, and this led to Husserl's phenomenology, a new method, which allows us a much more exciting approach to man than the way along which you have been tediously grinding away throughout your professional lifetime.

I replied, I understand that though much of Husserl's [1859-1938] work has been published, even more remains in manuscript—as much as forty-five thousand pages in shorthand. Husserl had a passion for certainty—

This was a symptom of a mild neurosis, interrupted Adeimantus. His elaborate investigations were nothing but complicated exercises in self-deception.

You would say that, remarked Polemarchus, but you forget that Husserl was still writing in 1935, the Nazis were in power, and Europe was again in crisis. This was thought by Husserl to be due to the decay of rational certainty. Philosophy for Husserl was not just his occupation; it was of the utmost seriousness to him. He spoke of it as some men speak of their call to the priesthood or others of their most sacred moral duties. Were he to waver in his devotion, he would be untrue to himself; were he to lose faith in philosophy, he would lose faith in himself.

This is not quite accurate, I said, for Husserl developed many of his ideas before the great crisis in Europe, although certainly while it was brewing. In fact, the later ideas of his phenomenology are already found in a series of five lectures he delivered from April 26 to May 2nd, 1907 [Husserl 1964]. You may be confusing him with Heidegger,

Polemarchus, and your description of "man" sounds more like Heidegger than Husserl.

Why is this important? asked Polemarchus.

Because a great many existential psychiatrists call themselves phenomenologists without realizing that Husserl's phenomenology has little to do with what they are talking about. Heidegger could not accept the phenomenological reduction of man, whereas Husserl insisted exactly on that. Existentialism, unlike phenomenology, does not aspire to be scientific; its subject matter is human existence or human reality, not consciousness as in phenomenology. Phenomenological existentialism goes beyond the phenomenological description of certain highly selective phenomena by a special kind of interpretation, the so-called hermeneutic method, which aspires to decipher their meaning for existence. Phenomenological reduction as practiced by Husserl is rejected by existentialist psychiatrists and even modern existentialist philosophers beginning with Heidegger. Also rejected is Husserl's concern for transcendental subjectivity as the absolute foundation of all being. Heidegger practically stopped using the term phenomenology in his own philosophizing, and yet the confusion is rampant among modern day psychotherapists who call themselves existential and phenomenological in their convictions. As a matter of fact, although phenomenology and existentialism are compatible in principle they certainly are not dependent on each other. The methods used by Jaspers and Heidegger are basically different than that used by Husserl.

Polemarchus, although rather crestfallen, continued, The ultimate objective of existentialism would not be theoretical justification then, but the awakening to a special way of life usually called "authentic existence."

That is more accurate, I replied, for although phenomenology and existentialism are compatible in principle, in actual practice Husserl's phenomenology is outspokenly rationalistic, whereas existential philosophy is opposed to all forms of intellectual or philosophical rationalism and deals with choice and commitment. Most important, Polemarchus, is to remember this quotation: "Existentialism may be on the trail of more vital, more fruitful insights than pure phenomenology. But it has still to learn a few lessons from the older phenomenology, particularly from Husserl. One of these is the injunction which I heard him address to an informal group of students when he criticized Max Scheler's much more rapid but not equally solid production: 'One needs bright ideas, but one must not publish them'. Another lesson is his insistence on the need of making sure of the epistemological groundwork: 'One must not consider oneself too good to work on the foundations.' It is such lessons, lessons of philosophical solidity, integrity, and humility, which both phenomenologists and existentialists still have to learn or to relearn" [Kockelmans 1967]. Husserl was an obscure writer; may I briefly review his main thesis for you?

Please do, replied Polemarchus.

Husserl went directly back to the Greeks. He argued that accepting the premises and methods of the natural sciences in philosophy and psychology is wrong and suggested instead that in philosophy and psychology we use the phenomenological method or "stance". This is characterized by "bracketing"—a special kind of seeing that discloses *objects originaliter*. Things are self-given when we bracket, and use the stance of *epoche*. *Epoche* is a term used by the Greek skeptics to express an attitude of suspension of judgment in the face of the uncertain world that Husserl calls "phenomenological doubt." Thus we refuse to accept the truth of "objects" as presented by experience. We *bracket* experience and a new, complex, fusing and merging set of experiences occurs. Husserl argued that this approach makes possible a new "science of being" and therefore by the use of the phenomenological method philosophy could be made a science and attain certainty.

Why in Husserl's view are the truths encountered in this phenomenological stance so important? asked Polemarchus.

Because whatever survives universal doubt is absolutely certain. Recall that Husserl held it to be his mission in life to resolve the crisis of European man by establishing philosophy as a rigorous science. According to Husserl, phenomenology *is* this rigorous science, insamuch as its method yields those certain truths that European man has been seeking. We need not follow Husserl in all his ramifications and refinements; indeed he insisted that it was impossible to follow him without extensive practice and training in phenomenological reduction. It will be enough for our purposes to understand Husserl's phenomenological method in a general way and to consider its implications for us.

Does the method really uncover apodeictically certain truths about the nature of being? asked Polemarchus. Husserl seems to differ profoundly from Wittgenstein about the relation between philosophy and language. For Wittgenstein all seeing is "language-ified;" all seeing is relative to "frames"—to presuppositions and values that have become congealed in language. In Husserl's view there is a special kind of seeing, wholly free from language, that occurs when we bracket properly. I have noted much discussion in your literature especially in attempting to understand schizophrenic phenomena this way. Certainly Husserl's view would undermine the entire program behind Wittgenstein's notion of philosophy as a therapy. And thus Husserl's phenomenology is, in effect and by anticipation, a direct answer to Wittgenstein's *Philosophical Investigations*.

I replied sadly, There is no way of adjudicating definitively between these interpretations. What seems to one party apodeictically certain because it is "there" seems to the other party a projection of the quest for certainty. Here we have reached a fundamental parting of ways in philosophical foundations. As Jones points out: "To speak in this fashion is to side with Wittgenstein rather than with Husserl. For instance, the language just used about their difference being a matter of 'interpretation' is language that is congenial to Wittgenstein, not to Husserl. Furthermore, Wittgenstein could accept, and Husserl had to reject, the notion that what is 'empirical evidence' remains an open issue; finally, Wittgenstein could agree, and Husserl could not, that there *are* partings of the ways" [1969].

This seems to create a negative impression of Husserl's philosophy, remarked Polemarchus. Certainly if his philosophy is judged by its own grandiose aims, its accomplishments seem to be meagre. Then why do we bother with it?

I replied, His influence on contemporary philosophy, psychology, and the social sciences has been great. He founded a school of psychology that, following his method more or less closely, has made detailed and often illuminating investigations of such phenomena as bad faith, anxiety, and inner time sense. The difficulties have occurred when psychotherapists who have the personal tendency to think in existentialist terms insist that their frame of reference is based on a "scientific" method that they call phenomenology. It is possible to argue on practical grounds that it is worthwhile to "stay with" patients and to attempt to awaken patients to a special way of life or authentic existence [for example see Havens 1974], but the ultimate justification of this in no sense can be called science or phenomenological method; it is much more an attempt by the convinced to convince others to make a psychological leap. This belongs in the category of persuasion and inspiration and may be thought of as a theological or imaginative or dramatic way of looking at human life. As a matter of fact, Husserl's notion of phenomenology is antithetic to this approach in many ways, and was developed for entirely different purposes. There is just as much confusion and disagreement among contemporary phenomenologists as there is among the adherents of any other fundamental philosophical or psychological schools of thought.

I understand you, said Polemarchus, but if this definition of phenomenology as the basic science of psychology and psychotherapy breaks down what other can be offered?

Several times in the course of the discussion Thrasymachus had made an attempt to get the argument into his own hands, and had been put down by the rest of the company, who wanted to hear the end. But when Polemarchus had done speaking and there was a pause, he could no longer hold his peace. Gathering himself up, he came at us like a wild beast seeking to devour us. We were quite panic stricken at the sight of him as he roared out to the whole company, What folly has taken possession of you all and why, dunces, do you knock under to one another? I say if you want really to know what psychology is all about you should quit confusing yourself with questions and answers about theoretical foundations. And now I will not have you say that there are theoretical foundations of any importance to psychology; this sort of nonsense will not do for me—I must have clearness, science, and accuracy.

I was panic stricken at his words, and could not look at him without trembling. Indeed I believe if I had not fixed my eye upon him, I should have been struck dumb. But when I saw his fury rising, I looked at him first, and was therefore able to reply to him. Thrasymachus, I said, with a quiver, don't be hard upon us. Polemarchus and I may have been guilty of a little mistake in the argument, but I can assure you that the error was not intentional. You people who know all things should pity us and not be angry with us.

You are starting to sound like Socrates, replied Thrasymachus, with a bitter laugh. Please don't imitate his ironical style as it is not suitable to mediocrities like us. I have proclaimed that justice is nothing else than the interest of the stronger, and the course of history since the time I proclaimed it is unquestionably very much in that direction. I now proclaim that the course of psychology is going in the same direction and you with all your fussing and concern over so-called humanistic values are soon to be swept away by the world of the future, which will be based on a scientific experimental psychology. In fact, you yourself have grudgingly admitted in your deservedly not very well known books, that conditioning has a vital role in the process of working through. You would get much farther and be much more popular and sell many more books if you gave conditioning the central role and dropped all this other nonsense. It seems to me that you are doing the wrong and irrelevant things in your psychotherapy and what little success you do have you are utterly misinterpreting.

Then you cannot accuse me of irony, Thrasymachus, when I agree that I know nothing like Socrates, since you have already stated that I know nothing. How can I answer you if I am told by you that even if I have some faint notions of my own, you, a man of authority, feel that they are nonsense and not worth uttering? The natural thing then is that someone like yourself, who professes to know, should tell me what he knows. Will you then kindly explain yourself for the edification of the company and myself?

Glaucon and the rest of the company joined in my request and Thrasymachus, as anyone might see, was in reality eager to speak, for he thought he had an excellent answer, and would distinguish himself. Listen, he said, by viewing all psychotherapy as fundamentally a form of instrumental conditioning you can free yourself from the unnecessary burden of nonsensical philosophical assumptions, and carry out a direct, clear-cut, and scientific method in the tradition of the physical sciences. You can statistically evaluate your work and develop an exact cause-and-effect technique that is amenable to laboratory investigation and development according to the classical methods of science. All this nonsense about authentic life and humanistic concerns can be left to the philosophers, and psychotherapists can become medical scientists again as they should have been all along until they were befuddled by the Jewish mystical imagination of Freud. Ever since Freud, psychotherapists seem to have forgotten what they are getting paid for—the removal of symptoms that cause distress to the patient. The patient comes complaining of symptoms. By deconditioning you remove these. He is happy and he pays you, for he got what he came for as in any other branch of medical science. A description of these scientific behavioristic techniques can be found in any standard textbook, and it is clear that the world of the future will be shaped by such techniques. So you better get with it or you will starve in your smoky little office.

Again Thrasymachus left me shaken. Please explain yourself in more detail, I requested. Behavioral psychotherapy does not seem quite so simple to me. I would appreciate it if you would outline for us the fundamental propositions upon which it is based. It is one thing to say that conditioning has an important role in the working-through process; it is another to maintain that conditioning or deconditioning is the whole of psychotherapy and that all else is nonsense.

I can see that you have learned something from Socrates and from history, smiled Thrasymachus, drawing himself up in a rather supercilious fashion. Socrates seemed to demolish my arguments in the *Republic,* but history shows that they have prevailed in practice. You seem genuinely interested in understanding the psychology of the future, and so I will outline it for you if you can be more silent than you were with Polemarchus, for I have noted that you have a tendency to write and pronounce on a great many subjects.

Thoroughly chastened I replied, speak Thrasymachus and I will listen.

II

In order to put this discussion into perspective, Thrasymachus asked Polemarchus to outline briefly the classical Greek philosophical positions on the mind and the brain.

He replied, these are psychophysical parallelism, interactionism, subjective idealism, solipsism, and epiphenomenalism. "Psychophysical parallelism presupposes that physical and psychic events move along together in a parallel but independent manner. Interactionism assumes, as the term implies, that physical and psychic events are capable of influencing one another. Subjective idealism assumes that there is no material world and that all reality is subjective, in human minds. Solipsism posits that there is only *one* mind, namely, one's own, and that not only the material world but other people are the creations thereof. And epiphenominalism posits that the physical world is the only true reality and that psychic events are inconsequential excrescences" [Mowrer 1972].

I have no problem with this, began Thrasymachus, because for me the only significant realities are events in the external world, and *the behavior* that they elicit in living organisms. Mental states are by-products and not to be mistaken for causes; I am against "freedom" and against "dignity" and against "feelings" and against "values." I am against anything that smacks of mind, because mind is soft and ghostly and gets in the way of clear thinking about the control of behavior. Furthermore, "The environment not only prods or lashes, it *selects*. Its role is similar to that of natural selection, though on a very different time scale, and was overlooked for the same reason. It is now clear that we must take into account what the environment does to an organism not only before but after it responds. Behavior is shaped and maintained by its consequences. By refusing to recognize that a person who responds in acceptable ways to weak forms of control may have been changed by contingencies which are no longer operative, the defenders of freedom and dignity encourage the misuse of controlling practices and block progress toward a more effective technology of behavior" [Skinner 1971]. All this foolishness about the Being of man as it runs for example through Book IX of Plato's *Republic*, or telling us that what is threatened is man *qua* man, or man in his humanity, or man as Thou not It, is nonsense. What is being abolished by my viewpoint is autonomous man: "the inner man, the homunculus, the possessing demon, the man defended by the literatures of freedom and dignity" [Skinner 1971]. The abolition of autonomous man has long been overdue, for he is nothing but a device used to explain what cannot be explained in any other way. He has been constructed from our ignorance, and as our understanding increases, he vanishes. To man *qua* man we readily say good riddance. Only by dispossessing him can we turn to the real causes of human behavior. Freedom and dignity and man *qua* man are cardboard verbal concepts expressing a fuzzy minded and false view of man which must be demolished if we are to understand how to make an improved society.

Oh Thrasymachus, I sadly replied, if Dr. Skinner had only limited his call for a new science of man to a plea for study and research of human behavior by way of an objective observational and inductive methodology, few would disagree with his thesis. It is when he gets involved in essentially philosophical areas that the romanticism of his thinking becomes apparent and the speculative nature of his utopia becomes controversial. What does the history of scientific institutional approaches to controlling behavior tell us about the future of scientific behavioral control?

In many ways we have been better served by happenstance than social design, added Polemarchus. One need only look at the state of our designed institutions today—our prisons, our mental institutions, our schools—to question the wisdom of social science and social engineering.

Yes Polemarchus, I replied, all that is predictable is minor in comparison with what is not predictable. I think the trouble comes from Skinner's dogmatic commitment to a radical positivism—bad philosophy rather than good science. "Feelings and intentions, cognitive processes, and inferred mental or neural dispositions of whatever kind are quite arbitrarily ruled out of the causal process—in the mode of a severely restricted philosophy of science more characteristic of Skinner's formative period than of today. All that is left, then, are behaviors and the environmental contingencies under which they occur. This arbitrary, pigeon-brained constriction of the psychologist's model of man puts some of the humanly most important questions out of bounds" [Smith 1972]. We can enjoy the challenge that Skinner poses to the more tender-minded in psychology, but do we need to accept Skinner's narrow preconceptions of the causal process as it involves human beings?

Freedom, dignity, and responsibility need not be conceived as epiphenomena, as humanistic relics in a scientific, technological age, insisted Polemarchus.

Do you not see Thasymachus, I asked, how Skinner's fusion of scientific determinism with a rigid positivism invites an unnecessary polarization of scientific as against humanistic psychology? "The humanistic attack on Skinner is warranted, not because of his 'scientism' but because he arbitrarily excludes from psychological analysis what people have often regarded as more important than their reinforcements" [Smith 1972].

It is hard to debate with that, replied Thrasymachus, more softly.

May I ask you, are these views based on a 'hard' or 'soft' determinism?

Skinner is a hard determinist, answered Thrasymachus.

If he is a hard determinist and his premise is correct, that is, if everything we do is strictly determined, then we cannot choose to master or control the environment, nor can we choose to follow Skinner's or your recommendations, unless we are determined to do so. If, on the other hand, we can influence or modify the environmental conditions under which we behave, then do we not have some measure of freedom?

I see what you mean, replied Thrasymachus.

"Soft determinism, holding the latter position (which, incidentally, most contemporary philosophers accept) is perfectly compatible with both scientific behaviorism and genuine freedom of choice. It allows that human behavior can be explained by reference to natural causes, *and* that we freely select goals and that our choices have consequences in future conduct. Skinner at times, appears to be following hard, rather than soft determinism. His rejection of individual freedom mistakenly follows from this premise. But behavioral science need not presuppose hard determinism nor need it reject freedom" [Kurtz 1971]. Also, can you see why strict determinism in the sense of being able to predict a sequence of future behaviors completely from a knowledge of the present state and past states of the organism is not acceptable?

Why? asked Thrasymachus.

First, because of statistical randomness, from cosmic rays, or somatic mutations, or thermal fluctuations in the nervous systems, which provides variations in behavior on which mechanisms of shaping actually depend—so they represent a necessary limitation on any exact determinism. Second, the initial state of a very complex organism, from which prediction starts, is unknowable by any observer of the same complexity. This is for two reasons, "complexity-indeterminacy" and "privacy-indeterminacy" [Platt 1972]. In a human brain of 10^{11} neurons and 10^{14} synapses one can never expect deterministically predictable results, Furthermore, complex and private operations determine each of our outcomes and behaviors in ways that no experimenter or controller can entirely measure or predict. "If anyone still wishes to say that we are behaving deterministically, 'in principle' he can; but it is operationally an empty statement if the prediction is in principle not possible itself because of incomplete information" [Platt 1972]. It may be further argued that these private inputs and operations interacting with the environment "can lead to new insight-closure of new organism-environment loops", as Platt [1972] explains.

I am getting confused, said Thrasymachus. Do you imply that stimulus-response theories have no place in the understanding of man?

They certainly do have a place, I replied, and the best way to put the place into perspective is to look at the overall development of stimulus-response theory. To quickly summarize stimulus-response theory first: "In classical conditioning a conditioned-stimulus (e. g. tone) is paired with an unconditioned stimulus (e.g., food) that evokes an unconditioned response (e.g. salivation). After repeated pairings of the two stimuli, the conditioned stimulus is by itself capable of evoking the unconditioned response. A conditioned response can be extinguished by presenting the conditioned stimulus in the absence of the unconditioned stimulus. . . . Basic phenomena in classical conditioning are spontaneous recovery (the reappearance of a conditioned response after the passage of time), stimulus generalization (the ability of stimuli similar to the conditioned stimulus to evoke the conditioned response), and conditioned discrimination (the application of acquisition and extinction methods to training an organism to respond to one stimulus but not to a similar one)" [Kendler and Kendler 1971].

A more important type of conditioning is known as instrumental conditioning, in which reinforcement occurs only after the subject makes an appropriate response. The main kinds of instrumental conditioning are reward, escape, and avoidance. Furthermore, "Whereas instrumental conditioning occurs with discreet trials, operant conditioning takes place in a free-responding situation. In operant conditioning, behavior is measured in terms of rate of responding, which is computed by dividing the number of responses by a constant unit of time. The rate of responding before conditioning takes place is known as the operant level of that response. . . . A major variable that determines the rate of responding is the schedule of reinforcement. In an intermittant schedule, reinforcements occur only after some responses, not after others. One consequence of an intermittant schedule is that it creates greater resistance to extinction than consistant reinforcement does" [Kendler and Kendler 1971].

I don't think "instrumental" is a very happy word, interrupted Thrasymachus, because it implies the use of instruments, and there are units of behavior where the word is really not appropriate at all. Skinner prefers the word "operant" in the sense of behavior which operates on the environment and produces reinforcing effects: "You define an operant in terms of its effects, and study it by means of its effects on your apparatus. Operant behavior, as I see it, is simply a study of what used to be dealt with by the concept of purpose. The purpose of an act is the consequences it is going to have. Actually, in the case of operant conditioning, we study the consequences an act has had in the past. Changes in the probability of response are brought about when an act is followed by a particular kind of consequence. It can be positive or negative reinforcement as the case may be, but the datum that you watch and follow is the probability that a response of a given type will indeed occur. An operant, then, is a class of responses, and a response is a single instance of that class" [Evans 1968].

The main point, I continued, is how different this all is from Pavlov's discovery in 1910 of the conditioned reflex and classical conditioning, although it is still confused with Skinner's work. Pavlov rang a bell as he presented food to a dog and then found that the dog would salivate to the bell alone. In this case, the experimenter does both things before-hand, not waiting for the animals "operant" behavior; and the animal does nothing but "associate" them, so the method is useless for shaping new behavior.

Thrasymachus still had trouble keeping still for he interrupted again and claimed, Shaping behavior is what this is all about. New behavior is produced by operant conditioning. The experimenter takes advantage of random variations in the operant response, reinforcing only those responses that are in the desired direction. The practical significance of partial reinforcement is very great. A child's mother is not always present to reward him for looking both ways before crossing the street. But the influence of reinforcemets are such that they persist against many non-reinforcements. Furthermore, any stimulus can be made reinforcing through association with a reinforcing event: "Once established, a secondary reinforcer can strengthen responses other than the response used during its original establishment and can do so with drives other than the one prevailing during the original training. . . . Secondary reinforcement greatly increases the range of possible conditioning. If everything we learn had to be followed by a primary reinforcer, the occasions for learning would be very much restricted.

As it is, however, any habit once learned can have other habits built upon it" [Hilgard et. al. 1971].

I thought we were going to review the development of stimulus-response theory! insisted Polemarchus.

During the very time when Freud's position was earning prominence, the behavioristic movement in psychology was announced with enthusiasm—and denounced with vigour. John Watson [1878-1958], inspired by the writings of Pavlov [1849-1936], disavowed the importance of consciousness and paved the way for a behavioristic psychology of learning. One of the major influences on Watson's thinking was Pavlov's concept of the conditioned reflex or conditioned response, which we have already discussed. Watson's manifesto in 1913 insisted that it was not enough to dignify the study of behavior to equal that of the study of consciousness in psychology, but rather that behavior was hereafter to be *the only method* of psychology; indeed, its study was to be the definition of psychology. "Anything smacking of the mental was anathema to Watson. It was as if to him the mental was outside this rational world of ours, dwelling in the dark with the other ghosts and goblins. His conception of the earlier work in psychology was simple and clear; the introspectionists assumed the soul or its substitute (consciousness) to exist and then proceed to study this airy nothing by introspection" [Watson 1963].

Exactly! declared Thrasymachus.

Pavlov, the son of a village priest, was born in Russia in 1849, and received his early education in a local seminary. In 1870, he entered the University of St. Petersburg with animal physiology as his specialty. In 1875, he enrolled in the medical school to prepare himself for a research post in physiology. He studied in Germany for two years and then returned to St. Petersburg for years of hard work in the laboratory with little financial return. Only at the age of forty-one, in 1890, was he made professor of pharmacology (later physiology) at the St. Petersburg Military Academy. He continued his research on the processes of digestion for which he received the Nobel prize in 1904. Only after the age of fifty did he study what became known as conditioning, which study covered a span of another thirty years. He died in 1936.

In 1913, Watson stood alone, but by 1930, his view, based on Pavlov's, had swept through psychology in the United States.

Thus we are dealing with really two questions, added Polemarchus. The first is the issue of developing a therapy *deliberately* based on behavioral psychology and the second is to what extent stimulus-response theory can be applied to psychoanalytically oriented psychotherapy. These are really two entirely different issues.

There is a third issue, I added, for a recent discovery by Miller and his associates [1969] has shown that glandular and visceral responses can be modified by instrumental conditioning procedures. This has enormous possibilities and consequences in the treatment of psychosomatic disorders, but it is so new at this time that little can be said in detail about it. A number of studies have appeared and the subject is beautifully reviewed by Jonas [1972]. At any rate, numerous attempts have been made to integrate stimulus-response theory, learning theory, and the process of psychotherapy. A tremendous unrealized wish has repeatedly been mentioned by numerous authors to recharacterize the process of psychoanalytic psychotherapy in terms of learning theory, but there is still so much disagreement about learning theory that it really accomplishes very little to try to do so at this time. The most famous effort in this direction has been made by Dollard and Miller [1950].

Thrasymachus insisted: Skinner has already characterized psycho-analytic psychotherapy as follows: "The therapist constitutes himself a non-punishing audience. Under these circumstances, responses repressed by punishment tend to return. Forgotten experiences may be recovered, the patient may act aggressively (or at least verbalize aggressive impulses), the patient may exhibit strong emotion. The appearance of previously punished behavior in the presence of the non-punishing therapist makes possible the extinction of some of the effects of punishment. . . . This plausible account calls for no 'explanatory fictions'—no id, ego, or superego, inhabiting a psychic or mental world" [Hilgard 1956]. For details you can read Skinner's *Science and Human Behavior*.

That is a good brief summary of Skinner's view Thrasymachus, I replied, but anyone who practices psychoanalytic psychotherapy can easily discover that a lot more goes on. The exact extent to which operant conditioning plays a role in the process of psychoanalytically oriented psychotherapy remains today a matter of major debate. There is no doubt, however, that the notion of operant conditioning is a great idea, but the trouble comes from always trying to oversimplify the extremely complex process of intensive psychotherapy. In a way I think it is better that the stimulus-response psychologist spend his energies in attempting to construct deliberately a therapy based on stimulus-response theory, instead of attempting to characterize psychoanalytic therapy as "nothing but" some form of deconditioning process, or reduce it down that way.

I could see that Thrasymachus was not quite subdued, for again the victory smile crossed his face as he announced, Just what I would expect you to say Richard. As a result of the immense contribution psychoanalysis has made to psychiatry, everyone is now aware of the widespread prevalence of psychiatric illness, and the urgent need for extensive therapeutic intervention. Still you insist on an unrealistic, impractical, and uneconomic procedure like psychoanalytically oriented psychotherapy in spite of the rapid gains made by behavior therapy in the quick cure of symptoms.

I do not minimize the importance of removing symptoms, I replied. But psychoanalytic psychotherapy is a humanistic therapy based on the importance of the individual [Bieber 1973], committed to resolving as much of the existing psychopathology in the total personality as possible. The influence of stimulus-response psychology on the practice of psychoanalytically oriented psychotherapy is and will remain small because of this fundamental polarization. For those patients who are motivated to develop their human potential to the best of their ability, intensive psychotherapy will be the treatment of choice; for those patients who wish to contract for specific symptom-removal, the carefully designed behavioral therapies will be more economical and efficient. There is some overlap, but not as much as is generally assumed.

It is best to clearly delineate the behavioral therapies. For example, Wolpe, a South African born physician and psychologist, believes that many forms of maladaptive behavior are nothing more or less than persistent learned habits. For Wolpe, anxiety is an inappropriate fear response to situations and events that carry no objective threat to the individual, and it plays a central role in the development and maintenance of a neurosis. Wolpe posits that anxiety is learned by classical conditioning. He offers [Wolpe 1959, 1969] a technique for alleviating anxiety called systematic desensitization, which is based on the principle of reciprocal inhibition, an attempt to follow Pavlov and Watson. It is no longer possible to argue against the fact that systematic desensitization has been shown to be a highly efficient and successful treatment method for the symptoms of certain disorders, most particularly phobias or irrational fears and furthermore, because of the specific nature of the problems treated, it has been possible to measure outcomes objectively.

And more scientifically, interrupted Thrasymachus. Reciprocal inhibition is based on the idea that an anxiety habit can be overcome by making some other response possible in the presence of the anxiety evoking stimulus. Systematic desensitization is a clear, simple, and scientific procedure. Other methods such as "flooding" and "aversion therapy" are currently coming into use, although they are not as generally accepted yet. Behavior therapy, at least for specific symptom complaints, is clearly superior to psychoanalytic therapy [Wolpe 1971]. Furthermore, operant conditioning has many other possible and as yet unexplored therapeutic applications.

This is not as simple as you are making it sound, Thrasymachus, I replied. It now seems clear that the stimulus-response formula, however powerful in the hands of a Hull or a Skinner, is at best incomplete. There must be the recognition that a great deal goes on *between* stimulus and response. "The great complexity of human behavior is currently a matter of stress. Accumulating evidence shows clearly that even the simplest conditioned response is controlled by a great many variables. Furthermore, these variables interact in ways which mean that a condition which has one effect under a certain set of circumstances, may have a different, even opposite effect under another" [Hilgard and Marquis 1961].

Furthermore, it is necessary for you to admit that among behavior therapists just as among psychotherapists there exists a broad range of differences, from adherents of Pavlov and Hull, to Skinnerians, eclectics, and to those who lean toward information theory and general systems theory. "At one end of each spectrum the theories of behavioral and dynamic psychotherapists tend to converge, while at the other end their divergence is very great. It is because adherents of these two approaches tend to define each other stereotypically in terms of their extremes that so much misunderstanding and heat are often generated between them" [Marmor 1971]. The problem lies in the oversimplified explanation by the behavior therapists of what goes on in the therapeutic transaction between patient and therapist and their insistence that the *essential core* of their behavior therapeutic processes rests on Pavlovian or Skinnerian conditioning and is also "more scientific" than traditional psychotherapies.

With these formulations goes a conception of mental illness that is quite simplistic. And the philosophical foundations of such explanations, involving naive realism or positivistic empiricism are also quite simplistic and easy to take apart. For example, evidence from recent work in linguistics [Chessick 1974g] indicates that the basic philosophical preconceptions of stimulus-response theory are untenable. In addition, Piaget's genetic epistemology demonstrates the crucial interaction between an intrinsic maturational sequence and learning and the role of *internal* reinforcements through self-regulation [Evans 1973].

From this discussion it ought to be clear to you Thrasymachus, that no theoretical position at this time has the right to make arrogant assertions about having all the answers. What is desperately needed is an integration of these various points of view so that they may be seen as a variety of ways of looking at the same process, without any point of view insisting on a claim to total or whole truth. This is supported by clinical evidence also, for as behavioral therapy techniques have been applied to a wider and wider spectrum of emotional disorders, the reported successes have fallen to the level of that of psychoanalytic psychotherapy. In fact, the behavioral therapists are guilty of the same error as the classical psychoanalysts at the beginning of their science; a tendency to explain everything and to promise more than they can deliver. As Marmor concludes, "The psychotherapeutic challenge of the future is to so improve our theoretical and diagnostic approaches in psychopathology as to be able to apply knowledgeably and flexibly to each patient the particular treatment technique and the particular kind of therapist that together most effectively achieve the desired therapeutic goal" [1971].

III

I am indebted to you Thrasymachus, I said, now that you have grown gentle towards me and have left off scolding. Nevertheless our discussion has not been entertaining, for we have not yet been able to arrive at any agreement on what should be a foundation for our psychological systems. The result of the whole discussion so far is that we know nothing at all of the subject.

With these words I thought that I had made an end of the discussion, but the end in truth only proved to be the beginning, for Glaucon was dissatisfied at Thrasymachus's retirement; he wanted to have the battle out.

You remember, he began, that in the *Republic* I argued that a man is just, not willingly or because he thinks that justice to him is any good individually, but of necessity, for whenever anyone thinks he can safely be unjust, there he is unjust. All men believe in their hearts that injustice is far more profitable to the individual than justice, and he who argues as I have been supposing will say that they are right. Thus justice is a mean or compromise between the best of all, which is to do injustice and not be punished, and the worst of all, which is to suffer injustice without the power of retaliation. Justice, being at a middle point between the two, is tolerated not as a good but as the lesser evil and honored by the reason of the inability of a man to do injustice without punishment. I am sure you can see the parallel to Freud's theory that all of us have instincts that press for discharge along the pleasure principle, but we come on the basis of the reality principle to make compromises. Perhaps Freud's approach to psychology then is still best of all.

As you know, Glaucon, my inclination is to agree with you, I replied, but we must be very aware that the foundations of psychodynamics are on a theoretical grounding every bit as vague and slippery as phenomenology. Some sort of epistemological foundation for psychodynamics can be developed from a combination of rationalism and empiricism; Freud felt he was a Kantian, and Rapaport has pursued that in later literature [see chapter 8]. My personal intuition is to follow Einstein on such concepts. According to Einstein, the nature of the external world is not immediately given in experience; what are given are data, the data of consciousness. This is exactly what Freud said in his final unfinished work, *An Outline of Psychoanalysis*. The only way to pass from the data of consciousness to knowledge of the external world is by way of *intellectual construction*. Brennan explains, "The most elementary concept of everyday experience is that of independently existing objects, such as the table in the room. The table, however, is not given to us as an independently existing object but rather as a complex of sensations to which we attribute the name and concept 'table.' In Einstein's words: 'In my opinion, it is of the greatest importance to be conscious of the fact that such a concept ("table"), like all other concepts, is of a speculative-constructive kind. Otherwise one cannot do justice to those concepts which in physics claim to describe reality, and one is in danger of being misled by the illusion that the "real" of our daily experience "exists really" and that certain concepts of physics are "mere ideas" separated from the real by an unbridgable gulf' " [1967].

Einstein maintains that although concepts such as that of independently existing physical objects are speculative-constructive they are not mere fancies. These concepts "stand in a relation of correspondence with our sensations," Einstein maintains. The correspondence or correlation between concepts and sensations becomes more and more indirect as science advances. Because the concepts of physics are highly abstract (just as the concepts of psychodynamics in psychiatry) and only indirectly correlated with ordinary experience, it does not follow that they are fictions. Thus scientific concepts are tied to experience in so far as they help us to establish correct and verifiable relations between the data of our experience. Einstein maintains a remarkably optimistic and realist position. He writes, "We believe in the possibility of a theory which is able to give a complete description of reality, the laws of which establish relations between the things themselves and not merely their probabilities" [Brennan 1967].

Worrying about the so-called scientific reality of psychodynamic constructs, maintained Glaucon, is what confuses and puts off many beginning students of psychological systems. Other systems have immediate emotional appeal. Basic psychodynamics on the other hand must be learned slowly and carefully and involves concepts such as "psychic energy" and "the repetition compulsion," which are difficult to grasp, often poorly phrased and explained, and lead the scientifically trained reader astray because he tries to characterize them in the language of the physical sciences and lacks the opportunity to fit these concepts into the personal clinical experience of therapeutic interaction. In addition, the pessimism and determinism of Freud's psychodynamics puts off many young students who, due to age or inclination, tend to be more optimistic and hopeful.

I was going to say something in answer to Glaucon, when Adeimantus, his brother, interposed and said, There is a way out of this dilemma.

What else is there? I answered.

The strongest point of all has not been even mentioned, he replied.

Well then, according to the proverb, Let brother help brother—if he fails in any part, you assist him; although I must confess that Glaucon has said quite enough to insure a lot of reflective thought.

Let me add something more, maintained Adeimantus. There is another side to Glaucon's argument. In the *Republic,* I pointed out that parents and tutors are always telling their sons and their wards that they are to be just. But why? Not for the sake of justice, but for the sake of character and reputation, in the hope of obtaining for him who is reputed just, some of those offices, marriages, and the like which Glaucon has enumerated among the advantages accruing to the unjust from the reputation of justice. My point was that men do not behave in certain ways of their own free will, but rather out of the early interpersonal relations that they experience and that ultimately causes their behavior. Our personality, our patterns of behavior are formed in the crucible of interpersonal interactions from birth. By observing these phenomena, we can avoid difficult issues involving combinations of rationalism and empiricism, which lie at the foundation of Freudian psychodynamics, since we can do away with "intra-psychic" postulates. In addition, we can bring psychotherapy back to the level of an observational science, for by participating and at the same time observing an interpersonal interaction, we can utilize the data so obtained for scientific investigation, experiment, and hypothesis formation. This gives us clear and observable data which may be seen by a group of observers and have a publicness that is necessary for any science to develop.

Thus, indeed, brother has helped brother, I agreed. Adeimantus seems to be attempting to retain the basic concepts of dynamic psychotherapy while replacing them with a language easier for the neophyte to understand because it is based on the data of interpersonal relations and avoids the postulations of intrapsychic phenomena. I hope Adeimantus can see however, that the philosophical foundations of this point of view are even more shaky.

Why, what do you mean? asked Glaucon and Adeimantus together.

For some reason Harry Stack Sullivan was always reluctant to admit his obvious debt to the philosophy of Dewey [see chapter 12]. I suspect this is because the philosophy of Dewey *is* rather shaky, and yet it is the only philosophy that can form an adequate foundation for the interpersonal theory of psychiatry. Dewey adopted the word "instrumentalism" as a label for the aspects of his own doctrine that are somewhat associated with pragmatism, but because of the misunderstandings and controversies around the word pragmatism he used a term of his own.

Adeimantus asked, What is the parallel between the philosophy of Dewey and interpersonal psychiatry?

Dewey's interpretation of experience forcefully rejects the notion that experience is sensation and that what we know are sense data. He has no patience with empiricists who tell us that when we look at a chair we really only experience a colored patch. A man experiences a chair, not when looking at it, but when he intends to sit down in it. Dewey explains, "Experience is what happens to us and what we do about it." He insists that the primary stress should be put on the *doing* rather than the *undergoing*. This is an exact parallel to Sullivan's point of view about human development and human interaction. Brennan explains, "Dewey sees man as an organism acting upon the being acted upon by the dual environment of Nature and society. . . . Man *acts* upon his environment, changing its character, and the environment, so modified, reacts upon him. Experience is the *product* of this interaction between the human organism and its natural and social environment. Experience is the outcome of transactions between man, Nature, and society" [1967]. This has proven to be a very weak explanation of knowledge—reducing all knowledge to problem solving, representing every worthwhile situation of human thought in terms of fixing an automobile engine.

I object, interposed Adeimantus. It is not to speculative knowledge that Dewey objects, but to knowledge that is *merely* speculative. Ideas, concepts, theories, and speculations are utterly necessary to productive knowledge. But unless they make some difference one way or another, they are just ideas and no more. Ideas which are not used as *instruments,* as operational plans to guide future action, are no better than day dreams.

This is still an unreasonable reductionism, I claimed, for you cannot get around the fact that observation and experiment and instruments and problem solving do not by themselves produce great scientific theories. These are the products of the creative, speculative, rational aspects of human thought stimulated by the problems and uncertainties of the world of sense. One does not know in advance where such theories, speculations, and ideas will lead, and often they are not generated for the purpose of problem solving at all, although they may be. In fact, sometimes a spectacular insight occurs to a person in which an idea generated for the purpose of solving one problem suddenly appears to explain another. Here is a fundamental disagreement. Dewey insists that knowledge does not spring up out of nothing. A problem, an obstacle, a sense of trouble and unease must exist to stimulate productive thought. We know from clinical experience that this sense of unease may have nothing to do, however, with unsolved practical problems but may be coming from internal conflicts and intra-psychic disturbances within. Conceptions, daydreams, and theories which arise as a result of intrapsychic phenomena may be found later in one context or another to have application to interpersonal problems or other problems of a practical nature, but it is unreasonable to argue backwards that *all* knowledge arises out of an effort to solve practical problems of living. It is sometimes said that the movement variously called pragmatism, instrumentalism, or radical empiricism is an expression of naive "Americanism."

I disagree, insisted Adeimantus. Certainly, although many leading pragmatists have been Americans, much more than local influence went into the development of pragmatism and Dewey's philosophy. Dewey insists that all knowledge is practical. He denied that intuition is knowledge. His definition of habit, for example, is typically Sullivanian: a habit is a "mechanism" for dealing with certain recurrent "classes of stimuli, standing predilections and aversions." A habit is a *function* between organism and environment by means of which life is furthered and maintained. He writes: "Very early in life sets of mind are formed without attentive thought, and these sets persist and control the mature mind. The child learns to avoid the shock of unpleasant disagreement, to find the easy way out, to appear to conform to customs which are wholly mysterious to him in order to get his own way—that is to display some natural impulse without exciting the unfavorable notice of those in authority. Adults distrust the intelligence which a child has while making upon him demands for a kind of conduct that requires a high order of intelligence, if it is to be intelligent at all. The inconsistency is reconciled by instilling in him "moral" habits, which have a maximum of emotional impressment and adamantine hold with a minimum of understanding. These habitudes . . . govern conscious later thought. They are usually deepest and most unget-at-able just where critical thought is most needed—in morals, religion, and politics. These 'infantilisms' account for the mass of irrationalities that prevail among men of otherwise rational tastes. . . . To list them would perhaps oust one from 'respectable' society" [Dewey 1922, pp. 98-99].

It is certainly true, I agreed, that Dewey emphasized men's fundamental urge to seek security. He insisted that the pursuit of security is the real problem, to which traditional philosophy provides only a pseudo-solution. Instead of looking for security in the control of the environment by scientific means, insists Dewey, traditional philosophers flee to a dream world of their own creation. Jones writes, "According to Dewey, philosophers of this type are unable to face up to the fact that security never is, and never can be, perfect—that even science never gives us *the* answers, and that life accordingly is a growing, living adventure. The traditional philosophers are simply men who are too weak to accept the world as it is, and their theories are nothing but a projection of their inner uneasiness, a flight from reality" [1969].

Exactly. exclaimed Adeimantus.

You would agree then Adeimantus, that Dewey and Nietzsche are greatly similar, for both philosophers insist—Dewey in a much more scholarly fashion—that the problems of life are the presence of change, decay, and death and that metaphysical thinking simply represents fictions to allay insecurity.

I agree, replied Adeimantus.

Would you agree Adeimantus, I asked, that according to Dewey the situation with respect to values is exactly the same as the situation with respect to physical objects?

.Yes, said Adeimantus.

In our perceptual fields are all sorts of perceptual experiences. Do we accept all of them at their face value?

We do not, said Adeimantus, for if we do so we are soon forced to become a bit more careful. However, we can make reasonable judgments. By intelligent action we can make the world better; we can change people's behavior by bringing their attention to their undesirable interpersonal interactions. Even though we can never be absolutely sure of what is good, nevertheless, knowledge that a particular experience is desirable will do. This knowledge is a reliable rule for guiding conduct, and that's all we need. Values are facts found in experience.

Here is where Dewey's own theory turns out to be untrue by its own criterion of truth, I said sadly. His theories are workable only on the assumption that fanaticism, neuroses, and the death wish are minority phenomena attributable only to a handful of the mentally ill. History shows that a more pessimistic estimate of human nature is correct. There is not really a consensus about what is good and how people ought to behave and wish to behave. Men are less socially conscious than they are selfish, aggressive, sadistic, and irrational, and far from being guided by a consideration of the consequences of their actions, they often deliberately choose to destroy themselves. Again we have a serious reductionism. Attributing all human behavior to the consequences of interpersonal interactions leaves many important aspects of human behavior poorly explained indeed. Only when we add to this the postulation of certain intrapsychic phenomena can we come out with a theory that fits a great deal more of the phenomena of human development and human behavior. Thus again Dewey's philosophical foundations are too narrow and too reductionistic.

I think I see what you mean, said Adeimantus, but it certainly goes against the Greek mind, for we Greeks always believed in the sovereignty of reason and the reasonableness of men—if they were not barbarians—who could be persuaded to take different positions in a decent conversational interaction. If you are right, then all men are barbarians.

What happened to the Greeks, I asked?

We committed suicide, he sadly admitted. In the Peloponnesian Wars we finally destroyed ourselves and our marvelous civilization. Even Thucydides in our own time recognized this.

It seems then my friends, that we are forced to remain with a theoretical structure that contains important intrapsychic postulates.

This is forced upon us not only by a consideration of the epistemological foundations of the great psychological systems but by the history of mankind itself, which again and again contradicts the hope that man is a rational malleable creature, and underscores his immense tendency towards irrationality, unbridled passion, aggression, and self destruction.

It is certainly true, added Glaucon, that the basic difference between your age and ours is the absence of hope in your time. In our Golden Age it seemed that man had reached the summit and would always stay there; in your dark age there seems to be no end to disappointment in humanity.

At the same time, insisted Polemarchus, the story is not over. Man is more than he appears to be, and he can never be completely explained by any deterministic or mechanical theory. The scientific explosion is still exploding. Who knows where it may lead?

Those are brave words in the dark, Polemarchus, I replied, but I have just come from the Piraeus; I did not find men like your father there, and I cannot conclude by consoling us with myths about the soul, as Socrates did in the *Republic*.

My friends looked sad and even Thrasymachus had lost his customary arrogance. I was about to try to say something to console them, when a loud high shriek jolted me. It was a boat whistle. I was back on the deck. The boat was moving over the water and my wife was standing over me laughing.

"What a troubled sleep you seemed to be having," she remarked. "Can't you even be contented when you sleep? Generations of men have come and gone and yet we go on and on begetting our children, loving them, caring for them, and nursing them. Men are constantly troubling their heads about what ought to be and about mysteries that they can never understand. Flies do not find their way out of fly-bottles; they just bang their heads against the glass. You seem tired. Come down to the cabin with me and take a nap. The pattern for what you are looking for on earth exists only in heaven."

Chapter 20

Ego-Feeling and
the Quest for Being

Teaching is even more difficult than learning. . . . Not because the teacher must have a larger store of information, and have it always ready. Teaching is more difficult than learning because what teaching calls for is this: to let learn. The real teacher, in fact, lets nothing else be learned than—learning. His conduct, therefore, often produces the impression that we properly learn nothing from him, if by "learning" we now suddenly understand merely the procurement of useful information. The teacher is ahead of his apprentices in this alone, that he has still far more to learn than they—he has to learn to let them learn. The teacher must be capable of being more teachable than the apprentices. The teacher is far less assured of his ground than those who learn are of theirs. If the relation between the teacher and the taught is genuine, therefore, there is never a place in it for the authority of the know-it-all or the authoritative sway of the official. It is still an exalted matter, then, to become a teacher—which is something else entirely than becoming a famous professor.

Heidegger, *What is Called Thinking?*

PATIENTS WHO LONG TO FEEL ALIVE

Nietzsche wrote, "A philosopher is a man who never ceases to experience, see, hear, suspect, hope, and dream extraordinary things.

. . . Philosophy is a voluntary living amid ice and mountain heights" (Heidegger 1961). In all the other chapters of this book we have reviewed relatively accepted and logical thinkers, who have in one way or another contributed great ideas to the practice of psychotherapy. In this final chapter, I am going to approach a philosopher who some have called an arrogant and spectacular failure but who has brought attention to an idea that will become increasingly important to the practice of intensive psychotherapy, especially with the borderline patient (see Chessick 1977).

I have been frequently confronted in my practice with a rather typical patient, as illustrated by the following two case vignettes. The first patient is a thirty-five-year-old woman who has reached a considerable degree of executive success in a well-known corporation. She is respected by those around her. Her efficiency and industry are often without equal, and she is responsible for the production of a number of items, with large sums of money hinging on her executive decisions. Yet she seeks therapy because, although she functions well, she has vague complaints of restlessness, dissatisfaction, and "of being alive but not alive." Her marriage has failed. Her husband has turned from her into some obscene perversion, taking her almost entirely by surprise. Her later relationships with men have consisted primarily of sexual promiscuity with an utter lack of any emotional relationship. Again and again, she has started out to form a relationship with this man or that man, and again and again it has deteriorated into merely promiscuous sexuality.

She writes in her diary: "It's no good, the walls are turning in, there is no one there. We all hang suspended over some kind of hell fire which no one remits and which finally becomes some sort of dull, thudding given, which has no meaning and from which there is no recourse. Please turn me around, please explain it. I can't function, I am not going to make it. Life is worthless, everything is lying around me, everything dying around me. I can't go on much longer. I need something I can't have. Please care, please don't go away, I will be all right. There is nowhere, nothing. I can't make it any way. Please, please help me. I am crying. I can't stand it, I don't know what to do. I don't want to turn on. I want out not in. I want to be with people, I don't want to be strung out where somebody can pinch and poke me and take away me from me. I'm afraid of tomorrow, I can't make it happen. I can only distract myself and that doesn't help any more."

After five turbulent years of psychotherapy, the patient begins to realize that her life has consisted essentially of *two phases* of existence, which alternate with each other. Either she cries herself into a state of exhaustion and then relatively enjoys the quiescent feeling, or she gets somebody to hold her, for which she trades sexual relations, and then experiences for a brief time the magical sensation that "everything will be all right." She remembers as a child being in bed with her sister and insists "I held on" by putting an arm around her sister in spite of her sister's repeated protests. Only while she was holding on could she go to sleep. There was nothing sexually arousing about this and no sexual play of any sort took place in this situation.

As it becomes clearer and clearer in the therapy that the patient seems to be compulsively reliving two phases of her destructive infancy, she has the intuitive idea of checking over her own medical records describing the period when she was an infant. In a true executive fashion, she tracks the matter down and discovers to her astonishment that she spent four months in the hospital as an infant suffering from severe eczema. During the months she was not in the hospital, there was very little holding, because allegedly the skin disease was rather repulsive to her rigid, obsessive mother, who was overwhelmed with problems of cleanliness. Being held became the occasional magical act, which suddenly introduced nirvana and serenity into an otherwise horrible abyss.

Let us turn to another case. A twenty-seven-year-old nun has spent the last six years in convent. She reports that she went about all her duties in exemplary fashion, gaining continual praise from her superiors. She was thought of as a pious, dedicated, hard working, reliable, and mature woman. She followed all the rules correctly. There was never any serious problem. At the same time, the patient felt continuously that she was dead. She went through the motions of living always with the strange almost indescribable feeling that she was not alive. This went on and on, and it seemed to the patient that it would always go on. She never consciously worried about it. She felt that somehow this was her perpetual fate, the background of her existence. One of her superiors began to seduce her. She was attractive and young and this superior, who had a history of some homosexual acting out in the past, began to encourage the patient to come in her room and to caress her. The patient refused to do any active caressing but did allow herself to be caressed, and a series of clandestine evening meetings began to take place in which the patient and superior would climb into bed, and the superior would hold the patient close and caress her breasts. The patient never allowed this to progress to anything further, in spite of the increased impassioned urging and pressures from the homosexual superior.

This stirred up a tremendous conflict in the patient, because she felt that what she was doing was really not in her best interest, although the superior kept describing this procedure as therapeutic for her and indeed, the patient noted with surprise and astonishment that while she was being caressed and held, the feeling of being dead would go away. Finally, the patient went to a higher superior and told the whole story. To her surprise, she was asked to leave the convent, and nothing was done about her seducer, who made large financial contributions to the order.

The sudden experience of being held and caressed caused an explosion inside the patient. She did not become psychotic, but she could no longer accept perpetually feeling dead. She began to realize there was something she was missing that she could have, and she began to strive for it. This was her chief reason for coming into therapy, namely "I feel dead all the time. I know I don't have to feel dead and I want to do something about it."

What were these women looking for? What was wrong? They were not overtly psychotic, they were not neurotic as far as the traditional diagnostic categories are concerned, yet they were severely disturbed individuals with deeply abnormal interpersonal relations. Their history also contained serious but transient psychosomatic disorders and various and other fleeting kinds of problems, which made it very easy to label them borderline patients though certainly *not* latent schizophrenics (Chessick 1974a, 1977).

Hollender et al (1969, 1970, 1970a) have written three papers on the need to be held in women. He reports that for a few women in his series, the need or wish to be held is so compelling that it resembles an addiction. Body contact commonly provides feelings of being loved, protected, and comforted. But it is not at all really clear what being held does for these patients or what is really wrong. In repeated cases such patients have begged me even to simply hold their hand because they insisted that *without the tactile stimulation they just do not feel alive*. It is *not* a sexual desire, and it does *not* seem to be directly related primarily to infantile wishes for tactile pleasure, although this is certainly a component. There seems to be an additional component, in which some sort of profound sensation of deadness can only be neutralized by the physical touching presence of another human being, and not by anything else including talk, psychotherapy, or interpretations of any kind. No other substitute will do, including drugs and sexual orgies. It is actually *destructive,* however, for the therapist to provide such tactile stimulation (Chessick 1974a, 1976), under any guise whatsoever (Langs 1974).

After a few cases of this sort, both male and female I inquired more carefully into my patient's habits regarding tactile contact and found to my surprise that a number of patients with predominantly existential complaints, such as difficulty in finding meaning to life, vague restlessness and discontent, or a sense of boredom and nausea, also often displayed in one way or another an extraordinary need to be held or for tactile contact even with a transitional object (see Winnicott 1958)—a need which could not be substituted for by anything else. Only after reading Martin Heidegger did certain aspects of metaphysics and psychoanalytic psychology begin to fall into place to provide what I consider to be another great idea in psychotherapy.

I will have to begin with a description of the philosophy of Martin Heidegger. Heidegger believed that only Greek and German were suitable languages of philosophizing. Any translation loses a certain coloration of what he is trying to say, since he is almost obsessively word conscious. His concepts are often poetical and rarely logical. His lines must be studied and repeated again and again and again; I have often found it helpful to read him out loud.

MARTIN HEIDEGGER

Of all the thinkers reviewed in this book, Heidegger has the least stature as a human being, and it is difficult to keep irritation with him personally from obscuring the fact that he is a genius who has had a truly original thought and has exerted a profound impact on current continental European philosophy.

Born in 1889 in Bayden, Heidegger became *Privatdozent* at the University of Freiburg in 1915, professor at Marburg in 1923, and professor at Freiburg in 1928. As a student at Freiburg, he was trained in the phenomenological method of Edmund Husserl. Though he later renounced Husserl because he was Jewish, his most significnant work *Being and Time* was dedicated to him. In 1933, Heidegger became the first National Socialist rector of the University of Freiburg and in a public lecture "Role of the University in the New Reich" celebrated the advent of a new and glorious Germany: "The highly touted 'academic freedom' is being banished from the German university; being merely negative, this freedom was spurious. It meant indifference, arbitrariness of goal and inclinations, actions with restraint" (Schmitt 1969). He eagerly adopted the slogans of the Third Reich and willingly began and ended all his lectures, as was the rule, with "Heil Hitler."

In 1935, he resigned this post not out of moral indignation with the horrors perpetrated by the Nazis but out of disagreement with their obviously foolish and superficial philosophy. Ten years after this, following Germany's surrender in the Second World War, Heidegger was dismissed from his chair of philosophy because of alleged Nazi sympathies. He thereupon retired to a life of seclusion near Freiburg.

There he lived, until his death in 1976, reading over and over again the work of the overtly schizophrenic German poet, Hölderlin. This closeness to Holderlin is no accident but an essential key to understanding Heidegger's philosophy. Brock writes: "For Hölderlin came from the same physical region, he faced the same spiritual problems, and he experienced more lucidly and bitterly the ultimate meaning of nothingness than any other person who could give expression to it in song. . . . On both occasions when I met Professor Heidegger, . . . I had to drive for an hour to the small town of Todtnau in the Black Forest Mountains, then to climb still further until the road became a patch and all human habitation scattered and invisible. There on top of a mountain, with the valley deep down below, with nothing but space and wilderness all around, in that small skiing hut, I spoke to the philosopher. He had not been to Freiburg for six months when I saw him for the second time. His living conditions were primitive; his books were few, and his only relationship to the world was a stack of writing paper. His whole life revolved within those white sheets and it seemed to me that he wanted nothing else but to be left in peace to cover those white sheets with his writing" (1968, pp. ix-xx).

There is no doubt that even in his latest writing Heidegger considered the Germans a superior race to the "barbarians"—Americans and Russians—whom he envisions as dangerous pincers possessed by "the same dreary technological frenzy, the same unrestricted organization of the average man," putting pressure on the German nation and endangering it. He considered the Germans "the most metaphysical of nations" and as having the historic mission to lead Europe to the unfolding of new spiritual energies arising from the German intellectual and geographical situation in the center of Europe.

Heidegger must also be accused of professional dishonesty. Numerous studies have demonstrated that his translations of Greek are incorrect—not only inaccurate and downright wrong for someone who should know better but clearly twisted for his own purposes. His readings of other philosophers, such as Plato and Kant, are clearly misreadings and at some points obvious fabrications in which the philosopher is deliberately misinterpreted to fit Heidegger's purpose.

Heidegger has emphatically denied that he was ever an existentialist, and I think in all fairness this is true. He has spent his life in the quest for Being, and his study of human being has been only in the service of this quest. At this point, it is necessary to make clear that the quest for Being is not merely a metaphysical abstraction but is a concept pertinent to psychotherapy today. Heidegger has had the primary responsibility for bringing it to our attention once again in our time.

It was fortunate for Heidegger that in his first major work *Being and Time* (1962a), which first appeared in 1927, he studied human being *(Dasein)* for the purpose of elucidating the concept of Being. It is this study of human being which has had the most influence on other philosophers and laid part of the groundwork for current existentialist philosophy. However, Heidegger insists again and again that the concentration of later philosophers on human being misses the point of what he is seeking, and this is why he refuses to be labelled an existentialist (see Heidegger 1962b).

BEING AND TIME

Being and Time is a work of true philosophical power if one is willing to forgive Heidegger's many faults. It contains incisive but rather rhetorical and devastating insights into the ultimate loneliness of individual existence. The philosophical formulation of the place of death in life is one of Heidegger's greatest concepts. He becomes the first philosopher since Plato to put death into the center of his philosophical thought.

It is written in a contorted and arbitrary style, hopelessly untranslatable into English. Experts in German and Greek have found it wholly unsatisfactory. Grene writes: "Yet for all its verbosity and arrogance, there is in it a direct driving compression: its words, though many, are less than the passion behind it" (1957). In Heidegger's later work he attempts to approach the problem of Being more directly, and when he does so the contents and the concepts become more poetic, more mystical, and more empty.

In order to approach the question What is meant by Being? Heidegger proposes to study first, using Husserl's phenomenological method, the kind of Being that belongs to persons. The Being that belongs to persons Heidegger labeled *Dasein,* which literally means being-there. The fundamental ontological characteristics of human being *(Dasein)* are existentiality, facticity, and forfeiture. The evidence for this, using the phenomenological method, is given as "simple awareness of something present at hand in its sheer presence at hand," which Heidegger claims was also the method of Parmenides (see chapter 1). Furthermore, ontology, or the study of Being, requires this phenomenological method and is impossible by the use of any other method. The meaning of Being must be "wrested" from the objects of phenomenology. Heidegger argues that the quest for Being can never end, and as if to prove this, his plans for a study of the question of Being called for both a third division to Part I and a Part II of *Being and Time* which have never appeared. Similarly, the famous ending to his book *An Introduction to Metaphysics* emphasizes, "To know how to question means to know how to wait, even a whole lifetime" (1961).

Returning to the being of man *(Dasein),* the concept of facticity represents the idea that human being is always being among others in the sense that it is being always already in a world, a world into which, beyond its willing, it has been cast *(Geworfen).* Thus the destiny of *Dasein* is bound up with the being of others and *Dasein* is always one being among others.

Existentiality implies that human being is always reaching out beyond itself. Its very being consists in aiming at what is not yet. In its very giveness there is the striving towards its own possibility of achievement, in its necessity, freedom.

Forefeiture involves the constant falling away from Being that Heidegger variously and effectively describes as distancing, averaging, leveling down, or publicness—ways of covering up our authentic being-in-the-world. There is a tendency to engage in idle talk, curiosity, and ambiguity, falling away into the world of others, or the "they." This forfeiture is tranquilizing, but the tempting tranquilizing aggrevates the falling and leads to a life of "hustle," alienation, and self-entanglement. It is a downward plunge toward "entities" within the world and away from Being. It is the self in flight from itself which is the starting point and principle theme of the "preparatory analysis," that constitutes the first division of *Being and Time*.

This division also contains the famous passages often quoted by existentialist therapists on Heidegger's concepts of care and solicitude. This discussion begins with Heidegger's insistence that in *Dasein* there lies an essential tendency toward closeness and reaches its rhetorical peak in the fourth chapter in a discussion of the two extremes of positive solicitude "that which leaps in and dominates, and that which leaps forth and liberates." It also contains Heidegger's interesting notion of empathy as a *secondary* phenomenon based primarily on the fact that *Dasein* is being-in-the-world. This is very close to Sullivan's description of empathic linkage (chapter 12).

In the second division of *Being and Time,* Heidegger emphasizes that the being of *Dasein* is being-towards-death. Thus falling (fleeing) is a constant fleeing in the face of death. Without going into many details we can briefly state that Heidegger conceives of *Dasein* as lost in the "they," potentially able to find itself by the presence of the voice of conscience "which speaks when one keeps silent." This voice of conscience is only in *Dasein's* kind of being. In response to this voice we can make an existential choice. We can choose a being-one's-self that Heidegger labels "resoluteness" or we can remain "lost in idle talk." *Dasein* can fail to hear its own self in listening to the they-self. So conscience summons *Dasein's* self from its lostness in the "they."

Kierkegaard's concept of dread reappears in the context of Heidegger's description of life facing death. Authentic *Dasein* is care, based on being-towards-death, and the reader interested in these notions should especially see page 237 of *Being and Time* (1962a). Finally, the book deals with the historicity of *Dasein*. Human being is found to be primarily historical: to possess a destiny. Great emphasis is placed on the concept of time—primary, personal existential time.

Time is the ontological ground of human being: this is what human being most truly and deeply is. Destiny is created by the individual. Conscience calls the self to be resolved among itself, to "pull itself together" in the face of being-towards-death. This is the individual with "anticipatory resoluteness" shaping his life in the face of being-towards-death, facing and creating his destiny, coming face-to-face with it in dread and silence.

Destiny is a mode of authentic, not forfeited existence. Grene writes, "It is not the portion meted out to each of us by the Fates who spin and measure and cut for all alike. It is a pattern achieved only by the rare individual who in dread and silence has come face to face with its own nothingness and has shaped his life in the light, or the darkness, of that encounter" (1957).

Innumerable criticisms can be leveled at *Being and Time*. The most obvious is that the authentic individual knows no friend or fellow, is alone for the sake of his own integrity, and faces his own death alone. Heidegger's resolute man is cut off not only from men, but from beasts—from the whole of living nature. "The personality of animals, the togetherness of men and animals, in work or play, enter nowhere for a moment in Heidegger's account of human being" (Grene 1957) (see Chessick 1971a).

Schmitt essentially agrees with Grene, "It is extremely doubtful therefore that *Being and Time* makes any contribution to reawakening our understanding of the question of what Being means. . . . The source of this failure does not lie in the particular concept recommended, but in the fact that concepts are recommended at all" (1969). The criticism and arguments leveled against his work seem to have been effective, because although *Being and Time* achieved fame in its rhetorical exposition of the being of man, as an elucidation of Being it failed miserably. Heidegger attempts unsuccessfully in all his later work to go beyond the being of man in order to somehow characterize the nature of Being itself.

HEIDEGGER ON KANT

Grene explains that the Kant-book (as *Kant and the Problem of Metaphysics* (1962) is usually called) is a transitional work, to a new—and for psychotherapists less interesting—phase in Heidegger's thought. Brock (1968) and other authors insist there has been *no* transition and that Heidegger is consistent from beginning to end. I leave this argument to the experts. At any rate, the Kant-book poses three theses about the work of Kant, especially the *Critique of Pure Reason* (see chapter 8). These are (1) that its central theme is the finitude of man; (2) that this theme is grounded in Kant's conception of the nature of our minds as (a) essentially temporal and (b) essentially active or creative; and (3) that in preparing the second edition of the *Critique of Pure Reason,* Kant turned back from his deepest insight to rely more heavily on the stable but deadening framework of logic.

Unquestionably, as Grene writes, "there is something right yet something wrong and twisted" about each of Heidegger's theses (1957). I think his characterization of Kant's concepts of intuition and creative imagination are *deliberately* dishonest and distorted for Heidegger's own purposes.

On the other hand there is a legitimate contribution to the study of Kant's *Critique of Pure Reason* in Heidegger's emphasis—the great importance of our subjective awareness of self in time as a basic premise that underlies Kant's entire depiction of human mental functioning. Heidegger tries to make this a major justification for his preoccupation with time and historicity in *Being and Time.* Gelvin (in a book that has been severely criticized by some experts) makes this contribution more understandable: "Heidegger is arguing that the meaning of human existence is based upon the temporality of man. The amazing thing about Heidegger's claim is that he does not leave the insight to a kind of intuition or mystical grasp. He painstakingly ferrets a temporal basis out of every single way in which man reflects upon himself or functions within the world. . . . He has accomplished a truly remarkable phenomenological account of how time is significant to man as an existing being. His accounts of the future as expectation or anticipation, the present as making—present by actions and situations—and the past as remembering and forgetting, are examples of interpretive philosophy at its best" (1970).

The remainder of Heidegger's work, which often consists of lectures given in the 1930's but published in the late 1950's and 1960's, attempts to answer the question How does it stand with Being? This is approached in two ways: (1) through metaphysical essays such as *An Introduction to Metaphysics, What is Philosophy?,* or *What is*

Metaphysics? (see Brock 1968) and (2) through an analysis of the poetry of Hölderlin.

THE CRUCIAL PROBLEM OF OUR ERA

The opening to *An Introduction to Metaphysics* is one of the most eloquent passages in all philosophical writing. Heidegger asks, "Why are there essents (things that are) rather than nothing? . . . Many men never encounter this question, if by encounter we mean not merely to hear and read about it as an interrogative formulation, but to ask the question, that is, to bring it about, to raise it, to feel its inevitability." It is much to Heidegger's credit that he insists that "each of us is grazed at least once, perhaps more than once, by the hidden power of this question, even if he is not aware of what's happening to him. The question looms in moments of great despair, when things tend to lose all their weight and all meaning becomes obscure. Perhaps it will strike but once like a muffled bell that rings into our life and gradually dies away. . . . The question is upon us in boredom, when we are equally removed from despair and joy and everything about us seems so hopelessly commonplace that we no longer care whether any thing is or is not" (1961).

Heidegger insists that the problem of our age is our falling away from Being and dogmatically asserts that this is a mistake that began in Greek philosophy after the pre-Socratic philosophers, who attempted to find universal principles to explain the whole of nature, from the origins and ultimate constituents of the universe to the place of man within it.

Heidegger argues that the pre-Socratic philosophers did *not* make a separation between truth and Being, but that all Western philosophy and science since that time has made such a separation, and this has led inevitably to materialism and the darkening of our world. His writing is very eloquent, but there is not much in the way of philosophical or psychological argument either for or against his contentions. Most of this material is presented as simple proclamation. It is apparently the German nation's role to bring Western civilization back to Being and to remove what Heidegger says is a dichotomy between Being and thought that is not present in the pre-Socratic philosophers.

In a later work on *What Is Called Thinking?*, Heidegger makes more of a personal exhortation to the individual to participate in thinking. He argues that thinking is a response to a call from Being and that "thinking is thinking only when it *recalls* in thought the *eon* ["the presence of that which is present"]. Furthermore, "What is most thought-provoking in our thought-provoking time is that we are still not thinking." This is a dark, threatening, and injurious situation, and he asserts it began with the philosophy of Plato (1968).

For the pre-Socratic philosophers, Heidegger claims, truth represented the unforgetfulness or the unhiddenness of Being. In Plato and Aristotle this concept was destroyed, ending with the view crystallized by Aristotle (see chapter 2) that truth is correctness, truth belongs now not to Being but to propositions and consists in correspondence with facts. This loosening of truth from Being, according to Heidegger, leads to the current concept that Being is meaningless.

CURE THROUGH POETRY

In order to get back to Being, argues Heidegger, only poetry can stand in the same order as philosophy. No one besides the poet cares so seriously and intently for using the right word as does the philosopher. He seeks to find the word out of which the truth of Being may be heard. Brock writes: "Only if he zealously guards his words, dwelling for a long time in the meditation of matters that command silence and cannot be worded until their realm becomes lucid, will he be able to speak in an authentic way and communicate what he has to say in terms that remain memorable. 'Dread' in the sense of horror and awe, opening up for man the abyss of 'nothingness,' is one of those great instances of speechless silence" (1968). The great magical faith that Heidegger puts on words and language is obvious. We should keep in mind Heidegger's insistence that language is one of the cardinal aspects of the being of man and note how close this is to Chomsky's concept of a language faculty as being unique for man.

Interestingly, Heidegger confines his discussion of poetry to "Hölderlin . . . and he alone." He insists on trying to find a universal essence of poetry in the work of one single poet and argues that "we take 'essence of poetry' to mean what is gathered together into a universal concept, which is then valid in the same way for every poem. . . . For us Hölderlin is in a pre-eminent sense *the poet of the poet"*(Brock 1968).

It is extremely interesting that he has chosen Holderlin, one of the greatest German lyric poets (1770-1843). Hölderlin spent a substantial portion of his life afflicted with chronic schizophrenia which gravely interfered with his work during acute flareups. By the age of thirty-six he was almost entirely incapacitated by schizophrenia. At first in his more lucid intervals he continued to write magnificent poetry, most of which was published by friends after he was hopelessly ill.

Hölderlin's work is characterized by an ardent love of ancient Greece and Greek dieties, fused by the poet with a pantheistic conception of nature into a prophetic and visionary whole. There are also some outstanding verse translations by Hölderlin of Sophocles' *Antigone* and *Oedipus Tyrannus,* published in 1804. He was preoccupied throughout with the "mystery of reality" (Salzberger 1952).

CRITICISM

How easy it is to criticize all this. An excellent summary of such criticism can be found in Kaufmann (1960). For example, he attacks Heidegger's authoritarianism as manifest in insisting that Hölderlin, or the pre-Socratics such as Heraclitus or Parmenides might never be mistaken. Any criticism of the pre-Socratic philosophers is out of the question. Heidegger does not display a truly philosophical critical spirit or carefulness or the virtues of the intellectual conscience. When in the end we ask what he really said, we come up either with nothing or with trivialities. At the same time Kaufmann admits the puzzling fact that students of Heidegger have often remained passionate devotees of philosophy. He does not destroy an initial interest; he increases it, "more precisely, he awakens and maintains it." He points out that anyone who reads *An Introduction to Metaphysics* will understand why so many men who have studied with him have kept for life a passion for philosophy and agree they never had a more fascinating teacher.

Heidegger recaptures the excitement of the first stages of Western philosophy. The problem is that he stirs up the reader to the pitch of feeling on the edge of a great discovery, but then suddenly we are let down with the uneasy feeling that we don't know much more about the subject when we finish than we knew when we began. Yet is is impossible to avoid the conviction that Heidegger is aiming at something here which has a validity on some level.

METAPSYCHOLOGY OF THE QUEST
FOR BEING AND FEELING ALIVE

It should be clear from the previous exposition that there is a parallel between the strivings and yearnings of the patients quoted at the beginning of this chapter and Heidegger's exciting and stimulating quest for Being. Can this now be put into psychodynamic terminology? I think it can, and we have various clues in this direction coming from Searles and the psychodynamic formulations of Weiss and Federn, which have fallen into general neglect in our modern day.

Let me begin with a crucial question from Winnicott. In his discussion of good-enough holding, he writes that good-enough holding "facilitates the formation of a psychosomatic partnership in the infant. This contributes to the sense of 'real' as opposed to 'unreal.' Faulty handling militates against the development of muscle tone, and that which is called 'coordination,' and against the capacity of the infant to enjoy the experience of body functioning, and of Being. . . . If the environment behaves well, the infant has a chance to maintain a sense of *continuity of being;* perhaps this may go right back to the first stirrings in the womb. When this exists the individual has a stability that can be gained in no other way" (1968). Now what, in psychodynamic terms is this sense of Being and the continuity of Being, which is clearly a function of good-enough holding in infants?

FEDERN'S CONCEPT OF EGO-FEELING

I am going to refer to the Federn-Weiss theory because it is not entirely clear what Federn (1952) is always talking about and the editing, introduction and expansion by Weiss (1960) may or may not present a clear picture of what Federn really meant. Federn became a member of Freud's circle in 1903. He left Vienna in 1938 and worked as a practicing psychoanalyst in New York. He is described by Weiss as "my first teacher in psychoanalysis," and his major field of interest already in the 1920s was in schizophrenia.

These authors present the concept of the ego as an *Erlebnis,* that is, a subjective experience. Weiss claims that Federn "equates" the ego with "the actual sensation of one's ego, which he calls ego feeling." However, this appears to me to be carrying Federn's concepts to an extreme.

At least part of the time Federn points out that the ego is "more inclusive" than the sum total of the usual ego functions that psychoanalysts talk about. He writes, "The ego, however, is more inclusive; more especially, it includes the subjective psychic experience of these functions with a characteristic sensation" (1952). For the purposes of our discussion let us label this subjective experience the ego-experience *(Icherlebnis).*

This phenomenon of the ego's experience of itself cannot be clearly explained. As long as the ego functions normally, one may ignore or be unaware of its functioning. So Federn says, normally there is no more awareness of the ego than the air one breathes; only when respiration becomes burdensome is the lack of air recognized. The subjective ego experience includes the feeling of unity in continuity, contiguity, and causality in the experiences of the individual. In waking life, the sensation of one's own ego is omnipresent, but it undergoes continuous changes in quality and intensity.

Federn sometimes distinguishes very clearly and carefully between ego-consciousness *(Ichbewusstsein)* and ego-feeling *(Ichgefühl).* This crucial neglected distinction is the key to a psychodynamic understanding of Heidegger's quest. Federn writes: "Ego feeling is the sensation, constantly present, of one's own person—the ego's own perception of itself. . . . We can distinguish, often accurately, between ego *feeling* and ego *conciousness.* Ego consciousness, in the pure state, remains only when there is a deficiency in ego feeling. And the mere empty knowledge of one's self is already a pathological state, known as estrangement or depersonalization" (1952).

Ego-consciousness represents an enduring feeling and knowledge that our ego is continuous and persistent, despite interruptions by sleep or unconsciousness, because we feel that processes within us, even though they may be interrupted by forgetting or unconsciousness, have a persistent origin within us, and that our body and psyche belong permanently to our ego. It is an entity involving the continuity of a person in respect to time, space, and causality. Our sense of ego consciousness plays a central role in the argument of Kant's *Critique of Pure Reason* (see chapter 8).

Ego feeling however, is the "totality of feeling which one has of one's own living person. It is the residual experience which persists after the subtraction of all ideational contents—a state which, in practice, occurs only for a very brief time. . . . Ego feeling, therefore, is the simplest and yet the most comprehensive psychic state which is produced in the personality by the fact of its own existence, even in the absence of external or internal stimuli" (1952).

To say the least, this is an extremely important and neglected concept for both philosophers and psychotherapists. Federn explains that ego-feeling is quite different from mere knowledge of one's self or of consciousness of the ego at work; it is primarily a *feeling* or *sensation,* normally taken for granted. This is exactly parallel to Heidegger's explanation that "the being of beings is the most apparent; and yet, we normally do not see it—and if we do, only with difficulty." Furthermore, both Heidegger and Federn would agree that "even the clearest *knowledge* of one's ego is experienced as something insufficient, uncomfortable, incomplete, and unsatisfying, even akin to fear" (1962a). Clearly we have returned to the starting point of this chapter, describing the complaint of our borderline patients.

Borrowing from Federn's not very well defined concept, the various pieces to the puzzle posed by these patients begin to fall into place. The relationship to Heidegger is now obvious. As a matter of fact, Federn pointed out—and I doubt if he read Heidegger—that the classical Greek language, in contrast for example to English, is necessary to get an intuitive verbal concept of ego feeling. This is because in the classical Greek language there is a middle voice, a neutral objectless form. In English grammar the middle voice is expressed by certain intransitive phrases such as I grow, I drive, I live, I prosper, I develop, I perish, I age, I die. The middle voice implies action involving one's self and not passing over to other objects.

Freud (1917) used the same term ego-feeling *(Ichgefühl)* for example in *Mourning and Melancholia,* but he used it to mean something akin to self-esteem, which is of course quite different. The careful reader will note that I am not discussing or advocating Federn's theory of schizophrenia as representing a deficiency of ego-libido here at all, nor am I developing Federn's metapsychological explanation of ego-feeling. This is a different discussion and rests on some different and highly controversial concepts. In my opinion Federn and Weiss left these concepts unnecessarily vague and at the same time pushed them too far in trying to explain the varied phenomena of schizophrenia; their theoretical conceptions have fallen into neglect as a result. Bellak (1958) describes Federn's thinking as "ingenious and original" but "semantically confused," and I agree.

The notion of ego-feeling however, is something extremely important to our modern work with borderline patients, *especially* when it is carefully differentiated from ego-consciousness as above. First, our intuitive conviction or grasp of the being of man, Heidegger's *Dasein,* comes from our inner ego-feeling. Second, our inner sense of existence, of being alive, our capacity to develop a sense of relatedness and of life having some sense of meaningfulness, requires a healthy development of ego-feeling.

APPLICATION TO SCHIZOPHRENIA: SEARLES

The final contribution comes from Searles in his book on *The Nonhuman Environment in Normal Development and Schizophrenia:* "It is my conviction that there is within the human individual a *sense,* [my italics] whether at a conscious or unconscious level, of *relatedness to his nonhuman environment,* that this relatedness is one of the transcendentally important facts of human living, that—as with other very important circumstances in human existence—it is a source of ambivalent feelings to him, and that, finally, if he tries to ignore its importance to himself, he does so at peril to his psychological well-being" (1960). This "sense of relatedness" is the psychodynamic equivalent of Heidegger's concept of the being of man. However the two authors are diametrically opposed in their view of the consequences of not falling away from Being. The careful reader will remember the major criticism of Heidegger's solution: Heidegger's authentic life cuts man off from animals and the nonhuman environment.

Searles writes in almost identical terms as Heidegger, although I doubt very much if he is a student of Heidegger. For example, he points out how the processes and products of technology tend to cause the individual to lose sight of the basic kinship between human and nonhuman, referring to this as "divorcement," which he contrasts to the pantheistic paganism of ancient Greece that preached how the revered dieties themselves often took the forms of various members of the animal kingdom or even the vegetable kingdom.

Searles argues that a chronic inability during infancy and early childhood to relate oneself to a relatively stable, relatively realistically perceived, relatively simple rather than overwhelmingly complex, world of inanimate objects may have much to do with one's inability in adult life to find fundamental, graspable realities and a tangible meaning in life. Conversely a mature relatedness with the nonhuman environment is very fruitful in the assuagement of anxiety, the fostering of self-realization, the deepening of feeling of one's reality, and the fostering of one's appreciation and acceptance of one's fellow men. There is again an extremely important parallel with Heidegger's conception of *Dasein* as being-in-the-world and his understanding of authentic and inauthentic existence, solicitude, and care.

Searles quotes Fromm and Tillich in describing the repercussions in various areas of human living which result from disjointedness in the individual's relationship with his nonhuman environment. In Heidegger-like terminology he describes the most important result of this disjointedness as causing the person to deal with his fellow men in a *noncherishing manner*. Human relations and material possessions are experienced in ways which are similarly impoverished of a sense of meaningfulness.

Again the parallel to Heidegger is obvious, as is the opposition present in Searles' conclusion about authentic life, which he borrows manifestly from Buber. Searles contends that a meaningful sense of personal relatedness with outer reality enables the individual to develop the highest order of human existence, the most mature orientation, which Buber calls the I-Thou relatedness. Buber's (1958) well-known concept of I-Thou relatedness is the diametric opposite of Heidegger's isolated authentic man.

SUMMARY

The capacity to develop a secure relationship to the nonhuman environment as well as an I-Thou relatedness is grounded in a healthy ego-feeling. The ego defect so frequently talked about in vague terms in describing the borderline patient to a great extent is a defect in ego-feeling or a severe falling away from Being as Heidegger describes it on a literary level. The cause of defect in ego-feeling or disturbance in the sense of Being can be traced clinically in the borderline patient to a lack of good enough holding in infancy. The result of such a falling away is that relationships become noncherishing and of the type that Buber calls I-It, and the individual often becomes immersed in an obsessive search for something he intuitively knows is missing but often cannot clearly describe in words.

For example, Heidegger spent his life in an obsessive intellectual search for Being which he projects as something at least in part outside himself that he can never find. The patient who is able to function well in business and mundane matters finds herself obsessed with the need for holding and a search for the magical sensation this produces. I submit that somehow this holding, at an extremely primitive level, offers a temporary sense of relatedness and ego feeling that is basically missing in the patient and cannot be replaced with any kind of intellectual or verbal exchange. One patient told me, "I have to at least touch you or hold your hand once in a while to really be sure I am alive and you are really here with me."

Those who have not experienced such problems have an extremely hard time understanding this set of concepts. The patients have to teach us. As Heidegger put it, "An age which regards as real only what goes fast and can be clutched with both hands looks on questioning as "remote from reality" and as something that does not pay, whose benefits cannot be numbered. But the essential is not number; the essential is the right time, i.e. the right moment, and the right perseverance" (1961).

This chapter also provides the psychodynamic answer to the important philosophical question posed by Wychogrod: "If Heidegger's concept of Being is now taken as the source of his non-existential—in the pathetic sense—approach to his enterprise, the question as to why it is the problem of Being that occupies his central interest is still not answered" (1969). Careful investigation of various aspects of the borderline patient's ego-feeling, as illustrated by clinically reported preoccupations such as those discussed, certain religious compulsions, and the obsessive philosophical quest for pure Being will reveal them to be based on the serious ego defect in many borderline patients—patients who enigmatically appear superficially so intact and yet suffer so intensely underneath.

FEDERN - WEISS	KANT	HEIDEGGER	CLINICAL SYMPTOMS OF DEFECT
Ego-consciousness (*Ichbewusstsein*)	Basis of the Transcendental Deduction of categories	Starting point of science and "darkening of the world"	Organic delirium states Dream-like states Feelings of unreality
Ego-feeling (*Ichgefühl*)	Retreated from in second edition of *Critique of Pure Reason*	Starting point of empathy and the quest for Being. pre-Socratic "thinking"	Vague borderline complaints Meaninglessness to life Inner deadness Quest for holding Noncherishing relationships to human and nonhuman environment
Ego mechanisms	Categories of the Understanding	Forfeiture and falling away from authentic self and the being-of-man (*Dasein*)	Ordinary psychopathology

In this contention I therefore disagree with the brief comments of Scharfstein and Ostow (Hanly and Lazerowitz 1970) who attempt to attribute Heidegger's search for Being to an unconscious oedipal sexual striving for his mother. The philosopher, according to these authors, is the "fearful lover of his mother." In my judgment, a careful reading of Heraclitus, Parmenides, and Heidegger yields much more the kind of "cosmic feeling" problems characteristic of borderline patients and some schizophrenic states, described psychodynamically by Federn and by Searles. For clarity, I have summarized the discussion of this chapter in figure 1.

The therapy of a defective sense of ego-feeling is an enormous challenge to all the personality resources of the psychotherapist. The best information so far indicates that it is the experience of the therapist's personality and the encounter with the therapist's *Dasein* or human being rather than any interpretations or other verbal exchange that makes the fundamental difference in the therapy of such patients. Nacht described this most accurately as the effect of the deep inner attitude of the therapist in such cases: "It seems to me that what is most important to obtain such a result is not so much what the analyst says as *what he is*. It is precisely what he is in the depths of himself—his real availability, his receptivity and his authentic acceptance of what the other is—which gives value, pungency and effectiveness to what he says" (1969, see also 1962).

The Challenge
from the Soviet Union

In the minds of millions, in the capitalist world, there is growing a new criterion by which to measure and compare the two world systems.

The comparisons are not now limited to industrial charts or prices of goods.

What is placed on the scales is the overall quality of life. Standards of physical comforts remain very important in determining the quality of life, but the yardstick is much broader now. It includes the total spectrum of human values, the order of priorities, dictated by the inherent laws of each system. It includes the moral, cultural and philosophical concepts nurtured by each system. Many of the new components that add up to a quality of life cannot be measured by charts.

G. Hall, *Our Friends Speak*

There is another possibly great idea which remains to be tested. Although it is usually presented as a matter of politics and the social sciences, in a very fundamental way the basic idea of Marxist-Leninist theory is potentially a psychological great idea. It is being implemented in several countries today, but with the most notable success in the Soviet Union. The courage, determination, and effort of the Russian people (see Salisbury 1974) deserves great admiration and the issue of whether the political system under which they live is or is not best suited for them is open to debate, but this is a matter for sociology and politics and not for psychology.

It is against the historical background of the utter devastation of Russia in World War II that one can much better understand statements by such writers as Sholokhov: "Humanism, love of man, of mankind. . . . How differently different people tend to interpret this concept depending on what forces of human society they represent: The artist's eternal theme is the struggle between good and evil, light and darkness. In our times this struggle has a distinct class meaning" (1973).

This is taken from a letter entitled, "A Humanist is the Man Who Fights." Humanism in his view is the willingness to fight, to be on guard, and to serve the State, and from these points of view the American concept of freedom is nonsense. For example as Sholokhov explains "Every Marxist and every worker who ponders over the forty years' experience of our revolution will say: "Let's look into this—*what sort* of freedom of the press? What *for?* For *which class?*'. . . The world is gripped by anxiety and alarm. And here someone wants freedom of the press for all—from monarchists to anarchists. What is this—pure naivete or cool brazenness? . . . The 'freedom mongers' are trying to corrupt our youth" (1973).

Only in Leningrad could I find anybody to admit that some of the things Lenin said might be wrong. The presence of Lenin is everywhere in the Soviet Union. What is important for psychotherapists in his teachings is his exhortation to a *radical change* in the psychology of man. "It was the declared aim of the old type of school,' writes Lenin, "to produce men with an all-round education, to teach the sciences in general. We know that this was utterly false, since the whole of society was based and maintained on the division of people into classes, into exploiters and oppressed" (1971).

Lenin argues, "Learn hatred of the old society, learn communism." Don't encumber young people's minds with immense amounts of knowledge which is "nine tenths useless and one tenth distorted." Learn the spirit of the class struggle in all art and education. All education for Lenin is political. "There is no such thing as an apolitical education" (1971).

The great challenge of the Soviet system is still presented best in the writings of Lenin. There must be, he insists, a change in the fundamental psychology of man. He hopes that this will be brought about by creating a different society. The purpose of psychotherapy becomes in such a situation entirely different. It has nothing to do with the unfolding of individual human potential but rather it concentrates on enabling the individual to function in the service of society, or the state. Thus psychotherapy in the Soviet system is *always fundamentally political* and has a primarily political purpose.

What we today call emotional illness is viewed in the Soviet system as either representing a physical problem of some kind with an organic etiology, or sheer malingering based on faulty education or more ominously a "bourgeois mentality" and "infection with capitalistic thought." The purpose of psychotherapy under such a system would be to cure this "infection" and to enable the individual to fit better into the service of the state and the community. Dissenters of all kinds, not just political dissenters, under this approach become labeled as mentally ill and it is understandable why the Soviets have a tendency to place dissenters in mental hospitals. In a society where there is so much intolerance of deviation, the appearance of deviation has to be explained either as a bourgeois plot which should be punished by jail sentences and even execution, or as a mental illness in need of cure. In the old days the tendency was to see *all* deviations as a sign of secret collusion with either Trotskyites (definition: anybody who disagrees even in the slightest with Stalin) or capitalists and to deal with it as treason; today with the greater softening of governmental power and less paranoia there is a willingness to see it more as "mental illness."

The Soviet challenge insists that the role of the psychotherapist in society is political and consists basically in changing the psychology and habits of an individual who is deviating from Lenin's view of sociology. As Lenin explains,

> The old society was based on the principle: rob or be robbed; work for others or make others work for you; be a slave-owner or a slave. Naturally, people brought up in such a society assimilate with their mother's milk, one might say, the psychology, the habit, the concept which says: you are either a slave-owner or a slave, or else, a small owner, a petty employee, a petty official, or an intellectual—in short, a man who is concerned only with himself, and does not care a rap for anybody else.

If I work this plot of land, I do not care a rap for anybody else; if others starve, all the better, I shall get the more for my grain. If I have a job as a doctor, engineer, teacher, or clerk, I do not care a rap for anybody else. If I toady to and please the powers that be, I may be able to keep my job, and even get on in life and become a bourgeois. A Communist cannot harbor such a psychology and such sentiments. When the workers and peasants proved that they were able, by their own efforts, to defend themselves and create a new society—that was the beginning of the new and communist education, education against the struggle of the exploiters, education in alliance with the proletariat against the self-seekers and petty proprietors, against the psychology and habits which say: I seek my own profit and don't care a rap for anything else. (1971, p. 615)

This is the challenge from the Soviet Union to American psychotherapy, and it is a challege which we must answer not through warfare but through debate, mutual enlightenment, and mutual change. The issues raised by this challenge in the practice of psychotherapy in the Western countries cannot ever again be avoided or ignored, for Soviet endurance and determination will never permit us to rest in what they consider to be a never-ending world-wide struggle of good against evil.

In this struggle, civilization itself is in danger. And civilization is really what this present book has been about, "the whole human effort towards beauty and truth, the love, the tender manners, the decency and seemliness that give form and substance to virtue" (Nef 1973). This concept of civilization began perhaps in eighteenth-century Europe and, as Nef explains, "It expressed a new hope: That the powers humans were achieving over nature could be used to raise humanity to a higher level of dignity and harmony than had ever existed. This gave both men and women a new and inspiring ideal." In the struggle between the great world political systems and between the "haves" and the "have-nots" in the world, civilization as a whole for the first time in a thousand years is seriously hanging on the balance (1973).

It is becoming harder and harder to integrate one's children into civilization, as the forces of darkness descend around us; the crushing deterioration of civilized life has produced the massive problem of the borderline patient who appears alone and isolated in our office—the rootless man overcome by nausea. And so this is a crucial matter for psychotherapists—to maintain and restore civilized values wherever possible, even in this terrible dark age.

Franz Alexander died a month after submitting his paper. "Social Significance of Psychoanalysis and Psychotherapy," in which he returns to the motto of the Renaissance humanists, "respect for the dignity of the individual" (chapter 5). In this final paper he explains, "Psychotherapy aims not only at enabling a person to adjust himself to existing conditions, but also to realize his unique potentials. Never was this aim more difficult and at the same time more essential. Psychoanalysis and psychotherapy in general are among the few still existing remedies against the relentlessly progressing levelization of industrial societies which tend to reduce the individual person to becoming an indistinguishable member of the faceless masses" (1964).

The world is desperately overpopulated, and overwhelming masses of people are living in conditions of unbelievable ignorance, misery, and wretchedness. Thus, when we speak of the goals of psychotherapy in the Western world we are talking only to a relatively tiny handful of the earth's population. The overwhelming majority are hopelessly mired in the problems of basic survival. As overpopulation increases and distances shrink under the impact of the jet planes, the fortunate minority that has enjoyed civilization is going to be overwhelmed very soon (see Raspail 1975).

It is no longer possible to take for granted the Western intellectual tradition, as described by Bronowski and Mazlish:

In the five hundred years since Leonardo, two ideas about man have been especially important. The first is the emphasis on the full development of the human personality. The individual is prized for himself. His creative powers are seen as the core of his being. The unfettered development of the individual personality is praised as the ideal, from the Renaissance artists through the Elizabethans, and through Locke and Voltaire and Rousseau. The vision of the freely developing man, happy in the unfolding of his own gifts, is shared by men as different in their conceptions as Thomas Jefferson and Edmund Burke. . . . This has come to be the unexpressed purpose of the life of individuals: fulfilling those special gifts with which a man is endowed.

The self-fulfillment of the individual has itself become part of a larger, more embracing idea, the self-fulfillment of man. We think of man as a species with special gifts, which are the human gifts. . . . The total of these gifts is man as a type or species, and the aspiration of man as a species has become the fulfillment of what is most human in these gifts. (1960, pp. 499-500)

Psychotherapists are involved whether they like it or not in the possible demise of civilization and of psychotherapy as a discipline altogether. Each psychotherapist must decide between his stomach and his conscience (see Eissler 1974). The loss of civilization itself is the greatest disaster that could befall mankind, because it means the loss of *hope.* It is hope that keeps our sickest patients going and trying to get well regardless of their suffering and anxiety; sometimes they have to go on the hope and faith of the therapist when theirs has been inundated by misery.

Psychotherapists must contribute to the hope and faith that civilization will not be allowed to die, or they also will perish. The absolute wretchedness of most human life today is impossible to exaggerate. A new sense of social conscience and a new sense of human values—of civilization in the eighteenth century sense—is going to have to be fostered and nurtured if our species is to survive with anything but a nasty, brutish, and short existence. Psychotherapists must take an active part in the universal establishment of a reverence for human life (Chessick 1973) in the face of the profound human struggle between man's proclivity to brutality and paranoia on the one side and on the other "the soft voice of intellect" as Freud called it—the enduring values of civilization. All the beauty that men and women have managed to create across several millenia, all the knowledge the spirit of continuing inquiry, all the sense of our heritage and participation in the greatest human pageant: these represent whatever is worthwhile in humanity and realize whatever capacities men contain for transcendence over the brief moment of their individual existence.

Bibliography

Abernathy, G., and Langford, T. 1970. *Introduction to Western Philosophy.* Belmont, California: Dickenson.

Alberti, L. 1966. *On Painting.* Trans. J. Spencer. New Haven, Conn: Yale University Press.

Alexander, F. 1930. *Psychoanalysis of the Total Personality.* New York: Nervous and Mental Disease.

———. 1948. *Fundamentals of Psychoanalysis.* New York: W. W. Norton.

———. 1950. *Psychosomatic Medicine.* New York: W. W. Norton.

———. 1951. *Our Age of Unreason.* Philadelphia: J. B. Lippincott.

———. 1956. *The Criminal, the Judge and the Public.* Glencoe, Ill.: Glencoe Free Press.

———. 1960. *The Western Mind in Transition.* New York: Random House.

———. 1961. *The Scope of Psychoanalysis.* New York: Basic Books.

———. 1964. Social significance of psychoanalysis and psychotherapy. *Archives Psychiatry* 11: 235-244.

———. 1966. *Psychoanalytic Pioneers.* New York: Basic Books.

Alexander, F., and Alexander, S. 1964. *The Berenson Collection.* Milan, Italy: Art Grafiche Ricordi.

Alexander, F., and French, T. 1946. *Psychoanalytic Therapy.* New York: Ronald.

Alexander F., and Healy, W. 1935. *Roots of Crime.* New York: Alfred A. Knopf.

Alexander, F., and Ross, H. 1952. *Dynamic Psychiatry.* Chicago: University of Chicago Press.

———. 1953. *Twenty Years of Psychoanalysis.* New York: W. W. Norton.

Alexander, F., and Selesnick, S. 1966. *The History of Psychiatry.* New York: Harper and Row.

Allen, D. 1952. *The Philosophy of Aristotle.* London: Oxford University Press.

Alsop, J. 1964. *From the Silent Earth.* New York: Harper and Row.

Anscombe, G. 1967. *An Introduction to Wittgenstein's Tractatus.* London: Hutchison University Library.

Ardrey, R. 1966. *The Territorial Imperative.* New York: Atheneum.

Aristotle. 1941. *The Basic Works.* Ed. R. McKeon. New York: Random.

Arlow, J., and Brenner, C. 1964. *Psychoanalytic Concepts and the Structural Theory.* New York: International Universities Press.

Arnett, W. 1955. *Santayana and the Sense of Beauty.* Bloomington: Indiana University Press.

Ash, M. 1971. Freud on feminine identity and female sexuality. *Psychiatry* 34: 322-329.

Augustine, St. 1952. *Confessions.* Trans. H. Gardiner. New York: Pocket Books.

―――. 1958. *On Christian Doctrine.* Trans. D. Robertson. Indianapolis: Bobbs-Merrill.

―――. 1972. *City of God.* Trans. H. Bettenson. Baltimore: Penguin.

Aurelius, M. 1964. *Meditations.* Trans. M. Staniforth. Baltimore: Penguin.

Ayer, A. 1952. *Language, Truth and Logic.* New York: Dover.

Babkin, B. 1949. *Pavlov.* Chicago: University of Chicago Press.

Bahm, A. 1963. *Tao Teh King.* New York: Ungar.

Bakan, D. 1969. *Sigmund Freud and the Jewish Mystical Tradition.* New York: Schocken.

Balint, M. 1968. *The Basic Fault.* London: Tavistock.

Balogh, P. 1971. *Freud.* New York: Scribner.

Barrett, W. 1958. *Irrational Man.* New York: Doubleday.

Bartley, W. 1973. *Wittgenstein.* Philadelphia: J. B. Lippincott.

Bellak, L. 1958. *Schizophrenia.* New York: Logos Press.

Benoit-Smullyan, E. 1966. *History of Political Theory.* Boston: Student Outline Company.

Berenson, B. 1952. *The Italian Painters of the Renaissance.* London: Phaidon.

―――. 1962. *The Bernard Berenson Treasury.* Ed. H. Kiel. New York: Simon and Schuster.

Bibring, E. 1963. The development and problems of the theory of the instincts. *Imago* 22: 147.

Bieber, I. 1973. On behavior therapy—a critique. *Journal of the American Academy of Psychoanalysis* 1: 39-52.

Birk, L.; Stolz, S.; Brady, J. P.; Brady, J. V.; Lazarus, A.; Lynch, J.; Rosenthal, A.; Skelton, W.; Stevens, J., and Thomas, E. 1973. *Behavior Therapy in Psychiatry.* Washington, D.C.: American Psychiatric Association.

Blackham, H. 1952. *Six Existentialist Thinkers.* London: Routledge and Kegan Paul.

Blos, P. 1962. *On Adolescence.* New York: The Free Press.

———. 1970. *The Young Adolescent.* New York: The Free Press.

———. 1971. The child analyst looks at the young adolescent. *Daedalus* 100: 961-978.

Bohm, D. 1971. *Causality and Chance in Modern Physics.* Philadelphia: University of Pennsylvania Press.

Bohr, N. 1934. *Atomic Theory and the Description of Nature.* Cambridge, Mass.: Cambridge University Press.

———. 1958. *Atomic Physics and Human Knowledge.* New York: John Wiley.

———. 1963. *Essays 1958-1962 on Atomic Physics and Human Knowledge.* New York: Interscience.

Bonnard, A. 1961. *Greek Civilization.* New York: Macmillan.

Booth, W. 1967. *The Knowledge Most Worth Having.* Chicago: University of Chicago Press.

Bowra, C. 1962. *The Greek Experience.* New York: Mentor.

———. 1965. *Classical Greece.* New York: Time-Life.

Bradley, F. 1951. *Appearance and Reality.* Oxford: Clarendon.

Brennan, J. 1967. *The Meaning of Philosophy.* New York: Harper and Row.

Brenner, C. 1955. *An Elementary Textbook of Psychoanalysis.* New York: International Universities Press.

———. 1973. *An Elementary Textbook of Psychoanalysis.* 2nd Ed. New York: International Universities Press.

Breuer, J., and Freud, S. 1893-1895. Studies on hysteria. *Standard Edition,* vol. 2 (1955).

Brewster, M. 1972. Beyond freedom and dignity. *American Scientist* 60: 80-83.

Brinton, C.; Christopher, J.; and Wolff, R. 1955. *A History of Civilization.* 2 vols. Englewood Cliffs, N.J.: Prentice Hall.

Brock, W. 1968. *Existence and Being.* Chicago, Ill: Henry Regnery.

Bromberg, W. 1954. *Man Above Humanity.* Philadelphia: J. B. Lippincott.

Bronowski, J., and Mazlish, B. 1960. *The Western Intellectual Tradition.* London: Hutchinson.

Brook-Rose, C. 1971. *A ZBC of Ezra Pound.* Los Angeles: University of California Press.

Brown, P. 1969. *Augustine of Hippo.* Berkeley: University of California Press.

Bruch, H. 1974. *Learning Psychotherapy.* Cambridge, Mass.: Harvard University Press.

Buber, M. 1958. *I and Thou.* New York: Charles Scribner.

Burckhardt, J. 1958. *The Civilization of the Renaissance in Italy.* 2 vols. New York: Harper Torchbooks.

Bury, J. 1913. *A History of Greece.* New York: Random House.

Camus, A. 1955. *The Myth of Sisyphus.* New York: Alfred A. Knopf.

Canaday, J. 1969. *The Lives of the Painters.* 4 vols. New York: W. W. Norton.

Cantor, N. 1969. *Western Civilization Its Genesis and Destiny.* Glenview, Ill.: Scott, Foresman.

Castell, A. 1966. *An Introduction to Modern Philosophy.* New York: Macmillan.

Castiglione, B. 1967. *The Book of the Courtier.* Trans. G. Bull. Baltimore: Penguin.

Cavendish, A. 1964. Early Greek philosophy. In *A Critical History of Western Philosophy,* ed. D. O'Connor. New York: Macmillan.

Chan, W. 1963. *A Source Book in Chinese Philosophy.* Princeton, N.J.: Princeton University Press.

———. 1968. Confucianism. *Encyclopedia Britannica* 5. Chicago: W. Benton.

Chein, I. 1972. *The Science of Behavior and the Image of Man.* New York: Basic Books.

Cherry, R., and Cherry, L. 1973. The Horney Heresy. *New York Times Magazine,* August 26.

Chessick, R. 1961. Some problems and pseudo-problems in psychiatry. *Psychiatric Quarterly* 35: 711-719.

———. 1965. Orgia and omophagia. *Journal of the American Medical Association* 192: 310-312.

———. 1967. Critique. *American Journal of Psychotherapy* 21: 130-132.

———. 1969a. *How Psychotherapy Heals.* New York: Jason Aronson.

———. 1969b. Was Machiavelli right? *American Journal of Psychotherapy* 23: 633-644.

———. 1971a. The being of man and the yowling of coyotes. *American Journal of Psychotherapy* 25: 643-645.

———. 1971b. The use of the couch in the psychotherapy of borderline patients. *Archives of General Psychiatry* 25: 306-313.

———. 1971c. *Why Psychotherapists Fail.* New York: Jason Aronson.

———. 1972. Externalization and existential anguish in the borderline patient. *Archives of General Psychiatry* 27: 764-770.

———. 1973. A la recherche d'un bonheur humain. *Le Greours Medical,* May 19, 1973.

———. 1974a. The borderline patient. In *American Handbook of Psychiatry,* vol. 3, ed. S. Arieti, 2nd ed. New York: Basic Books.

———. 1974b. Europe in the twentieth century. *American Journal of Psychotherapy* 28: 144-146.

———. 1974c. Mahler and the human condition. *Medikon International* 28 Feb., pp. 5-8.

———. 1974d. The principle of complementarity. *American Journal of Psychotherapy* 28: 292-294.

———. 1974e. Psychotherapeutic interaction. *American Journal of Psychotherapy* 28: 243-251.

———. 1974f. The special theory of psychotherapeutic interaction. *Psychotherapy and Psychosomatics* 24: 433-438.

———. 1974g. *The Technique and Practice of Intensive Psychotherapy.* New York: Jason Aronson.

———. 1976. *Agonie: Diary of a Twentieth Century Man.* Ghent, Belgium: European Press.

———. 1977. *Intensive Psychotherapy of the Borderline Patient.* New York: Jason Aronson.

Churchill, W. 1942. *The World Crisis 1911-1918.* New York: Macmillan.

Claman, H. 1964. Karl Jaspers—modern existentialist. *New England Journal of Medicine* 271: 513-514.

Clapp, J. 1967. John Locke. In *Encyclopedia of Philosophy,* ed. P. Edwards. New York: Macmillan.

Clark, K. 1969. *Civilisation.* New York: Harper and Row.

Cole, J. 1971. *The Problematic Self in Kierkegaard and Freud.* New Haven: Yale University Press.

Coles, R. 1970. *Erik H. Erikson.* Boston: Little, Brown.

Confucius. 1938. *Analects.* Trans. A. Whaley. New York: Vintage.

Conrad, J. 1966. *Great Short Works.* New York: Harper and Row.

Coope, C.; Geach, P.; Potts, T.; and White, R. 1970. *A Wittgenstein Workbook.* Berkeley: University of California Press.

Copleston, F. 1946. *Arthur Schopenhauer's Philosophy of Pessimism.* London: Methuen.

———. 1962a. *A History of Philosophy.* Vol. 1, Part 1. Garden City: Doubleday.

———. 1962b. *A History of Philosophy.* Vol. 1, Part 2. Garden City: Doubleday.

———. 1964. *A History of Philosophy.* Vol. 6, Part 2. Garden City: Image Books.

————. 1965. *A History of Philosophy.* Vol. 7, Part 2. Garden City: Image Books.

Creel, H. 1960. *Confucius and the Chinese Way.* New York: Harper Torchbooks.

Crombie, I. 1966. *An Examination of Plato's Doctrines.* Vol. 1. London: Routledge and Kegan Paul.

Crowley, R. 1971. *Harry Stack Sullivan.* New Jersey: Hoffman-La Roche.

Danto, A. 1964. Nietzsche. Chapter 21 In *A Critical History of Western Philosophy,* ed. D. J. O'Connor. New York: Macmillan.

————. 1965. *Nietzsche as Philosopher.* New York: Macmillan.

Decker, H. 1967. *The Renaissance in Italy.* New York: Viking.

Decter, M. 1972. *The New Chastity and Other Arguments Against Women's Liberation.* New York: Coward, McCann and Geoghegan.

Deutsch, F. 1957. Footnote to Freud's "Fragment of an analysis of a case of hysteria." *Psychoanalytic Quarterly* 26: 159-167.

Deutsch, H. 1944. *The Psychology of Women.* 2 vols. New York: Grune and Stratton.

————. 1973. *Confrontations With Myself.* New York: W. W. Norton.

DeWald, E. 1961. *Italian Painting 1200-1600.* New York: Holt, Rinehart and Winston.

Dewey, J. 1922. *Human Nature and Conduct.* New York: Henry Holt.

————. 1958. *Art as Experience.* New York: Capricorn Books.

Dewey, J.; Hook, S.; and Nagel, E. 1943. The new failure of nerve. *Partisan Review* 10: 2-23.

DeWitt, N. 1967. *Epicurus and His Philosophy.* New York: Meridian Books.

Dollard, J., and Miller, N. 1950. *Personality and Psychotherapy.* New York: McGraw, Hill.

Durant, W. 1939. *The Life of Greece.* New York: Simon and Schuster.

————. 1953. *The Renaissance.* New York: Simon and Schuster.

Edwards, P., ed. 1965. *Encyclopedia of Philosophy.* New York: Macmillan.

Einstein, A., and Infeld, L. 1938. *The Evolution of Physics.* New York: Simon and Schuster.

Eissler, K. 1974. On some theoretical and technical problems regarding the payment of fees for psychoanalytic treatment. *International Review of Psycho-Analysis* 1: 73-101.

Eldred, S. 1972. Intensive psychotherapy with schizophrenic patients. *Contemporary Psychoanalysis* 8: 149-164.

Elkind, D. 1972. Good me or bad me—the Sullivan approach to personality. *New York Times Magazine,* Sept. 24.

————. 1973. Erik Erikson's eight ages of man. *New York Times Magazine,* April 7.

Ellenberger, H. 1970. *The Discovery of the Unconscious.* New York: Basic Books.

Erikson, E. 1950. *Childhood and Society.* New York: W. W. Norton.

———. 1958. *Young Man Luther.* New York: W. W. Norton.

———. 1959. *Identity and the Life Cycle.* New York: International Universities Press.

———. 1964. *Insight and Responsibility.* New York: W. W. Norton.

———. 1968. *Identity, Youth and Crisis.* New York: W. W. Norton.

———. 1969. *Gandhi's Truth.* New York: W. W. Norton.

———. 1974. *Dimensions of a New Identity.* New York: W. W. Norton.

———. 1975. *Life History and the Historical Moment.* New York: W. W. Norton.

Evans, R. 1967. *Dialogue with Erik Erikson.* New York: Harper and Row.

———. 1968. *B. F. Skinner.* New York: E. P. Dutton.

———. 1973. *Jean Piaget.* New York: E. P. Dutton.

Ewing, A. 1967. *A Short Commentary on Kant's Critique of Pure Reason.* Bloomington: Indiana University Press.

Fann, K. 1971. *Wittgenstein's Conception of Philosophy.* Berkeley: University of California Press.

Farrington, B. 1970. *Aristotle.* New York: Praeger.

Federn, P. 1952. *Ego Psychology and the Psychoses.* New York: Basic Books.

Fisher, S. 1973. *The Female Orgasm: Psychology, Physiology, Fantasy.* New York: Basic Books.

Fleming, W. 1968. *Arts and Ideas.* 3rd ed. New York: Holt, Rinehart and Winston.

———. 1970. *Art, Music and Ideas.* New York: Holt, Rinehart and Winston.

Fliegel, Z. 1973. Feminine psychosexual development in Freudian theory. *Psychoanalytic Quarterly* 42: 385-406.

Fleiss, R. 1948. *The Psychoanalytic Reader.* New York: International Universities Press.

Frame, D. 1965. *Montaigne.* New York: Harcourt Brace.

Frank, J. 1961. *Persuasion and Healing.* Baltimore: Johns Hopkins University Press.

Freedman, A., and Kaplan, H., eds. 1972. *Interpreting Personality.* New York: Atheneum.

Freud, A. 1946. *The Ego and the Mechanisms of Defense.* New York: International Universities Press.

———. 1969. *Difficulties in the Path of Psychoanalysis.* New York: International Universities Press.

———. 1972. *The Writings of Anna Freud.* 7 vols. New York: International Universities Press.

Freud, S. 1896. The aetiology of hysteria. *Standard Edition* 3: 189-224 (1962).

———. 1900. The interpretation of dreams. *Standard Edition* 4/5: 1-630 (1953).

———. 1901. The psychopathology of everyday life. *Standard Edition* 6 (1960).

———. 1905a. A case of hysteria. *Standard Edition* 7: 7-124 (1953).

———. 1905b. Three essays on sexuality. *Standard Edition* 7: 136-243 (1953).

———. 1909a. Analysis of a phobia in a five-year-old boy. *Standard Edition* 10: 3-152 (1955).

———. 1909b. Notes upon a case of obsessional neurosis. *Standard Edition* 10: 153-318.

———. 1910a. The future prospects of psychoanalytic therapy. *Standard Edition* 11: 139-152 (1957).

———. 1910b. Leonardo da Vinci. *Standard Edition* 11: 63-138 (1957).

———. 1910c. 'Wild' psychoanalysis. *Standard Edition* 11: 219-230 (1957).

———. 1911. The case of Schreber. *Standard Edition* 12: 3-84 (1958).

———. 1911-1915. Papers on technique. *Standard Edition* 12: 89-174 (1958).

———. 1914a. The Moses of Michelangelo. *Standard Edition* 13: 209-240 (1955).

———. 1914b. On narcissism. *Standard Edition* 14: 73-104 (1957).

———. 1915. The unconscious. *Standard Edition* 14: 159-204 (1957).

———. 1916. Some character types met with in psychoanalytic work. *Standard Edition* 14: 311-336 (1957).

———. 1916-1917. Introductory lectures on psychoanalysis. *Standard Edition* Vols. 15 and 16 (1963).

———. 1917. Mourning and melancholia. *Standard Edition* 14: 237-260 (1957).

———. 1918. From the history of an infantile neurosis. *Standard Edition* 17: 3-124 (1955).

———. 1919a. A child is being beaten. *Standard Edition* 17: 175-204 (1955).

———. 1919b. Lines of advance in psychoanalytic therapy. *Standard Edition* 17: 157-168 (1955).

———. 1920. Beyond the pleasure principle. *Standard Edition* 18: 3-66 (1955).

———. 1923. The ego and the id. *Standard Edition* 19: 3-68 (1961).

———. 1924. The dissolution of the Oedipus complex. *Standard Edition* 19: 173-182 (1961).

———. 1925a. An autobiographical study. *Standard Edition* 20: 3-76 (1959).

———. 1925b. Negation. *Standard Edition* 19: 235-242 (1961).

———. 1925c. A note upon the mystic writing pad. *Standard Edition* 19: 227-234 (1961).

———. 1925d. The resistance to psychoanalysis. *Standard Edition* 19: 213-226 (1961).

———. 1925e. Some psychical consequences of the anatomical distinction between the sexes. *Standard Edition* 19: 243-260 (1961).

———. 1926. Inhibitions, symptoms and anxiety. *Standard Edition* 20: 91-178 (1959).

———. 1927. Future of an illusion. *Standard Edition* 21: 3-58 (1961).

———. 1930. Civilisation and its discontents. *Standard Edition* 21: 59-148 (1961).

———. 1931. Female sexuality. *Standard Edition* 21: 223-246 (1961).

———. 1933. New introductory lectures on psychoanalysis. *Standard Edition* 22: 3-184 (1964).

———. 1937a. Analysis terminable and interminable. *Standard Edition* 23: 209-254 (1966).

———. 1937b. Constructions in analysis. *Standard Edition* 23: 255-270 (1966).

———. 1940. An outline of psychoanalysis. *Standard Edition* 23: 141-208 (1966).

———. 1953-1966. *The Standard Edition of the Complete Psychological Works of Sigmund Freud.* 23 vols. Trans. James Strachey. London: Hogarth Press.

———. 1954. *Letters.* Ed. E. Kris. New York: Basic Books.

———. 1960. *Letters.* Ed. E. Freud. New York: Basic Books.

Friedlander, P. 1958. *Plato: An Introduction.* New York: Harper Torchbooks.

———. 1969. *Plato: The Dialogues—Second and Third Periods.* Princeton, N.J.: Princeton University Press.

Frings, M. 1968. *Heidegger and the Quest for Truth.* Chicago, Ill.: Quadrangle Books.

Fromm, E. 1955. *The Sane Society.* New York: Holt, Rinehart and Winston.

———. 1963. *The Art of Loving.* New York: Bantam.

Fromm-Reichmann, F. 1950. *Principles of the Intensive Psychotherapy.* Chicago: University of Chicago Press.

———. 1959. *Psychoanalysis and Psychotherapy.* Chicago: University of Chicago Press.

Fuss, P., and Shapiro, H. 1971. *Nietzsche.* Cambridge, Mass.: Harvard University Press.

Gardiner, M. 1955. Feminine masochism and passivity. *Bulletin of the Philadelphia Association for Psychoanalysis* 5: 74-79.

———. 1971. *The Wolf-Man.* New York: Basic Books.

Gardiner, P. 1971. *Schopenhauer.* Middlesex, England: Penguin.

Gedo, J. 1973. Kant's way: The psychoanalytic contribution of David Rapaport. *Psychoanalytic Quarterly* 62: 409-433.

Geleerd, E. 1967. Book Review of D. W. Winnicott: The Family and Individual Development. *International Journal of Psycho-Analysis* 48: 108-111.

Gelven, M. 1970. *A Commentary on Heidegger's Being and Time.* New York: Harper Torchbooks.

Glynn, E. 1971. Erik Erikson. *American Journal of Orthopsychiatry* 41: 683-685.

Goble, F. 1970. *The Third Force.* New York: Grossman.

Gould, R. 1972. The phases of adult life. *American Journal of Psychiatry* 129: 521-531.

Green, H. 1964. *I Never Promised You a Rose Garden.* New York: Signet Books.

Green, P. 1973. *In the Shadow of the Parthenon.* Berkeley, Cal.: University of California Press.

Greenson, R. 1965. The working alliance and the transference neurosis. *Psychoanalytic Quarterly* 34: 155-181.

———. 1967. *The Technique and Practice of Psychoanalysis.* New York: International Universities Press.

Greenson, R., and Wexler, M. 1969. The non-transference relationship in the psychoanalytic situation. *International Journal of Psycho-Analysis* 50: 27-40.

Greenson, R., and Wexler, M. 1970. Discussion of the nontransference relationship in psychoanalytic situation. *International Journal of Psycho-Analysis* 51: 143-150.

Grene, D., and Lattimore, R. 1959. *The Complete Greek Tragedies.* 4 vols. Chicago: University of Chicago Press.

Grene, M. 1957. *Heidegger.* London: Bowes and Bowes.

———. 1963. *A Portrait of Aristotle.* Chicago: University of Chicago Press.

———. 1967. Martin Heidegger. In *The Encyclopedia of Philosophy,* ed. P. Edwards, vol. 3. New York: Macmillan.

———. 1970. *Introduction to Existentialism.* Chicago: University of Chicago Press.

Groddeck, G. 1961. *The Book of the It.* New York: Mentor Books.

Guillemin, V. 1968. *The Story of Quantum Mechanics.* New York: Charles Scribner's.

Guntrip, H. 1968. *Schizoid Phenomena, Object Relations and the Self.* New York: International Universities Press.

———. 1971. *Psychoanalytic Theory, Therapy and the Self.* New York: Basic Books.

———. 1975. My experience of analysis with Fairbairn and Winnicott. *International Review of Psychoanalysis* 2: 145-156.

Guthrie, W. 1960. *The Greek Philosophers.* New York: Harper Torchbooks.

———. 1965. Pre-Socratic philosophy. In *The Encyclopedia of Philosophy,* ed. P. Edwards. New York: Macmillan.

Hale, J. 1960. *Machiavelli and Renaissance Italy.* New York: Macmillan.

Hall, C., and Lindzey, G. 1957. *Theories of Personality.* New York: John Wiley.

Hall, G. 1971. *Our Friends Speak.* Moscow: Novostoi Press.

Hamilton, E. 1973. *The Greek Way.* New York: Avon Books.

Hampshire, S., and Grene, M. 1958. On Heidegger. *Encounter Magazine,* April, pp. 67-69.

Hanley, C., and Lazerowitz, M. 1970. *Psychoanalysis and Philosophy.* New York: International Universities Press.

Hartmann, H. 1960. Towards a concept of mental health. *British Journal of Medical Psychology* 33: 243-248.

Hartnack, J. 1965. *Wittgenstein and Modern Philosophy.* New York: New York University Press.

Hartt, F. 1969. *History of Italian Renaissance Art.* New York: Harry N. Abrams.

Havens, L. 1973. *Approaches to the Mind.* Boston: Little, Brown.

———. 1974. The existential use of the self. *American Journal of Psychiatry* 131: 1-10.

Heidegger, M. 1956. *What is Philosophy.* Trans. J. Wilde and W. Kluback. New Haven, Conn.: College and University Press.

———. 1958. *The Question of Being.* Trans. J. Wilde and W. Kluback. New Haven, Conn.: College and University Press.

———. 1961. *An Introduction to Metaphysics.* Trans. R. Manheim. New York: Anchor Books.

———. 1962a. *Being and Time.* Trans. J. Macquarrie and E. Robinson. New York: Harper and Row.

———. 1962b. Letter on humanism. In *Philosophy in the Twentieth Century,* vol. 3, eds. W. Barrett and H. Aiken. New York: Random House.

———. 1962c. *Kant and the Problem of Metaphysics.* Trans. J. Churchill. Bloomington, Ind.: Indiana University Press.

———. 1962d. Plato's doctrine of truth. In *Philosophy in the Twentieth Century,* vol. 3, eds. W. Barrett and H. Aiken. New York: Random House.

———. 1966. *Discourse on Thinking.* Trans. J. Anderson and H. Freund. New York: Harper and Row.

———. 1967. *What is a Thing?* Trans. W. Barton and V. Deutsch. Chicago: Henry Regnery.

————. 1968. *What is Called Thinking?* Trans. F. Wieck and J. Gray. New York: Harper and Row.

Heisenberg, W. 1971. *Physics and Beyond.* New York: Harper and Row.

Hendy, P. 1968. *Piero della Francesca and the Early Renaissance.* New York: Macmillan.

Henry, P. 1960. *St. Augustine on Personality.* New York: Macmillan.

Highet, G. 1971. *Explorations.* New York: Oxford University Press.

Hilgard, E. 1956. *Theories of Learning.* New York: Appleton-Century-Crofts.

Hilgard, E., Atkinson, R., and Atkinson, R. 1971. *Introduction to Psychology.* 5th ed. New York: Harcourt Brace Jovanovich.

Hilgard, E., and Marquis, D. 1961. *Conditioning and Learning.* New York: Appleton-Century-Crofts.

Holderlin, F. 1943. *Selected Poems.* Trans. F. Proskosch. Norfolk, Conn.: New Directions.

————. 1965. *Hyperion.* New York: Signet Classics.

————. 1968. *Poems and Fragments.* Trans. M. Hamburger. Ann Arbor: University of Michigan Press.

Hollender, M. 1970. The need or wish to be held. *Archives of General Psychiatry* 22: 445-453.

Hollender, M., Luborsky, L. and Harvey, R. 1970. Correlates of the desire to be held in women. *Journal of Psychosomatic Research* 14: 387-390.

Hollender, M.; Luborsky, L.; and Scaramella, T. 1969. Body contact and sexual enticement. *Archives of General Psychiatry* 20: 188-191.

Hollingdale, R. 1965. *Nietzsche.* Baton Rouge: Louisiana State University Press.

Holton, G. 1973. *Thematic Origins of Scientific Thought.* Cambridge, Mass.: Harvard University Press.

Horney, K. 1937. *The Neurotic Personality of Our Time.* New York: W. W. Norton.

————. 1939. *New Ways in Psychoanalysis.* New York: W. W. Norton.

————. 1942. *Self-Analysis.* New York: W. W. Norton.

————. 1945. *Our Inner Conflicts.* New York: W. W. Norton.

————. 1950. *Neurosis and Human Growth.* New York: W. W. Norton.

————. 1967. *Feminine Psychology.* New York: W. W. Norton.

Housman, A. 1947. *A Shropshire Lad.* New York: World.

Howie, G. 1969. *St. Augustine On Education.* Chicago: Henry Regnery.

Husserl, E. 1964. *The Idea of Phenomenology.* The Hague: Martinus Nijhoff.

Jacobsen, E. 1964. *The Self and the Object World.* New York: International Universities Press.

Jacques, E. 1964. Death and the midlife crisis. *International Journal of Psycho-Analysis* 46: 502-514.

Jaeger, W. 1960. *Paideia: The Ideals of Greek Culture*. Trans. G. Highet. New York: Oxford University Press.

Janeway, E. 1971. *Man's World. Woman's Place*. New York: Dell.

Janik, A., and Toulmin, S. 1973. *Wittgenstein's Vienna*. New York: Simon and Schuster.

Janson, H. 1967. *History of Art*. Englewood Cliffs, N.J.: Prentice-Hall.

Jaspers, K. 1913. *General Psychopathology*. Chicago: University of Chicago Press (1963).

———. 1931. *Man in the Modern Age*. Garden City, New York: Anchor Books (1957).

———. 1932a. *Philosophy*. Vol. 1. Chicago: University of Chicago Press (1969).

———. 1932b. *Philosophy*. Vol. 2. Chicago: University of Chicago Press (1970).

———. 1932c. *Philosophy*. Vol. 3. Chicago: University of Chicago Press (1971).

———. 1935a. *Nietzsche*. Tucson: The Arizona University Press (1966).

———. 1935b. *Reason and Existenz*. New York: Farrar, Strauss and Giroux.

———. 1941. Existenzphilosophie. In *Existentialism from Dostoevski to Sartre*, ed. W. Kaufmann. New York: Meridian Books (1957).

———. 1948. *The Perennial Scope of Philosophy*. New York: Philosophical Library (1968).

———. 1954. *The Way to Wisdom*. New Haven, Conn.: Yale University Press.

———. 1962. *The Great Philosophers*. Vol. 1. New York: Harcourt, Brace and World.

———. 1963. *The Nature of Psychotherapy*. Chicago: University of Chicago Press.

———. 1966. *The Great Philosophers*. Vol. 2. New York: Harcourt, Brace and World.

Jonas, G. 1972. Visceral Learning. *New Yorker Magazine,* August 19 and August 26.

Jones, E. 1957. *The Life and Works of Sigmund Freud*. 3 vols. New York: Basic Books.

———. 1963. *The Life and Works of Sigmund Freud*. Ed. and abridged L. Trilling and S. Marcus. New York: Anchor Books.

Jones, W. 1967. *The Sciences and the Humanities*. Berkeley: University of California Press.

Jones, W. T. 1969. *A History of Western Philosophy*. 3 vols. New York: Harcourt Brace and World.

Kahn, E. 1963. On crises. *Psychiatry Quarterly* 27: 297-305.

Kahn, M. 1971. Donald W. Winnicott. *International Journal of Psycho-Analysis* 52: 225-226.

Kaltenmark, M. 1969. *Lao Tzu and Taoism.* Stanford, Cal.: Stanford University Press.

Kant, I. 1950. *Prolegomena to Any Future Metaphysics.* Ed. L. Beck. New York: Library of Liberal Arts.

―――. 1960. *An Immanuel Kant Reader.* Ed. and trans. R. Blakney. New York: Harper and Bros.

―――. 1965. *Critique of Pure Reason.* Trans. Norman Kemp Smith. New York: St. Martin's Press.

Kaufmann, W. 1958. *Existentialism from Dostoyevsky to Sartre.* New York: Meridian Books.

―――. 1960. *From Shakespeare to Existentialism.* New York: Anchor Books.

―――. 1967. Nietzsche. *The Encyclopedia of Philosophy,* ed. P. Edwards. New York: Macmillian.

―――. 1968. *Nietzsche.* New York: Vantage Books.

Kelman, H. 1971. *Helping People: Karen Horney's Psychoanalytic Approach.* New York: Jason Aronson.

Kendler, H. and Kendler, T. 1971. *Basic Psychology: Brief Edition.* New York: Meridith.

Kenny, A. 1973. *Wittgenstein.* Cambridge, Mass.: Harvard University Press.

Kierkegaard, S. 1946. *The Concept of Dread.* Trans. W. Lowrie. Princeton, N.J.: Princeton University Press.

―――. 1947. *A Kierkegaard Anthology.* Ed. R. Bretall. Princeton: Princeton University Press.

―――. 1954. *Fear and Trembling and Sickness Unto Death.* New York: Anchor Books.

―――. 1959. *Journals.* Ed. A. Dru. New York: Harper Torchbooks.

―――. 1967. *Stages on Life's Way.* New York: Schocken Books.

―――. 1971a. *Concluding Unscientific Postscript.* Trans. D. Swenson and W. Lowrie. Princeton, N.J.: Princeton University Press.

―――. 1971b. *Either/Or.* Trans. W. Lowrie, 2 vols. Princeton, N.J.: Princeton University Press.

King, C.; May, A.; and Fletcher, A. 1969. *A History of Civilization.* New York: Scribner.

Kirk, G., and Raven, J. 1971. *The Presocratic Philosophers.* New York: Cambridge University Press.

Kitto, H. 1972. *The Greeks.* Middlesex, England: Penguin.

Klein, D. 1970. *A History of Scientific Psychology.* New York: Basic Books.

Kligerman, C. 1957. The confessions of St. Augustine. *Journal of American Psychoanalytic Association* 5: 469-484.

Kockelmans, J., ed. 1967. *Phenomenology*. New York: Doubleday, Anchor Books.

Koestenbaum, P. 1967. Karl Jaspers. In *the Encyclopedia of Philosophy*, ed. P. Edwards. New York: Macmillan.

Kohut, H. 1971. The *Analysis of the Self*. New York: International Universities Press.

Koller, J. 1970. *Oriental Philosophies*. New York: Scribner.

Korner S. 1970. *Kant*. Baltimore, Md.: Penguin.

Kuhn, T. 1962. *The Structure of Scientific Revolutions*. Chicago: University of Chicago Press.

Kurtz, P. 1971. Democracy and the technology of control. *The Humanist,* November-December, pp. 33-34.

Lakatos, I., and Musgrave, A. E., eds. 1970. *Criticism and the Growth of Knowledge*. London: Cambridge University Press.

Lambert, K., and Brittan, G. 1970. *An Introduction to the Philosophy of Science*. Englewood Cliffs, N.J.: Prentice-Hall.

Lampl–de Groot, J. 1967. On obstacles standing in the way of psychoanalytic cure. *Psychoanalytic Study of the Child* 22: 20-35. New York: International Universities Press.

Langs, R. 1974. *The Technique of Psychoanalytic Psychotherapy*. 2 vols. New York: Jason Aronson.

Laurin, J. 1971. *Nietzsche*. New York: Scribner.

Lee, J. 1970. On the existential viewpoint of Karl Jaspers. *Existential Psychiatry* 7: 7-28.

Legge, J. 1935. *The Chinese Classics*. 5 vols. Fairlawn, N.J.: Oxford University Press.

Lenin, V. 1971. *Selected Works*. Moscow: Progress Publishers.

Leonard, W. 1915. *Socrates, Master of Life*. London: Open Court.

Levi, A. 1959. *Philosophy and the Modern World*. Bloomington, Ind.: Indiana University Press.

———. 1969. *Literature, Philosophy and the Imagination*. Bloomington, Ind.: Indiana University Press.

Lichtheim, G. 1972. *Europe in the Twentieth Century*. New York: Praeger.

Liebert, R., and Spiegler M. 1970. *Personality*. Homewood, Ill.: The Dorsey Press.

Locke, J. 1969. *An Essay Concerning Human Understanding*. Ed. and abridged A. Woozley. New York: Meridian Books.

Lowrie, W. 1971. *A Short Life of Kierkegaard*. Princeton, N.J.: Princeton University Press.

Lucretius. 1924. *On the Nature of Things.* Trans. C. Bailey. Oxford: Clarendon.

McCarthy, M. 1957. *Venice Observed.* New York: Reynal.

McDaniel, S. 1965. *The Philosophy of Nietzsche.* New York: Monarch.

Machiavelli, N. 1950a. *The Discourses.* New York: Random House, Modern Library.

———. 1950b. *The Prince.* New York: Random House, Modern Library.

———. 1960. *History of Florence.* New York: Harper and Row.

———. 1961. *Literary Works.* London: Oxford University Press.

———. 1965. *The Art of War.* Indianapolis, Ind.: Bobbs-Merrill.

McInerny, R. 1963. *From the Beginnings of Philosophy to Plotinus.* Notre Dame, Ind.: University of Notre Dame Press.

McNeill, W. 1963. *The Rise of the West.* Chicago: University of Chicago Press.

———. 1967a. *History Handbook of Western Civilization.* Chicago: University of Chicago Press.

———. 1967b. *A World History.* New York: Oxford University Press.

Magee, B. 1973. *Karl Popper.* New York: Viking.

Malcolm, N. 1967. Wittgenstein. In *Encyclopedia of Philosophy*, ed. P. Edwards. New York: Macmillan.

———. 1970. *Ludwig Wittgenstein.* London: Oxford University Press.

Mannoni, O. 1971. *Freud.* New York: Pantheon.

Markus, R. 1964. Augustine. In *A Critical History of Western Philosophy,* ed. D. J. O'Connor. New York: The Free Press.

Markus, R., ed. 1972. *Augustine.* New York: Doubleday, Anchor Books.

Marmor, J. 1971. Dynamic psychotherapy and behavior therapy. *Archives of Psychiatry* 24: 22-28.

———. 1973. *The Contributions of Franz Alexander to Modern Psychotherapy.* Nutley, N.J.: Roche Laboratories.

Maslow, A. 1968. *Toward a Psychology of Being.* New York: Van Nostrand Reinhold.

———. 1971. *The Farther Reaches of Human Nature.* New York: Viking.

Masters, W., and Johnson, V. 1966. *Human Sexual Response.* Boston: Little, Brown.

———. 1970. *Human Sexual Inadequacy.* Boston: Little Brown.

Maugham, W. 1946. *The Summing Up.* New York: Mentor Books.

May, R. 1958. *Existence.* New York: Basic Books.

Mehta, J. 1971. *The Philosophy of Martin Heidegger.* New York: Harper Torchbooks.

Merejcovski, D. 1938. *The Romance of Leonardo da Vinci.* New York: Heritage Press.

Milch, R., and Patterson, C. 1966. *Nicomachean Ethics.* Lincoln, Nebr.: Cliff's Notes.

Miller, H. 1941. *The Colossus of Maroussi.* New York: New Directions.

Miller, J., ed. 1973. *Psychoanalysis and Women.* New York: Brunnel/Mazel.

Miller, N. 1969. Learning of visceral and glandular responses. *Science* 163: 434-445.

Montaigne. 1957. *The Complete Works.* Trans. D. Frame. Stanford: Stanford University Press.

———. 1958. *The Complete Essays.* Trans. D. Frame. Stanford: Stanford University Press.

Moore, G. 1966. *Principia Ethica.* New York: Cambridge University Press.

Moravcsik, J. 1967. *Aristotle.* New York, Doubleday.

Morgan, G. 1965. *What Nietzsche Means.* New York: Harper Torchbooks.

Morris, C. 1946. *Signs, Language and Behavior.* Englewood Cliffs, N.J.: Braziller.

Mowrer, O. 1972. Beyond freedom and dignity. *Contemporary Psychology* 17: 469-472.

Mullahy, P. 1948. *Oedipus, Myth and Complex.* New York: Hermitage Press.

———. 1970. *Psychoanalysis and Interpersonal Psychiatry.* New York: Jason Aronson.

———, ed. 1949. *A Study of Interpersonal Relations.* New York: Grove Press, Inc.

Muller, H. 1971. *In Pursuit of Relevance.* Bloomington: Indiana University Press.

Mullins, E. 1961. *Ezra Pound.* New York: Fleet.

Munroe, R. 1955. *Schools of Psychoanalytic Thought.* New York: Dryden.

Muraro, M. and Grabar, A. 1963. *Treasures of Venice.* Cleveland, Ohio: World.

Murphy, G. and Murphy, L. 1969. *Western Psychology.* New York: Basic Books.

Muslin, H. 1971. The superego in women. In *Moral Values and the Superego Concept in Psychoanalysis,* ed. S. Post. New York: International Universities Press.

Nacht, S. 1962. The curative factors in psycho-analysis. *International Journal of Psycho-Analysis* 43: 206-211.

———. 1969. Reflections on the evolution of psychoanalytic knowledge. *International Journal of Psycho-Analysis* 50: 597.

Nagera, H. 1975. *Female Sexuality and The Oedipus Complex.* New York: Jason Aronson.

———, ed. 1970. *Basic Psychoanalytic Concepts.* 4 vols. New York: Basic Books.

Nef, J. 1967. *The United States and Civilization*. Chicago: University of Chicago Press.

———. 1973. *Search for Meaning*. Washington: Public Affairs Press.

Nietzsche, F. 1968a. *Basic Writings*. Trans. W. Kaufmann. New York: Modern Library.

———. 1968b. *The Portable Nietzsche*. Trans. W. Kaufmann. New York: Viking.

———. 1968c. *The Will to Power*. Trans. W. Kaufmann. New York: Vintage Books.

———. 1969. *Selected Letters*. Trans. C. Middleton. Chicago: University of Chicago Press.

Nunberg, H. 1962. *Minutes of the Vienna Psychoanalytic Society*. Vol. 1. New York: International Universities Press.

Oates, W., ed. 1940. *The Stoic and Epicurean Philosophers*. New York: Random House.

O'Connor, D. 1964. *A Critical History of Western Philosophy*. New York: Macmillan.

Offenkrantz, W., and Tobin, A. 1974. Psychoanalytic psychotherapy. *Archives of General Psychiatry* 30: 593-606.

Pater, W. 1959. *The Renaissance*. New York: Mentor Books.

Paton, H. 1951. *Kant's Metaphysics of Experience*. 2 vols. London: George Allen and Unwin.

Pavlov, I. 1957. *Experimental Psychology*. New York: Philosophical Library.

Pears, D. 1970. *Ludwig Wittgenstein*. New York: Viking.

Pico della Mirandola, G. 1956. *Oration on the Dignity of Man*. Trans. R. Caponigri. Chicago: Henry Regnery.

Pieper, J. 1954. *Fortitude and Temperance*. New York: Pantheon Books.

Pitcher, G. 1964. *The Philosophy of Wittgenstein*. Englewood Cliffs, N.J.: Prentice-Hall.

———, ed. 1966. *Wittgenstein: The Philosophical Investigations*. New York: Doubleday, Anchor Books.

Plato. 1932. *The Dialogues of Plato*. 2 vols. Trans. B. Jowett. New York: Random House.

Platt, J. 1972. A revolutionary manifesto. *The Center Magazine* 5: 34-52.

Plutarch. 1932. *Lives*. Ed. H. Clough. Trans. J. Dryden. New York: Modern Library.

Polanyi, M. 1958. *Personal Knowledge*. Chicago: University of Chicago Press.

———. 1974. *Scientific Thought and Social Reality*. New York: International Universities Press.

Popper, K. 1964. *The Poverty of Historicism*. New York: Harper Torchbooks.

———. 1965. *Conjectures and Refutations.* New York: Basic Books.

———. 1966. *The Open Society and Its Enemies.* Princeton, N.J.: Princeton University Press.

———. 1968. *The Logic of Scientific Discovery.* New York: Harper Torchbooks.

———. 1972. *Objective Knowledge.* New York: Oxford University Press.

Pound, E. 1951a. *The Confucian Analects.* Washington, D.C.: Square Dollar Series.

———. 1951b. *The Unwobbling Pivot.* Washington, D.C.: Square Dollar Series.

Prezzolini, G. 1967. *Machiavelli.* New York: Farrar Strauss and Giroux.

Price, R. 1967. *Decline and Fall.* New York: Random House.

Prosen, H. 1972. The remembered mother and the phantasized mother. *Archives of Psychiatry* 27: 791-793.

Randall, J. 1960. *Aristotle.* New York: Columbia University Press.

Rapaport, D. 1951. *Organization and Pathology of Thought.* New York: Columbia Universities Press.

———. 1960. *The Structure of Psychoanalytic Theory.* New York: International Universities Press.

———. 1961. *Emotions and Memory.* New York: Science Editions.

———. 1967. *Collected Papers.* New York: Basic Books.

Raspail, J. 1975. *The Camp of the Saints.* Trans. N. Shapiro. New York: Scribner.

Rausch, L. 1965. *The Philosophy of Kant.* New York: Monarch.

Reichenbach,. H. 1951. *The Rise of Scientific Philosophy.* Berkeley, Calif.: University of California Press.

Renault, M. 1959. *The King Must Die.* New York: Pocket Books.

———. 1972. *The Bull From the Sea.* New York: Pocket Books.

Ricoeur, P. 1970. *Freud.* New Haven, Conn.: Yale University Press.

Ridolfi, R. 1954. *The Life of Niccolo Machiavelli.* Chicago: University of Chicago Press.

Rieff, P. 1961. *Freud: The Mind of the Moralist.* New York: Doubleday, Anchor Books.

Roazen, P. 1968. *Freud: Political and Social Thought.* New York: Alfred A. Knopf.

———. 1974. *Freud and His Followers.* New York: Alfred A. Knopf.

Robert, M. 1966. *The Psychoanalytic Revolution.* New York: Harcourt Brace and World.

Rodes, J. 1970. *A Short History of the Western World.* New York: Scribner.

Ross, N. 1966. Book Review of Insight and Responsibility. *International Journal of Psycho-Analysis* 47: 562-569.

Ross, W. 1963. *Aristotle.* New York: Meridian Books.

Rothgeb, C., ed. 1973. *Abstracts of the Standard Edition of the Complete Psychological Works of Sigmund Freud.* New York: Jason Aronson.

Roubiczek, P. 1964. *Existentialism.* Cambridge, England: Cambridge University Press.

Rubin, T. 1962. *Lisa and David.* New York: Ballantine Books.

Rubins, J. 1972. Karen Horney. In *Interpreting Personality,* ed. A. Freedman and H. Kaplan. New York: Atheneum Publishers.

Russell, B. 1945. *A History of Western Philosophy.* New York: Simon and Schuster.

———. 1948. *Human Knowledge Its Scope and Limits.* New York: Simon and Schuster.

———. 1951. *The Conquest of Happiness.* New York: Signet Books.

———. 1959. *Wisdom of the West.* Garden City: Doubleday.

———. 1961. *Basic Writings.* New York: Simon and Schuster.

———. 1962. *Human Society in Ethics and Politics.* New York: Mentor.

———. 1964. *Wisdom of the West.* Greenwich, Conn.: Fawcett.

———. 1967. *Why I Am Not a Christian.* New York: Simon and Schuster.

———. 1968. *Autobiography.* Vol. 2. Boston: Little, Brown.

Russell, P. 1950. *An Examination of Ezra Pound.* New York: New Directions.

Ryle, G. 1949. *The Concept of Mind.* New York: Barnes and Noble.

Salisbury, C. 1974. *Russian Diary.* New York: Walker.

Salzberger, L. 1952. *Holderlin.* Cambridge, Mass.: Bowes and Bowes.

Salzman, L. 1967. Psychology of the female. *Archives of Psychiatry* 17: 195-203.

Santayana, G. 1936. *The Sense of Beauty.* New York: Scribner.

Sartre, J. 1964. *Nausea.* New York: New Directions.

Saul, L. 1958. *Technic and Practice of Psychoanalysis.* Philadelphia: J. B. Lippincott.

———. 1966. The concept of emotional maturity. *International Journal of Psychiatry* 2: 446-469.

Schafer, R. 1974. Problems in Freud's Psychology of Women. *Journal of the American Psychoanalytic Association* 22: 459-485.

Schilpp, P., ed. 1951. *The Philosophy of George Santayana.* New York: Tudor.

———. 1957. *The Philosophy of Karl Jaspers.* New York: Tudor.

———. 1968. *The Philosophy of G. E. Moore.* New York: Tudor.

———. 1974. *The Philosophy of Karl Popper.* LaSalle, Ill.: Open Court.

Schmitt, R. 1969. *Martin Heidegger on Being Human.* New York: Random House.

Schopenhauer, A. 1883. *The World as Will and Idea.* Trans. R. Haldane and

J. Kemp. 3 vols. London: Routledge and Kegan Paul.

———. 1928. *The Philosophy of Schopenhauer*. Ed. I. Ednan. New York: Modern Library.

———. 1958. *The World as Will and Representation*. Trans. E. Payne. 2 vols. Indiana Hills, Colo.: Falcon's Wing Press.

———. 1970. *Essays and Aphorisms*. Trans. R. Hollingdale. Middlesex, England: Penguin.

———. 1974. *The Fourfold Root of the Principle of Sufficient Reason*. Trans. E. Payne. LaSalle, Ill.: Open Court.

Schott, R. 1962. *Michelangelo*, New York: Harry N. Abrams.

Schur, M. 1972. *Freud: Living and Dying*. New York: International Universities Press.

Searles, H. 1960. *The Nonhuman Environment in Normal Development and Schizophrenia*. New York: International Universities Press.

Sechehaye, M. 1951. *Autobiography of a Schizophrenic Girl*. New York: Grune and Stratton.

Shands, H. 1960. *Thinking and Psychotherapy*. Cambridge, Mass.: Harvard University Press.

———. 1970. *Semiotic Approaches to Psychiatry*. The Hague: Mouton.

———. 1971. *The War With Words*. The Hague: Mouton.

Sherfey, M. 1973. *The Nature and Evolution of Female Sexuality*. New York: Random House.

Sholokhov, M. 1973. *At The Bidding of the Heart*. Moscow: Progress Publishers.

Shorey, P. 1965. *What Plato Said*. Chicago: University of Chicago Press.

Simpson, C. 1968. *Greece*. New York: Fielding.

Skinner, B. 1948. *Walden Two*. New York: Macmillan.

———. 1960. *Science and Human Behavior*. New York: Macmillan.

———. 1971. *Beyond Freedom and Dignity*. New York: Alfred A. Knopf.

———. 1972. *Cumulative Record*. New York: Appleton-Centry-Crofts.

———. 1974. *About Behaviorism*. New York: Knopf.

Smith, B. 1972. Book review of Beyond Freedom and Dignity. *American Scientist* 60: 80-82.

Smith, N. 1950. *A Commentary to Kant's Critique of Pure Reason*. 2nd ed. New York: Humanities Press.

Solomon, R., ed. 1973. *Nietzsche*. New York: Anchor Books.

Spence, D. 1972. Book review of Semiotic Approaches to Psychiatry. *Psychoanalytic Quarterly* 41: 458-460.

Spengler, O. 1962. *The Decline of the West*. New York: Alfred A. Knopf.

Stafford-Clark, D. 1965. *What Freud Really Said*. New York: Schocken.

Stambaugh, J. 1972. *Nietzsche's Thought of Eternal Return*. Baltimore, Md.: Johns Hopkins University Press.

Stegmuller, W. 1970. *Main Currents in Contemporary German, British and American Philosophy.* Bloomington, Ind.: Indiana University Press.

Stoller, R. 1973. Sex Research and psychoanalysis. *American Journal of Psychiatry* 130: 241-251.

Stone, I. 1971. *The Passions of the Mind.* New York: Doubleday.

Stone, L. 1961. *The Psychoanalytic Situation.* New York: International Universities Press.

Stumpf, S. 1966. *Socrates to Sartre.* New York: McGraw-Hill.

Sullivan, H. 1947. *Conceptions of Modern Psychiatry.* Washington, D. C.: W. A. White Foundation.

————. 1953. *The Interpersonal Theory of Psychiatry.* New York: W. W. Norton.

————. 1954. *The Psychiatric Interview.* New York: W. W. Norton.

————. 1956. *Clinical Studies in Psychiatry.* W. W. Norton.

————. 1962. *Schizophrenia as a Human Process.* New York: W. W. Norton.

————. 1964. *The Fusion of Psychiatry and Social Science.* New York: W. W. Norton.

————. 1972. *Personal Psychopathology.* New York: W. W. Norton.

Taaffe, T. 1965. *The Philosophy of Arthur Schopenhauer.* New York: Monarch.

Taylor, A. 1953. *Socrates.* New York: Anchor Books.

Taylor, A. and Heiser, J. 1971. Phenomenology. *Comprehensive Psychiatry* 12: 480-486.

Taylor, R. 1964. Schopenhauer. In *A Critical History of Western Philosophy,* ed. J. O'Connor. New York: The Free Press.

Thompson, C. 1964. *Interpersonal Psychoanalysis.* New York: Basic Books.

Thompson, J. 1973. *Kierkegaard.* New York: Alfred A. Knopf.

————, ed. 1972. *Kierkegaard.* New York: Anchor Books.

Tolstoy, L. 1942. *War and Peace.* Trans. L. Maude and A. Maude. New York: Simon and Schuster.

————. 1951. *The Death of Ivan Ilych.* Trans. L. Maude and A. Maude. London: Oxford University Press.

Tseng, W. 1973. The concept of personality in Confucian thought. *Psychiatry* 36: 191-202.

Usdin, G., ed. 1973. *The Psychiatric Forum.* New York: Brunner/Mazel.

Van Peursen, C. 1970. *Ludwig Wittgenstein.* New York: Dutton.

Vasari, G. 1967. *The Lives of the Most Eminent Painters.* 2 vols. Trans. M. Lavin. New York: The Heritage Press.

Veatch, H. 1966. *Rational Man.* Bloomington, Ind.: Indiana University Press.

————. 1974. *Aristotle* Bloomington, Ind.: Indiana University Press.

Venturi, L. 1950. *The Creators of the Renaissance.* Geneva: Skira.
―――. 1961. *The Renaissance.* Geneva: Skira.
Waley, A. 1965. *The Way and Its Power.* London: George Allen and Unwin.
Wallace, W. 1890. *Life of Arthur Schopenhauer.* London: Walter Scott.
Wallbank, T.; Taylor, A.; and Bailkey, N. 1967. *Civilization.* Glenview, Ill.: Scott Foresman.
Walsh, J. and Shapiro, H. 1967. *Aristotle's Ethics.* Belmont, Calif.: Wadsworth.
Walsh, W. 1967. Kant. In *The Encyclopedia of Philosophy,* ed. P. Edwards. New York: Macmillan.
Warner, R. 1973. *Men of Athens.* New York: Viking.
Warnock, G. 1964. Kant. In *A Critical History of Western Philosophy,* ed. D. J. O'Connor. New York: The Free Press.
Watson, R. 1963. *The Great Psychologists.* Philadelphia: J. B. Lippincott.
Waugaman, R. 1973. The intellectual relationship between Nietzsche and Freud. *Psychiatry* 36: 458-467.
Weiss, E. 1960. *The Structure and Dynamics of the Human Mind.* New York: Grune and Stratton.
Weldon, T. 1958. *Kant's Critique of Pure Reason.* New York: Clarendon Press.
Wheelis, A. 1958. *The Quest for Identity.* New York: W. W. Norton.
Wheelwright, P. 1968. *Heraclitus.* New York: Atheneum Press.
Widlocher, D. 1970. On Winnicott's The Maturational Processes and the Facilitating Environment. *International Journal of Psycho-Analysis* 51: 526-530.
Wiegert, E. 1960. Soren Kierkegaard's mood swings. *International Journal of Psycho-Analysis* 41: 521-525.
Wiener, P., ed. 1953. *Readings in Philosophy of Science.* New York: Scribner.
Wilhelm, R. 1931. *Confucius and Confucianism.* New York: Harcourt Brace Jovanovich.
Winnicott, D. W. 1958. *Collected Papers.* New York: Basic Books.
―――. 1966. *The Maturational Processes and the Facilitating Environment.* New York: International Universities Press.
―――. 1968. *The Family and Individual Development.* London: Tavistock.
―――. 1971a. *Playing and Reality.* New York: Basic Books.
―――. 1971b. *Therapeutic Consultations in Child Psychiatry.* New York: Basic Books.
Wisdom, J. 1952. *Other Minds.* New York: Oxford University Press.
―――. 1953. *Philosophy and Psychoanalysis.* New York: Oxford University Press.

Wittgenstein, L. 1962. *Philosophical Investigations.* New York: Macmillan.

———. 1965. Lectures on ethics. *The Philosophical Review* 74: 3-12.

———. 1967. *Lectures and Conversations.* Berkeley: University of California Press.

———. 1969a. *The Blue and Brown Books.* New York: Barnes and Noble.

———. 1969b. *Notebooks 1914-1916.* New York: Harper and Row.

———. 1969c. *Tractatus Logico-Philosophicus.* Trans. D. Pears and B. McGuinness. New York: The Humanities Press.

———. 1970. *Zettel.* Berkeley: University of California Press.

———. 1972. *On Certainty.* New York: Harper Torchbooks.

Wolff, R. 1969. *Kant's Theory of Mental Activity.* Cambridge, Mass.: Harvard University Press.

———. 1973. *The Autonomy of Reason.* New York: Harper and Row.

———., ed. 1967. *Kant: A Collection of Critical Essays.* New York: Anchor Books.

Wollheim, R. 1971. *Sigmund Freud.* New York: Viking.

Wolman, B., ed. 1972. *Handbook of Child Psychoanalysis.* New York: Van Nostrand Reinhold.

Wolpe, J. 1959. *Psychotherapy by Reciprocal Inhibition.* Stanford, Calif.: Stanford University Press.

———. 1969. *The Practice of Behavior Therapy.* New York: Pergamon.

———. 1971. *Orientation to Behavior Therapy.* New Jersey: Hoffmann-LaRoche.

Wychogrod, M. 1969. *Kierkegaard and Heidegger.* New York: Humanities.

Zetzel, E. 1970. *The Capacity for Emotional Growth.* New York: International University Press.

Zilboorg, B. 1941. *A History of Medical Psychology.* New York: W. W. Norton.

Index